MORE PRAISE FOR

SPEAK NOW

"The beauty and elegance of Yoshino's writing about law at times stops you short. There will likely be no more important trial about same-sex marriage than *Hollingsworth v. Perry* and there will likely be no more important book about that trial than this one."

—DALE CARPENTER, author of *Flagrant Conduct;*
Earl R. Larson Professor of Civil Rights and Civil
Liberties Law, University of Minnesota Law School

"Beautifully crafted . . . A celebration of the power of the adversarial system, at its best, to distinguish fact from bombast. In Kenji Yoshino, *Hollingsworth v. Perry* has found its ideal chronicler."

—ANTHONY APPIAH, author of *The Honor Code;* Professor
of Philosophy and Law, New York University

"*Speak Now* shows how trial courts are uniquely well positioned to evaluate the truth or falsehood of 'legislative facts'—broad empirical propositions that are often politically contested—in ways that can advance equality and liberty. 'Let there be a trial,' Yoshino concludes, and by vividly describing the gay rights trial of the new century, he has created a gripping and memorable constitutional narrative."

—JEFFREY ROSEN, author of *The Supreme Court;*
Professor of Law, George Washington University Law School

"Kenji Yoshino seamlessly weaves together the story of the landmark litigation over same-sex marriage in California, incisive insights about the power of trials, and personal reflections about his own marriage and parenting. The result is a captivating introduction to the issues of fact, law, and meaning surrounding marriage equality."

—MARTHA MINOW, Morgan and Helen Chu
Dean and Professor, Harvard Law School

NOW

MARRIAGE EQUALITY ON TRIAL

THE STORY OF

HOLLINGSWORTH V. PERRY

KENJI
YOSHINO

CROWN PUBLISHERS
NEW YORK

Library of Congress Cataloging-in-Publication Data
Yoshino, Kenji, author.
Speak now : marriage equality on trial / Kenji Yoshino
1. Hollingsworth, Dennis, 1967– Trials, litigation, etc.
2. Perry, Kristin—Trials, litigation, etc. 3. Same-sex
marriage—Law and legislation—United States—Cases.
4. Gay couples—Legal status, laws, etc.—United States—
Cases. 5. United States. Defense of Marriage Act.
6. California. Proposition 8 (2008) I. Title.
KF228.H645Y67   2015
346.79401'68—dc23   2014042967

ISBN 978-0-385-34880-5
eBook ISBN 978-0-385-34881-2

Printed in the United States of America

Book design by Barbara Sturman
Jacket design by Ben Wiseman

10 9 8 7 6 5 4 3 2 1

First Edition

for
Ron, again
and
Sophia and Luke, anew

CONTENTS

SPEAK NOW

EMBRACED BY LAW

I married my husband, Ron Stoneham, on August 8, 2009. Guido Calabresi, a federal appellate judge, performed the ceremony on his farm in Woodbridge, Connecticut. Guido was dean when I enrolled as a student at Yale Law School. By the time I graduated in 1996, President Clinton had appointed him to the Second Circuit Court of Appeals. I worked for him after graduation as a clerk, then joined the Yale Law School faculty. He mentored me on the path to tenure, which I received in 2003. In 2006, I became the inaugural Guido Calabresi Professor of Law. My husband ribs me for having taken Guido's name but not his.

Guido took me and Ron aside before the ceremony. At the time, Connecticut recognized same-sex marriage, but the federal government did not, due to a law styled the Defense of Marriage Act (DOMA). Guido said: "You're the first same-sex couple I've married. When I've married couples in the past, I've always said, 'By the power vested in me by the state of Connecticut and the United States of America, I now pronounce you married.' Now, because of

DOMA, I can't marry you under federal law. But I also can't find it in my heart to treat you differently from any other couple." The skin around his blue-gray eyes crinkled with lawyerly pleasure. "So when I speak of 'the power vested in me by the United States of America,' I will be referring to my authority as a federal judge to marry you under state law. But the words will remain the same."

Then he hugged us. I could feel his heart beating through his judge's robe. I thought how odd it was to be embraced by the law. The great law professor Robert Cover wrote that judges sit atop a pyramid of violence "dealing pain and death." Usually, being "apprehended" by the law is a terrifying experience. Yet at that moment, I understood marriage as the rare place where law and love converge.

Marriage is a major life event for most people. Yet I think it still carries an extra jolt of wonder for same-sex couples. It runs so counter to what we have been told about the lives possible for us. I was born in 1969, the year of the Stonewall Riots. Had I been born a generation earlier, or in a different country, my current life would be unimaginable. Monique Wittig, born in 1935, wrote in 1980 that the heterosexual contract was simple: "you-will-be-straight-or-you-will-not-be." Paul Monette, born in 1945, wrote in his 1992 memoir: "Until I was twenty-five, I was the only man I knew who had no story at all. I'd long since accepted the fact that nothing had ever happened to me and nothing ever would." Andrew Sullivan, born in 1963, gave the gay community more hope in his indispensable 1995 work *Virtually Normal*, which argued for same-sex marriage. Yet even that manifesto ended by touting how the tendency of gay people not to have families of our own benefited society: "The displacement of family affection onto a broader community also makes the homosexual an ideal person to devote him- or herself to a social institution: the university, the school, the little league, the Boy Scouts, the church, the sports team." He concluded: "Scratch most of these institutions and you'll find a homosexual or two sustaining many of its vital functions."

I remember reading Sullivan's book when it was published. I had just embarked on my legal career. While I did not consciously take his words as a prescription for my life, I recognized that they captured how many expected me to live. Yale was then considered the Ivy with the highest gay population (as one wag put it: "One in four, maybe more; one in three, maybe me; one in two, maybe you!"). Yet even pro-gay colleagues would ask if I wanted a family, in a twist on how my straight female classmates would be asked if they wanted a career. In 1998, many colleagues assumed I would not settle down or have children. One encouraged me to become dean because I would have no family to balance against the rigors of the job.

These expectations fulfilled themselves. I repeatedly chose work over relationships. Work brought pleasure—stature, awards, promotions, raises. Relationships caused pain in my family of origin, and, because of my own internal conflicts, in me. Put differently, achievements that might seem unusual—attending good schools, getting tenure, writing books—have seemed relatively ordinary to me. Because I had been given every advantage growing up, these paths were marked. In contrast, the more common milestones—falling in love, marrying, raising children—seemed unattainable. Long after I achieved tenure, I retained a devotional relationship to my career. I worked every weekend, accepted every committee assignment, and assumed extra student supervisions. The school handsomely rewarded me. Still, I risked marrying an institution.

Thankfully, this changed in my thirties. While such atmospheric shifts are hard to pinpoint, I think of 2003, when the United States Supreme Court struck down criminal bans on sodomy and, in the wake of that decision, the Massachusetts high court issued a decision legalizing same-sex marriage in that state. As same-sex marriage became a possibility, friends and family began to push me to get my personal life in order. They imposed the social discipline to which I had seen my peers subjected in their twenties. I welcomed the chivvying. I finally had not only the permission but also the pressure to go the way I yearned to go.

I left Yale in 2008 to move to New York University. I had met Ron during a sabbatical visit to that institution. I was in my late thirties, he in his late forties. The first thing I noticed about him were his eyes—one gray and one gray streaked with copper—like light breaking a storm. I thought: *This landscape could keep me indoors.* I felt attracted to him in the most literal sense—I knew I would rather be in the same state as he, the same city, the same building, the same room. I knew, quickly, that I would marry him, if he would have me.

Ron and I are ideologically progressive but temperamentally conservative. We both wanted what our parents had modeled for us—life-long marriage and children. "Don't wait," Guido said during our wedding. "You were born to be parents." We needed no encouragement. We had already started attending sessions of "Men Having Babies" at Manhattan's Lesbian, Gay, Bisexual and Transgender (LGBT) Community Center. One reason we wanted to get married was to provide our children the protections of the institution. We now have a daughter and a son.

I always wear a suit to teach. A colleague once asked why. I said I did so out of respect for an honorable profession. He guffawed, observing that most of my students would become big-firm lawyers whose profession would consist of helping corporations wage war. I remain unrepentant. My own life has deprived me of any capacity to be cynical about the law. Every time I needed a legal gate to open, it opened. When I first came out as gay in the early 1990s, the law had changed in most states to decriminalize sexual acts between men; when Ron and I wished to marry, the law in Connecticut allowed it; when we wished to have children, surrogacy and adoption laws permitted us to do so. To be sure, those legal changes did not happen independently of cultural and political transformations. Still, without concrete legal reform, I might have had no husband, no daughter, and no son. Now it is that life that seems unimaginable.

When Ron and I married, a major legal development was unfolding on the other coast. Filed on May 22, 2009, *Perry v. Schwarzenegger* challenged the constitutionality of California's Proposition 8, which had amended the state's constitution to limit marriage to one man and one woman. The amendment withdrew equal marriage rights from same-sex couples six months after the state's supreme court had recognized them. The *Perry* case was distinctive because it assailed a state's prohibition of same-sex marriage on federal constitutional grounds. That meant the case could reach the United States Supreme Court. It also created a media frenzy because it was filed by the odd couple of David Boies and Ted Olson, the superlawyers who had squared off in *Bush v. Gore*.

At the time, only four states had legalized same-sex marriage. Moreover, a majority of states had in recent years enacted or reinforced bans on same-sex marriage. The Supreme Court generally does not tread far ahead of public opinion. For this reason, leaders of the major gay-rights organizations—many of whom I regarded as friends and colleagues—passionately opposed the suit. The movement lawyers worried that Boies and Olson would rush this case to a defeat at the Supreme Court. They could then return to their lucrative corporate practices, leaving the gay-rights lawyers to pick up the pieces. Those shards could scatter far, given that the consequences of an adverse ruling might not be confined to marriage. As gay-rights advocates had witnessed in the aftermath of a devastating loss before the high court in 1986, the constitutional logic that justifies discrimination in one area can be extended—by lower courts, state officials, and others—to fuel discrimination in different realms. Undoing the effects of an adverse ruling could also take years—perhaps decades. Even if a new majority believes that a case was wrongly decided, the Supreme Court is loath to overrule its precedents. To support the Boies and Olson case seemed like a betrayal of my community.

For this reason, I kept a wary distance: I did not attend the trial in January 2010, and publicly expressed my reservations about it. Yet I was naïve to think I could evade it. David Boies was a trustee of my law school. My students lobbied me to get him on campus—primarily to challenge what he had done. In April 2010, I moderated a discussion that included him, Matt Coles, and Paula Ettelbrick. Coles, an American Civil Liberties Union (ACLU) attorney, had helped formulate the national LGBT movement's incremental strategy for marriage equality—the strategy that Boies and Olson, by filing *Perry*, had upended. Ettelbrick, who had served in the leadership of Lambda Legal and other LGBT organizations, brought additional critiques to the table: She had long cautioned against making marriage equality the primary goal of the LGBT movement, arguing that privileging rights for married couples marginalized those who defined family in other ways. The debate was civil, but heated. Boies was unflappable.

In hindsight, Boies and Olson have been vindicated. On August 4, 2010, federal judge Vaughn R. Walker struck down California's state ban on same-sex marriage. Only when I read the 136-page decision did I realize the magnitude of what had occurred. The opinion relied not just on legal precedent but also on the judge's eighty findings of fact, which in turn were supported with extensive citations to exhibits, testimony, and other evidence. I personally knew several of the nineteen witnesses—including University of Massachusetts economist Lee Badgett, Yale historian George Chauncey, and Harvard historian Nancy Cott. The opinion made me curious about the twelve-day trial. Only one same-sex marriage case had gone to trial before—in Hawaii in the 1990s. While that trial ended with a ruling for the plaintiffs, a state constitutional amendment superseded the decision before it could take effect. I decided to dig further into *Perry*.

I vividly recall reading the three-thousand-page transcript in the case. It is the experience many readers have—perhaps the experience that defines us as readers—of "falling into" a text and not resurfacing into everyday life until we have turned the last page. Drawing on months of pre-trial proceedings (and years of arguments advanced by LGBT activists) the transcripts captured the best conversation I had seen on same-sex marriage—better than any legislative hearing, any academic debate, or any media exchange. What distinguished it from these other dialogues was the intellectual rigor of the proceedings—the submission of expert reports, the daylong pre-trial depositions of the witnesses, the testimony under penalty of perjury, the record that swallowed every word in its maw, and perhaps above all the cross-examination of witnesses on the stand. The transcript was a luminous civil-rights document. Any resentment I felt toward Boies or Olson evaporated.

My intent is not to revisit the shopworn dispute over whether courts or legislatures or direct votes by the people are the best place to resolve the question of same-sex marriage. As a practical matter, that argument is moot. Around the world the debate is occurring—and will continue to occur—in all these forums. My question is where the best conversation—meaning the most enlightening, comprehensive, and meticulous one—is happening. In this instance, the best dialogue took place in the courtroom—and more broadly, through the entire adversarial process that culminated in Judge Walker's trial.

Immediately after Judge Walker's decision, Boies extolled the trial form in an interview on *Face the Nation*. In political debates, he argued, it was too easy to "throw around opinions, appeal to people's fear and prejudice," and "cite studies that either don't exist or don't say what you say they do." In a trial, he observed, "you've got to stand up under oath and cross-examination," which made it impossible for opponents of marriage equality to prevail based on misrepresentations, speculation, and hyperbole. He continued:

When they come into court and they have to support those opinions and they have to defend those opinions under oath and cross-examination, those opinions just melt away. And that's what happened here. There simply wasn't any evidence. There weren't any of those studies. There weren't any empirical studies. That's just made up. That's junk science.

And it's easy to say that on television. But a witness stand is a lonely place to lie. And when you come into court, you can't do that. And that's what we proved. We put fear and prejudice on trial, and fear and prejudice lost.

Journalists who covered the trial echoed Boies's theme. Writing for the *New Yorker,* Margaret Talbot acknowledged the conventional wisdom that the culture wars should be fought out in the legislature, the ballot box, or even the blogosphere. However, she observed that the *Perry* trial showed that the courtroom could be a classroom "where the values of thoroughness, precision in speech, and the obligation to reply have a way of laying bare the fundamentals of certain rhetorical positions." More recently, law professor Dale Carpenter criticized Boies and Olson and disputed their assessment of *Perry*'s import but lauded the trial itself, contending that it had revealed "the thin logic, unsubstantiated assertions and stereotypes that undergird the opposition to same-sex marriage in a way that only litigation, including testimony subject to cross-examination under oath, can do."

Such tributes are particularly important now, when the civil trial is quietly going the way of the dodo. In the 1930s, about 20 percent of civil cases filed in federal courts were resolved at trial; in the 2000s, the figure had plummeted to less than 2 percent. Part of the reason is that courts have significantly expanded pre-trial procedures, giving litigants substantial opportunity to interrogate witnesses, review their opponents' documents, and conduct formal settlement negotiations. Some scholars celebrate this development as a triumph of judicial efficiency, and indeed it is. Many benefits of adversarial litigation are now available without the expense and delay associated with trials. But nothing captures the full range of a trial's advantages other than a trial itself. We must confront what is lost in surrendering this great American tradition. As much as anything, this book is a paean to the civil trial.

The proponents of Prop 8, who were the effective defendants in the suit, objected to the trial on several grounds. At various points in the proceedings—and afterward—they contended that the disputed sociological issues could not be resolved through the judicial process, that four of their witnesses decided not to testify out of concerns for their safety, and that the judge was biased because he was gay and in a same-sex relationship. I will address these criticisms as they arose in the proceedings. For now, let me say that compared to a Platonic ideal of discourse, the trial will fall short. Compared to the real alternatives, it shines.

I initially tried to write this book in my "constitutional law professor" voice. Yet withholding my personal reactions made the narrative feel incomplete, even slightly dishonest. I could not have been more affected by the issues in this case. During the four-year span between the filing of *Perry* and its ultimate resolution, Ron and I married, welcomed our daughter into the world, and then welcomed our son. When we traveled to the Supreme Court on March 26, 2013, to hear oral arguments in the case, we were riven with anxiety. Those nerves stemmed as much from the choking panic of having left our young children in a different city for the first time as they did from the case. And of course, my parental and professional anxieties were intertwined—whether we would be able to offer crucial protections to our children could be determined by the Court's decision.

Some may question whether an individual with such a stake in the outcome could evaluate the trial dispassionately. When I consider that objection, I recall a moment on the first day of trial.

Boies asked plaintiff Paul Katami if being granted the right to marry would change his relationship to his community. Opposing counsel lodged an objection, arguing that Katami was just a plaintiff, not an expert. Katami stood his ground with a cri de coeur: "I can't speak as an expert. I can speak as a human being that's lived it." I speak in this book not only as an expert in constitutional law but also as a human being who has lived it. Just as our life experience may dull our faculties of perception, so too it may sharpen them.

To supplement my own perspective, I crisscrossed North America conducting over forty interviews with counsel, witnesses (including withdrawn witnesses), and other stakeholders on both sides of this debate. Piecing together this puzzle has been one of the signal pleasures of my professional life. It was also an occasion for personal transformation, as I found myself connecting at some level with every person with whom I spoke, even when we disagreed vehemently about the question at hand.

Many individuals believe the same-sex marriage debate will soon come to a close. While the Supreme Court will make a decision affecting all fifty states in the next few months, the idea that it will end the debate is fanciful. Resistance to the Supreme Court's 1967 decision striking down bans on interracial marriage endured long past that case. And if we take a more global perspective, same-sex marriage is currently available nationwide in fewer than twenty out of some two hundred countries, while same-sex sexual conduct is still illegal in more than seventy. In eight countries, gay sex is punishable by death. I expect to be arguing for marriage equality for the rest of my life, during which time the validity of my own marriage will fade in and out like a radio signal depending on where in the world I am making the argument.

At the same time, the debate seems mature. Now that the arguments have been articulated, parsed, and refined, we can drive toward closure. Much of this occurred, of course, before and independently of *Perry,* through decades of litigation, grassroots activism, and political and academic debate. What struck me as I read *Perry* was not that the proceedings had generated new arguments but that they had forced an unusually direct, disciplined, and comprehensive confrontation between the opposing sides.

In marriage ceremonies, there is that tremulous moment where the officiant states: "If any of you can show just cause why these two may not be married, speak now, or else forever hold your peace." As we planned our ceremony, we learned that most couples dispensed with this line. But we asked Guido to leave it in, a subtle reminder to ourselves and our guests that many of our fellow citizens felt they had just cause to object to our marriage. (I had no qualms in the ringing pause after the question was posed, though I did think wildly of that scene in *Jane Eyre,* when a stranger declares: "The marriage cannot go on: I declare the existence of an impediment.") Like marriage ceremonies, trials—of any kind—are moments of cultural compression, where one must speak or bear the consequences of one's silence. We should want both sides to have a full and fair opportunity to speak. Yet after those conditions are in place—as they were in *Perry*—we should want both sides to live with the consequences of what they have said—no less for a marriage trial than for a marriage.

For the processional to our wedding, Ron and I chose the Bach cantata *Sleepers Wake.* We both felt we were stirring from a slumber. And we felt the country and world were on the cusp of a shift comparable to the Great Awakening. As we raise our children, we feel renewed responsibility to press for that enlarged awareness. No scholar wants to exhaust his life on one argument. Yet in a real sense, we are arguing for our lives, our children's lives, and the lives of our community. Today, when I think of what I would place before the open-minded but uncertain individual, I think of the *Perry* trial. I do not think any such person could read what transpired there without ending with a more favorable view of same-sex marriage. Because few will read the full transcript, this book seeks to bring the trial to the reader. Clarifying the key issues in an inflamed social controversy is something trials can do for us. Memorializing such trials is what we can do for them.

PART I

BEFORE

1

THE PLAINTIFFS

On November 4, 2008, Ron and I watched the election returns. On the historic day that swept President Barack Obama into office, California voters passed an amendment to the state constitution banning same-sex marriage by a 52–48 margin. One cartoonist portrayed the moment as one of "Yes We Can" for Democrats across the nation but one of "No You Can't" for same-sex couples in California. For us, the passage of Prop 8 was personal. Ron's sister Donna and her wife had married after the California Supreme Court had legalized same-sex marriage earlier that year. Because Prop 8 might apply retroactively, it called the validity of their marriage into question.

When Ron asked what would happen next, I felt confident in my answer. I said we would move on to other states: "In California, we'll see another ballot initiative to repeal Prop 8 in a few years." He asked if someone would bring a federal lawsuit. "No," I said. "It's too soon." I pointed out that the movement groups were all against a federal suit, and that they would talk any rogue plaintiffs out of filing, like the National Association for the Advancement of Colored People (NAACP) did on the road to *Brown v. Board of Education.*

I could not have been more wrong. A thirty-five-year-old political strategist named Chad Griffin disagreed that a federal challenge was premature. Griffin had watched the election returns with San Francisco mayor Gavin Newsom. The result devastated Griffin, a gay man who had raised millions to defeat Prop 8: "All I could think about was the message this sent to the kid I used to be, growing up in Arkansas."

Born in 1973, Griffin grew up in Arkadelphia, a town of 10,000 people. Based on his volunteer work for the Clinton campaign, Press Secretary Dee Dee Myers hired Griffin when he was nineteen. One Sunday, Griffin gave a tour of the White House to Hollywood director Rob Reiner, who wished to authenticate the sets for his upcoming film *The American President.* The meeting sparked an important friendship. After Griffin graduated from college, Reiner and his wife, Michele, persuaded him to help them launch a foundation. Griffin shuttled between New York and Los Angeles, a commute that reflected his budding capacity to span the worlds of politics and entertainment.

With his crew cut and square glasses, Griffin looks like a head boy at an English prep school—one whose rise was preordained. In Los Angeles, Griffin established a public-relations firm that represented the Walmart Foundation and Al Gore's Live Earth global concert series. Griffin also worked on California ballot initiatives concerning clean energy, stem-cell research, and early childhood education. In October 2008, just weeks before voters went to the polls, Griffin was tapped to turn around the flagging campaign to defeat Prop 8.

The roots of Prop 8 trail back to at least the mid-1990s, when it appeared that a Hawaii court ruling would lead that state to recognize same-sex marriage. The ruling mobilized opponents of same-sex marriage around the country, including in California, where

Republican State Assembly member William "Pete" Knight—who would later become a state senator—introduced a bill to prevent the state from recognizing out-of-state marriages of same-sex couples. After his legislative efforts failed, Knight formed the Protection of Marriage Committee, which sought to accomplish the same goal through a ballot initiative that went directly to the people. Prop 22, also known as the Knight Initiative, would become a prototype for Prop 8. It passed with 61 percent of the vote in 2000, adding a provision to the California Family Code stating: "Only marriage between a man and a woman is valid or recognized in California."

Pro-gay advocates fought back. In 2003, the California legislature bolstered the state's 1999 domestic-partnership law. The legislation largely reduced the discrepancy between marriages and domestic partnerships to the word "marriage."

For some, the reform fell short. On February 10, 2004, Mayor Gavin Newsom unilaterally decided to issue marriage licenses to San Francisco same-sex couples. The first couple to be married was Phyllis Lyon and Del Martin, two activists who had formed the nation's first lesbian organization, the Daughters of Bilitis, in 1955. They had been a couple for more than half a century. Newsom's move made national headlines. Under our system of separation of powers, the judicial branch, not the executive one, wields the power to invalidate laws as unconstitutional. Yet Newsom felt that he, too, had a "sworn duty to uphold the California Constitution, including specifically its equal protection clause."

From mid-February to mid-March, San Francisco issued marriage licenses to roughly four thousand same-sex couples, inaugurating San Francisco's "winter of love." Terry Stewart, the chief deputy attorney for San Francisco, sought to extend that season. A lawyer who had worked for twenty years as a commercial litigator in San Francisco, Stewart had served as the first openly gay president of the City Bar Association. She left private practice in 2002 to move to city hall. At that point, Stewart believed San Francisco had done "all it could do" for LGBT rights and figured her portfolio would contain no such work. Little did she know that her gay-rights docket was about to explode.

Earnest and diminutive, Stewart has short blond hair and pale blue eyes that snap whenever she touches on an issue of controversy. When she spoke of the days after the mayor's declaration, however, her eyes grew soft. The atmosphere at city hall was like a "dream state." "It was wet and cold and drizzly," she recalled, but "people came pouring in from all over the Bay Area and other parts of the state and other states, and probably other countries." Staffed with volunteers, the clerk's office kept city hall open over the weekend. The volume of calls shut down the voicemail system. "I think everyone figured that it would be likely that a court would be approached and would issue some kind of injunction, and so they didn't think they could do it for long," Stewart reflected. A line of same-sex couples wound tightly around the entire perimeter of city hall, waiting all night with sleeping bags, outdoor chairs, and umbrellas to get into the building in the morning. Firefighters and police officers volunteered to protect those in line. Cars drove by honking their horns.

The heady spirit outside city hall did not cross the threshold. Inside, Stewart recounted, it was "like a cathedral." In every corner, quiet, solemn ceremonies took place. A volunteer in the Midwest had arranged for florists to send flowers to the couples. Stewart described the feelings it unleashed even—perhaps especially—in those not expecting them: "People I spoke to said they had come to get married essentially for political reasons. But it had a much deeper emotional impact on them than they expected. You'll see pictures of people in tears." Stewart understood the welter of sentiment: "You don't realize the depth of emotion you have about the issue, because it's something out of reach and you don't want to have to feel that sadness all that time. It's such a universal human experience that gay people have been denied. So when it's finally within reach, you finally kind of fall apart and think—*Oh my God*. It's a mixture of grief and joy all at once."

I knew what she meant. While I never opposed marriage equality, I routinely covered critiques of marriage in my early years of teaching. For me personally, however, much of my skepticism about marriage turned out to be sour grapes. A way to maintain social equanimity when one cannot participate in such a universal experience is to dismiss its importance. When Guido married us, some internal wall of denial crumbled. Usually, one sets goals and then attains them (or not). Yet I understood marriage as my heart's desire only at the moment that desire was satisfied.

In March 2004, the California Supreme Court ordered San Francisco to cease issuing marriage licenses to same-sex couples pending its decision. Five months later, the court found the Newsom marriages had never been valid. It pointed out that allowing mayors to enforce their own interpretations of the constitution would undermine the rule of law; a mayor could just as easily refuse to enforce restrictions on assault weapons if, in his or her personal view, such restrictions violated the Second Amendment.

The reasoning was cogent; its effect, devastating. The state sent each of the four thousand same-sex couples a notice that their marriages were void. The letters asked if the couples wanted their registration fees refunded or donated to charity. As Lyon observed: "Del is eighty-three years old and I am seventy-nine. After being together for more than fifty years, it is a terrible blow to have the rights and protections of marriage taken away from us. At our age, we do not have the luxury of time."

Nevertheless, the ruling placed an almost coy emphasis on the court's openness to a challenge to Prop 22 brought through proper channels. The mainstream LGBT litigation groups, including the National Center for Lesbian Rights (NCLR), Lambda Legal, and the ACLU, took the hint. In March 2005, a state trial court duly entertained such a challenge in a group of cases, ultimately known as the *In re Marriage Cases*. Stewart pushed for a trial, but said (with a short laugh) that she "failed miserably." On the basis of written submissions alone, Judge Richard Kramer held that the California Constitution required that same-sex couples be allowed to marry. The California legislature also got involved, becoming the first in the nation to pass a bill legalizing same-sex marriage. Gov. Arnold Schwarzenegger vetoed the bill. In 2006, the California Court of Appeals reversed the lower court in a 2–1 decision. In October 2007, the legislature passed another bill, which Schwarzenegger also vetoed.

Finally, on May 15, 2008, the California Supreme Court ruled 4–3 that barring same-sex couples from marrying violated the state's constitution. Chief Justice Ronald George found that marriage was a fundamental right and that the state presented no compelling reason to bar gays from " 'the most socially productive and individually fulfilling relationship that one can enjoy in the course of a lifetime.' " The court could have decided the case on this basis alone, but it had greater ambitions. It explicitly found that the California Constitution required the courts to review discrimination based on sexual orientation under the same standard used to review discrimination based on race.

The opinion was revolutionary. One of the most respected state courts in the country, the California high court often acts as a harbinger. As Chief Justice George noted, the California Supreme Court struck down a ban on interracial marriage in 1948, long before the US Supreme Court did so in *Loving v. Virginia*. In pragmatic terms, California is the most populous state in the nation, with an economy comparable in size to that of Brazil, Canada, or Italy.

Opponents of same-sex marriage were braced for this ruling. Senator Knight had already established the Proposition 22 Legal Defense and Education Fund. By 2002, the fund held the domain name Protectmarriage.com, which would later become the official name of the coalition defending Prop 8. In anticipation of the ruling, the Protect Marriage coalition had begun the petition process to qualify a state constitutional amendment restricting marriage to opposite-sex couples. Five individuals stepped forward to serve as the official proponents—Martin Gutierrez, Dennis Hollingsworth, Mark Jansson, Gail Knight, and Hak-Shing "Bill" Tam. Gail Knight had been married to Sen. Pete Knight until his death in 2004, and Dennis Hollingsworth, like Knight, was a conservative California senator. The other individuals represented constituencies in California that largely opposed same-sex marriage—Bill Tam, for instance, was a significant figure in the Chinese evangelical community.

On June 2, 2008, the California secretary of state certified Prop 8 for the November general election ballot. Prop 8 sought to revise the California Constitution to provide: "Only marriage between a man and a woman is valid or recognized in California." These fourteen words tracked those in Prop 22, but the proponents now aspired to entrench them in the state's highest law. By doing so, they would place the definition of marriage beyond the reach of California's courts or legislature.

Gay-rights advocates challenged Prop 8 on the grounds that the measure was not an "amendment" but a "revision." Under California's constitution, amendments can be passed by a simple majority of the electorate through a process that bypasses the legislature, while "revisions," which go to the heart of the state's structure of governance, require a two-thirds vote of the legislature before going to the voters. While seemingly plausible, this challenge confronted adverse precedents. California's constitution has been amended more than five hundred times. Some amendments concern fateful issues, including the death penalty, gun control, and affirmative action. The argument that Prop 8 could not be considered an "amendment" was a heavy lift from the start. The California high court allowed Prop 8 to go forward.

On November 4, 2008, Prop 8 passed with 52.3 percent of the vote, devastating Chad Griffin and millions across the nation. The next day, gay-rights supporters filed several lawsuits, renewing the argument that such a change was a revision, not an amendment. Led by Shannon Minter of the NCLR, the suits also asked the court to grandparent in the eighteen thousand marriages that had occurred between June and November of that year. The California Supreme Court consolidated these cases under the title *Strauss v. Horton.*

～

Ten days after the election, Rob Reiner and Michele Singer Reiner invited Chad Griffin to lunch at the Polo Lounge in the Beverly Hills Hotel. Inevitably, the conversation turned to Prop 8. Outraged that the right to marry had been withdrawn by a popular vote, the group discussed the possibility of a federal lawsuit.

Because Prop 8 was now enshrined in the state constitution, advocates of same-sex marriage had no substantive judicial challenges left under state law. The only viable claims were procedural ones, like *Strauss,* which contested whether Prop 8 had been enacted in the proper manner. Advocates of same-sex marriage could always bring a *federal* challenge to Prop 8, given that federal law trumps state law when the two conflict. But here lay dragons. Unlike a state constitutional challenge, a federal constitutional challenge could ascend to the United States Supreme Court. Any decision there would bind the entire nation, either way. A win could permit same-sex couples to marry in all fifty states. A loss could foreclose a fifty-state solution for the foreseeable future.

After Griffin left, an acquaintance of the Reiners, Kate Moulene, stopped by the table. Later that afternoon, Moulene phoned Michele Reiner to suggest that they speak to her former brother-in-law, the lawyer Ted Olson. "Ted Olson?" Michele Reiner exclaimed. "Why on earth would I want to talk to him?"

Olson, who was sixty-eight when Prop 8 passed, is a central figure in the conservative establishment. He is still most famous for winning *Bush v. Gore,* the blockbuster 2000 case that ensconced George W. Bush in the Oval Office. Olson had become active in the Republican Party as a student in California in the 1960s, valuing small government and individual liberty. He was one of a few law students at the ultra-liberal University of California at Berkeley to support Barry Goldwater's 1964 presidential bid.

Many of Olson's causes over the years had set him at odds with progressive communities. In Reagan's Justice Department, Olson worked to end race-based affirmative action in federal contracting. On behalf of the state of Virginia, he argued against allowing women into the Virginia Military Institute (VMI), losing that case in the Supreme Court in 1996. As President George W. Bush's solicitor general, Olson pressed for broad interpretations of the executive branch's wartime powers. Indeed, Olson had been approached about *defending* Prop 8 in the California Supreme Court after he returned to the multinational law firm of Gibson, Dunn & Crutcher. When he declined, fellow conservative eminence Kenneth Starr got the job. Like Justice Clarence Thomas and former Supreme Court nominee Robert Bork, Starr was a close friend of Olson's. Legal reporter Jeffrey Toobin described Olson and his wife Barbara—who perished on one of the hijacked airplanes on 9/11— as the "first couple of the legal conservative world." "If Hillary Clinton's vast right-wing conspiracy had a headquarters," Toobin wrote in 2008, "it was their estate in Great Falls, Virginia."

Wherever one stands politically, it is next to impossible to dislike Olson. He has a canine quality, with his slightly jowly face and matted sandy hair. Debating him is like debating a golden retriever with a genius IQ. Time and again, liberal participants in the trial carried this refrain. The plaintiffs' political science expert Gary Segura took the stand in *Perry* on January 21, 2010, the day Olson won the *Citizens United* case—a huge blow to many progressives in its invalidation of significant restrictions on what could be spent in political campaigns. Segura recalled: "Other people on his team were trying to explain why the case was correctly decided. And I said, 'Get away from me, I teach this stuff at Stanford; you've just destroyed democracy.' But Ted? Ted is a hell of a guy."

Despite his conservative reputation, Olson was no stranger to gay rights. While working in the Reagan Justice Department, he wrote a legal opinion maintaining that a prosecutor could not be denied a promotion just because he was gay. During the Bush administration, Olson slammed a proposed amendment to the federal Constitution that would have banned same-sex marriage. Olson also believed religious convictions could not justify governmental restrictions on civil marriage. Having grown up and practiced law in California, Olson was shocked when the voters passed Prop 8.

Olson finalized his participation in December 2008 at the Reiners' Los Angeles home, where he assured the assembled group of elated but confused progressives that he would not "just be some hired gun." Olson later acknowledged that in certain progressive circles, he was known as "the devil." "Now," he observed, "I'm the devil to a different group of people." He was. Bork declared he could not speak to Olson on this topic. Ed Whelan, a prominent conservative lawyer who would follow the case closely, predicted on CNN that Olson would never recover his conservative reputation, given that the lawsuit was "a betrayal of everything that Ted Olson has purported to stand for." Apparently, Olson's support for the case was like the thirteenth chime of the clock that calls all that preceded it into question.

Olson had neither the time nor the temperament to let the naysayers get to him. The belief that other federal lawsuits would soon be filed imbued Griffin and Olson with urgency. By early spring, the Gibson Dunn Prop 8 team had members in offices in Los Angeles, San Francisco, and Washington, DC. By April, the legal team had vetted the issues from all angles and concluded it could win at the US Supreme Court. In Olson's words, the key to Supreme Court litigation was the ability to "count to five." Olson believed he could find that majority on the nine-member Court.

But which five? In April 2009, the Supreme Court had a bloc of four solid conservatives: Chief Justice John Roberts, Justice Samuel Alito, Justice Antonin Scalia, and Justice Clarence Thomas. Most pundits assumed all four would vote against marriage equality. The Court had an equally solid bloc of four liberals: Justice Stephen Breyer, Justice Ruth Bader Ginsburg, Justice David Souter, and Justice John Paul Stevens. Court watchers predicted Justice Souter and Justice Stevens would retire before the case reached the Court.

However, they correctly assumed President Obama would replace these liberal jurists with like-minded colleagues. In 2009, Justice Sonia Sotomayor replaced Justice Souter; in 2010, Justice Elena Kagan replaced Justice Stevens. Although many commentators presumed the four liberals would vote for marriage equality, others challenged that premise—not because they thought the liberal justices were ideologically opposed to same-sex marriage but because those justices might be wary of moving too far ahead of public opinion. In particular, Justice Ginsburg had expressed concern over the years that *Roe v. Wade*'s "heavy-handed" intervention had triggered a backlash that had endangered the right to abortion. (Ginsburg would just have struck down the draconian Texas law, letting the debate about less-restrictive abortion regulations percolate.) Some considered her frequent invocation of this point to be a worrisome omen for *Perry.*

The Gibson Dunn team's greatest cause for optimism lay in two pro-gay majority decisions penned by Justice Kennedy. In the 1996 case of *Romer v. Evans,* the Supreme Court struck down an amendment to the Colorado Constitution under the federal Equal Protection Clause. Amendment 2 represented the successful attempt of anti-gay groups to wash out the pro-gay laws in three cities—Denver, Boulder, and Aspen—and to bar pro-gay measures moving forward. The amendment's impact was harsh and far-reaching. Under Amendment 2, neither the state legislature nor any local government could enact a policy protecting gay men, lesbians, or bisexuals from discrimination in any context. They could, however, enact such policies protecting heterosexuals. So after the amendment passed, a landlord in Aspen could post a sign saying NO GAYS ALLOWED in his yard. Yet he was arguably still barred from posting a sign saying NO STRAIGHTS ALLOWED. At oral argument, Justice Ginsburg asked the lawyer for Colorado if he could think of another law of this kind in the nation's history. The lawyer acknowledged that the law was "unusual."

Writing for a six-member majority of the Court, Justice Kennedy struck down Amendment 2, deeming it "unprecedented in our jurisprudence." He found the measure to be "at once too narrow and too broad," because "it identifies persons by a single trait and then denies them protection across the board." Such laws, Kennedy wrote, "raise the inevitable inference that the disadvantage imposed is born of animosity toward the class of persons affected." Kennedy observed that a 1973 precedent established that "bare . . . desire to harm a politically unpopular group cannot constitute a legitimate governmental interest."

Kennedy's categorization of anti-gay sentiment marked a major advance for gay rights. Moral objections to homosexuality had long been used to justify laws burdening gays and lesbians. In the same year that the Court handed down *Romer,* a report from the House of Representatives justified DOMA as an appropriate expression of "moral disapproval" of homosexuality. Justice Kennedy's opinion reframed disapprobation of gay people as "animus," and held that such animus was not a constitutionally legitimate basis for law. In doing so, it adopted an analysis comparable to the Court's approach in cases protecting the rights of other minorities, such as individuals with disabilities. It gave gays and lesbians a newfound dignity in constitutional jurisprudence.

Still, legal analysts warned against overestimating the pro-gay dimensions of *Romer.* Kennedy stressed that the harms the Colorado amendment inflicted on gays and lesbians were "broad and undifferentiated," a universal pox. Barring Colorado from making gay individuals "strangers to our laws" did not prevent any state from saddling gays with lesser harms. Adhering to that view, state supreme courts in liberal states like Washington and Maryland read *Romer* narrowly in upholding bans on same-sex marriage.

Olson's optimism about Justice Kennedy's vote stemmed above all from the epochal 2003 case of *Lawrence v. Texas,* often touted as the *Brown v. Board of Education* of the gay-rights movement. In this case, the Court considered the constitutionality of state laws that criminalized same-sex sodomy (even if that activity occurred between consenting adults in the privacy of the home). In *Lawrence,* Justice Kennedy again wrote a stirring majority opinion striking down those laws. Along the way, he overruled *Bowers v. Hardwick.* In the infamous 1986 *Bowers* decision, the Court had rejected the argument that the Constitution's right to privacy protected "homosexual sodomy" as "at best, facetious." In *Lawrence,* Justice Kennedy reiterated that moral objections, standing alone, could not justify such restrictions on individual liberty.

While Kennedy noted that the case did not raise—and therefore did not decide—whether same-sex relationships were entitled to "formal recognition," his colleague Justice Scalia was having none of it. In his dissent, Justice Scalia asked: "If moral disapprobation of homosexual conduct is 'no legitimate state interest' . . . what justification could there possibly be for denying the benefits of marriage to homosexual couples exercising the liberty protected by the Constitution? Surely not the encouragement of procreation, since the sterile and the elderly are allowed to marry." He concluded: "This case 'does not involve' the issue of homosexual marriage only if one entertains the belief that principle and logic have nothing to do with the decisions of this Court."

Although many opponents of same-sex marriage doubtless grimaced over Justice Scalia's analysis, many disagreed with Scalia, distinguishing the freedom from governmental condemnation from the freedom to secure governmental affirmation. As the main opinion of the New York high court said in denying same-sex couples the right to marry under the state constitution in 2006: "Plaintiffs here do not, as the petitioners in *Lawrence* did, seek protection against state intrusion on intimate, private activity. They seek from the courts access to a state-conferred benefit."

So while *Romer* and *Lawrence* were both pro-gay decisions written by Justice Kennedy, and while Kennedy was a vital vote, it did not follow that Kennedy would be the fifth vote to invalidate Prop 8.

~

Whether or not Olson was reading Kennedy correctly, the endeavor had reached the point of no return. In April 2009, Griffin's team officially incorporated the American Foundation for Equal Rights (AFER). As gay-rights magazine *The Advocate* noted, "The foundation's website is nearly indistinguishable from, say, the Tea Party movement's site: no rainbow hues, no equality symbols, just American flags—something Griffin was adamant about. 'That's my flag too. That's the LGBT community's flag as much as any other group's.' "

In addition to a public-relations function, AFER performed a major fund-raising role. While Gibson Dunn donated the first $100,000 of its services, it required flat fees thereafter. In one four-week period in 2009, AFER raised millions of dollars from fewer than a dozen donors—"gay *and* straight," as Griffin emphasized. The total fees ended up exceeding $6 million—a price tag that has generated some controversy, given that many lawyers argue significant public-interest cases for free. Griffin explained early in the litigation that he had sought "the lawyers Microsoft is going to want, not the lawyers who are going to do it pro bono." But the need for quality representation does not fully explain the steep price. Paul Smith of the law firm Jenner & Block successfully argued *Lawrence v. Texas* pro bono before the Supreme Court in 2003. Ten years later, Robbie Kaplan of Paul Weiss brought *United States v. Windsor,* a case challenging the federal Defense of Marriage Act, without, in her words, "billing a penny." And of course many of the LGBT public-interest organizations also have exceptional lawyers, who have litigated the movement's most significant victories without charge.

The tireless Griffin also found the four plaintiffs. Griffin knew Kristin Perry and Sandra Stier through his work on a ballot initiative to support early childhood education. Perry was then the executive director of a statewide commission created by that initiative. Perry had wed Stier in 2004 in a civil ceremony in San Francisco after Newsom's announcement. After the court invalidated their marriage just months later, the couple could not bear to repeat the process in 2008, when the California Supreme Court gave them another opportunity to marry.

Griffin found Paul Katami and Jeffrey Zarrillo through the couple's activism. In April 2009, an organization called the National Organization for Marriage (NOM), which opposes same-sex marriage, released a video titled *The Gathering Storm*. Set against lowering clouds and portentous music, the film depicted individuals fearful of what the advent of same-sex marriage would mean for them. "I am a California doctor who must choose between my faith and my job," said one. Frank Rich, then a columnist at the *New York Times,* dubbed it an "Internet camp classic," a cross between *The Village of the Damned* and *A Chorus Line.* In Stephen Colbert's parody, lightning from "the homo storm" turns an Arkansas teacher gay, while a New Jersey pastor complains that gays had converted his church into an Abercrombie & Fitch. Katami and Zarrillo wanted to respond more seriously. Katami, a fitness expert, had made several films, and Zarrillo worked in the entertainment industry. Within two days of viewing *The Gathering Storm,* the couple produced a video called *Weathering the Storm* that provided point-for-point rebuttals to the claims made in the NOM video. When Griffin saw the response video, he sought the couple responsible for it.

These two couples were a lawyer's dream. They represented different genders at different stages of life. At the time of trial in early 2010, Perry, who was forty-five, and Stier, who was forty-seven, had been together for eleven years and were raising four sons together. Katami, who was thirty-seven, and Zarrillo, who was thirty-six, had been together eight years. They tracked social sensibilities—then as now, it was more familiar to see two women raising children than to see two men doing so. Perry had also spent her entire career protecting children. There was only one serious wrinkle. Stier had previously been married to a man, a fact that could undercut one of the plaintiffs' key arguments: that homosexuality was an immutable trait.

Faith in the judicial process underwrote the plaintiffs' participation. When first asked whether she was interested in a project to restore marriage equality, Perry pled "gay-marriage fatigue." Informed it was a federal lawsuit, she changed her mind: "We get to talk about this in a nonpolitical way? Now I'm really interested." Katami had a similar reaction. He felt the lawsuit would "put a respectable face to the fight," elaborating—"I didn't want to just come out with my arms swinging." It may seem odd to think of a judicial proceeding as a "nonpolitical" event, or an adversarial proceeding as not requiring a participant to come out with "arms swinging." Yet both Perry and Katami correctly intuited that federal litigation would be more civilized than a political debate. And it would certainly offer more decorum than the physical violence Katami had experienced in the past—as he would testify during trial, Katami had been pelted with rocks and eggs during his first visit to a gay establishment.

Meanwhile, AFER searched for co-counsel to balance Olson's reputation as a staunch conservative. The AFER team worried that if Olson brought the suit alone, he would be viewed as trying to throw the case in favor of the opponents of same-sex marriage. In a May conference call with AFER principals, Olson suggested David Boies. The reaction was explosive: "Everyone on the call said, 'Oh my God, do you think he would do it? That would be fantastic.'" Olson would later write: "California's motto, 'Eureka' ('We have found it'), leapt to mind."

David Boies was sixty-seven when approached to be co-counsel in *Perry*. If Olson has a canine quality, Boies's profile is more avian—a domed balding head and an aquiline nose. The president of the Young Republicans club while in college in the 1960s, Boies soon realized he "was on the wrong side" of the battle for civil rights. He became a Democrat soon after graduating from Northwestern University, and went to work defending civil-rights workers arrested in Jacksonville, Mississippi.

Although he was, like Olson, a private lawyer in a large firm,

Boies had significant credentials as a liberal litigator. In 1986, he won an injunction barring the Republican National Committee from suppressing the vote of racial minorities through unevenly enforced ballot security measures. In the early 1990s, Boies recovered $1.2 billion from companies that sold junk bonds to failed savings and loan associations. And of course, there was *Bush v. Gore.* Or, as Boies put it: "Every lawyer is used to losing cases. I lost the whole fucking country." Several days after the conference call among AFER principals, Boies received a call from his former adversary. Boies says it took him fifteen seconds to accept Olson's invitation. Olson says it took him less than one.

From a public-relations perspective, the match was inspired. The coming together of these lawyers symbolically reunited the two halves of the country. Far from downplaying their legendary clash, Olson and Boies used *Bush v. Gore* as a leitmotif throughout the public-relations strategy that accompanied the litigation. Boies would joke that he would be responsible for persuading the four justices who voted with him in that case, while Olson would be responsible for the other five. The pairing was less odd than it seemed. In the wake of *Bush v. Gore,* the two lawyers had become friends who vacationed together with their families. As Boies reflected, "You get so deeply involved in a case that about the only person that really appreciates what's going on is the lawyer on the other side, who's just as deep into the weeds as you are." Sherlock Holmes might have said the same of Professor Moriarty.

The plaintiffs began to lay the foundation for their case. On May 20, Katami and Zarrillo met a Gibson Dunn associate at the Los Angeles County Clerk's Office. The men submitted an application for a marriage license, which was, as expected, denied. The next day, Perry and Stier went through the same exercise at the Alameda County Clerk-Recorder's Office. On May 22, a Gibson Dunn associate quietly filed the suit.

The California Supreme Court upheld Prop 8 against the procedural challenge, as expected, on May 26. But it did preserve the

18,000 same-sex marriages performed from June to November 2008. Ron's sister Donna and her wife, Julie, were safe. The court reasoned that, unlike the 2004 Newsom weddings, these weddings were valid when performed. Nevertheless, this decision left California with an odd patchwork of marriage law. If Donna and Julie had divorced and then sought to remarry each other, they would not have been permitted to do so.

The next morning, the *Perry* plaintiffs and their lawyers held a press conference to announce their suit. They assembled at the Millennium Biltmore Hotel in Los Angeles, before an audience bristling with national media, including CNN, Fox News, the *New York Times,* and NPR. Nary a rainbow flag flew. The conservatively attired lawyers and plaintiffs lined up before alternating California and American flags. Griffin introduced Olson and Boies. Both lawyers heralded the bipartisan nature of the suit, declaring that they sought to vindicate the right to marry for all Americans. "Creating a second class of citizens is discrimination, plain and simple," Olson boomed. "The Constitution of Thomas Jefferson, James Madison, and Abraham Lincoln does not permit it." When they opened the floor for questions, gay-rights activist Karen Ocamb immediately challenged Olson: "There's tremendous suspicion in the LGBT community about your involvement in this because we never thought you were pro-gay."

The major gay-rights organizations also gave *Perry* a frosty reception. On the day AFER announced its lawsuit, nine LGBT advocacy groups—including the ACLU, the Gay and Lesbian Advocates and Defenders (GLAD), the Human Rights Campaign (HRC), Lambda Legal, and the NCLR—released a joint statement responding to the California Supreme Court's decision to uphold Prop 8. The statement exhorted individuals "to go back to the voters." While acknowledging the allure of a federal lawsuit, the groups described it as "a temptation we should resist." The statement made no mention of *Perry.* However, Griffin and his colleagues interpreted it as an assault.

It was a fair inference. The advocacy groups had trumpeted their disapproval of *Perry* to the media. The *New York Times* quoted Jennifer Pizer of Lambda Legal as saying, "We think it's risky and premature," and Matt Coles of the ACLU as remarking sarcastically, "Federal court? Wow. Never thought of that." In an interview with *The Advocate,* Coles elaborated that *Perry* was "an attempt to short-circuit the process, to go all the way to the end." To movement lawyers who had spent years painstakingly assembling the foundation for a federal case, *Perry* seemed like a risk and usurpation. Their harsh reaction can only be understood against the backdrop of the national movement for same-sex marriage.

2

THE MOVEMENT LAWYERS

In 1983, when few took same-sex marriage seriously, a Harvard law student named Evan Wolfson wrote a thesis that made an impassioned case for it. The handwritten corrections in the margins show its vintage. Yet Wolfson's arguments—based on equality and liberty—seem clairvoyant. Its last paragraph ties both themes to the importance of love.

> People are born different, into different circumstances, but are inherently equal in moral terms and in the eyes of the law, as our Constitution confirms. According this equality is perhaps most vital when it comes to love, the great leveler, which comes to each of us not wholly by choice or design. The choice we do and should have is what to make of what we are. For gay women and men, who also love, same-sex marriage is a human aspiration, and a human right. The Constitution and real morality demand its recognition. By freeing gay individuals as our

constitutional morality requires, we will more fully free our ideas of love, and thus more fully free ourselves.

Wolfson had difficulty finding a professor to supervise this paper. Even the more progressive ones balked. "It's not that they were against it," he said. "I think they didn't see it as that important or that likely to happen, and in some cases a little bit trivial." The professor who ultimately supervised his paper gave him a B.

Often called the godfather of the same-sex marriage movement, Wolfson has dedicated his life to this cause. He served for more than a decade at Lambda Legal and directed its marriage efforts until 2001, after which he established the prominent organization Freedom to Marry. Freedom to Marry adopted a three-track strategy to secure nationwide marriage equality: win more states, build and grow the majority of the public who would support same-sex marriage, and end federal discrimination against same-sex couples by fully overturning DOMA. Wolfson's work, including the 2004 book *Why Marriage Matters,* has been crucial in bringing same-sex marriage from the margins to the mainstream.

As Wolfson knew when he wrote his thesis, however, the struggle would take decades. In the early '80s, a majority of states still criminalized same-sex sexual conduct, and only one state—Wisconsin—had enacted a non-discrimination law covering sexual orientation. On the rare occasions when courts considered the issue of same-sex marriage, they treated it with scorn.

While lawsuits seeking same-sex marriage may seem like a recent innovation, they date back to the 1970s. In the wake of *Loving v. Virginia,* decided in 1967, and the Stonewall Riots of 1969, same-sex couples in Kentucky, Minnesota, Washington, and Wisconsin brought lawsuits seeking the right to marry. One of these couples, Jack Baker and James Michael McConnell, brought their case all the way to the Supreme Court in a case captioned *Baker v. Nelson.*

Baker and McConnell met in Oklahoma in 1966, later moving to Minnesota, where Baker attended law school. On New Year's Eve, 1969, Baker proposed to McConnell, and the couple applied for a marriage license the next May in Minnesota's Hennepin County. The County Clerk denied their application, and the couple filed suit later that year, alleging violations of the federal Constitution. They lost all the way to the Minnesota Supreme Court. "The institution of marriage as a union of man and woman," the court wrote, "is as old as the book of Genesis." With the assistance of the Minnesota Civil Liberties Union, they then appealed to the US Supreme Court, which in 1972 ruled against them in a single sentence: "The appeal is dismissed for want of a substantial federal question." Yet that lone sentence was technically binding precedent. In more recent cases involving same-sex marriage, including *Perry,* opponents of same-sex marriage have argued that *Baker* precludes lower courts from ruling in favor of same-sex marriage under any provision of the federal Constitution.

In addition to losing his marriage case, McConnell also lost his job: After the media reported on the couple's application for a marriage license—"Prospective Newlyweds Really in a Gay Mood," a local paper blared—the University of Minnesota Board of Regents rescinded an offer it had extended to McConnell to work in the university's library. Though McConnell filed a lawsuit and won an injunction from a federal district court, the US Court of Appeals for the Eighth Circuit reversed it, in a decision that accused him of trying "to foist tacit approval of [a] socially repugnant concept upon his employer." Over the lone dissent of Justice William Douglas, the Supreme Court declined to review the decision.

Though the ACLU's Minnesota affiliate represented McConnell in his marriage and employment discrimination suits, the national office of the ACLU did not appear in either case. The ACLU had supported gay rights in principle since 1966. In an internal memo about the marriage case, however, one ACLU attorney wrote that bringing the matter to the Supreme Court could "jeopardize" the organization's "more serious efforts on behalf of the homophile movement."

The *Baker* plaintiffs had few other organizations to which they could turn. The national LGBT litigation shops—GLAD, Lambda Legal, and NCLR—would not materialize until later in the '70s, and the national office of the ACLU would not establish its Lesbian and Gay Rights Project until 1986. Even if those organizations had existed in 1970, they probably would not have jumped to take *Baker v. Nelson*. In their early years, the groups' immediate aspirations were perforce more modest. One group had to litigate its right to exist: In 1972, a panel of New York judges denied Lambda Legal's petition to form as a nonprofit corporation. In the judges' view, the organization's "stated purposes"—which included defending the "legal rights of homosexuals" free of charge—were neither "benevolent nor charitable" as required for nonprofit groups under state law. (The state's highest court reversed that decision in 1973.) The other gay-rights groups also largely played defense. GLAD was founded in response to aggressive police targeting and entrapment, including an arrest of 103 men on charges ranging from indecent exposure to "open and gross lewdness." The organization's first case charged the Boston Public Library and police officials with violating the rights of a man arrested at the library.

When gays faced widespread police harassment, when courts debated whether a gay-rights group could exist as a nonprofit, and when the few judges to consider same-sex marriage viewed it as "socially repugnant," constitutional litigation seeking nationwide marriage equality seemed a quixotic goal.

During the years that followed, marriage equality for same-sex couples seemed to slide even further from reach. In 1986, the Supreme Court dealt the gay-rights movement a devastating setback in the *Bowers* case, which upheld the constitutionality of sodomy statutes. The case did not result in many subsequent arrests for sodomy. It did, however, create a ripple effect. *Bowers* caused many courts to rule that gays could not receive any meaningful protection under the Constitution, much less the heightened protection accorded to some minorities. These courts reasoned that a Constitution that allowed homosexual conduct to be criminalized could not bar other forms of discrimination against gays.

Until the Supreme Court's *Lawrence* decision overruled *Bowers* in 2003, courts and public officials relied on this line of reasoning—and the sodomy laws that *Bowers* had left in place—to rule against gay individuals in cases involving a panoply of issues, from adoption to military service. I once asked Coles whether *Bowers* had made the movement groups unduly cautious. "It made us rightly cautious," Coles replied evenly. "Litigating under *Bowers* was hell."

The parenting cases were especially wrenching. In one case, a Virginia trial judge relied on the state's sodomy law to remove a three-year-old child from the custody of his mother, Sharon Bottoms. The mother's "homosexual conduct," the court found, was both "illegal" and "immoral," rendering her an unfit parent. The judge awarded custody to the child's grandmother, who had become estranged from Bottoms after learning she was gay. Though an intermediate appellate court sided with the mother, she lost in 1995 before the Supreme Court of Virginia, which reinstated the trial judge's order. While purporting to agree in principle that "a lesbian mother is not per se an unfit parent," the court wrote that her lesbian conduct counted against her because it was a felony in Virginia.

Given that movement lawyers were still fighting—and often losing—battles involving *Bowers* and state sodomy laws well into the 1990s, they understandably felt skittish when approached in the early 1990s by same-sex couples seeking to file a marriage suit in Hawaii. The couples had reached out to the ACLU and to Lambda Legal. Both groups initially declined to represent them, deeming the suit premature. In the end, a straight attorney named Dan Foley brought the case in 1991. When the case found its way to the Supreme Court of Hawaii, Lambda Legal stepped in through its attorney Evan Wolfson.

In 1993, the Hawaii Supreme Court issued its ruling—a watershed decision that subjected bans on same-sex marriage to heightened judicial scrutiny under the state's Equal Protection Clause. In a manner that would distinguish it from most later courts, the court found the ban discriminated on the basis of sex, not sexual orientation.

The debate about whether bans on same-sex marriage should be challenged as sex discrimination or sexual-orientation discrimination rages to this day. The sex-discrimination argument focuses on how the bans refer only to men and women, not gays and lesbians. Prop 8, for instance, stated that "only marriage between a man and a woman is valid or recognized in California." Under these bans, a lesbian is free to marry a gay man, while two straight men cannot marry each other. Advocates of the sex-discrimination argument maintain that this terminology is enough to trigger the heightened review drawn by sex classifications. Opponents counter that the law does not treat the sexes unequally just because it mentions them. As is so often the case in law, how you frame the issue makes all the difference. If you define the act as "marrying a woman," then the bans discriminate on the basis of sex, as John, but not Jane, can marry Jill. If you define the act as "marrying someone of the same sex," the law treats John and Jane the same.

Yet as Andrew Koppelman—the legal scholar probably most responsible for developing the sex-discrimination theory—has pointed out, this "equal application" defense was made and rejected in the interracial marriage context. The state of Virginia argued in *Loving* that its law did not violate the Equal Protection Clause because both whites and non-whites were prohibited from marrying outside their groups. The Court cut through the noise and said that everyone knew that the laws were enacted to enforce "white supremacy."

For the analogy to carry over to same-sex marriage, critics of Koppelman have argued, one would have to say that bans on same-sex marriage were about "male supremacy," when they appear to be more about "heterosexual supremacy." Yet Koppelman persuasively responds that much of homophobia is driven by male supremacy, contending that in a world without sex discrimination, we would see little if any sexual-orientation discrimination. Marshaling studies that reveal a correlation between homophobia and rigid, stereotypical views about gender roles, he argues that much of the antipathy toward gay and lesbian people flows from their perceived failure to adhere to gender expectations. By policing the boundary between the sexes, homophobia preserves the hierarchy of men over women.

As convincing as I find Koppelman's argument, I understand why most courts have preferred to analyze marriage-equality cases as a form of discrimination on the basis of sexual orientation. As Oliver Wendell Holmes once said, "The life of the law has not been logic; it has been experience." Even if the bans on same-sex marriage do not mention gays or lesbians, they are experienced— correctly—as targeting that population. Yes, two straight men and two gay men are equally prohibited from marrying, but only in the manner that the rich and the poor are equally prohibited from sleeping under bridges.

The real puzzle is why anyone would view these claims to be mutually exclusive rather than mutually reinforcing. Courts can—and should—rule on both grounds. Throughout *Perry*, the argument focused on sexual-orientation discrimination, but the sex-discrimination argument could be heard as a tantalizing grace note all along the way.

After embracing the sex-discrimination argument, the Hawaii high court sent the case back downstairs, ordering the trial court to apply the more stringent standard of judicial review used in sex-discrimination cases to the ban on same-sex marriage. Under this standard, the trial court would have to find Hawaii's ban unconstitutional unless the state demonstrated that it advanced "compelling state interests" that were "narrowly drawn to avoid unnecessary abridgements of constitutional rights." Judge Kevin Chang presided over a nine-day trial in which four expert witnesses testified on each side, mostly about child rearing. The trial court found that the government could not meet the high standard set by the state supreme court. It stayed—or delayed the implementation of—this decision, pending appeal. To the elation of many gay couples, it seemed Hawaii would soon permit same-sex marriage.

Instead, the Hawaii case generated a seismic backlash. To preempt a final court decision guaranteeing same-sex marriage, Hawaii enacted a constitutional amendment that authorized the legislature to define marriage as it wished, thereby shutting down the possibility of same-sex marriage for the time being. The 1993 Hawaii decision also triggered a national panic, causing Congress to pass DOMA three years later. Most people are familiar with the section of DOMA that defined marriage for all federal purposes as a relationship between one man and one woman. Fewer recall that DOMA contains another provision as well: It allows states not to recognize same-sex marriages legally performed in other states. DOMA sailed through both houses of Congress on a lopsided vote, with the House of Representatives approving it 342–67, and the Senate 85–14. Reiterating his "long-standing" opposition to same-sex marriage, President Clinton promised to sign the bill even before it passed the House. Clinton would later say that he supported DOMA in part because he believed it would defuse a push to enact a federal constitutional amendment banning marriage for same-sex couples. Perhaps he read the zeitgeist correctly: By the end of the Hawaii litigation in 1998, thirty-one states had enacted statutory or state constitutional bans on same-sex marriage (often called mini-DOMAs). California followed suit shortly thereafter with the March 2000 passage of the Knight Initiative.

Throughout the Hawaii litigation and legislative backlash, gay-rights supporters were embroiled in their own internal battle. Starting in 1989, Lambda colleagues Tom Stoddard and Paula Ettelbrick engaged in a long, public, and celebrated debate about whether lesbians and gay men should strive for marriage at all. While Stoddard argued that the movement should "aggressively" pursue legal recognition, Ettelbrick contended that same-sex marriage would "force our assimilation into the mainstream," undermining the goals of the movement, including the "validation of many forms of relationships."

Meanwhile, Andrew Sullivan published a trailblazing article in 1989 making the first "conservative" case for same-sex marriage in the *New Republic,* arguing that gay marriage would "foster social cohesion, emotional security, and economic prudence." Sullivan expanded on this theme in his 1995 book, *Virtually Normal,* and other conservatives joined in—including Jonathan Rauch, who argued that marriage would offer "stabilizing influences" on gay relationships.

Not everyone was convinced, however. Echoing Paula Ettelbrick, Michael Warner maintained in *The Trouble with Normal* that same-sex marriage would leave "unmarried queers looking more deviant." In a similar vein, Nancy Polikoff expressed concern that embracing same-sex marriage would obscure the limitations of a "social system valuing one form of human relationship above all others." Polikoff argued not for the elimination of marriage itself, but for the elimination of marriage as the determinant of whether a family could access legal benefits. In many instances, she noted, the law gave privileges to married couples—such as estate tax exemptions, adoption rights, survivor benefits—that it denied to unmarried partners and to individuals in nonsexual relationships. Polikoff contended that instead of using marriage as a "rigid dividing line between who is in and who is out," we should identify the purpose of laws that currently elevate marriage above other families, and extend legal privileges to nonmarital relationships that fulfill the same purpose.

Gay-rights litigation groups took these perspectives seriously. Lambda Legal, for instance, argued for legal recognition of nontraditional family units without regard to "arbitrary distinctions" such as "marital relation" or "genetic history." At the same time, the movement lawyers steadily pursued a strategy aimed at achieving marriage equality. Meeting every six months, they settled on an inch-by-inch approach. When the groups challenged state bans on same-sex marriage, they argued solely on the basis of state constitutional law. Because state supreme courts are the ultimate authorities on state law, this strategy insulated these cases from review by the United States Supreme Court, protecting the groups from another *Bowers*. The gay-rights groups planned to proceed incrementally until a critical mass of jurisdictions legalized same-sex marriage. Then, and only then, did the groups plan to "make a federal case" out of state bans on same-sex marriage, bringing a suit that would cause the Supreme Court to wash out the outlier states.

The movement lawyers chose to litigate in states in which they could not only prevail in court but also preserve a win from being wiped out by a state constitutional amendment. To this end, they analyzed the marriage law and constitutional amendment procedures in all fifty states. The states vary widely with respect to how easily their constitutions can be amended. As a general rule, states that joined the Union earlier have constitutions more difficult to amend than states that joined later. The difference can be explained in part by the Populist and Progressive movements that swept the nation starting in the 1890s. During that period, voters became increasingly distrustful of their elected representatives. They created mechanisms of direct democracy through which ordinary citizens could participate in lawmaking, including ballot initiatives that bypassed the legislature altogether.

The great benefit of direct democracy is that it allows citizens to check legislatures captured by special interests. The great downside is that citizens can sidestep legislatures to disadvantage minorities. Ballot initiatives originally sought to keep powerful minorities at the top of society—such as corporations—from hijacking the lawmaking process. Yet the same procedures have increasingly been used to hurt minorities at the bottom of society—such as racial minorities, undocumented immigrants, or gays. Legislatures have passed laws safeguarding vulnerable groups from the masses, only to see those masses override those protections. One reason direct democracy often leads to populist attacks on minorities is that unlike legislators, whose debates are publicly recorded and scrutinized by the media, voters need not disclose their reasons for supporting a ballot initiative.

Consequently, the movement lawyers targeted states that did not permit voters to amend the constitution without input from the legislature. The New England states, which generally had stringent amendment procedures, presented the natural "second front" of litigation after Hawaii. A few states outside of New England also had constitutions that were hard to amend, which explained why Lambda Legal targeted New Jersey and Iowa for early lawsuits.

Mary Bonauto of GLAD, rightly called the Thurgood Marshall of the gay-rights movement by fellow pioneer Rep. Barney Frank, drove the New England strategy. The first victory came in Vermont: In 1999, the Supreme Court of Vermont ruled unanimously that the state constitution did not allow the state to "exclude same-sex couples from the benefits and protections that its laws provide to opposite-sex married couples." Yet a majority of the court declined to mandate marriage equality, leaving it to the legislature to provide either same-sex marriage or "some equivalent statutory alternative." In 2000, Vermont enacted a civil-unions law, becoming the first state in the nation to provide comprehensive relationship recognition (minus the word "marriage") to same-sex couples.

GLAD's breakthrough, however, came in 2003, when the Massachusetts Supreme Judicial Court became the first high court in the nation to hold that a state constitution granted same-sex couples the right to marry. In a 4–3 decision written by Chief Justice Margaret Marshall, the court gave the state legislature 180 days to change the law.

The wisdom of the movement strategy then revealed itself. Massachusetts's amendment procedure is exacting. A proposed amendment to its constitution must be approved by a joint session of the lawmakers during two successive legislative sessions, after which it must still go to the voters. In 2004, before any same-sex couples could marry, the legislature voted 105 to 92 in favor of a constitutional ban on same-sex marriage. To go into effect, however, the proposed amendment would need to get another majority in the state legislature in 2005, and then to prevail in a popular vote in November 2006. In short, Chief Justice Marshall knew when she imposed the six-month deadline that same-sex couples would be able to marry for at least the period between May 2004 and November 2006. Couples began to marry on May 17, 2004, when Gov. Mitt Romney ordered town clerks to begin issuing marriage licenses to same-sex couples. On the one-year anniversary of that day, a headline in *USA Today* said it all: "The Sky Didn't Fall in Mass." Later that year, the second legislative vote defeated the amendment 157–39, meaning it would never go before the voters. Even a co-sponsor of the original amendment, Sen. Brian P. Lees, voted against it the second time. In 2007, a separate attempt to put the issue before voters also failed.

Like the Hawaii decision, the Massachusetts decision provoked a rash of legislation. Citing concern that "activist judges" would strike down DOMA, President George W. Bush called for a federal constitutional amendment to prohibit any state from legalizing same-sex marriage, whether by judicial, legislative, or other means. While the Federal Marriage Amendment failed in both the House and Senate to secure the two-thirds supermajority required for constitutional amendments, it secured symbolically important majority votes from the House in both 2004 and 2006. Motivated by the same desire to hang the issue beyond the reach of their courts or legislatures, states elevated their bans into their constitutions. In the 2004 national elections, eleven out of eleven proposed bans on same-sex marriage found their way into state constitutions. In 2006, eight more states enacted such prohibitions.

Prop 8 sought to make California the twenty-seventh state with such a ban. California's amendment process is as easy as

Massachusetts's is difficult. The California Constitution can be changed through a ballot initiative that entirely circumvents the legislature. Proponents of an initiative need to collect signatures from only 8 percent of the citizens who voted in the last gubernatorial election to place their proposal on the ballot. A raw majority of voters can then enshrine the measure in the constitution.

Despite the odds against them, California was too large a prize for the movement lawyers to ignore. In 2003, they convened an invitation-only meeting at UCLA called the California Marriage Litigation Roundtable. Briefing papers analyzed the California case law relating to gay rights and to marriage, profiled the California Supreme Court justices, and outlined the threat posed by the amendment process. The roundtable concluded that while same-sex couples would prevail in the California Supreme Court, a subsequent initiative would wash out that victory. In short, the movement lawyers predicted exactly what would happen in 2008.

The LGBT advocates took their battles elsewhere—with mixed results. They lost their cases in the high courts of Washington and New York in 2006, and in the Maryland Supreme Court in 2007. In Connecticut, however, the state Supreme Court issued an October 2008 decision requiring the state to allow same-sex marriage. The Iowa Supreme Court ruled unanimously in favor of same-sex couples seeking the right to marry in April 2009. Four days later, the Vermont legislature authorized same-sex marriage, overriding a gubernatorial veto and becoming the first state to attain marriage equality through legislative rather than judicial means. New Hampshire and the District of Columbia quickly followed suit. In several other states—including states where efforts to win marriage equality initially faltered—LGBT advocates secured other forms of relationship recognition, such as civil unions and domestic partnerships.

Some movement lawyers also turned their attention to the section of DOMA that banned federal recognition of same-sex marriages lawfully entered at the state level. In early March 2009, more than two months before *Perry* was filed, Bonauto and her colleagues at

GLAD filed a federal constitutional challenge in Massachusetts to that provision—the same provision the Supreme Court ultimately declared unconstitutional in its historic *Windsor* decision in 2013. The often-repeated claim that gay-rights advocates avoided federal courts in the fight for marriage equality, then, is untrue—they only avoided challenging state bans in that forum.

Nonetheless, the gay-rights groups looked down a torturous road. With regard to state bans, the formula that many gay-rights advocates bandied about was "ten-ten-ten-twenty." As James Esseks of the ACLU put it, the plan was to move state by state until they had "ten states with marriage, ten states with full partnership, ten states with more limited domestic partnership protections, and twenty states where we don't think we're going to get marriage." Some movement lawyers thought even this plan was too slow, and none saw it as anything more than a guideline. Yet the strategy was significantly more bullish than the strategy that stamped out bans on interracial marriage. When *Loving v. Virginia* was filed, thirty-three states already permitted interracial marriage. When AFER filed its lawsuit, only four states had marriage equality. Just as important, many states had upheld bans on same-sex marriage—even liberal ones like Maryland, New York, and Washington. No wonder, then, that the gay-rights groups found *Perry* "premature."

In AFER's defense, the organization conferred extensively with these groups before filing suit—a fact that often gets lost because the conversations were confidential. In the fall of 2008, a representative from AFER reached out to Paul Smith, because he had won *Lawrence* at the Supreme Court. Smith declined to play a role in *Perry*. Similarly, in May 2009, an AFER board member met with Ramona Ripston and Mark Rosenbaum of the ACLU and Jennifer Pizer and Jon Davidson of Lambda Legal. Both groups advised AFER not to file.

AFER stood its ground, refusing to withdraw its suit. In the end, the gay-rights groups petitioned the court to intervene as co-counsel in the case. Intervention would not allow them to shut down the case, but it would allow them a say in how it was argued. Griffin responded with a scalding public letter, which concluded: "You have unrelentingly and unequivocally acted to undermine this case even before it was filed. In light of this, it is inconceivable that you would zealously and effectively litigate this case if you were successful in intervening. Therefore, we will vigorously oppose any motion to intervene." Even Boies and Olson would later write that he showed "perhaps a little too much zeal." The LGBT groups declined to respond. They had spent decades laying the groundwork for a Supreme Court challenge; now they felt control wrested from them by corporate lawyers who might or might not know how to bring a successful civil-rights suit. What's more, those lawyers were publicly denouncing them.

This conflict shows how much civil-rights litigation has changed. In the fight to overturn the Jim Crow laws, civil-rights groups like the NAACP had much more control over the pace of litigation. After *Plessy v. Ferguson*, the 1896 case that upheld the constitutionality of "separate but equal" on the basis of race, the NAACP orchestrated its litigation to the last detail. Working in the 1930s and '40s, Charles Hamilton Houston and Thurgood Marshall decided it was too soon to ask the Court to reconsider the constitutionality of "separate but equal." They instead focused on ensuring that the separate facilities created for African Americans were truly equal. Moreover, they sequenced the cases so that each successive decision asked more of the institutions being sued.

In one of the early "equalization" cases, *Missouri v. Gaines*, the NAACP challenged an all-white Missouri graduate school's practice of sending African Americans to out-of-state schools. The NAACP lawyers argued that the state had not met the requirements of "separate but equal" if it had to ship racial minorities across state lines to grant them equality. In 1938, the Supreme Court agreed. In the wake of *Gaines*, states had to create all-black equivalents of their all-white universities within state borders. The "separate but equal" policy began to collapse under its own impracticability—the state could not conjure up "equal" educational institutions overnight. When the University of Texas hastily constructed an in-state all-black cognate, the NAACP brought suit. In 1950, the Supreme Court ruled for the plaintiffs, noting that the jerry-built school lacked the University of Texas's physical plant, reputation, alumni networks, and faculty. Other schools tried a different tack, allowing African Americans into the building, but adopting a "velvet rope" strategy, in which blacks had to sit in different areas of the classrooms, libraries, and cafeterias. The Court also rejected this arrangement. At that point, graduate education was essentially integrated. Then, and only then, did the NAACP directly attack the constitutionality of "separate but equal" in *Brown v. Board of Education.*

Such institutionally choreographed civil-rights litigation may no longer be possible. When rogue plaintiffs sought to disrupt the movement strategy, the NAACP told them to stand down. Almost without exception, the private lawyers withdrew their cases. In a much more litigious age, no coalition of LGBT groups can sequence cases as the NAACP did on the road to *Brown.* Olson defended bringing the suit on this ground, noting that some rogue plaintiff would inevitably file a federal suit against Prop 8. If so, that rogue might as well be him. "We've all seen people bringing cases in the Supreme Court who don't know what they're doing," he said. Ultimately, the movement lawyers had no choice but to be philosophical about AFER's decision. The groups pooled their expertise. On one conference call, Kate Kendell of the NCLR dubbed Olson an "honorary lesbian."

Scholars have spilled much ink over the question of whether private litigants like Olson and Boies have an ethical obligation to defer to movement lawyers. Jon Davidson of Lambda Legal observed: "Imagine a lot of white lawyers not affiliated with the NAACP bringing desegregation cases on their own from big law firms not involved in civil-rights work. Would they have not felt like they should have gotten the blessing of the NAACP before they ventured off and did it?" Yet Davidson also acknowledged that had Olson and Boies not challenged Prop 8, someone else without their resources or acumen would have done so: "If somebody was going to do it—and somebody was—it was good that they did it." A rock paperweight on his desk reminded us both of the flexibility required of every civil-rights litigator. Etched in the surface of the rock were the words: NOTHING IS WRITTEN IN STONE.

3

THE PROPONENTS

With their star wattage, Boies and Olson largely overshadowed their opponents. Yet although their greater visibility drew more attention to the infighting in their camp, the conflicts among the defense attorneys were also dramatic.

For starters, the government officials sued in *Perry* refused to defend Prop 8. The plaintiffs' complaint named California governor Arnold Schwarzenegger as the primary defendant. Schwarzenegger had previously vetoed same-sex marriage bills passed by the California legislature, stating that he believed marriage should be between a man and a woman. By the time Prop 8 passed, Schwarzenegger had come to support same-sex marriage—a gradual conversion that would prefigure the "evolving" views of President Obama, Bill and Hillary Clinton, and umpteen other political figures. The governor compared the stamina needed to secure marriage equality to that needed in bodybuilding. "I learned that you should never, ever give up," he asserted. "They should be on it and on it until they get it done." And when *Perry* was filed, his attorney general, Jerry Brown, decided not to defend the law. (That position would later prove critical.) When Brown succeeded Schwarzenegger as governor in 2011, his attorney general, Kamala Harris, took the same position.

The task of defending a state constitutional amendment, usually assumed by government officials, fell to the proponents of the ballot initiative. It fell most immediately on the shoulders of a solo practitioner in Sacramento named Andrew Pugno. If one were looking to cast Chad Griffin's party opposite, it would probably be Pugno, who was also only thirty-five years old when Prop 8 passed. With his round glasses and cherubic face, he looks like the Eagle Scout and Young Republican that he is. After graduating from UC Davis, Pugno worked in the California Capitol. He started as a legislative consultant to then assemblyman Pete Knight. Shortly after Knight was elected to the state senate in 1996, Pugno became his chief of staff. In Knight, Pugno found a staunch mentor until Knight's death in 2004.

Pugno's first assignment with Knight was same-sex marriage. In 1995, conservatives around the country were aghast at how close Hawaii appeared to legalization. A marriage is usually valid in all fifty states if valid in the state where it was performed. Opponents feared that if one state permitted same-sex marriage, gay couples around the nation would marry there and demand recognition at home. Knight asked Pugno to work on a bill that would block California from recognizing same-sex marriages performed outside the state. The California legislature voted down the measure, but Pugno had found a calling. He would draft and defend laws against same-sex marriage for the next fifteen years.

After failing three times in the legislature, Knight's organization took the issue directly to the people through a ballot initiative—Prop 22. Prop 22 passed in 2000 with a 22-point margin—a classic case of the voters burdening a minority after their elected representatives had declined to do so. In 2001, Pugno completed law school and stopped working for Knight. Yet when his mentor asked him to defend Prop 22 in court, Pugno loyally returned to service. That defense began when San Francisco mayor Gavin Newsom began issuing marriage licenses. Arguing that Newsom's actions violated Prop 22, Pugno and his allies prevailed at the California Supreme Court in 2004.

Pugno's relationship with other potential allies, however, was not always so harmonious. As early as 2005, conservative groups predicted the California Supreme Court would overturn Prop 22 on state constitutional grounds. They decided to bring a constitutional amendment before the California voters. The groups fiercely disputed the scope of the amendment. Pugno simply wanted to bake the language of Prop 22 into the constitution. Randy Thomasson, who headed the Campaign for California Families (CCF), pressed for a measure that would not only bar same-sex marriage but also extinguish existing domestic-partnership rights, including those pertaining to child custody, community property, and hospital visitation.

"It was like the nuclear option to obliterate the entire domestic-partners law," Pugno observed. "We were constantly hassled by that organization, who thought we weren't aggressive enough." Each group partnered with religious-liberties groups that reflected their approaches. For Thomasson, that group was the Liberty Counsel, a group based at Jerry Falwell's Liberty University. For Pugno, it was the religious-liberties juggernaut called the Alliance Defense Fund (ADF).

In 1994, a who's who of New Christian Right leaders—including Bill Bright of the Campus Crusade for Christ, D. James Kennedy of Coral Ridge Ministries, and Marlin Maddoux of the *Point of View* radio program—founded the ADF. In all, more than thirty ministries joined this umbrella organization. Since its inception, the organization has been led by Alan Sears, a former prosecutor who served in Ronald Reagan's Department of Justice.

When the ADF launched, the Associated Press reported that it sought "to raise $25 million a year to fight what they perceived to be anti-Christian litigation." According to James Kennedy, "It was just years of seeing the ACLU and its cronies attacking religious organizations or religious exercise. And, very frequently, there was nobody that even showed up to defend the Christian position." The ADF has maintained a laser-sharp focus on the ACLU. Maddoux said the ADF would "out-swamp them so bad that they'll wonder why they ever went into this business." The ADF has amply fulfilled its financial aspirations, with annual revenues over $39 million in 2013.

During its infancy, the ADF focused on funding other religious-litigation outfits and training a new generation of lawyers. It founded its Legal Academy, a five-day seminar that created a "farm team" of Christian lawyers, in 1997. In return for educating them without charge on how to "defend religious freedom, the sanctity of life, and marriage and family," the ADF required these attorneys to commit to 450 hours of free legal work "on behalf of the Body of Christ." Since 2000, the ADF has also sponsored the Blackstone Fellowship, which trains law students in "constitutional law and a biblical world view" before they head to clerkships and other influential posts. Such programs have created a network of 2,200 "allied attorneys," including Pugno.

Around 2002, the ADF's operational model changed. While still funding cases handled by other firms, the ADF began litigating in its own name. To reflect this shift, the organization changed its name in 2012 from the Alliance Defense Fund to the Alliance Defending Freedom. That year, it boasted forty-four staff attorneys—more than GLAD, Lambda Legal, and the NCLR combined.

The ADF promotes itself as a defender of "religious liberty." Yet as Barry Lynn, the executive director of Americans United for Separation of Church and State, has noted: "They're not for some form of generic religious freedom. They're for Christian superiority." The ADF may sometimes downplay its Christian focus, but does not deny it. As Alan Sears has stated, "The Alliance Defense Fund was founded to defend the right to hear and speak the Truth—that truth is the Gospel of Jesus Christ." The organization only hires Christians (as it can, because it designates itself a ministry), and all allied attorneys must sign a "statement of faith." The first tenet is: "We believe the Bible to be the inspired, infallible, authoritative Word of God."

The ADF believes the Supreme Court has grossly misinterpreted the Establishment Clause of the Constitution, which states that "Congress shall make no law respecting an establishment of religion." In several cases, the Court has interpreted that text to require a "wall of separation between church and state." Sears maintains that the Founders only intended the clause to stop Congress from declaring a national religion. (Even on the current Supreme Court, which has done some work to dismantle the wall, only Justice Thomas shares Sears's view.)

A major setback for this narrow reading dates back to 1971, when the Supreme Court maintained in *Lemon v. Kurtzman* that laws had to be justified by "a secular legislative purpose." To be sure, the Court has used the *Lemon* test opportunistically, generally invoking it only when it wishes to invalidate state action. In 1983, the Court flatly ignored *Lemon* in a case involving legislative prayer, which could hardly be said to have a secular purpose. When the issue came up again in 2014, the Court did the same thing. Nonetheless, the Court's decision to avoid *Lemon* (as opposed to overruling it or creating an explicit exception to it) suggests the Court's enduring commitment to the idea that the laws that bind us all cannot codify the beliefs of a particular sect.

This may not be the case in the future. Through the work of the ADF, Sears contends, "one by one, more and more bricks that make up the artificial 'wall of separation' are being removed." The ADF has participated in a vast array of religious-liberties cases in the federal courts and boasts an 80 percent success rate. Lynn believes this rate is misleading: "They do a lot of no-brainer cases

where some school has made an obvious error. . . . Then they go
in and file a lawsuit and prevail and claim they've won this great
victory." Still, the ADF's effectiveness is undeniable. Its cases have
involved religious symbols, religious groups and prayer in schools,
abortion, and end-of-life issues. And, of course, homosexuality.

The ADF's interest in sexual orientation intensified in the mid-
1990s. It participated on the winning side of Supreme Court
cases concerning LGBT issues, such as a 1995 case permitting organizers to ban gays from marching openly in South Boston's St.
Patrick's Day parade and a 2000 case finding that the Boy Scouts
could exclude openly gay adults. That participation ramped up dramatically when same-sex marriage became a matter of national debate. Sears published *The Homosexual Agenda* in 2003, the same
year Massachusetts legalized same-sex marriage. By 2004, the
ADF maintained a "Marriage Litigation Center."

While more extreme organizations issue scorching condemna-
tions of homosexuality, the ADF adopts a posture of pity. Sears's
book begins with an authors' note underscoring that "both authors and the ministry of the Alliance Defense Fund have nothing but respect, compassion, and sensitivity toward those ensnared
in homosexual behavior. . . . Both of us have family members, respected acquaintances, and friends who have been trapped in this
behavior and know something of the incredible pain and sorrow it
has brought to them and their families." Sears castigates individuals like Fred Phelps of the Westboro Baptist Church "who would
picket the funerals of AIDS victims, post messages that 'God Hates
Fags' on the World Wide Web, condemn those who have compassion for those trapped in homosexual behavior, and state that there
is no redemption for the homosexual."

Even as the ADF affirms gay individuals, it condemns the homosexual activity in which those individuals are "ensnared." Sears
acknowledges the tension: "With God's grace we carefully balance

this love and respect for these individuals with warnings about the carrying out, promotion, and demand for legal approval for homosexual behavior that will stifle religious freedom and trap millions of more people in its deadly grip." The tension lies entirely between status and conduct. Sears brooks no ambivalence about the conduct itself. Obedience to God requires understanding certain "crystal-clear, non-debatable issues." Sears avows that one of those issues is "homosexual behavior," which God "undeniably condemns."

The dual certainties of the ADF foreclose a "live and let live" détente. Having a loving attitude toward gay individuals requires intervention on their behalf, lest they lose their eternal souls. It would be much easier for the ADF to coexist with "unrepentant" gays if the ADF did not "love" them. In Sears's words: "As Christians, we cannot sit idly by as individuals engage in behavior that will result in their eternal demise."

The ADF therefore must—and does—oppose same-sex marriage. From its perspective, validating such relationships would lock gay people into a sinful lifestyle. Of course, the ADF's objection to same-sex marriage extends far beyond its perceived negative effects on gay people. Same-sex marriage also violates "God's plan for marriage and the family." The ADF routinely places same-sex "marriage" in scare quotes to distinguish it from what the organization calls "true" marriage. It argues that marriage just *is* an opposite-sex institution. Opponents have countered that this is a circular argument. Yet from the ADF's point of view, the critique is incorrect, given that the definition flows from God. In a 2011 brochure, the ADF observed that marriage is "the first institution ordained by God," "a crowning achievement of His Creation," and a reflection of "the relationship of Christ and His Bride, the Church."

Given what the ADF believes, its capacity to translate its views into secular terms is dazzling. Throughout the *Perry* trial, the ADF toggled away from claims about "sin" or "God's plan" or "Christ and His Bride, the Church," to arguments about "optimal parenting" or "responsible procreation." The ADF doubtless believes those secular reasons. However, it does not lead with them when speaking to its members. The enduring power of the wall of separation appears in how the ADF engages audiences on either side of that divide, reserving its explicitly sectarian language for its flock.

The desire to cloak religious intent may explain why faith-based opposition to same-sex marriage has turned to ballot initiatives. In debating legislation, such opponents risk leaving a paper trail about the religious basis for their vote, and courts or voters may call them to account. For an ecclesiastical majority with lawmaking ambitions, a ballot initiative is the friendliest forum. Shielded, often literally, by a curtain, voters may cast their ballots on whatever grounds they wish, including religious ones. If the law is challenged in court, it will be much harder to discern whether it was passed with the requisite secular purpose because it will be harder to discern purpose of any kind. As gay people have emerged from the closet, some religious opponents of gay rights have retreated into the closet of the voting booth to express their views.

Because many lawmaking bodies are not receptive to religiously based arguments, it is good strategy for opponents of same-sex marriage to insist on direct democracy. But these opponents sometimes overplay their hand, suggesting that even representative democracy is somehow undemocratic. After the New York legislature legalized same-sex marriage in 2011, NOM—the same group responsible for the *Gathering Storm* video—mounted a counter-campaign that turned on the slogan "Let the People Vote." Even an editorial board member of the right-leaning *Wall Street Journal* called foul, stating that the slogan was the political equivalent of "deceptive advertising." "Let the People Vote" is a protest usually lodged against unelected "activist" judges. In this instance, however, the people *had* voted—through their elected representatives. The rallying cry would make more sense if direct democracy were the only form of legitimate democracy. The United States, of course, does not subscribe to that theory.

Although the ADF dutifully scrubbed its rhetoric of any religious allusions when it entered the courtroom, Pugno remained unsatisfied. He looked elsewhere for lead counsel.

G riffin had hired lawyers not associated with gay-rights causes—Supreme Court litigators who gave press conferences in front of American—not rainbow—flags. Pugno sought the equivalent on the other side—lawyers who routinely argued before the Supreme Court and would give press conferences with no religious symbols in sight. Pugno never sought to serve as lead counsel himself. As one reporter put it: "He is a good enough lawyer to understand that he shouldn't argue directly with the fancy attorneys trying to derail Proposition 8."

Finding fancy lawyers to defend Prop 8 proved challenging. In a 2003 salvo that must have cheered the ADF, Justice Scalia accused the legal profession of having been taken over by the "so-called homosexual agenda." The accusation held some force. All the amicus briefs ("friend of the court" briefs submitted by outside groups or individuals) filed by large firms in the California Supreme Court took the pro-gay position. Princeton professor Robert George, a founder of NOM, came to the rescue, as he would several times during *Perry*. On George's advice, Pugno tapped Chuck Cooper, the name partner of the small but sterling firm of Cooper & Kirk in Washington, DC.

When the lawsuit was filed, Cooper was fifty-seven. A native of Alabama, Cooper had given up on his dream of becoming a professional baseball player as an undergraduate at the University of Alabama. He attended law school at the same university, serving as editor in chief of the law review. He went on to clerk in 1978 for Justice William Rehnquist, and still speaks with reverence of "The

Boss," as Rehnquist was known to his clerks. With his silver hair firmly parted in the middle, he looks like a Southern gentleman lawyer sent from Central Casting.

Following in Rehnquist's footsteps, Cooper took a position in the Department of Justice soon after his clerkship. In 1985, President Reagan appointed him to lead the Office of Legal Counsel (OLC), the body that tenders legal advice to the president. This prestigious post had been held in the past by Justices Rehnquist and Scalia. Cooper's immediate predecessor in that role was his close friend Ted Olson. As one reporter described it, the swap eliminated "a certain libertarian squishiness at the Office." Today, portraits of Olson and Cooper hang side by side in the conference room of OLC.

After leaving government in 1988, Cooper served as a partner in two different law firms before founding his own litigation shop in 1996. From the outset, Cooper & Kirk adopted certain flamboyant gestures, such as the practice of running up a red-and-white flag with the firm motto—*Vincere Aut Mori* ("Victory or Death")—when it posted a victory. (The phrase comes from a famously defiant letter written by Lt. Col. William B. Travis at the Alamo.) The firm's male attorneys wear cufflinks embossed with the motto, featuring a laurel wreath encircling a sword. When associates sign with the firm, they receive a sword along with their laptop. Tea Party favorite Sen. Ted Cruz, who was Cooper & Kirk's first associate, has his sword hanging in his Senate office.

Unlike many large firms that eschew an ideological brand, Cooper & Kirk is unabashedly conservative. It defended Michigan's Proposal 2, which barred state schools from engaging in affirmative action on the basis of race or gender. It represented the Citadel, an all-male military academy, when a woman named Shannon Faulkner attempted to enroll. And it defended the National Rifle Association's Political Victory Fund in a case alleging violation of campaign contribution limits.

In an era when large firms are merging into megafirms, Cooper & Kirk has remained lean, employing fewer than a dozen lawyers.

Pugno selected Cooper & Kirk to defend Prop 8 in part because of its size. Cooper noted that his larger competitors could not take the case: "The issue is too volatile, too controversial, too much of a tear in the fabric of the partnership." Cooper was right: attorney Paul Clement chose to move from a large firm to a small one after his original firm barred him from defending the provision of DOMA pertaining to the federal definition of marriage.

When he took the case, Cooper refused to confirm that he personally opposed same-sex marriage, but stated: "Most people could look at me, look at my background, look at my general political history and make an educated guess." They could. While he led OLC, Cooper wrote a 1986 policy memorandum opining that employers could fire employees with AIDS based on fears that they could spread the virus, even if that fear was irrational. The OLC repudiated that memorandum in 1988. In 1994, Cooper filed an amicus brief on behalf of several states defending the constitutionality of the anti-gay Colorado amendment invalidated in *Romer*. In 1997, Cooper represented Hawaii when same-sex couples sued the state for the right to marry. Even then, the plaintiffs' attorney, Dan Foley, criticized the state for choosing a lawyer "known for taking anti-gay positions in courts."

By 2010, Cooper had moderated his public positions. Throughout *Perry*, he stressed that one could be pro-gay and still oppose same-sex marriage. His main argument for Prop 8 concerned its status as a democratic enactment that should not be overturned by the courts. He even said he would defend an initiative that went the other way: "I would not hesitate to defend the constitutional right of the people of Vermont to decide this issue the way they did, quite contrary to the way the people of California have, if that were challenged on some federal constitutional basis." To be sure, it is hard to think of a constitutional ground on which a law granting marriage equality could be challenged. Nonetheless, Cooper's polish and prowess would be extraordinary assets for the proponents.

Pugno saw Cooper's "demeanor and civilized tone" as an

extension of the campaign, and contrasted it with the "combative" tone adopted by "fringe" organizations. One such group was the Liberty Counsel, which represented CCF. Liberty Counsel had been founded by Mathew Staver, a minister turned lawyer who initially focused on issues relating to abortion. Although ADF support had enabled Liberty Counsel to grow from a regional organization to a national one, the two organizations drifted apart over time. In 2000, Liberty Counsel found a new patron in Rev. Jerry Falwell. Under an agreement with Falwell, Staver became the dean of the Liberty University Law School, which also housed an office for Liberty Counsel. By 2004, Staver had no association with the ADF. Under Staver's leadership, Liberty University built a replica of the Supreme Court bench at a cost of $1 million. The nine high-backed chairs, the red curtains, and the mahogany fixtures are virtually identical to those in the actual Court, two hundred miles away. Georgetown Law Center has a similar reproduction, though its purpose is perhaps different from Staver's. "Basically, this courtroom represents our vision of restoring the rule of law," Staver says.

The Southern Poverty Law Center considers Liberty Counsel, but not the ADF, to be a "hate group." Liberty Counsel is certainly more extreme. In 2000, it threatened to sue a public library for issuing certificates "for completion of term in Hogwarts School of Witchcraft and Wizardry" to children who had finished a book in the Harry Potter series. Staver maintained: "Witchcraft is a religion, and the certificate of witchcraft endorsed a particular religion in violation of the First Amendment establishment clause." Three years later, Liberty Counsel sought to prevent a mentally disabled Miami woman who had become pregnant as a result of rape from having an abortion. The woman's mother had been advised by a physician that her daughter risked death if she carried the pregnancy to term. Liberty Counsel sought unsuccessfully to intervene as guardians of the fetus.

With regard to homosexuality, the Liberty Counsel's views

mirror those of the ADF, but again, it seems willing to go further. For years, the organization represented Lisa Miller in her efforts to block her former partner, Janet Jenkins, from visiting with the couple's daughter, Isabella. Miller had given birth to Isabella shortly after Miller and Jenkins entered into a civil union in Vermont. Miller later converted to a conservative form of Christianity, renounced her homosexuality, and the couple dissolved their union. Miller's legal team at Liberty Counsel then tried to strip Jenkins of her parental rights, even though Miller had already conceded to a Vermont court that Jenkins was Isabella's lawful parent. Miller had also already agreed to visitation and sought child support from Jenkins. Even after the high courts of Vermont and Virginia both ruled unanimously against Miller and the US Supreme Court twice declined to get involved, Miller continued to flout court orders requiring visitation and ultimately made a cloak-and-dagger escape to Nicaragua with Isabella. She now faces criminal charges for kidnapping.

In a 2011 book about the legal saga titled *Only One Mommy*, Liberty Counsel attorney Rena Lindevaldsen castigates "activist judges," although the courts merely ruled that Jenkins's status as a legal parent entitled her to visitation rights. If anything, Lindevaldsen wanted the judges to be *more* activist, observing "one exception to this principle that judges are required to follow the law, even if they don't like it: judges are not bound to follow laws that violate the higher law—God's law." In a similar vein, she told the *New York Times* in 2012 that the courts had mishandled the Miller case by "turning a child over to a person who lives contrary to biblical truths."

In same-sex marriage litigation, the Liberty Counsel has continuously jockeyed for position with the ADF. In the state court proceedings challenging Mayor Newsom's weddings, Staver's organization rushed into court first, but was rebuffed because it failed to give proper notice to city officials. The ADF slipped past it to bring the successful challenge. Following that incident, the two organizations sniped at each other. Staver argued that many of the cases claimed by the ADF had been litigated by the Liberty Counsel; the ADF's counsel highlighted the deficiencies in the Liberty Counsel's work that had led the court to reject its challenge.

Given that history, the proponents had some clear priorities. The goal was to put Cooper & Kirk on center stage. The ADF would be given the relatively minor role of putting on the lay witnesses. And the Liberty Counsel would be excluded outright.

The media loved to describe Boies and Olson as counterintuitive lead counsel for the plaintiffs. Yet Cooper was similarly a much more mainstream lawyer than the groups that had been waging the marriage wars in California. The two groups—gays and conservative Christians—both often expressed feelings of marginalization in American society. But in *Perry*, their champions hailed from the most elite and mainstream segments of the Bar. On the force of their names alone, these champions would help draw the conversation about same-sex marriage onto the center of the American legal and political stage.

4

GETTING TO TRIAL

On Friday, May 22, 2009, a nervous Gibson Dunn associate named Enrique Monagas went to the court clerk's office in San Francisco to file the complaint in *Perry*. The California Supreme Court had announced that it would release its opinion in *Strauss*—the case addressing the procedural challenge to Prop 8— on the Tuesday after the Memorial Day weekend. To ensure that they were the first to mount a federal challenge to Prop 8, the plaintiffs wanted to file before the *Strauss* decision came down. Monagas was sworn to secrecy and instructed to wait until the last possible moment to file.

Monagas did not talk about the case with anyone, not even his family. He loitered near the desk, inching as close as possible to the deadline of 3:30. Finally, with about five minutes to go, he handed the papers to the clerk. The clerk entered the filing data into the computer, which randomly assigned the judge who would preside over the case. Monagas saw that the complaint was stamped with the time—3:25 p.m.—and the initials VRW. The case had gone to Chief Judge Vaughn R. Walker.

T he first time he was up for a seat on the federal bench, Walker did not emerge from the Judiciary Committee, in part because of allegations that he was anti-gay. It was 1987, and President Ronald Reagan had nominated him to be a district judge. Walker, then forty-three, had strong credentials. A graduate of the University of Michigan and Stanford Law School, he had clerked for a district judge in California before joining the establishment firm of Pillsbury Madison & Sutro in San Francisco. He climbed the ladder there, making partner in 1978.

Walker's confirmation hearing became mired in two issues. One was his membership in San Francisco's Olympic Club. At the time, the Olympic Club had only recently begun to admit black members and still did not grant full membership to women. Unfortunately for Walker, the club had just made national headlines. Fellow member Anthony Kennedy had gone through his confirmation hearing for the Supreme Court earlier that year. Kennedy had resigned from the club a month before his nomination, citing a failed vote to make the club more inclusive. Walker remained a member.

Opponents also challenged Walker's involvement in the "Gay Olympics" case. Former Olympic decathlete Dr. Thomas Waddell had founded the Gay Olympic Games—now called the Gay Games—to help "homosexual men and women to move into the mainstreams of their respective societies." Walker represented the United States Olympic Committee (USOC) in trademark litigation seeking to ban the organization from using the word "Olympics." Waddell's lawyers argued that the USOC's uneven enforcement of the trademark reflected anti-gay animus, given that the USOC had not sued either the Police Olympics or the Armenian Olympics. The Olympic Committee prevailed at the Supreme Court. Susan McGreivy, a former Olympian turned ACLU lawyer, pointed out that the committee had not objected to "Olympic" games for rats or cockroaches: "I guess the moral is that if you're gay, in the next life you'd better be born a rat."

Attacked for his involvement in the case, Walker gave the classic lawyerly defense: "A lawyer acting in a professional way must divorce himself from personal views." Undeterred, Walker's opponents condemned Walker's litigation tactics. While representing the USOC, Walker had a lien placed on Waddell's property to secure attorneys' fees while Waddell was dying of AIDS. A beloved figure in the gay community, Waddell died without knowing whether he had been able to bequeath his estate to his daughter. Waddell's attorney told the *New York Times* that Walker's "inhumanity and coerciveness" should be disqualifying.

Over the four hours of Walker's confirmation hearing, witnesses accused Walker of being anti-black, anti-woman, and, particularly, anti-gay. In an intervention whose full irony would only be revealed two decades later, one pro-gay witness floated the idea of conditioning Walker's confirmation on his agreement "not to handle any lesbian or gay cases." Walker never came up for a confirmation vote before the Senate.

Two years later, President George H. W. Bush renewed the nomination. One week beforehand, Walker had resigned from the Olympic Club, and the passage of time had effaced the Waddell incident. The Senate Judiciary Committee voted for Walker 11 to 2. He sailed through the Senate and received his commission in 1989.

By the time the Prop 8 case landed on his docket, Walker had been on the bench for two decades, serving as Chief Judge of the Northern District of California since 2004. Over time, Walker had revealed himself to be more of a libertarian than a social conservative. In 2006, he ruled against the federal government and AT&T in a case involving alleged warrantless surveillance of customer communications. Off the bench, Judge Walker expressed his skepticism about the criminalization of drugs. He had also earned a reputation as a tough-minded jurist. As one lawyer put it, Walker pulled each argument "apart straw by straw, piece by piece, and [gave] it back to you." Another noted: "You don't hear a lot about fairness from him. You hear a lot about the law."

When it became public that he was the judge in the Prop 8 case, however, one biographical detail about Walker overshadowed all others: By this time, he was widely known to be gay. He had not publicly acknowledged this fact, but he also made no attempt to hide it—he brought his longtime partner, a physician, to professional events. His random assignment to the case was remarkable, given that more than a dozen judges were eligible to be chosen (indeed, at the time, only one federal judge sitting on a district or appellate court—Deborah Batts of the Southern District of New York—was openly gay).

Both sides feared reading too much into the sexual orientation of the irascible judge with the piercing blue eyes and the Van Dyke beard. "Everyone knew about the Olympics case," said James Esseks of the ACLU. "And there is that stereotype that closeted judges can be much harder on gay causes than openly gay individuals or straight judges." When asked whether they intended to make an issue of Walker's sexual orientation, the proponents' team replied in the negative.

Walker had almost failed to make it onto the bench because of his involvement in the controversy about whether gays could have access to the word "Olympics." A circuit court opinion in that case noted that the word "Olympics" possessed "a meaning unique within our language" and challenged the idea that "Congress can deny all of us that word, and the ideas it embodies." Now, at the end of his career as a judge, Chief Judge Walker confronted the question of whether gays could access the prestige of a different word—"marriage."

Legal disputes are often resolved without going to trial, even in the most high-stakes cases. The parties may settle out of court, or the judge may issue a ruling based on documents filed by the lawyers, sometimes without the cross-examination of witnesses, or without any witness testimony at all. Even if a case goes to trial, the parties must jump through a series of procedural hoops to get there, which can take months or even years.

Both sides in *Perry* wanted the case to cruise to the Supreme Court, not drift in a district court in California. The plaintiffs' desire for speed seemed counterintuitive. In May 2009, only four states had legalized same-sex marriage—Connecticut, Iowa, Massachusetts, and Vermont. Even then, it was clear that more states would permit same-sex marriage in time, creating momentum that would help the Supreme Court feel more comfortable ruling for the plaintiffs.

Some believed Boies and Olson wanted the case to reach the Court while Justice Stevens remained on it, because Stevens allegedly had Justice Kennedy's ear. Yet the more likely explanation was that AFER feared another litigant would beat them to the finish. The *Perry* plaintiffs had successfully filed first. However, if they got bogged down in a trial, someone who filed later could reach the Supreme Court earlier.

On May 27, 2009, the plaintiffs requested a preliminary injunction. A preliminary injunction is a court order that requires a party to perform (or abstain from) an action until the court makes a final decision in a case. The *Perry* plaintiffs asked Judge Walker to restrain California officials from enforcing Prop 8 until the court had ruled on its constitutionality. A successful motion would have permitted same-sex couples to marry while the court assessed the merits of the case. If the plaintiffs ultimately won the case, same-sex couples could continue marrying; if they lost, same-sex marriage in California would be stopped in its tracks yet again.

Because a preliminary injunction grants parties what they want pending final decisions, the court hands them out sparingly. It generally requires the party to show a substantial likelihood of winning the case, "irreparable injury" if the motion is denied, a balance of harms (as between the plaintiff and defendant) that tips in the plaintiff's favor, and a public interest served by the grant. If, for example, the *Perry* plaintiffs were unlikely to succeed in their ultimate claim, there was little point allowing same-sex couples to marry in the meantime. Similarly, if it would cause more harm to grant an injunction than to deny it, the court would decline the request. Boies and Olson argued that they met this stringent standard, claiming that every day their clients could not marry irreparably harmed them.

The plaintiffs hoped to use the preliminary injunction as a vehicle to rocket their case to the Supreme Court. Because of the risk of irreparable harm, courts usually decide such requests quickly. If Judge Walker denied the plaintiffs' motion, they could appeal immediately to a federal appellate court and, from there, to the Supreme Court. Crucially, the Supreme Court can—and does—flip requests for preliminary injunctions (which do not render an ultimate decision about the substance of the case) into requests for a final "merits" decision (which does). Left to the ordinary course of litigation, a case can take three or four years to reach the high court. With a preliminary injunction ruling, it can zip up in less than a year.

While generally passive throughout this litigation, the Governor's Office ardently opposed the preliminary injunction motion. Schwarzenegger remembered the chaos created by the Newsom ceremonies and the California court's invalidation of them. Enjoining Prop 8 temporarily while the court decided what to do risked a similar outcome.

On June 30, 2009, Judge Walker issued a significant order. He first permitted the proponents to intervene, transforming them into the effective defendants, given that state officials had declined to defend Prop 8. Judge Walker then declared his "tentative plan" to go "expeditiously to trial."

The care with which the judge's order set forth the factual disputes in the case suggested that the plan to go to trial was a good deal more than tentative. The judge asked the parties to prepare evidence on three subjects. First, he requested evidence on the nature of the "right to marry"—a fundamental constitutional right recognized in a series of Supreme Court decisions. The plaintiffs claimed that same-sex couples sought access to this right, just as interracial couples had successfully done in *Loving*. The proponents argued that the analogy was not apt, because the capacity to procreate within a marriage was one of its defining features. As the judge pointed out, the two definitions of marriage were fundamentally at odds.

Second, Judge Walker invited both sides to demonstrate the level of scrutiny that state discrimination based on sexual orientation should receive under the Fourteenth Amendment's Equal Protection Clause. In interpreting that clause, the Supreme Court has given certain classifications (such as race or sex) "heightened scrutiny," which means groups that fall under those classifications get enhanced judicial protection. The Supreme Court has never formally decided whether discrimination based on sexual orientation merits heightened scrutiny. In determining whether a new classification should receive such scrutiny, the Court often considers four factors—whether the group traditionally disadvantaged by the classification has suffered a history of discrimination, whether it is marked by an "obvious, immutable, or distinguishing characteristic," whether it is "politically powerless," and whether it has the same capacity to contribute to society as a group without the trait. Judge Walker asked for evidence about whether sexual orientation met these criteria.

If the plaintiffs could show that they were being denied the fundamental right to marry or that sexual orientation triggered heightened scrutiny under the Equal Protection Clause, they would almost certainly prevail. However, even if they could not win on those grounds, the Supreme Court's precedents—including *Romer v. Evans*—established that Prop 8 still needed to rest on some conceivably legitimate government rationale. It could not rest on simple "animus" toward the targeted group. For this reason, Judge Walker also asked for evidence supporting the justifications for Prop 8, including the oft-touted claim that it promoted the best environment for raising children.

On July 2, the parties gathered before the judge for the first time. Olson and a team of lawyers from Gibson Dunn were there; Boies was not, although several lawyers from his firm, Boies Schiller, were. Charles Cooper appeared with his colleague David Thompson, the fortyish, bespectacled managing partner of Cooper & Kirk. Several attorneys from the ADF were also present. Terry Stewart represented the City of San Francisco.

The city's desire to sue the state perplexed some observers; Thompson would later memorably criticize San Francisco for attacking "its creator like a Frankenstein monster." Nonetheless, San Francisco had significant experience litigating for marriage equality, most prominently through its defense of Mayor Newsom's actions. It sought a place at the plaintiffs' table on the strength of that experience.

Facing one another in court, the plaintiffs and proponents agreed on one point: they wished to avoid a trial. Cooper recalled that Olson pulled him into a corner of the courtroom that morning. "Chuck, we don't see any reason to have a trial," he said. "We don't want to have another Scopes monkey trial here, do we?" Cooper agreed. Yet the two sides were arrayed against a judge strongly leaning in the other direction.

At the top of the hearing, Judge Walker reiterated that he found the governor's position against a preliminary injunction persuasive. In the wake of Newsom's 2004 order, he observed, both county authorities and same-sex couples were in a state of confusion when it came to the validity of their marriages. To definitively resolve that uncertainty, he inclined toward a trial. He elaborated:

> Now, this is a trial court, this is not the Supreme Court of the United States where we deal with these boxcar philosophical issues. We deal with facts; we deal with evidence; we deal with

testimony of witnesses. . . . I'm reasonably sure, given the issues involved and given the personnel that are in the courtroom, that this case is only touching down in this court, that it will have a life after this court, and what happens here, in many ways, is only a prelude to what is going to happen later. So I am inclined to think that how we do things here is more important than what we do, that our job in this case, at this point, is to make a record.

Rebuffing a final sally from Olson, the judge denied the motion for a preliminary injunction.

That denial did not guarantee a trial. Judge Walker could still render summary judgment. Unlike a preliminary injunction, a summary judgment is a final determination of the merits of the case. The purpose of summary judgments is to preserve trials only for cases requiring courtroom testing of disputed facts. A party seeking summary judgment can still engage in various forms of fact-finding, such as offering and deposing experts. After that, if the judge deems that no "genuine issue of material fact" remains, he or she issues judgment without a trial. With that in mind, Olson sought to engage in the most expeditious fact-finding possible, hoping that summary judgment would deliver him the fast track to the Supreme Court that his preliminary injunction motion had not secured. He and Cooper could narrow the scope of their disagreements, he said, especially given that some of the relevant issues had already been settled in state litigation. Walker pounced on this reference, asking Olson if the California litigation had included a trial. Olson acknowledged that it had not. He said he did not oppose a trial per se, but believed that he and Cooper could streamline the issues requiring expert testimony. The two old friends would soon discover how few were the facts about marriage—same-sex or otherwise—on which they could agree.

Returning to the issue of a trial, Walker asked whether discovery would be necessary. Discovery is the process through which each side obtains relevant information from the other. It is often agonizingly time consuming, involving the exchange of large numbers of documents, disputes over what each side must provide the other, and even side litigation to settle those disputes. Olson responded that he was not sure whether discovery was needed, or if so, what form it should take.

Cooper also wanted to resolve the case through summary judgment. He returned to Walker's point that the California marriage cases had not gone to trial. "As far as our research has been able to turn up," he pointed out, "we can't find that any of the marriage cases, the dozen or so of them that have proceeded around the country, actually submitted issues of fact to trial, as opposed to having gone off on summary judgment." On its face, the argument was plausible—*Other courts have not gone to trial, so neither should you.* In fact, Cooper's statement was startling. The Hawaii case in 1996 had gone to a nine-day trial, and Cooper had handled the appeal.

The judge could not be distracted: "I think you and Mr. Olson agree that what's going on here is basically a prelude to further proceedings, and shouldn't those further proceedings be based on a fully developed record here?" As Cooper began to respond, the judge cut him off: "We develop records with trials."

Cooper replied with an argument that he would return to in the years ahead—that trial procedures were appropriate for adjudicative facts but not legislative ones. An adjudicative fact might be whether a driver exceeded the speed limit, whether a signature was forged, or whether a person read a contract before he signed it. Cooper quoted celebrated appellate judge Richard Posner, who had once offered this definition: "facts germane to the specific dispute, which often are best developed through testimony and cross-examination."

Legislative facts are, on the other hand, broader claims about the world, such as whether underage drivers are more likely to speed, whether forged signatures are easy to detect, or whether people generally sign standardized contracts without reading them. Posner had described them as "facts relevant to shaping a general rule," which are "more often facts reported in books and other documents not prepared specially for litigation or refined in its fires." As this description suggests, calling these *legislative facts* is a terrible (but hopelessly entrenched) misnomer, as they are facts found not by a legislature but by a court.

In *Perry,* the question of whether the plaintiffs had been denied marriage licenses was an adjudicative fact. This is not to say that all adjudicative facts are easy to determine—whether Prop 8 was enacted due to "animus" against gay people was also an adjudicative fact because it was specific to *Perry.* In contrast, the question of whether marriage by definition involved the ability to produce children involved a legislative fact. Cooper argued that facts about the nature of marriage, like all legislative facts, were not appropriate for trial. They were better established through ordinary research: "You need only go back to your chambers, Your Honor, and pull down any dictionary, pull down any book that discusses marriage and you will find this procreative purpose at its heart wherever you go."

Yet a blanket rule that trials cannot resolve legislative facts makes little sense. If a trial's clash of proofs works for adjudicative facts, it should also work for legislative ones. Even Posner's decision granted that if an evidentiary hearing was necessary with regard to legislative facts, one should be held. The appellate courts have generally come to this sensible conclusion: that contested adjudicative facts *must be* subjected to trial, while contested legislative facts *need not be* (which, of course, is different from saying that they *may not be*).

While the Supreme Court has not opined directly on this point, it has shown its hand through its practice. The Court has repeatedly relied on legislative facts established in trials in landmark cases. In *Brown v. Board of Education,* which desegregated public schools, the Court relied on psychological evidence mustered at trial about the negative effects of segregation. In the 1992 case of *Planned Parenthood v. Casey,* which upheld *Roe v. Wade,* the Court relied on more than a dozen of the trial court's findings on legislative facts gleaned from expert testimony. For instance, it accepted the finding that the "vast majority of women consult their husbands prior to deciding to terminate their pregnancy." And in the 2003 case of *Grutter v. Bollinger,* which upheld an affirmative-action program at the University of Michigan Law School, the Court relied on trial court findings showing the educational benefits of a diverse student body.

Indeed, I suspect Cooper's unease about using trials to resolve legislative facts would not come into play in the arena of the natural sciences, where people feel that they can reach some objective answer untainted by ideology. This trial, however, would rely on evidence from the social sciences, which, as one of his witnesses would say, can sometimes be social *science* and, at other times, be *social* science. Conservatives sometimes voice the fear that the liberal ideology of the academy will be adopted by a liberal district judge, and then, because of the deference appellate courts generally give to facts found by trial courts, become the accepted wisdom of the land.

But of course, any discussion of the trial as a fact-finding procedure must ask whether superior alternatives exist. Cooper's position raised a critical question: How does the law know? More specifically, how do judges—many of whom lead cloistered lives, come from privileged backgrounds, and are of an older generation—learn facts about the world? (When asked what he thought his greatest challenge in this case would be, Boies had an immediate answer: the age of the judges deciding it.) One intuitive answer is what the law professor Karl Llewellyn has called "situation sense"—judges' commonsense understanding of the world. A judge could also do his or her own research, or rely on the party or amicus briefs submitted in the case, or speak to his or her clerks. Yet all these avenues have faced mounting criticism because they are not susceptible to adversarial testing, and because one judge's common sense may differ markedly from another's, or from the common sense of the average American.

Judge Walker believed that the most thorough way to vet the

facts was through a full-dress trial. Still, at the end of the hearing, he left the issue open. He told the parties to confer and figure out what facts, if any, were truly in dispute. He set a hearing for mid-August, at which time he would revisit the question of how to proceed.

The rumblings about a trial dumbfounded the four plaintiffs, They had expected to play a passive role in the case—they would allow their names to be used in the filings, give some press conferences, and let their lawyers do the rest. The AFER lawyers now informed Katami, Perry, Stier, and Zarrillo that they could be called as witnesses and would have to prepare for depositions. " 'Deposition' was the word that sent us spinning," Perry later recalled. They had myriad questions for their lawyers, and the answers did not reassure them. In preparation for trial, opposing counsel would scour publicly available data—from newspapers to Facebook accounts—for damaging information. To prepare for the worst, the plaintiffs' attorneys needed to be equally intrusive. Stier would be asked in a prep session if she knew how one of her sons had spent the weekend—her attorney had found an account by one of his classmates stating that her son had been at an event where underage drinking had occurred. Depositions could last for up to seven hours, and the plaintiffs could be asked to testify for open-ended periods of time on the stand.

For the LGBT movement lawyers, the June 30 order and July 2 hearing were game changers for a different reason. The groups had originally intended only to file amicus briefs, but after the hearing they decided they would move to intervene in the case. Authors of an amicus brief make their opinion heard once, in the written material submitted to the court, leaving the parties to chart their own course. If allowed in, intervenors participate much like any other party. The difference between writing an amicus brief and intervening is the difference between being a backseat driver and having a hand on the steering wheel.

Led by James Esseks of the ACLU, the groups fired off a motion to intervene on behalf of three organizations, the most prominent of which was Parents, Families and Friends of Lesbians and Gays (PFLAG), a nationwide coalition of LGBT allies. His main argument was that these organizations represented people and interests ranging beyond those of the plaintiffs in *Perry*—an important factor in persuading a court to allow intervention.

Esseks had recently become a true believer in the importance of trials in gay-rights cases. In earlier marriage cases, he had not requested them. Trials require immense investments of time and money. Experts have to be found, vetted, hired. They have to be paid to research and write reports. They have to be prepped for deposition and trial. Even in the 2005 California same-sex marriage case—where San Francisco's attorney Terry Stewart had pushed for a trial—Esseks had not.

Subsequent experience had changed his view. In 2006 and 2007, the movement lost same-sex marriage cases in the high courts of New York, Maryland, and Washington State. With characteristic understatement, the tall, low-key Esseks described the run of losses as "dispiriting." It was a wake-up call that their strategy was not working. During roughly the same period, the movement lawyers had won a string of gay-rights cases pertaining to foster parenting and adoption in relatively conservative states. In 2004, a judge in Arkansas struck down a regulation barring gays from serving as foster parents. In 2006, the Arkansas Supreme Court unanimously upheld that decision. In 2008, the ACLU brought a case challenging Florida's ban on adoption by gay couples. Again, they prevailed.

Esseks asked himself why the movement lawyers were losing gay-rights cases in blue states and winning them in red or purple ones. He thought he saw a pattern—the plaintiffs had won the cases with a trial and lost the cases without one. In both the Arkansas and Florida cases, the judges touted the trials as educational experiences. Judge Timothy Fox, who presided over the Arkansas trial, wrote: "[The psychologist] Jerome Bruner has suggested that one of the reasons that people believe in our system of justice may be as simple as 'our faith that confrontation is a good way to get to the bottom of things.' The 'confrontation' in this case has presented us all with an excellent opportunity to replace ignorance with knowledge." For "those truly interested in reaching an informed decision" about the issue, he recommended "careful reading of the information and expert opinions assembled in the record of this case."

Now Judge Walker had issued an invitation to hold a trial on a plate with watercress around it. Both Olson and Cooper were steadfastly declining it. It would be a travesty, Esseks felt, if the lead counsel prevailed.

The City of San Francisco also filed a motion to intervene on the side of the plaintiffs, arguing that it could bring a governmental perspective to the proceedings. The motion noted that as a local government entity, San Francisco "bears the financial and public health consequences" of anti-gay discrimination and the denial of marriage to same-sex couples. This formulation was a fig leaf—the real expertise that San Francisco brought to the case was its experience litigating a marriage case (which the AFER team lacked). Stewart believed the plaintiffs would be much more willing to draw on that expertise if it came from the city rather than from the movement lawyers.

She was right. While the Boies/Olson team did not want any intervenors on their side, it was vastly more receptive to the City of San Francisco than to the LGBT groups. The plaintiffs' team was still smarting from the criticism heaped on them by the gay-rights lawyers. Boies and Olson told Stewart that while they would oppose both motions, they would oppose the city less vigorously.

By the time of the mid-August hearing, Olson and Cooper's agreement to bypass a trial had imploded. The plaintiffs stated: "A prompt, thorough trial on all disputed factual issues is the most effective and efficient way to present the record on which this case will be decided." Their position could not have been clearer: *You can have your trial, but please make it fast.* The proponents steadfastly resisted trial, noting that the plaintiffs had done an about-face without explanation, and suggesting that "a trial in this case would likely stretch on for weeks."

The plaintiffs' shift can be attributed to several factors. As Stewart put it, having the gay groups in the case was "the *last* thing Ted and David wanted." Their desire to exclude these groups placed pressure on their strategy. If they continued to oppose a trial, the judge, who clearly wanted one, might let the movement groups join the case. Stewart also used her collegial relationship with the Boies/Olson team to warm them up to the idea of the trial. She arranged for a conference call between Chris Dusseault of Gibson Dunn and Jean Dubofsky, the attorney who had litigated *Romer*. While the Supreme Court's opinion in *Romer* made no explicit reference to the trial in that case, Dubofsky believed that the record—with its descriptions of rank animus toward gays—had influenced the Court. Finally, Olson, who had never litigated a gay-rights case, may not have anticipated the degree to which the parties would differ on "genuine issues of material fact," making quick disposal of the case on summary judgment impossible.

For their part, attorneys on Cooper's team may have taken a less conciliatory position because of conflicts on their own side. The Liberty Counsel, the ADF's nemesis, had filed a motion to intervene on behalf of the CCF. If the Cooper team conceded too many facts to Olson, the case for intervention would be stronger, because CCF would then offer a perspective not adequately represented by the proponents.

On August 19, the parties were back in court. The main question to be resolved was whether the three groups seeking intervention—a coalition of LGBT-rights groups represented by the ACLU, Lambda Legal, and the NCLR; the City of San Francisco represented by its own lawyers; and the CCF represented by Liberty Counsel—would be permitted to do so.

In the hearing, Rena Lindevaldsen of the Liberty Counsel argued that the CCF should be permitted to intervene because the proponents were "willing to concede too much of the Plaintiffs' case." Lindevaldsen chastised the proponents for conceding that homosexuality was not a medical disorder, that being gay "does not result in any impairment of judgment," and that "gay individuals, including Plaintiffs, have formed lasting, committed relationships."

The proponents' lawyers did not want Liberty Counsel or their clients anywhere near their case. Thompson of Cooper & Kirk argued that the CCF wanted to intervene to force a futile strategy: "They say it's a tactical mistake not to contest each one of these points that the Plaintiffs could make the rubber bounce on, and that we need to be in the trenches fighting every war, even battles that can't be won." Many of the plaintiffs' lawyers, in contrast, desperately wanted Judge Walker to grant intervention to the CCF. City attorney Ronald Flynn archly referred to Lindevaldsen as "hair on fire"—a reference to her flyaway blond hair and vehement style of speaking. He observed that something "weird" happened during trial preparation: "The more crazy and hateful that I found things, the happier I got. . . . You find a pamphlet that is comparing us to horses or incest and you're like—'This is phenomenal!' " Flynn predicted that unlike Cooper, who maintained the "façade" that he was simply trying to "uphold the will of the people," the CCF would "explode" at trial. In *Romer,* the lawyers defending Amendment 2 let Gary Bauer, president of the conservative Family Research Council, make unvarnished anti-gay statements from the stand. Now, Flynn lamented, mainstream opponents of gay rights "don't bring the crazies to the courtroom anymore."

After hearing both sides, Walker ruled from the bench. He excluded the groups represented by both the Liberty Counsel and the LGBT movement lawyers. He found that each failed to show that it held interests that would be inadequately represented by the parties already in the case. In contrast, Walker permitted the City of San Francisco to intervene on the ground that it represented a governmental perspective.

Like a casting director, the judge had determined the protagonists

for the rest of the litigation. He then set an aggressive schedule for
the trial. "We commence discovery in this case today," he said.
Expert reports were due on October 2. Any motion for summary
judgment would be heard on October 14. Unless summary judgment obviated the need for it, the trial would begin on January 11.

O n September 9, 2009, proponents filed a 127-page brief for
     summary judgment. They excused their failure to adhere to
the 25-page limit imposed by the Northern District by alluding to
the "momentous importance" of the case. The apoplectic plaintiffs
urged Walker to reject the proponents' submission outright. Judge
Walker allowed the proponents their brief. He gave the plaintiffs
the same number of pages, but drily encouraged them "to resist the
temptation to match proponents." The plaintiffs' response clocked
in at 57 pages.

The proponents' tome reflected the intensity of their desire to
avoid a trial. They raised one claim that would have scotched the
entire case—the argument that the 1972 Supreme Court case of
Baker v. Nelson barred the district court from even considering
the challenge. The proponents also argued that there was no right
to same-sex marriage and that the Equal Protection Clause did
not give heightened scrutiny to classifications based on sexual
orientation. Turning to government justifications, the proponents
argued that Prop 8 was supported by many rational bases, and
not motivated by animus. At times the brief slipped into hyperbole, as when the proponents compared same-sex parenting to
the "radical idea" from Plato's *Dialogues* that children should be
raised communally. The proponents also argued that "severing the
link between parents and children" had been "persuasively portrayed as distinctly dystopian," in Aldous Huxley's *Brave New
World*. In the section of the book they cited, the government has
taken over the business of procreation, abolishing the concepts of

marriage and family and growing fetuses in test tubes in state-run "Hatcheries."

Ruling from the bench, the judge denied the motion for summary judgment, taking nothing off the table. He first addressed the 1972 *Baker* decision. Judge Walker observed that substantial doctrinal developments—including *Romer* and *Lawrence*—suggested that the legal landscape had shifted dramatically since 1972, meaning that *Baker* did not block him from further consideration of the case. After losing that argument, the proponents had an uphill battle. Any "genuine issue of material fact" would require a trial. Judge Walker found that this case teemed with such factual controversies, including whether procreation was the main purpose of marriage, whether sexual orientation met the factors for heightened scrutiny, whether any legitimate justification supported Prop 8, or whether the initiative was based on animus. Cooper's effort to "skinny down" the proceedings through summary judgment failed spectacularly.

The summary-judgment hearing had its moments of levity. When Cooper reiterated his argument that the purpose of marriage was essentially procreative, Judge Walker responded: "Well, the last marriage that I performed, Mr. Cooper, involved a groom who was ninety-five and the bride was eighty-three. I did not demand that they prove that they intended to engage in procreative activity. Now, was I missing something?" Cooper replied that no, he was not. Judge Walker continued: "And I might say it was a very happy relationship." Cooper suavely responded: "I rejoice to hear that, Your Honor."

Walker then asked how permitting same-sex marriages would harm the institution of marriage: "Assume I agree with you that the state's interest in marriage is essentially procreative. . . . How does permitting same-sex marriages impair or adversely affect that interest?" Cooper responded that the question was irrelevant. Under existing law, he said, all the state needed to justify was the *inclusion* of opposite-sex couples, not the *exclusion* of same-sex couples. Judge Walker was not so easily distracted: "I'm asking you to tell me how it would harm opposite-sex marriages."

Cooper answered: "Your Honor, my answer is: I don't know. I don't know."

This answer would haunt him. During closing arguments, he would say that he heard those words—"I don't know"—quoted back to him more than any others he had uttered in his life. That brief sentence became an enormous talking point for the plaintiffs. As Olson wrote in a *Newsweek* essay some months later: "Tellingly, when the judge in our case asked our opponent to identify the ways in which same-sex marriage would harm heterosexual marriage, to his credit he answered honestly: he could not think of any." The moment was catnip for the media, which revisited it throughout the litigation.

Cooper later claimed that Olson had deliberately taken his words out of context. His face a rictus of pain, he said to me: "I'll never forgive Ted, as dearly as I love him as my friend." He pointed out that shortly after he said "I don't know," he elaborated on the point. A few lines down, the transcript does state: "Same-sex marriage is a very recent innovation. Its implications of a social and cultural nature, not to mention its impact on marriage over time, can't possibly be known now." In other words, Cooper claimed that when he said "I don't know," he was saying that "no one knows" or "society doesn't know."

In the hearing, Judge Walker pressed onward, asking what the *potential* harms of same-sex marriage might be. Cooper observed that allowing same-sex marriage would mean that domestic-partnership agreements would have to be open to heterosexuals. Walker asked why that would be harmful. Cooper responded that it appeared to have had negative effects in the Netherlands. Relentless, Walker inquired what those negative effects might be—would it hurt children, or society at large? Cooper said he had not come with a presentation on these issues. In other words, "genuine issues of material fact" remained. Unlike Cooper, Judge Walker believed the answers were unknown, not unknowable. Same-sex marriage was going to trial.

O n the eve of trial, a final skirmish arose about how public the proceedings would be. Various media outlets had asked whether the proceedings could be streamed on video to other courthouses or broadcast on the Internet. Though Judge Walker seemed eager to make the trial as accessible to the public as possible, the district court's rules prohibited broadcasting of trials beyond the confines of the courthouse. The judge sought to change this rule. For a time, it looked as if individuals in five courthouses in the country—or indeed anywhere, if the recording were posted on YouTube—might have access to the trial.

But in the end, Judge Walker's bid for transparency failed. The proponents took an emergency appeal to the US Supreme Court, which blocked the live video streaming (and by implication the YouTube video). The Court split 5–4, which some gay-rights advocates took to be an ominous portent. The five more conservative justices, including Justice Kennedy, all joined an unsigned opinion "by the court." The majority opinion underscored that it was not taking a position on the propriety of cameras in the courtroom. Instead, it was intervening because the district court had not followed the proper procedure under federal law to change the local rule. The majority stated that the proponents allegedly feared that their witnesses would not testify if the proceedings were broadcast. The majority credited this view, noting that some "witnesses have already said that they will not testify if the trial is broadcast, and they have substantiated their concerns by citing incidents of past harassment." The support consisted of an exhibit of seventy-one articles, mostly culled from newspapers.

Justice Breyer's dissent responded skeptically to the alleged fears and their effect on the trial, emphasizing that the disputed "broadcast" was a limited video transmission to five other court-rooms, which viewers would not be permitted to photograph, and which could not be retransmitted. The witnesses in question, he pointed out, were "all experts or advocates who have either al-ready appeared on television or Internet broadcasts, already toured the state advocating a 'yes' vote on Proposition 8, or already en-gaged in extensive public commentary far more likely to make them well known than a closed-circuit broadcast to another federal courthouse."

As for the articles that the proponents had submitted to sub-stantiate their fears of harassment, many were repetitious. While the weaknesses in these submissions did not trouble a majority of the Supreme Court in the video-transmission dispute, the propo-nents ran into difficulties when they relied on similar evidence in other cases.

One of those other cases, *ProtectMarriage.com v. Bowen*, had been filed by the Prop 8 proponents in early 2009. In *Bowen*, the proponents challenged a California law that required certain po-litical organizations to disclose information about people who con-tributed more than $100 to their campaigns. The proponents said that the forced disclosure of their financial supporters would lead to harassment. To back up their claims, they relied on a series of anonymous affidavits and a portfolio of articles purporting to show past threats against opponents of same-sex marriage. These materi-als covered the same events on which they relied in the dispute over video-transmission in *Perry*. Unlike the Supreme Court, the district court in *Bowen* had time to inspect the record.

Judge Morrison England of the Eastern District of Califor-nia rejected the *Bowen* challenge, upholding the state's disclo-sure law. His 2011 decision scrutinized the proponents' evidence of harassment and found it wanting. Many of their materials, he commented, were "highly repetitive, and perhaps deceptively over-whelming." True, there were reports of two death threats, but the threats came from the same individual and received an immediate police response. Two Mormon temples received a white powdery substance in the mail, but the FBI discerned no link to Prop 8. A trove of articles discussed "Yes on 8" yard signs that had disappeared. But the Orange County sheriff's department had received reports of such pilfering from both sides, attesting that such thefts were commonplace in political battles.

Judge England also stated that many of the harassment claims concerned acts that were "mechanisms relied upon, both historically and lawfully, to voice dissent." One California creamery, whose owner and his family had donated $20,000 to Prop 8, faced a boycott and protest where organizers handed out free rainbow sherbet. Leaders of the American River College student council confronted a recall vote after they officially endorsed Prop 8. Other complainants included a hotel that lost several conventions, a Palo Alto dentist who lost two patients, and an artistic director who chose to resign after prominent artists announced they could no longer work with his musical theater. Still others complained of "phone calls, emails and letters voicing disagreement" with their positions.

A whiff of hypocrisy hung about the proponents' harassment claims. Weeks before the November ballot, Protect Marriage had sent a letter to companies that donated to the No on 8 campaign. The letter threatened to expose them as opponents of traditional marriage if they failed to make a "donation of a like amount to ProtectMarriage.com." Members of Protect Marriage's executive committee, including Andrew Pugno, signed the letter.

The Constitution does not, of course, protect individuals from receiving disagreeable letters, nor does it generally protect them even from more confrontational forms of nonviolent protest. "Harsh criticism," Justice Scalia had written the previous year in a case in Washington State raising similar issues, "is a price our people have traditionally been willing to pay for self-governance. Requiring people to stand up in public for their political acts fosters civic courage, without which democracy is doomed." In her plainspoken way, Terry Stewart would say that this was one of the few things Justice Scalia had ever written with which she agreed. She paraphrased the holding of the case: "If you want to get in the game, you can't be a weenie."

The Supreme Court's acceptance of the proponents' harassment claims in *Perry* hit the movement lawyers hard. Bonauto of GLAD, whose team combed through and rebutted the allegations of harassment, called the claims a "base slur." Davidson of Lambda Legal described it as a "You-hurt-my-fist-when-I-punched-your-face" argument. Yet this salvo was only the first of the proponents' claims that they, not gays, were the true victims in this battle.

In the meantime, Judge Walker interpreted his uncontested prerogative to stream the trial within his courthouse to include the power to create a digital recording of the trial for use in chambers. That recording still exists, safely in the custody of Judge Walker's successor. However, it is unlikely to see the light of day, given that Judge Walker promised that the proceedings would not be broadcast. While it would undeniably be fascinating to see and hear the trial, I suspect few people would watch the entire proceeding. Rather, each side of this debate would doubtless blast out the clips that favored it. Yet it is only by considering the trial holistically that we can grasp its full import. In the transcript, we already have the raw materials to see this historic event clear and whole.

PART II

THE TRIAL

5

CURTAIN UP

On the first day of trial, January 11, 2010, Ted Olson and Charles Cooper embraced outside the courtroom. They would repeat this ritual on each morning of the twelve-day trial. After a roll call of the parties present, Judge Walker invited Olson to begin. Opening statements are promises of what the trial will show—advocates are technically not allowed to argue, only to describe. Under Judge Walker's rules, the same lawyer who opened had to close. Olson and Cooper knew they would be held to their words.

Olson opened with a claim that this case was about "marriage and equality." He framed the right to marry as "an intimate choice, an expression of emotional support and public commitment, the exercise of spiritual unity, and the fulfillment of one's self." Turning to the equality claim, Olson stressed the endless humiliations that second-class citizenship had imposed on his clients, saying: "What Prop 8 does is label gay and lesbian persons as different, inferior, unequal and disfavored." Domestic partnerships are pale alternatives to marriage, he said, because they inflict badges of inferiority on gay and lesbian people that "forever stigmatize their loving relationships" as "something akin to a commercial venture."

Judge Walker flashed his libertarian colors. Why, he asked, did the state not just get out of the marriage business? A constitutional right to marry, he said, did not necessarily entail a right to a marriage license from the government. Moreover, if the state denied everyone a license, it would treat everyone equally. Judge Walker would sound this theme repeatedly throughout the trial. While neither side wanted this outcome, it would hurt the plaintiffs more. A decision abolishing legal marriage would definitely be overruled. Olson reacted pragmatically, saying that the people of California would never accept such a ruling.

Olson then turned to another major theme: Allowing same-sex couples to marry would not, he argued, harm opposite-sex couples. Asked if it would change the institution, he countered that it would "fulfill the institution." To drive home that change should not be equated with harm, he observed that if President Obama's parents had tried to marry in Virginia before his birth, it would have been illegal.

Olson also proposed a California-specific solution, offering Judge Walker a narrower ground on which to rule. He mentioned that Prop 8 had extinguished the right of same-sex couples to marry in California after the state supreme court had granted it. Judge Walker retorted that the right had not existed for long— "mere months" separated the California Supreme Court decision in May 2008 from the ballot that reversed it. Olson parried: The California Supreme Court had not *created* the right; it had *recognized* a right. Perhaps because of Olson's reputation as a staunch originalist, Judge Walker wryly responded that some people found the discovery of constitutional rights previously thought nonexistent to be "surprising." Olson pivoted, noting that we are "constantly surprised by education." Expressing the belief that the *Perry* trial itself could teach the nation, Olson observed that "attitudes change when people are educated."

When he took the podium, Cooper argued for the legitimacy of the political process. Fourteen million Californians had voted on Prop 8. At the time, only four states had legalized same-sex marriage. Judge Walker should not insouciantly set aside the will of the people of California, who, Cooper claimed, were "entitled to await the results of that experiment in those few places where it is being tried."

Where Olson highlighted change, Cooper emphasized continuity. "The limitation of marriage to a man and woman is something that has been universal," he argued, "across history, across cultures, across society." The central and defining purpose of marriage, he contended, is "to promote procreation" and to channel procreative sexual activity between men and women into "stable, enduring unions." Cooper maintained that allowing same-sex couples to marry would change the institution by transforming marriage from a "pro-child societal institution into a private relationship designed simply to provide adult couples with . . . personal fulfillment."

Judge Walker asked Cooper about Olson's claim that marriage has evolved.

"That's what they have ballot booths for, Your Honor," responded Cooper.

Judge Walker turned to the consequences of such a transformation. In a written submission to the court, the proponents argued that if the sequel to being gay was same-sex marriage, then the sequel to being bisexual must be group marriage. Judge Walker asked what evidence supported that finding. Cooper explained that the argument flowed from "logical precepts," because a bisexual in love with two people might want to marry both of them. When Walker said this argument assumed simultaneous relationships, Cooper stated that the assumption was not farfetched in light of "modern conceptions of family." Cooper did not explain why a bisexual would want to marry a man and a woman at the same time any more than a heterosexual man would want to marry two women at the same time. Cooper never returned to this line of argument, perhaps sensing that it was a dead end.

Cooper concluded by arguing that the decision of the people of California to pass Prop 8 was not grounded in "ill will or animosity toward gays and lesbians," but rather a "special regard for this venerable institution." Cooper deftly flipped Olson's reference to President Obama, using him to illustrate that a gay-rights supporter could nonetheless draw the line at marriage. At the time of trial, the president supported civil unions for gay and lesbian people but opposed same-sex marriage.

After opening statements, the AFER team began their case with the four plaintiffs. They introduced the judge early to the human faces of the trial—not just to Katami, Perry, Stier, and Zarrillo, but also to lead counsel. Boies put the two men on the stand; then Olson put on the two women.

At their best, trials can be exercises in crystalline argumentation. But they are not only that. They are also human events, in which living, breathing protagonists embody the claims they make. There is great virtue in combining, as trials do, authentic human stories with abstract argumentation. The literary scholar Elaine Scarry distinguishes "narrative compassion," which flows from individual stories, from "statistical compassion," which flows from aggregate data. In her view, President Ronald Reagan had the former but not the latter. He could, for instance, immediately and genuinely relate to an individual's story about homelessness, as even his detractors admitted. Yet in Scarry's view, President Reagan lacked statistical compassion. He could be offered sheaves of statistics about homelessness but not be able to apprehend the suffering represented therein. Scarry argues that a just decision-maker must have both faculties.

At many points during the trial, the AFER team drew on individual stories to activate narrative compassion. In most trials, the plaintiffs provide the human face of the issue. City attorney Terry Stewart self-consciously amplified this strategy. Stewart did not want the human element to vanish after the plaintiffs had finished testifying on the first day. With that in mind, she interspersed lay witnesses with experts throughout the trial. The lay witnesses kept the testimony from feeling dry, while the experts kept the testimony from feeling idiosyncratic.

On the stand, Zarrillo observed that he loved Katami "probably more than I love myself." He continued: "I would do anything for him. I would put his needs ahead of my own." Katami said that he wanted to get married because he had found someone "I know I can dedicate the rest of my life to." Perry and Stier made similar professions of love. After the trial, Boies said that the proponents' lawyers could not meet the eyes of the plaintiffs during this testimony.

The proponents repeatedly argued that same-sex marriage privileged the selfish desires of adults over the needs of children. Yet it is hard to read the testimony of the plaintiffs and sustain this view. Is loving another adult more than you love yourself selfish? The proponents believed that such love, at least between two adults of the same sex, necessarily came at the cost of a child's best interests. Yet this belief raised further questions. Perry and Stier were raising four sons together—each woman had brought two sons into the relationship. How might they have behaved more selflessly? Should Stier have stayed in her previous marriage to a man? Should Perry, who had conceived her twins through artificial reproductive technology, not have had them in the first place? Should heterosexual couples be banned from using sperm or egg donors? Should the women have ended their eleven-year relationship and married men? Such questions would be raised with the expert witnesses. But the proponents did not ask the plaintiffs a single question on the stand about their personal lives.

This choice marked a shift from the strategy at deposition, in which ADF attorney Brian Raum had grilled all four plaintiffs about their sex lives. Because she had previously been married to a man, Stier fielded the most aggressive questions, such as whether she would go back to dating men if Perry died. Stier recalled that Raum had used baseball analogies—getting to "first base, second base, or hitting it out of the park"—to ask about her sexual experience with men. Stier found this idiom undignified and did not respond using his language, instead framing her answers as if her mother—a conservative Midwesterner—were in the room.

"Brian Raum seemed upset," she recollected. "I felt like, boy, this is upsetting you so much more than it is upsetting me." She speculated that at some level it was because she did not look the way he expected a gay person to look: "And by that I mean I walked in wearing a skirt and a jacket and I have long hair and high heels and I look like his neighbor or ladies in his church."

By trial, the proponents had decided this game was not worth playing. They were doubtless correct—it is hard to cross-examine someone on how much they love another person. Asking about the plaintiffs' sex lives would also have raised strategic risks because it was such an intrusion on their privacy.

The treatment of the couples at trial mirrored a major shift in gay-rights discourse. In 1993, law professor Mary Anne Case observed that gay couples tended to fare better in cases where sex was taken out of the picture—where the gay plaintiff's partner was dead, disabled, or incarcerated. She speculated that such fact patterns helped judges not to think about gay sex, making the litigant instantly more sympathetic.

For better and for worse, marriage has the same desexualizing effect. In 2003, when the Supreme Court struck down sodomy statutes in *Lawrence,* I was invited onto a couple television shows to analyze the decision. In one green room, I overheard a panelist say to another: "Well, at least we don't have to talk about sodomy." I wished I did not have to talk about it either. Today, in the marriage debates, the ground has shifted. Gay people talk about love, about commitment, about raising children. In prepping for trial, Stier feared "being cast as a bad parent," not discussing her sex life. Now opponents of same-sex marriage must speak about "getting to first base, second base, or hitting it out of the park," or (as a later amicus brief would argue) about why only male genitals and female genitals coming together in "coitus" create the special one-flesh union between the parties necessary to a "true" marriage. Call it bluenosed, but it is a rule of these debates: Whoever says "coitus" first has the steeper climb.

The right to marry may be a more comfortable topic of conversation than the right to engage in sodomy for another reason: marriage is accompanied by significant legal responsibilities. The right to engage in private sexual activity is essentially a "negative liberty"—a demand to be left alone to do as one pleases. The right to marry is what legal philosopher Jeremy Waldron calls a "responsibility-right." Waldron notes that the right to vote, for instance, is not only a prerogative but a duty. Similarly, exercising the right to marry binds individuals with responsibilities, such as the duty to care for one's spouse and children. So while granting access to marriage gives more affirmation to gay individuals than the decriminalization of sodomy, it also places more responsibilities on them.

The proponents' response was that California had already given plaintiffs both the rights and responsibilities of marriage, just not under that name. In his opening statement, Cooper observed that California had been "generous" toward same-sex couples by affording them domestic partnerships. I wince whenever I read that word—"generous." The point about civil rights is that you do not have to rely on the state's largesse to exercise them. Yet I take Cooper's point, which is that California's domestic partnership scheme—unlike that of most other states—effectively gave same-sex couples all the tangible legal benefits and burdens of marriage, withholding only the word "marriage." Given that California had closed the material gap, the plaintiffs had to show that the dignitary gap still mattered.

The plaintiffs all testified to the daily humiliations they encountered because they could not marry. Zarrillo gave the example of walking into a bank and saying, "My partner and I want to open a joint bank account," only to have the bank employee respond, "Is it a business account?" Similarly, Katami noted that when he introduced Zarrillo as his partner, listeners would ask if theirs was "an LLC or an S Corporation." Perry described traveling on a plane and being asked for whom she was saving a seat. When she answered "My partner," the other passenger asked her to move so he could sit with his wife. Stier described the frustration of having to fill out forms that had no designation for her relationship status.

Having taught a seminar on the trial twice, I am struck by the variance in student responses to the plaintiffs' testimony of their daily humiliations. Even at liberal NYU, some students feel the plaintiffs should have been able to muster better examples. Some were convinced by an analogy Olson made later. "What if you had all the rights of citizenship," he asked, "but could not call yourself a citizen?" Others were not. Finally, one of my gay students spoke up, citing Katami's claim: "Unless you have to deal with that, unless you have to go through a constant validation of self, there's no way to really describe how it feels." The student wrote that he had set up a blog to detail this death by a thousand cuts to shatter the same incredulity. The contemporary term for these "thousand cuts" is *microaggressions,* defined as brief and commonplace daily indignities imposed on marginalized groups. Though subtle, microaggressions may have serious cumulative effects on the recipients, including lower self-esteem, physical health problems, and shortened life expectancy.

Given the tendency to trivialize microaggressions, the plaintiffs' lawyers called in an expert, social epidemiologist Ilan Meyer, to analyze the plaintiffs' testimony. Meyer recognized that many of the interactions that the plaintiffs had described might seem inconsequential. However, he testified that these seemingly small indignities have an aggregate effect. Meyer said that in his own research on stigma, gay individuals consistently complained about filling out forms that required information about spouses but contained no designation that described their relationships. "You have to ask yourself, why would a person remember that type of minor incident?" he said, in reference to Stier's testimony. If there had been a random error on the form, he said, Stier would not have recalled it. What made the form memorable was its reminder of inequality. "The message," he said, was "I'm not equal to other people, to most people who fill [out] this form."

Meyer also observed that these humiliations were magnified when they came from the state. He said that because law is a teacher (another point on which both sides agreed), Prop 8 sent a message to the gay community that "propagates the stigma." He made the less intuitive point that it sent a message to heterosexuals that it was not only permissible, but also "highly valued by our Constitution to reject gay people, to designate them a different class of people in terms of their intimate relationships." It was perhaps predictable that Meyer's testimony was itself trivialized—the ADF posted on its blog that Meyer "spoke at length about how same-sex couples feel when they get funny looks."

Boies said that he and Olson held one question in reserve: "What would it mean to you to be married?" They had not asked this question in their practice sessions because they sought unscripted responses. Perry said that "if Prop 8 were undone and kids like me growing up in Bakersfield right now could never know what this felt like, then I assume that their entire lives would be on a higher arc. They would live with a higher sense of themselves that would improve the quality of their entire life." Stier said that as someone who had grown up in "one of those conservative little pockets of the country," she thought of the impact it would have on kids there "to at least feel like the option to be true to yourself is an option that they can have too." She continued: "I hope for something for Kris and I, but we are big, strong women. You know, we are in a good place in our lives right now. So we would benefit from it greatly, but other people over time, I think, would benefit in such a more profound, life-changing way."

6

THE RIGHT TO MARRY

The US Constitution contains no reference to the "right to marry." Yet even the staunchest textualists in our judiciary agree it is a fundamental right, meaning the government cannot restrict it without a compelling interest. Neither party in the *Perry* case disputed its fundamental nature. In their proposed stipulations, the plaintiffs quoted the dignified formulation of *Loving*: "The freedom to marry has long been recognized as one of the vital personal rights essential to the orderly pursuit of happiness by free men." The proponents agreed.

Lacking explicit recognition in the Constitution, the right to marry—like most other unenumerated rights—is housed under the Due Process Clauses of the Fifth and Fourteenth Amendments, which prohibit deprivation of "life, liberty, or property, without due process of law." The clauses safeguard procedural fairness by requiring the government to provide notice and an opportunity to be heard before it takes life, liberty, or property. Less intuitively, the Supreme Court has interpreted the Due Process guarantees to protect substantive rights, not just rights to fair procedure. In other words, even if the government provides you with notice and an adequate hearing, it must also offer a strong justification for restricting certain rights at all, one of which is the right to marry.

The dispute in this case lay in whether same-sex couples were seeking access to the established right to marry, or asking for the separate right of "same-sex marriage." The Supreme Court does recognize "new" unenumerated rights from time to time, as it did with the right to privacy in 1965. Yet the standard is stringent, perhaps ever more so. In 1997, the Court observed that to receive constitutional protection as a "fundamental right" under the due process guarantees, the right at issue must be "deeply rooted in this Nation's history and traditions," and "implicit in the concept of ordered liberty." The proponents argued that the right to same-sex marriage was not "deeply rooted" in the country's traditions. The plaintiffs did not dispute this point.

Instead, the plaintiffs contended that they sought to access an existing right, not to fashion a new one. They observed that when the Supreme Court granted interracial couples the right to marry in 1967, or allowed prisoners to marry in 1987, it did not speak of the "right to interracial marriage" or the "right to inmate marriage." Rather, the Court cast itself as expanding access to an existing right.

Though advocates for same-sex couples had argued in several cases that bans on same-sex marriage violated gay couples' fundamental right to marry, most courts had either rejected that argument or disposed of the case on other grounds. Even the Hawaii Supreme Court's 1993 decision in favor of same-sex couples had refused to interpret the right to marry expansively, commenting that federal cases recognizing marriage as a "fundamental right" had linked marriage to heterosexual procreation.

In *Perry*, the proponents emphasized this purported link to procreation, arguing that same-sex couples, unlike interracial couples or inmates, could not fulfill the defining purpose of marriage—the capacity to procreate. The question of whether same-sex couples had the right to marry depended on the nature of marriage itself.

The plaintiffs called Nancy Cott as their first expert witness. Cott has been a history professor at Harvard since 2002. Before that, she had spent twenty-six years teaching history at Yale. Her specialties include the history of women, gender, family, and marriage. Her main research on the history of marriage began in the 1990s and she published *Public Vows: A History of Marriage in the Nation* the following decade. Cott approached her topic from a vantage she thought others had neglected—the state's perspective. Because Cott's interest lay in what the state—as opposed to individuals—got out of marriage, she was well suited to address whether the state could still achieve those objectives if it allowed same-sex couples to marry.

Gibson Dunn's Ted Boutrous opened his examination by having Cott establish that secular law has "reigned supreme" in defining civil marriage. She acknowledged that religion has shaped how many Americans view marriage. However, Cott clarified, such understandings do not affect the legal validity of marriages, and religious officials can perform civil marriages (as opposed to religious marriages) only because the state has authorized them to do so.

Cott's opening gambit was crucial. Many individuals still believe that marriage—even in its legal guise—is a religious institution in the United States. When a 2010 poll asked opponents of "marriage" for gay couples whether they would support "civil marriage" for gay couples, more than a third said yes. Yet the only kind of marriage at issue in same-sex marriage litigation is civil marriage. No mainstream advocate of same-sex marriage has ever argued, to my knowledge, that the government can tell a sect how to conduct religious marriages—and with good reason, as he or she would slam up against insuperable objections based on the First Amendment.

By establishing that government-sanctioned marriage in this

country has always meant civil marriage, Cott sidelined the religious conceptions of marriage that dominated the Prop 8 campaign. For example, one ad portrays a train hurtling toward the viewer. The three narrators—including Ron Prentice, the executive director of Protect Marriage—all urge viewers, in overtly religious terms, to vote for Prop 8. "The devil wants to blur the lines between right and wrong when it comes to the family structure," pastor Miles McPherson says. "If someone believes in same-sex marriage, you say you believe in biblical marriage. Stand up for Jesus Christ. Do what he did. He stood up for you in a public forum, now you stand up for him. Don't be like Peter and deny him." The ad ends with the tag: "Stand up for righteousness. Vote 'yes' on Prop 8." Boies played this ad on the same day as Cott's testimony. When asked to comment on McPherson's term "biblical marriage," Cott said she found it "amusing" because the Bible features plenty of examples of polygamy.

Confronted with Cooper's statement that the limitation of marriage to a man and woman was "universal" across history, culture, and society, Cott again vividly countered with polygamy, which was, she explained, prevalent in ancient Judaic and contemporary Muslim cultures. "It's fairly clear, I think, to anyone who has looked at all at world history, that this is not an accurate statement," she remarked. Even if the proponents retreated from the millennia to speak about "traditional" marriage in the United States, they did so at their peril. Defending "traditional" marriage has broad intuitive appeal until one realizes that until the last century, marriage laws made women the property of their husbands, permitted spousal rape, and heavily restricted divorce.

Boutrous next asked Cott to address the social meaning of marriage in the United States. Cott underscored that marriage holds unparalleled importance in this country as a social institution. She observed that it serves as "the principal happy ending of all of our romantic tales," with a "cultural polish" reinforced by ubiquitous images billing marriage "as a destination to be gained by any couple who love one another." She also sounded a more pragmatic note—in this country, the state channels many legal benefits through the institution. Boutrous invited her to compare the social meaning of marriage to that of domestic partnerships. Cott was unequivocal: "There is nothing that is like marriage except marriage."

Boutrous asked Cott to react to Cooper's description of marriage's purpose: promoting procreation and channeling procreative activity into stable unions. Cott testified that procreation is one but not *the* defining purpose of the institution. After all, the state has never required fertility as a prerequisite to marriage.

Rather, Cott said, the state's purpose in licensing and encouraging marriage is to create "stable households" in which committed adults support each other and their dependents. Such mutual interdependence would diminish the dependence of individuals on the state. To bolster that point, Cott underscored that marriage has always been about supporting adults as much as children. At a time when women could not work outside the home, marriage was essential to their economic survival. The head of the married household would be expected to support not only biological children but also "stepchildren, nieces and nephews whose parents might be absent or dead, maiden aunts, unmarried sisters, [and] aged parents." Cott testified that while the "blended family" seems like a modern phenomenon, such families were in fact common in the nation's past due to early death and remarriage.

Cott also discussed the nature of marriage as a civil right. Just as the state had a stake in marriage, so too did individuals. Here Cott's narrative shifted. In the first part of her exchange with Boutrous, she had established the basic features of civil marriage in the United States—its secular nature, its cultural prestige, and its stabilizing function. Now she used the concept of marriage as a civil right to consider how the institution had evolved, observing that the state had given individuals seeking to marry increasing freedom to choose their partners.

Cott began this narrative by observing that slaves could not legally marry. A slave could not give himself to another person in marriage because he already belonged to someone else. Once emancipated, slaves "flocked to get married" because it was "the most everyday exhibit" that they finally owned themselves. Long after the government allowed racial minorities to marry, Cott continued, it prohibited them from marrying across the color line. Legal restrictions on white persons marrying persons of color pre-dated America's founding, multiplying after the Civil War, before dwindling, then being struck down by the Supreme Court in 1967. Boutrous asked how legislators justified these laws. Cott answered that they were usually justified according to God's plan that the races not mix.

Indeed, the trial judge who sentenced Richard and Mildred Loving in 1959 for violating Virginia's ban on interracial marriages opined: "Almighty God created the races white, black, yellow, malay and red, and he placed them on separate continents. And but for the interference with his arrangement there would be no cause for such marriages. The fact that he separated the races shows that he did not intend for the races to mix." (I have often wondered if the judge realized what a dangerous game he was playing—one way to restore God's arrangement, of course, would be to ship whites back to Europe.)

Boutrous asked Cott if she saw parallels between race-based restrictions on marriage and Prop 8. "The most direct parallel," she said, "is that the racially restrictive laws prevented individuals from having complete choice on whom they married, in a way that designated some groups as less worthy than other groups, and some marriages as less worthy than other marriages." Boutrous asked whether opponents of interracial marriage sounded alarms when the state stopped restricting such marriages. Yes, she replied, observing that interracial marriage was extremely controversial for decades and that the Supreme Court long delayed taking it up.

Cott was right—in the wake of *Brown v. Board of Education*, which abolished segregation in public education, the Court dealt out a series of short opinions as if from a deck of cards. These rulings extended desegregation from public education to other state-controlled domains, such as public transportation and public parks. In 1955, a case relating to interracial marriage came before the Court. Apparently deeming the issue too volatile, the Court found a procedural escape hatch to avoid deciding the case. It would be another twelve years before the Court established the right of interracial couples to marry.

Turning to gender-based regulation of marriage, Boutrous asked Cott to describe the ancient legal doctrine of coverture. Cott testified that under coverture, the state mandated marital roles and duties. The husband had to support his wife and dependents and provide them with basic material goods. The wife had to serve and obey her husband, surrender her property and income to him, and allow him to represent her in economic and legal transactions. The complementary duties of husband and wife enabled the survival of the household.

As the economy shifted toward mechanized work, however, and as gender roles became more flexible, the sexual division of labor faded. By the middle of the twentieth century, gender-differentiated spousal roles were seen by most as archaic. Today, Cott observed, spousal roles are "gender-neutral" before the law. She testified that the more symmetrical spousal roles have become, the more that same-sex marriage seems "perfectly capable of fulfilling the purposes" of the institution. She acknowledged that these changes were highly controversial, but perceived "no apparent damage" to marriage as a result. "In fact," she added, the changes redounded "to the benefit of the institution."

Unfortunately, Cott's point is often lost. Most everyone wants to compare same-sex marriage to interracial marriage. There is nothing wrong with the analogy. However, it was not the struggle for racial equality, but the struggle for sex equality, that led most directly to same-sex marriage. In an age when men were breadwinners and women were homemakers, pairing two individuals of the same sex would have been untenable. Only in an age when women could be breadwinners and men could be homemakers did same-sex marriage become viable. Opponents of same-sex marriage seem more conscious of this link (though they cast it pejoratively), emphasizing that only a "genderless" society could produce same-sex marriage. Cott strove heroically to make the point that real equality of the sexes entailed same-sex marriage (as Koppelman and others have argued in the legal literature), but her claim was often overlooked in subsequent argumentation.

If there was a discernible trend in the history of marriage in this nation, Cott said, "the direction has been away from governance and toward liberty." Over time, as the state lifted the restrictions she had enumerated in her testimony, marriage had become increasingly about equality within the relationship and before the state.

David Thompson of Cooper & Kirk cross-examined Cott for the defendants. "You feel that you're somewhat between a neutral party and an advocate, correct?" he began, implying bias on her part. When Cott declined to call herself an advocate, Thompson quoted from a deposition of Cott taken in another case: "You said: 'So I feel I'm somewhat between a neutral party and an advocate, in that I feel I'm led by my particular historical expertise to feel that this is the direction.'" With that exchange, Thompson, whom other witnesses would describe as both "brilliant" and "methodical to the point of being maddeningly plodding," introduced Cott to a key strategy in cross-examination. The examiner often asks the witness to agree with a controversial statement. If she disagrees, he might undermine her credibility by revealing the statement to be her own. If she agrees, she is on record for that position, even if it is not hers. Cott would later ask: "Are you reading my testimony?" Thompson returned: "I don't have to tell you."

Thompson then intimated that Cott's beliefs were more radical than she had portrayed. He revealed that she had donated money to the Alternatives to Marriage Project, an organization that advocates social recognition of "healthy relationships in all their diversity," including unmarried cohabiting couples. One of the project's annual reports had mentioned that couples "in relationships of more than two people" are "unable to marry." Thompson asked if Cott's support meant she supported polyamory. Cott said that she had been unaware of this report when she had donated to the organization.

In a similar vein, Thompson suggested that same-sex marriage broke more starkly with tradition than Cott would have it. He played an NPR interview in which Cott said of *Goodridge* (the Massachusetts decision legalizing same-sex marriage in 2003) that "one could point to earlier watersheds, but perhaps none quite so explicit as this particular turning point." Thompson produced quotations from several other scholars who believed that recognition of same-sex marriage would drastically change the institution.

Thompson also suggested that the line between civil and religious definitions of marriage had been less than distinct throughout American history. Cott agreed that marriage had a religious provenance, but held fast to her point that civil marriage was governed by secular law. Thompson wrapped up his examination by pressing Cott on the consequences of her claim that social mores around marriage had become "more flexible" in recent generations. In a bid to show the dark side of this flexibility, he pointed out that her book described how some Mormon sects had revived polygamy.

On redirect examination, Boutrous allowed Cott to expand on her answers to Thompson. Unlike live media debates, where the allotted time can expire with a gaffe still lingering in the air, a trial offers the opportunity to "rehabilitate" the witness, correcting misimpressions lingering from cross-examination. So Cott had the chance to address Thompson's description of her as an advocate. She explained that when she embarked on her research, it had been "a great shock" to see how punitively marriage laws had been used to regulate groups. That realization had led her to move "very solidly into the direction of" supporting same-sex marriage. Cott testified that she did not support polygamy, noting that the passage in her book about the rise of polygamy had been a description, not an endorsement.

D avid Blankenhorn, the president of the Institute for American Values, served as the proponents' primary expert. He had been an amateur boxer, which showed up in his kinetic, at times pugnacious, demeanor. Although he testified only once, the proponents employed him over two days to counter several of the plaintiffs' witnesses across a wide range of subjects. He faced off against Nancy Cott on the nature of marriage.

Cooper rose to handle the examination. The court learned that Blankenhorn had graduated from Harvard in 1977 and completed a master's while on a fellowship at the University of Warwick. After returning to the United States, he had worked as a volunteer for VISTA, the domestic equivalent of the Peace Corps—an experience that had made him passionate about the plight of the American family. He then served for four years as a community organizer in Massachusetts and Virginia. In 1987, he founded the Institute for American Values, a think tank focusing on issues relating to the American family, and in subsequent years he wrote two books: *Fatherless America* and *The Future of Marriage*.

A self-described "liberal Democrat" who favored gay rights but opposed same-sex marriage, Blankenhorn was initially perceived as an ace witness for the proponents. As ADF lawyer Austin Nimocks observed in his blog coverage of the trial: "Mr. Blankenhorn throws a *huge* wrench into the plaintiffs' case since, as described by some, he's 'one of them' and yet doesn't believe that same-sex 'marriage' is good for society." Some members of the mainstream media agreed that Blankenhorn offered strengths as a witness. Margaret Talbot of the *New Yorker* observed that Blankenhorn was probably the best advocate on the proponents' side, given the subtlety of his arguments and his "record of genuine concern for the well-being of children."

Yet Blankenhorn had some critical weaknesses, which Boies exposed through a process called voir dire. Derived from the Old French for "to speak the truth," voir dire enables lawyers to challenge the qualifications of a witness before they are permitted to testify. Boies established that Blankenhorn had earned his master's degree in comparative labor history and had written his thesis on nineteenth-century British cabinetmakers' unions. He had published no peer-reviewed work relevant to the litigation. He had never held a university post, nor had he taught a course in any college or university on marriage, parenting, or family structure. He did not hold a degree in any field relevant to the subject of his expertise, such as anthropology, psychology, or sociology. When Boies asked whether Blankenhorn had ever studied the effects of same-sex marriage in countries that had legalized it, Blankenhorn responded that he had read articles, tried to be an informed person, and had conversed with people. "I haven't developed a methodology or a set of expert, you know, findings about the topic," he admitted.

Boies broke off his questioning: "Okay. Your Honor, I would object."

Walker overruled Boies. He stated that the standard for admitting an expert rested on several factors—whether the witness's work met standards of intellectual rigor, whether his testimony was based on special skills as opposed to the insights of an "intelligent layperson," and whether the testimony would assist the judge or jury. Applying that standard to Blankenhorn, Judge Walker observed that if this were "a jury trial, the question might be a close one." However, given that the case was being tried before a judge, he permitted Blankenhorn to testify. (Judges often give more leeway with regard to witness testimony in non-jury trials on the assumption that, as courtroom veterans, they are less likely to be influenced by irrelevant testimony.) Blankenhorn later commented that if he were the proponents' counsel and knew how seriously law took formal credentials, he would not have put himself on the stand.

Despite Judge Walker's decision to admit Blankenhorn's testimony, the process that allowed Boies to challenge Blankenhorn reveals another advantage of trials, and of litigation generally. In popular debates, a lengthy, searching examination of an opponent's expertise might be considered impractical or even rude, and it is often seen as elitist to insist that only well-credentialed scholars offer opinions, even on technical subjects. All too often, in television debates in particular, an expert will be matched against a dilettante to give the impression that a contested issue has two equally respectable "sides."

A trial, by contrast, distinguishes between the testimony that lay and expert witnesses may give. Lay witnesses may speak to matters of firsthand knowledge or observation, such as the plaintiffs' experiences of microaggression and their desire to be married. However, only expert witnesses may speak to matters requiring scientific, technical, or specialized knowledge.

By imposing such standards, the rules of evidence recognize that experienced scholars applying rigorous methodology will help a judge determine the facts in technical fields more accurately than will laypersons, however intelligent. Furthermore, the law also restricts experts to their field of specialization. If they venture into other subjects or offer personal reflections, their testimony can be challenged and set aside. Even seasoned scholars like George Chauncey and Nancy Cott said they had not experienced the intensity of their *Perry* cross-examinations since their oral examinations in graduate school.

Cooper began his direct examination by asking Blankenhorn about the nature of marriage. Blankenhorn defined marriage as "a socially approved sexual relationship between a man and a woman." The most important function of marriage, he testified, is to "regulate filiation" by establishing the child's "legal and social parents." Blankenhorn said: "If you don't mind the poetry, we think of it as a gift that we give to children. We say: You as a child are being given this gift of being able to know and be known by the two people who brought you into this world."

Like Cott, Blankenhorn acknowledged that marriage has many purposes and has changed over time. However, he observed that marriage has always and everywhere been primarily organized to unite the "biological, social, and legal dimensions of parenthood." Blankenhorn cited authorities who held the view that marriage was distinctively about child rearing, including sociologist Kingsley Davis, anthropologist Bronisław Malinowski, and anthropologist Claude Lévi-Strauss. (That almost all the cited authorities were active in the twentieth century and deceased at the time of the *Perry* trial went unmentioned.)

Cooper then inquired whether an alternative view of marriage existed. Blankenhorn responded that under the alternative vision, "marriage is fundamentally a private adult commitment." He then argued that this view was inaccurate—that while the "affective private dimensions" of marriage are often important, they do not represent "the sum and substance of marriage."

David Boies cross-examined Blankenhorn. He observed that Blankenhorn had elsewhere described marriage as having three universal "rules": the rule of opposites (that it is between a man and woman); the rule of two (that it is between two people); and the rule of sex (that it is a sexual relationship). Of the three, Blankenhorn had earlier said under direct examination that the rule of two was "probably the weakest," as it is "already tested significantly by polygamy."

Boies challenged Blankenhorn on the universality of his definition, asking him whether exceptions existed to the rule of opposites in societies prior to the last fifty years. Blankenhorn produced only "one instance" of a society that may have had same-sex marriage. Boies asked whether he was familiar with the work of Katherine Young, one of the proponents' witnesses who had withdrawn—for reasons later hotly disputed—from the proceedings before trial.

Although she was on the same side as Blankenhorn, Young had given many examples of societies with same-sex marriage in her deposition. Blankenhorn said he was not familiar with her work.

Turning to the rule of two, Boies suggested that Blankenhorn would "obviously" be aware of a "lot of examples" of marriages inconsistent with that rule. Blankenhorn demurred. "You are not?" Boies inquired, apparently puzzled. He then asked Blankenhorn what societies prior to the last hundred years had "polygamy as a regular course." Blankenhorn replied that, "according to the best scholarly estimates," 83 percent of societies had done so—a strikingly specific number, given that he never named any of the scholars. Boies pressed the point:

> *Boies:* If you have a man who has five wives at the same time—
> *Blankenhorn:* He doesn't marry them at the same time.
> *Boies:* But he has them at the same time.
> *Blankenhorn:* After he has married the fifth, he has five.
> *Boies:* Right.
> *Blankenhorn:* After he has married one, he has one.
> *Boies:* After he's married two—
> *Blankenhorn:* . . . has two. That's how it works.
> *Boies:* And after he has married his fifth wife, assuming they all continue to live and there has been no divorce, he has five wives, right?
> *Blankenhorn:* Yes, sir.
> *Boies:* Now, it's your testimony that that man with five wives is consistent—that marriage is consistent—with what you say is your rule of two; is that correct? . . .
> *Blankenhorn:* Based on the findings of the anthropologists who've actually studied this, yes, the answer to your question is yes.

Blankenhorn clarified that polygamy is consistent with the rule of two because it is not a "group marriage." He continued: "It permits certain men that have access to power to marry more than one woman. Each marriage is a separate marriage of one man and one woman." Blankenhorn did not explain how this claim jibed with his earlier statement that polygamy "tested" the rule of two.

Finally, Boies turned to the rule of sex, asking whether Blankenhorn knew of marriages inconsistent with that rule. Blankenhorn emphasized that "the presumption of sex is one of the foundational elements of marriage. And failure to consummate the marriage through sexual intercourse, in the overwhelming majority of societies, in both law and custom, is grounds for divorce." Boies asked whether Blankenhorn was aware of any married couples who do not have sex. "That's really easy, right?" Boies said. Apparently it was not. After a pause, Blankenhorn produced the instance, which he described as hypothetical, of an incarcerated man "unable to have a conjugal visit." Boies pointed out that this scenario was not a hypothetical. In the 1987 Supreme Court case of *Turner v. Safley*, invoked repeatedly by both sides in *Perry*, the Court invalidated a prison regulation in Missouri that generally prohibited marriage between inmates. The Court ruled that prisoners retained their constitutional right to marry despite the restraints of incarceration. Blankenhorn disclaimed knowledge of the case. Soon after, Boies concluded his cross-examination.

T o develop Nancy Cott's point about how "there is nothing like marriage except marriage," the plaintiffs called lay witness Helen Zia. Zia was part of Terry Stewart's strategy of bringing the expert testimony to life through personal stories. Stewart realized that none of the plaintiffs, by definition, could compare a domestic partnership to a marriage. Unlike the plaintiffs, however, Zia and her partner, Lia Shigemura, had availed themselves of the five-month period in 2008 in which same-sex couples could marry in California. As one of the City of San Francisco attorneys said, Zia represented the "after" of marriage.

A writer who focuses on Asian American issues, Zia offered

an account that was by turns sobering and rollicking. She told the courtroom that she had known she was gay even as a young girl because she knew she did not want to get married. In other words, as Ilan Meyer had said, marriage is such an important life event that some children come to know they are gay by realizing that becoming a spouse is not part of their "possible self." Zia then described what she called her "lesbian trial," in which the community organizers with whom she worked after college staged an intervention and grilled her about rumors that she was a lesbian. Terrified, Zia denied the allegations. After that, she burned her diaries out of fear that they would expose her same-sex desires.

By the time she fell in love with Shigemura, however, Zia was willing to leave her executive position at *Ms.* magazine so that the two could live together in California. After California offered domestic partnerships to same-sex couples, Zia and Shigemura applied for a license at city hall. When asked whether her domestic partnership was like a marriage, Zia testified (as Perry and Stier had done) that it was strictly bureaucratic. She noticed that the city was issuing dog licenses from the same window. When she married in 2008, Zia reflected that the experience was different in kind. She came to understand that marriage is not just a union of two individuals, but of two families. She also spoke more concretely than Cott had about the global reach of the term, observing that her Chinese mother finally had a word for her relationship with Shigemura.

Stewart wanted Zia to testify in part because she worried that past gay-rights cases had showcased a parade of white plaintiffs. (The four plaintiffs in *Perry* identified as Caucasian, although Katami is of Jordanian and Brazilian descent.) As a first-generation Chinese American lesbian, Zia contributed a perspective that might not otherwise have been expressed. She spoke to the international reach of the concept of marriage.

Ron and I have our own version of this experience. We had both been in long-term relationships before. Yet it was only when

Guido married us that my parents, who are Japanese nationals, gave me and Ron a family heirloom I had not even known existed. My great-uncle, who was a calligrapher, had given my parents a scroll when they married. When I asked my parents what the ornate script meant, my father sheepishly said he had no idea. We have asked other Japanese friends, who have also been unable to decipher it. Nonetheless, that scroll now hangs under archival glass in our home. It is the first object each of us sees when we walk through the door. We do not know what it says, but we know what it means.

7

A HISTORY OF DISCRIMINATION

Advocates for same-sex marriage have largely succeeded in framing it as a campaign for equality. Yet if the concept of marriage equality has captured the public imagination, it deeply frustrates conservative opponents of same-sex marriage, who feel it is an empty slogan. They argue that a claim of equality is incoherent without a proper understanding of the essence of what one is trying to equalize. If, as the proponents in *Perry* contended, the purpose of marriage is to channel naturally procreative sexual activity into stable unions, it makes no sense to "equalize" the institution by extending it to same-sex couples, who cannot "naturally" procreate. The trial made this issue inescapable, and the value of Cott's testimony was that it met the proponents where they were, putting forward an alternative working definition of marriage.

Conversely, opponents focused on the definition of marriage often display less appreciation of what equality means to gays. Each side, then, focuses on one side of the debate to the detriment of the other. "This may seem like a ridiculous thing for me to say," Blankenhorn would later report, "but I never really viewed this [case] as about gays." The power of this trial was that it gave gay-rights advocates the opportunity to establish irrevocably that it was.

The equality principle of our Constitution is housed primarily in the Equal Protection Clause of the Fourteenth Amendment, originally framed to grant equality to the freed slaves. Yet as any progressive constitutional scholar will tell you, the framers of the clause made no mention of race, even though they did so in the roughly contemporaneous Fifteenth Amendment, which guaranteed the right to vote without regard to "race, color, or previous condition of servitude." By speaking of "equal protection of the laws" in general terms, the clause left the meaning of equality to the intelligence of later generations.

As its equality jurisprudence has developed (particularly over the past eight decades), the Supreme Court has found that five classifications—race, national origin, sex, alienage, and non-marital parentage—should receive what is known as "heightened scrutiny." Broadly speaking, heightened scrutiny means that these five classifications are so seldom relevant to any legitimate government purpose that the courts take a hard look whenever the government uses them to allocate benefits or burdens. The result, almost invariably, is that the Court invalidates the legislation. For example, in *Loving*, the Supreme Court applied the "most rigid scrutiny" to a ban on interracial marriage, and swiftly disposed of it. Applying heightened scrutiny in the 1996 case of *United States v. Virginia*, the Court struck down the male-only admissions policy at VMI, concluding that Virginia had failed to demonstrate an "exceedingly persuasive justification" for its gender-based classification.

Beyond these five, most classifications by government draw only "rational-basis review." In practice, this means that courts usually uphold the law if any conceivable rationale would justify it. This passivity is understandable, given that every law creates some kind of classification, and scrutinizing all laws would be a crushing

burden. In a famous 1955 case, the Supreme Court upheld a statute allowing only licensed optometrists or ophthalmologists to fit
old eyeglass lenses into new frames, against a challenge brought
by opticians. To a layperson, classifying different professions could
be seen as "irrational," given that opticians could easily fit lenses.
The law was a piece of pork passed by a strong doctors' lobby.
But the Court upheld it, saying the law would be valid as long as a
legislature "might have" had a plausible rationale for it. One such
rationale was that while fitting a lens, an ophthalmologist might
recognize that the person needed a stronger prescription, while
the humble optician might not. To be clear, the legislature never
provided such a rationale—an obliging Court supplied one on the
legislature's behalf. This case highlights a key difference between
heightened scrutiny and rational basis. Under heightened scrutiny,
if the legislature does not come forward with rationales, it will lose
its case; under rational-basis review, it may remain silent and the
Court must gin up rationales that "may have" or "might have"
motivated it. For that reason, as a colleague of mine is fond of saying, a law will generally survive rational-basis review if framed in
grammatically complete sentences.

Heightened scrutiny is the holy grail of equal-protection litigation—if a litigant can persuade a court to apply it, he or she will
generally prevail. The Supreme Court has never clarified whether
classifications based on sexual orientation should receive heightened scrutiny; in fact, it has dodged the issue twice. The Court
invalidated Colorado's Amendment 2 (in *Romer v. Evans*) and
Texas's Homosexual Conduct Law (in *Lawrence v. Texas*) without
clearly establishing a standard of review. In *Perry,* the plaintiffs
brought the issue to a head. They pushed for heightened scrutiny,
though they also contended that Prop 8 failed rational-basis review.

While the Supreme Court's approach to identifying heightened-
scrutiny classifications has been fitful, it has isolated four relevant
factors. As Judge Walker outlined in the summary judgment hearing, the Court asks whether the group typically disadvantaged by

the classification has suffered from a history of discrimination; whether the group is marked by "an obvious, immutable, or distinguishing" characteristic; whether the group is politically powerless; and whether the group has an equal capacity to contribute or to perform in society.

These four factors can be traced back to an opinion in 1973, where the Court confronted the question of whether gender-based classifications deserved heightened scrutiny. Represented by Ruth Bader Ginsburg, then an ACLU lawyer, Lt. Sharron Frontiero had challenged a military regulation that extended certain benefits to military men but not military women. In a plurality opinion, Justice William Brennan maintained that heightened scrutiny was appropriate, based on commonalities women shared with racial and national-origin minorities. While Brennan's opinion in *Frontiero v. Richardson* did not command a majority, subsequent majorities of the Court adopted the portion describing the four commonalities.

I must admit that when I came to *Perry* I was skeptical about the heightened-scrutiny factors. It seemed—and still seems—dangerous to generate criteria by using only a few classifications (sex, national origin, race) and then impose them across the board, given that governmental oppression takes many forms. A more fine-grained analysis should take into account, among other factors, a group's socioeconomic status, its health and longevity, and its susceptibility to private and public violence. Given that the Court has not granted formal heightened scrutiny to a group since the late 1970s, it also seemed to me increasingly unlikely that it would add a new classification.

However, observing the movement lawyers—as well as Boies and Olson—as they argued the four factors has tempered my view. In the right hands, the factors allow a group to introduce itself to the judiciary. This is especially true in the context of a trial, where the plaintiffs have the opportunity to expand the definition of a factor—for example, to show that political powerlessness should take into account a group's susceptibility to violence. Moreover, given that an increasing number of state and lower federal courts have granted heightened scrutiny to sexual orientation, we may be seeing a renaissance of the doctrine.

In addition, many of the heightened-scrutiny factors are relevant in political debates even if they are not decisive in court. A discussion during trial about the immutability of sexual orientation, for example, will almost always be more rigorous than the legislative or popular equivalent. I have often wished that the relevant discussions in the *Perry* trial could be air-dropped into popular debates.

Judge Walker gave the plaintiffs the crucial opportunity to prove the existence of the four heightened-scrutiny factors at trial. Unlike the Liberty Counsel, the proponents did not seriously contest the idea that gay people had an equal capacity to contribute to society. (This concession showed how much progress had been made since the medical establishment deemed homosexuality a mental disorder.) Both sides directed their energies to the three remaining factors: the history of discrimination, immutability, and political powerlessness.

Most courts have found it uncontroversial that gays have suffered a history of discrimination. The proponents offered to concede that "as a historical matter, gays and lesbians have faced discrimination on account of their sexual conduct." Nonetheless, the proponents refused to acknowledge that this history extended into the present. Lambda Legal's Kevin Cathcart has correctly observed that while new civil-rights movements are always beginning, no civil-rights movement has ever ended. In the proponents' view, however, discrimination against gay people sputtered out sometime before the enactment of Prop 8.

Erring on the side of caution, the plaintiffs fielded a witness on this topic—Yale history professor George Chauncey. Soft-spoken and rosy-cheeked, Chauncey's modest affect hides his intellectual courage. With Nancy Cott as his dissertation supervisor, he wrote about gay rights at a time when it could have been career suicide. In 1994, he published an award-winning book titled *Gay New York,* focusing on the world of gay men during the fifty-year period from 1890 to 1940. Like Cott, who testified on the nature of marriage, he had been "discovered" by the movement groups and had already testified in major gay-rights cases, including the *Romer* trial. In *Perry,* he offered opinions on four topics in gay and lesbian history: criminalization, discrimination, censorship, and demonization. City attorney Terry Stewart conducted the examination.

Chauncey began with the criminalization of homosexual behavior. Sodomy laws, he noted, had existed since the early American colonies. For most of our nation's history, these laws reflected a comprehensive Puritanism, prohibiting oral and anal sex for opposite-sex as well as same-sex couples. Over the course of the twentieth century, however, these laws were rewritten or reinterpreted to apply only to gay sex. Chauncey testified that roughly half of the more than seventy-five gay men he had interviewed for his book had been arrested on a gay-related charge. Although the criminal penalties imposed on these individuals were not necessarily severe, convictions would frequently lead to loss of employment or rifts in family life.

Stewart then moved Chauncey to a discussion of other forms of discrimination, beginning with public accommodations. Because they had few places to congregate openly, bars were important venues for gay people. However, beginning with New York in 1933, states cracked down, prohibiting any institution with a liquor license from serving gay people. Bar owners posted signs— IF YOU ARE GAY, PLEASE STAY AWAY. It paid to be risk-averse, given that state officials shuttered establishments on feeble evidence. Chauncey described an officer who justified the revocation of a liquor license because "he had overheard two men talking about the opera; something that no real man would do in the 1950s."

Discrimination in the US military became systematic with the start of the Second World War. At that time, Chauncey noted, the military established screening procedures to exclude gay people. A 1942 regulation authorized examiners to profile men at military induction stations, looking for "feminine body characteristics" or "effeminacy in dress and manner." After World War II, Congress and President Eisenhower similarly ferreted out gays and lesbians in civilian public employment. According to one study, the State Department expelled more alleged homosexuals than Communists in the heyday of McCarthyism. In 1953, President Eisenhower formalized these efforts by prohibiting the federal government from employing gays. Similar policies spread through state and local governments, as well as through the private sector.

Turning to censorship, Chauncey described how film-industry production codes banned gay characters in movies until the 1960s. Through less formal means, television networks kept most depictions of gays and lesbians off-screen well into the 1990s. In 1989, when the hit show *thirtysomething* showed two men in bed together, it ignited a firestorm—religious organizations boycotted the show, sponsors withdrew, and affiliates refused to air it. Chauncey reminded the court that when Ellen DeGeneres came out in 1997, she made the cover of *Time* magazine. The prevailing media blackout profoundly isolated gay individuals, he said. It meant that many "young gay people had no idea that there were other people like themselves in the world." It reminded older gay people that society despised them. For the general public, the lack of positive images enabled alarming stereotypes to emerge.

Stewart turned to those frightening stereotypes, taking up Chauncey's final topic of "demonization." Stewart asked how gays came to be seen as "frightening" as opposed to merely "pathetic," "amusing," or "sick." Chauncey pointed to articles in the press that whipped up a furor about child assault in the late 1940s and early '50s. The articles focused on "sex deviants," of which the quintessential example was "the homosexual." When Stewart asked if the charge had any foundation, Chauncey answered that most of the reported assaults concerned men attacking girls.

Stewart pointed Chauncey to an especially vivid example of such demonization from *Coronet,* a popular magazine. Chauncey read from a 1950 piece: "Once a man assumes the role of homosexual, he often throws off all moral restraints. Some male sex deviants do not stop with infecting their often innocent partners. They descend through perversions to other forms of depravity, such as drug addiction, burglary, sadism, and even murder." Government officials endorsed this impression. In 1949, the assistant attorney general of California characterized "the homosexual" as an "inveterate seducer of the young." A 1950 US Senate policy statement titled "Employment of Homosexuals and Other Sex Perverts in Government" stated: "One homosexual can pollute a government office."

Chauncey went on to describe a storied instance of such demonization—a 1977 campaign in Florida styled Save Our Children. Helmed by singer Anita Bryant, the campaign used the referendum process to overturn a law enacted in Dade County, Florida, that banned discrimination based on sexual orientation. Chauncey testified that the campaign fastened on the law's effect on children, with allusions to recruitment and predation. To support these claims, Chauncey read from two newspaper advertisements endorsed by Bryant. The first stated: "This recruitment of our children is absolutely necessary for the survival and growth of homosexuality, for since homosexuals cannot reproduce, they must recruit, must freshen their ranks." The second advertisement described "a hair-raising pattern of recruitment and outright seduction and molestation, a growing pattern that predictably will intensify if society approves laws bringing legitimacy to the sexually perverted." The success of this campaign spawned about sixty similar ones over the next two decades. The Save Our Children effort also led Florida's legislature to enact a law in 1977 categorically barring gay individuals from adopting.

The discussion of Save Our Children positioned Stewart to pivot dramatically toward the present. She asked Chauncey to review the messaging in the Prop 8 campaign in light of the history he had outlined. Stewart concentrated on the "protect our children" theme that pervaded the Prop 8 campaign. She first asked Chauncey to read from California's official Voter Guide: "[Prop 8] protects our children from being taught in public schools that same-sex marriage is the same as traditional marriage." She played several ads for Chauncey that focused on children. One ended with an adult narrator asking "Have you thought about what same-sex marriage means?" before cutting to a little girl who asks plaintively: "To me?" Another emphasized that gay marriage would "be taught in public schools." Still another had a mother stating: "After Massachusetts legalized gay marriage, our son came home and told us the school taught him that boys can marry other boys. He's in second grade."

Of these ads, one dominated not only the Prop 8 campaign but also other campaigns across the nation. Forceful in its simplicity, the thirty-second "It's Already Happened" ad (more popularly known as "the Princess ad") opens on a pigtailed girl bouncing into the brightly lit kitchen of her home, saying, "Mom, guess what I learned in school today?" The set radiates suburban domesticity— the mother stands behind a counter adorned with a careful formation of bell peppers. If you listen for it, you can hear birds chirping in the background. The mother asks, "What, sweetie?" Passing a book titled *King & King* over the counter, the girl enthusiastically responds, "I learned how a prince married a prince, and I can marry a princess." The mother's eyes widen with alarm as she looks at the book. She then leans over the counter to her child. At that point, Professor Richard Peterson of Pepperdine University Law School emerges into the foreground, although viewers continue to see the woman remonstrating with her daughter. "Think it can't happen?" he says. "It's already happened. When Massachusetts legalized gay marriage, schools began teaching second-graders that boys can marry boys. The courts ruled parents had no right to object." A judge's gavel bangs over a legal citation to a case entitled *Parker v. Hurley*. A female voice takes up the thread: "Under California law, public schools instruct kids about marriage. Teaching children about gay marriage *will* happen here unless we pass Proposition 8. Yes on 8." The ad ends with the woman still speaking to her daughter, while a Protect Marriage logo flashes on the screen.

The claim that parents "had no right to object" was, of course, false. Nothing in the courts' opinions prevented parents from objecting—they could go to their local school board or legislature and object all they wanted. They could also campaign to replace school board members or legislators who did not share their views. They simply did not have the right to see their objections automatically control the school's curriculum or the right to opt out of every portion of it with which they disagreed.

Stewart pressed on, using Chauncey's historical expertise to tie the Protect Our Children Prop 8 campaign to the earlier Save Our Children campaign. Asked to interpret the "protect our children" language in the official ballot materials, Chauncey responded: "Well, you have to ask the question: protect against what?" He answered that for him it evoked "the need to protect children from exposure to homosexuality; not just from exposure to homosexuals as presumed child molesters, but protecting them from . . . the idea of openly gay people." The Protect Marriage ads were "more polite" than Anita Bryant's, Chauncey said, but they were variations on her theme.

In an important 1996 article, legal scholar Reva Siegel describes a dynamic she calls "preservation-through-transformation." As a status hierarchy is contested, she posits, the dominant group protects the hierarchy by changing the rhetoric used to support it. She offers the example of domestic violence, noting that under eighteenth-century English law, a husband had the prerogative to beat his wife. The American legal system adopted that prerogative in qualified form, but advocates for women's rights successfully abolished it in the nineteenth century. After retiring wife-beating as a husband's right, however, courts replaced the rhetoric of prerogative with the rhetoric of privacy. Judges noted that it was improper to make husbands liable for domestic violence, because such judgments would impinge on the privacy of the marital relationship. Men continued to beat their wives with impunity. Siegel argues that the legal subordination endured not in spite of, but because of, the change to more contemporary rhetoric.

Similarly, as Chauncey's analysis revealed, it was possible in the 1970s to justify the subordination of gays by using "save our children" language that cast them as predators or molesters. After that view had been discredited, anti-gay groups had to find a kinder, gentler argot. As a theme, "protect our children" sounded much better, given that it was capacious enough to cover everything from "protect our children from learning about sexuality too early" to "protect our children from becoming gay," while sounding the dog whistle of "protect our children from being molested by gay people" to those who still held that view. However, as Chauncey observed, the "more polite" rhetoric kept the same hierarchy in place.

In cross-examining Chauncey, David Thompson of Cooper & Kirk rose gamely to a difficult task. The proponents had already conceded that gays and lesbians had suffered a history of discrimination. However, Thompson needed to qualify that history to block the plaintiffs' path to heightened scrutiny. To do that, he employed a sort of legal jujitsu, using Chauncey's expertise to blazon how much progress gays had made over time. Thompson established that homosexuality was no longer criminalized; that 90 percent of the largest employers in the United States had adopted antidiscrimination measures protecting gays; that the gay-themed movies *Philadelphia* and *Brokeback Mountain* had enjoyed critical and commercial success (gliding over how the protagonists of both films die); and that many churches no longer demonized gays. Thompson invoked Chauncey himself as a beneficiary of this "sea change in attitudes," pointing out that as a graduate student, Chauncey's decision to write on gay history met with skepticism, but that Yale hired him twenty years later because of that work.

Chauncey offered a mild qualification: "I would hardly take Yale as a bellwether for the entire United States."

"Thank heavens," Thompson responded.

To challenge Chauncey's characterization of Protect Our Children, the proponents played their own clip. In this video, a Massachusetts couple named Robb and Robin Wirthlin talk about the aftermath of marriage equality in Massachusetts. Introduced by a solemn presenter in a dark suit, the Wirthlins nestle on their living room sofa, clothed in pastel colors. With her husband's arm wrapped around her shoulder, Robin Wirthlin recounts how in March 2006, their son came home from school and said: " 'Our teacher read us the silliest book in school today, it was so funny, it was about a prince who married another prince, not a princess, and they became the king and the king.' " (The book, *King & King,* is the same one featured in the Princess ad.) Prompted by the presenter's concerned nods, Robin says: "We were surprised and really astonished because we felt like second grade is very young to be introducing the concept of homosexuality and gay marriage. We thought they would at least wait until they had sex ed in fifth or sixth grade."

Robb says: "We decided that our only recourse was to turn to the courts. And so we went to the First District Court here in Massachusetts and the judge ruled against us. And some of the ruling I thought was very troubling. To paraphrase, he suggested that the state *must* teach these things to children before they've had a chance to make up their own minds."

His wife adds: "The hate, the disparaging remarks, the hostility that we face, were so astonishing, when we sincerely wanted to just protect our children while they're children, not have them face adult issues while they're children." She concludes: "There's a long enough time in their life that they can work through adult issues, but we just wanted them to have a carefree and protected childhood."

The ad made it sound like Protect Our Children meant Protect Our Children from Premature Sexual Education. Moreover, unlike the "Oncoming Train" commercial, the ad does not disclose that the Wirthlins' legal objections to *King & King* were grounded in their Mormon faith. Some scrubbing of the religious motivations behind Prop 8 apparently occurred during the campaign itself, not just when the measure was challenged in court. The litigation in Massachusetts, however, had little to do with sex education and much to do with whether the Wirthlins' religious objections allowed them to opt out of a mandatory curriculum. Massachusetts allowed—and still allows—parents to choose not to participate in sex education in public schools. The school district did not provide the option in this case because it did not consider *King & King* to constitute sexual education. (If anything, *King & King* arguably concedes too *much* to tradition: when the kings kiss at the end of the book, their mouths are obscured by a heart.) The federal district and appellate courts deferred to that assessment. Both courts held that parents could not exercise a roving license to evade lessons they found offensive on religious grounds. Instead, the courts observed that parents retained the right to educate their children differently at home.

On the stand, Chauncey nailed this point. Thompson asked, "Is it reasonable for parents who morally disapprove of homosexuality to want to wait until the fifth or sixth grade for those sorts of issues to be taught in public school?" Chauncey asked whether one would say that people who morally disapprove of racial equality or interracial marriage should be able to ban such topics from schools. He continued: "I think the understanding is that schools are free to and are encouraged to teach broader social values. And in this case the child is simply being exposed to the existence of gay people." Thompson asked if parents had a right to object. Chauncey gave the only sensible answer: they could certainly object, but they could not expect their objection always to be binding. Thompson concluded his cross-examination.

King & King is not the first time a children's book has served as a lightning rod in the marriage wars. Published in 1958, Garth Williams's picture book *The Rabbits' Wedding* depicts a marriage between a white rabbit and a black rabbit. Sen. E. O. Eddins of Alabama railed against it, arguing that the book should be "taken off the shelves and burned" for its anti-segregationist theme. The controversy perplexed Williams, who is perhaps best known for illustrating the children's classic *Stuart Little*. He replied that he was "completely unaware that animals with white fur, such as white polar bears and white dogs and white rabbits, were considered blood relations of white human beings."

On a brief redirect, Stewart returned to the point that children were constantly taught about heterosexual relationships in ways unrelated to sex education. She asked if fairy tales existed about men and women falling in love. Chauncey answered that he believed so. "Do children sometimes even play a role in heterosexual weddings?" she continued. "I believe they have been exposed to heterosexual weddings, yes," he answered. (The word "exposed" was a nice touch.) Stewart asked if Chauncey had ever heard of a flower girl or ring bearer. Yes, yes, Chauncey answered amid background laughter.

Before he left the stand, Chauncey told the court that when he landed a tenure-track job at the University of Chicago in 1991, he was only the second person in the country to be hired in a history department based on a dissertation on gay and lesbian history. While he acknowledged the progress since that time, he said that when he pulled together materials for his course on that topic, he was still struck by the dearth of available work. He further observed that one of the most consistent observations he receives in class evaluations is that his students had never heard of "any of this" history in their prior education. "And so it's pretty clear to me," he concluded, "that the erasure of this history, the history of discrimination and of gay life itself, continues to be very prevalent in our culture."

The plaintiffs could easily have forgone a presentation on the history of discrimination, as the proponents had arguably conceded the point. Chauncey's testimony showed why the plaintiffs were wise not to do so. Without that knowledge, it would be difficult to understand why the LGBT community bridles at claims that its opponents are the real victims in the struggle or to evaluate whether seemingly innocuous phrases like "protect our children" might contain a more sinister echo.

8

IMMUTABILITY

In 1973, when Justice William Brennan was writing the ground-breaking opinion about the heightened-scrutiny factors, he keyed in on immutability. "Because sex, like race and national origin, is an immutable characteristic determined solely by the accident of birth," he wrote, "the imposition of special disabilities upon the members of a particular sex because of their sex would seem to violate 'the basic concept of our system that legal burdens should bear some relationship to individual responsibility.' " In other words, it was unfair for the government to punish individuals for traits they could not control.

Many scholars (including me) have criticized this factor for overemphasizing whether a group *can* change without asking the more relevant question: whether it *should have to* change. As legal scholar Laurence Tribe argued long ago, even if individuals could easily change their race, they should not be deprived of heightened scrutiny. Some appellate courts have taken such critiques to heart and broadened the immutability factor. The Ninth Circuit, which

includes California, defined an immutable trait in 2000 as "an innate characteristic that is so fundamental to the identities or con-
sciences of its members that members either cannot *or should not*
be required to change it." Yet because the Supreme Court has not
clarified what the immutability factor means, litigants still tend to
interpret it more narrowly.

In the context of same-sex marriage litigation, the immutability
of sexual orientation is a contentious topic. As one of my colleagues
has brilliantly argued, this may be because the combatants have different views about the immutability of *marriage*. Generally, advocates of same-sex marriage view homosexuality to be immutable
and marriage to be mutable—a legal construct that can change with
evolving social mores. In contrast, many opponents of same-sex
marriage view homosexuality to be mutable and marriage to be immutable—that is, a universal, eternal institution ordained by God.

These crisscrossing views freight the arguments over the immutability of homosexuality. If homosexuality is immutable, then it
seems cruel to say to gay people that they cannot marry (or can
marry only someone of the opposite sex). As gay-rights advocate
Jonathan Rauch puts it, one of the most potent arguments in favor
of same-sex marriage can be summarized in two words: "Homosexuals exist." Since that is the case, human dignity requires that
gays be given a chance at a decent life. ("Things that exist, exist,"
sculptor Donald Judd once said, "and everything is on their side.")

Recognizing the force of this argument, opponents of same-sex
marriage like NOM, who ostensibly lobby only against marriage
equality, have poured energy into making the case for conversion
therapy. They oppose, for instance, the rising effort in some states
to ban conversion therapy for minors. At first blush, it might seem
they have strayed from their stated mission, but the two issues are
linked. If homosexuality is mutable, the cruelty of bans on same-
sex marriage is mitigated; gay men and women have only to convert to heterosexuality to avail themselves of traditional marriage.
Affirming the immutability of homosexuality is how some gays

implicitly apologize for being gay; affirming its mutability is how some opponents of gay rights implicitly apologize for their anti-gay positions.

For this reason, much rode on the question of immutability, not just for the parties in the San Francisco courtroom but in the nation—indeed the world—beyond it.

To address the issue of whether sexual orientation was immutable, the plaintiffs called Ryan Kendall, a gay man from Colorado. Kendall, who was twenty-six at the time, appeared as a lay witness. Ronald Flynn, an attorney for the City of San Francisco, handled the direct examination.

A short man with a shaved head and stocky build, Kendall testified that he was born into a conservative Christian family in Colorado Springs. Kendall grew up learning that homosexuals were evil people whose existence threatened his family. To his alarm, he realized he was such a person at the age of eleven or twelve, after he looked up the word in the dictionary. Soon afterward, his parents discovered he was gay by reading his journal.

Flynn asked Kendall what happened next. "My parents flipped out," Kendall recounted. "Before all this started, I had the kind of parents who would drive me to school, and make my lunches, and write notes and put them in my lunch. And after this, they were always yelling at me." Flynn asked for examples. "My mother would tell me that she hated me, or that I was disgusting, or that I was repulsive. Once she told me that she wished she had had an abortion instead of a gay son." A gasp rippled through the courtroom.

Kendall's parents sent him to a local Christian therapist for "reversal therapy." The therapist told him that God did not want him to be gay. Kendall did not try to become heterosexual, because he did not consider it possible: "I knew I was gay just like I knew I'm short and I'm half Hispanic. And I just never thought those facts would change."

After Kendall's sessions with the local therapist proved unsuccessful, Kendall's parents sought advice from Focus on the Family, a Christian organization based in Colorado Springs. The organization recommended the California-based National Association for Research & Therapy of Homosexuality (NARTH). From the ages of fourteen to sixteen, Kendall worked with Dr. Joseph Nicolosi, the head of NARTH, mostly over the phone. Kendall testified that Nicolosi offered him no "specific technique" for change, telling him only that God did not want him to be gay.

Kendall related how, at age sixteen, he felt "just as gay as when [he] started" and realized that if he did not stop his therapy sessions, he would not survive. Flynn asked what he meant by that. "I would have probably killed myself," Kendall replied. Kendall worked with the state to emancipate himself from his parents. He then spent four or five years "in and out" of school and jobs. "I was very lost . . . suicidal and depressed. I hated my entire life. At one point, I turned to drugs as an escape from reality and because I was, you know, trying to kill myself." Flynn inquired whether Kendall was now stable and able to support himself. "Yes. It's been a—a long, hard journey. . . . [But] I've been able to do that," Kendall concluded.

Kendall's testimony will resonate with many, if not most, gay adults. The argument that homosexuality can be changed is a killing discourse. If homosexuality must be extinguished, and if homosexuality is inextinguishable, then the only way of accomplishing the mandate is to extinguish oneself. Recent studies show that gay youth are approximately two to five times more likely to commit suicide than their straight peers.

James Campbell of the ADF cross-examined Kendall for the defendants. He too kept it short. Campbell pointed out that Kendall had never lived in California (though it was unclear what difference this would have made) and that Kendall had "never studied whether a person's sexual orientation can change." He implied that therapy had not worked on Kendall because Kendall had never tried to change: "Your only goal for conversion therapy was to survive the experience; isn't that true?" Kendall said: "Absolutely." Campbell then asked if some people willingly participate in conversion therapy programs. Kendall denied ever having met such people. Pressed by Campbell, however, Kendall conceded that some people reported "effective results with conversion therapy."

Campbell had inadvertently opened a door. Flynn returned to elicit one final point: "While you were in conversion therapy, were you introduced to any people who purported . . . to have successfully undergone conversion therapy?" Kendall answered that he was. "Nicolosi trotted out his perfect patient, the guy who had been cured of his homosexuality," he recalled. The man's name was Kelly. Flynn asked Kendall if Nicolosi's model pupil affected Kendall's views. "I remember once, when Nicolosi stepped out of the room . . . Kelly told me that later that night he was going to a gay bar and that he was, essentially, just pretending to be cured for the sake of his family," Kendall answered. "I knew I was gay. I knew that could not be changed. And this just confirmed that this wasn't going to be effective for me."

Two days after Kendall testified, the plaintiffs brought forward their immutability expert—Gregory Herek, a professor of psychology at the University of California–Davis. The plaintiffs offered Herek as "an expert on social psychology, with a focus on sexual orientation." Gibson Dunn lawyer Ethan Dettmer conducted the direct examination and Howard Nielson of Cooper & Kirk handled the cross-examination.

Herek began by explaining that social scientists defined sexual orientation by looking at attraction, self-identification, and behavior. Researchers might favor one definition over another, depending on their goals. A scholar studying sexually transmitted disease would focus on behavior, while one interested in the effects of discrimination would focus on self-identification.

Herek also testified about whether people can choose or change their sexual orientation. He said that the vast majority of gay and lesbian people he had studied reported experiencing no or very little choice. Dettmer asked Herek if therapy to change one's orientation was effective. Herek said it was not. He observed that a special task force of the American Psychological Association had released a report in 2009 stating that lasting change in sexual orientation is rare and that many individuals felt harmed by change therapies, describing higher levels of anxiety and depression. Herek was not aware of any major mental health organization that had endorsed change therapies. Most, including the American Psychological Association and American Psychiatric Association, had expressed concern about forcing adolescents through them against their will.

During cross-examination, Nielson picked apart the three metrics, asking Herek to confirm that not everyone displays consistency among sexual feelings, behavior, and identity. Herek agreed. "Many men, for example, regularly have sex with other men, but never label themselves as gay or bisexual, correct?" Nielson asked. Herek agreed, but clarified that, overwhelmingly, people are consistent across the three dimensions. The two men spent hours arguing the point, with Nielson casting inconsistency as the rule, and Herek casting it as the exception. Herek noted that about 90 percent of people in the National Health and Social Life Survey were consistently heterosexual and another "core group" of 1 to 2 percent were consistently lesbian, gay, or bisexual across all three dimensions. The inconsistencies only arose with the other 8 to 9 percent of the population.

Nielson then turned to the sources of homosexuality. Here the proponents won some ground—Herek freely conceded that the origins of homosexuality were not known. He did not embrace theories that a gay gene had been discovered. Research claiming a genetic source for homosexuality—led by scientists like Simon LeVay and Dean Hamer—had burgeoned in the 1990s. After scholars pointed out flaws in the methodology of such studies, however, this line of inquiry seemed to wither on the vine in the ensuing decade.

On redirect, Dettmer inquired whether the challenges of assigning individuals to identity groups are specific to sexual orientation. Herek answered that, in fact, the question is common, such as when people try to define race. People who are "mixed," or whose "skin color may not be very revealing," have particular difficulty labeling themselves. In other words, although some people do not neatly fit into a single racial classification, the law still recognizes the classifications themselves.

Dettmer revisited Nielson's questions on change therapy by reading excerpts from the deposition testimony of Daniel Robinson, a professor of psychology with a joint appointment at Oxford and Georgetown. Robinson was one of the four proponents' experts who withdrew from the proceedings after deposition but before trial. Asked whether he believed that "sexual orientation is readily subject to change," Professor Robinson had said simply, "No." Dettmer asked Herek whether he agreed. "I would give the same response," Herek answered.

The trial once again proved eloquent in its synthesis of the human and the statistical—Kendall told his story, then Herek backed it up with data. At the same time, Kendall's experience showed how trials can produce truth quite aside from their outcomes. Stewart had found Kendall after reaching out through her networks, seeking "somebody who has been subjected to reparative therapy but who isn't so destroyed by it that they can't testify." After hearing Kendall's story, Stewart thought he would be a powerful witness but worried the trial would re-traumatize him. She spoke bluntly to Kendall at the outset, checking that he had adequate emotional support before he made the decision to testify. Kendall insisted on participating.

City attorneys Ron Flynn and Mollie Lee assumed the task of

preparing Kendall for trial. They quickly hit a snag—Kendall had wholly dissociated from his experiences. "He was telling someone else's story," Flynn observed. Flynn worried about how Kendall's reserve would play at trial: "He had to be one hundred percent truthful and honest, because you can tell when someone is not . . . you can look at them and say 'this is horseshit.' " Lee broke the log-jam, realizing they would never elicit an authentic reaction while they treated him with kid gloves. In one session, she told Kendall she would impersonate David Boies. Describing that session, Kendall recalled: "I just had to relate immediately, and I broke down in tears. It was just overwhelming. I had to reconcile the fact that this story that existed had happened and it had happened to a real person and it had had truly negative consequences in their life and that person was me." The trajectory of that sentence—from detachment to identification—mirrored Kendall's emotional journey during the trial. Kendall's performance on the stand was, according to Flynn, "phenomenal." When he came off the stand, Olson gave him a bear hug. (In speaking about the case, Olson would often refer—always with horror—to the young man whose mother said she would rather have had an abortion than a gay son.)

Kendall's participation in the trial had serious ramifications. Right after he left the courtroom, he flew back to his job in Colorado, which he described as being a "glorified secretary" for the Denver Police Department. "One minute I was talking with the smartest people in the legal profession and the next minute I'm entering pawn tickets in Denver," he recalled. "I was reprocessing my testimony. I did become re-traumatized; they were right to worry about that."

Five months after the trial, Kendall resolved to commit suicide. However, his sister was about to take the bar exam, and he decided to wait until she had completed it so as not to affect her performance. While he was waiting for his sister to finish, Lee called to check on him. Horrified by his condition, Lee asked how she could help. Kendall said he wanted to become a lawyer, but did not see how he could, given that he had never finished his undergraduate degree. With Lee's encouragement, Kendall successfully applied to Columbia University, graduating summa cum laude in 2014. When I last spoke to him, he had recently taken the LSAT and submitted his application to law schools.

The purpose of a federal trial, of course, is not to help people find their personal truths. Yet Kendall's story underscores how powerful the truth-finding mechanisms of the trial can be. As Kendall observed: "The trial saved my life." Everything about his life is now different, he noted, except, he says, "I'm just as gay as when I started."

9

POLITICAL POWERLESSNESS

By 2010, when the *Perry* case went to trial, gay families populated celebrated TV shows like *Modern Family,* gay politicians like Barney Frank served openly in Congress, President Obama had signed legislation prohibiting hate crimes against gay individuals, and gay-rights lobbying groups like the Human Rights Campaign (HRC) routinely raised millions. Alongside these major advances were myriad smaller ones—from the passage of a municipal ordinance to the coming out of less well-known public figures. All of these were broadcast in loving detail: As someone who belongs to various LGBT lists and feeds, I began to feel that if a gay man won a pie-eating contest in Peoria, I would hear about it before his face was clean. But I understood the impulse. The canvas had been blank for centuries. So the activists documented every tiny advance, painting a pointillist mural of a movement whose time had finally come.

The great irony of the heightened-scrutiny argument was that the plaintiffs had to show the court that gays were politically powerless, which meant that the triumphal narratives that played so well in the streets could harm them on the stand. The plaintiffs did not need to shade the truth—much work remained. But they had to flip the script: the glass was now half empty, not half full.

The proponents faced the same predicament. In public, they constantly emphasized that public sentiment was on their side—that every time same-sex marriage had come up in a ballot initiative, the people had (with only one exception) voted it down. But in court, the proponents began to sound like the HRC in talking about the popularity of *Will & Grace* or the twenty-one states that barred discrimination against gays. It was a game of "loser wins," imposed by the political powerlessness inquiry. As the lawyers tied themselves in knots, I was reminded of those movies where the protagonists swap bodies.

Although both sides wrestled with this challenge, the plaintiffs struggled more. They had the burden of proving that gays were politically powerless. As if this were not bad enough, the proponents offered a credible expert on this issue: Kenneth Miller, a professor of government from Claremont McKenna College, who held a PhD from Berkeley and a law degree from Harvard. Finally, Supreme Court case law cut sharply against the plaintiffs—a 1985 case defined political powerlessness as the condition of having "no ability to get the attention of the lawmakers."

In the face of these challenges, many lawyers would have surrendered the point. Not so Boies and his team.

Miller began his testimony by offering a panoramic view of the many allies of gay rights or marriage equality. In 2008, the California Democratic Party had expressed support for LGBT equality; a year later, it took a stance against Prop 8. Every major labor organization that Miller could think of supported LGBT rights. Miller had also done a study on twenty-three major newspapers in California, finding that twenty-one of them had opposed Prop 8 (the other two took no position). Many major companies—including AT&T, Kaiser Permanente, and Time Warner Cable—had donated funds to the

"No on 8" campaign. Miller also cataloged various celebrity advocates, mentioning Ellen DeGeneres, Brad Pitt, and Steven Spielberg, before alluding to Rob Reiner's presence in the courtroom. Associations of psychologists, psychiatrists, and other professionals had endorsed marriage equality. And the most powerful person in the country, President Obama, had expressed "significant support" for gay rights, Miller said, citing his appointment of openly gay people to positions in his administration, a "major address" to the HRC, and his recognition of Gay Pride Month.

After Miller's testimony, Boies asked how Prop 8 could possibly have passed with such a phalanx amassed against it. The plaintiffs had tasked Stanford political scientist Gary Segura with responding to that question. Segura had a ready answer: socially conservative churches and the ballot-initiative process.

Segura observed that "after government, it's difficult to think of a more powerful social entity in American society than the church." Churches are massively influential grassroots institutions, he said, because their leaders speak to their congregants weekly and because they are "in large measure . . . arrayed against the interests of gays and lesbians." He painstakingly walked through a series of exhibits showing that the Catholic Church hierarchy, influential Evangelical denominations, and the Church of Latter Day Saints (Mormons) had backed Prop 8. Segura read aloud a Protect Marriage e-mail celebrating the "substantial role" of the Roman Catholic Church, which had raised millions of dollars for the campaign. He described a conference call that convened 1,700 pastors in more than a hundred locations across the state. Segura also reviewed a document noting that the Mormon Church had a campaign coordinator "in every zip code." Segura could think of only one other issue—abortion—that could create such a coalition.

Miller hit back on this point. Progressive religious communities increasingly supported LGBT rights and same-sex marriage, he said. He noted that the California Council of Churches, which included members of the Presbyterian Church USA, the United

Church of Christ, and the United Methodist Church—generally supported gay rights. Miller also observed that California is one of the ten least religious states in the United States, with more than 20 percent of the population reporting no religious affiliation.

Yet Segura had another point. It was not just that conservative churches largely opposed same-sex marriage, but that they had found a way to codify their beliefs into law: ballot initiatives. The federal Constitution prohibits legislation based solely on religious belief or prejudice against a particular group. But because it is nearly impossible to ascertain why a citizen voted for a specific initiative, such initiatives allow voters to evade these restrictions.

Segura testified that prejudice against gays—whether based in religion or not—explained why gay-rights issues fared so poorly in ballot initiatives. Since the 1970s, gays and lesbians had been subjected to about two hundred ballot initiatives across the nation. Gays had lost about 70 percent overall, and almost 100 percent of the initiatives pertaining to marriage. Segura told the court that gays and lesbians had been targeted by ballot initiatives more than any other group in American society. He described the ballot initiative as the "Waterloo" of the battle for LGBT equality.

As a counterpoint, Miller provided some examples of ballot initiatives that gays had defeated. However, many of his examples seemed too extreme to have had a chance of succeeding—such as three initiatives in the 1980s aimed at quarantining people with HIV. Miller's analysis also did not venture beyond California. Because the Supreme Court has suggested that political powerlessness is measured nationally, Miller's neglect of the rest of the nation was conspicuous. Perhaps most important, Miller could not deny that his examples were the exceptions, while Segura's were the rule.

Nonetheless, the arguments on both sides were strong. Miller had produced significant evidence of gay political mobilization. Segura had countered that a combination of religion and referendums had hampered that mobilization. But it was a fair fight with respect to the credentials of its combatants. Miller was a tenured professor

of political science; moreover, unlike Segura, his particular spe-
cialty was direct democracy. If the plaintiffs were to prevail, they
would have to neutralize him.

Boies began his attempt to defang Miller by asking him to
open his binder to his expert report. He directed the professor toward the list of materials considered—an impressive 427
sources. Boies asked if some of the materials were provided to him
by counsel. Miller said yes. Boies then told Miller to circle the
sources in his bibliography he had found himself. It is difficult to
imagine a forum other than a trial in which one party to a debate
could force an opponent through such an exercise: Miller painstakingly went through the list for about fifteen minutes as the entire
courtroom silently observed him.

Miller knew he could expect trouble here. The plaintiffs had filed
a pre-trial motion to exclude Miller's testimony because his report
was heavily duplicative of the report of a withdrawn expert witness
for the proponents, Paul Nathanson. Miller and Nathanson had
listed more than 150 sources in common. Twenty-eight of the websites listed in Miller's report featured the same "date last visited" as
the websites listed in Nathanson's report. The two documents even
shared typos.

On the stand, Miller confronted two unpalatable alternatives.
If he circled too many sources that could be traced to Nathanson's
report, he risked perjury. If he circled too few, he would effectively
admit that he had not researched his own report. Of the 427 references listed, he circled 100. Boies entered the marked-up document
as an exhibit without going after Miller. The strategy was clear—
the plaintiffs' team would pore over the exhibit that evening, given
that Miller's testimony would spill over into the next morning.
Boies may as well have clambered onto the witness stand and hung
a Damoclean sword over Miller's head.

When Boies revisited the bibliography on the following day, he observed that Miller had circled fewer than a quarter of the sources listed. He then pointed out that between 140 and 150 of the sources had shown up on withdrawn witness Paul Nathanson's report. "It's not just a pure coincidence that the two of you came up with exactly the same list of documents, correct?" Boies asked. Miller said he "wouldn't know what to say about where the documents came from," but conceded that some came from his counsel.

In an e-mail, Miller responded to Boies's charge that he had lifted materials from Nathanson's report: "As I was completing work on my expert report, it appeared that Dr. Nathanson might be withdrawing from the case and that, as a consequence, the evidence he cited might be excluded at trial. I concluded that some of his evidence was relevant to my analysis of the political power of the LGBT movement and that it was an important contribution to the trial. I thus incorporated it into my report." Miller nonetheless insisted that he analyzed the evidence and the issue himself.

When I shared this explanation with Segura, he would have none of it: "Inside a student judicial process at Stanford and many other universities I have taught at, that would be sufficient for student judicial proceedings against that student for academic misconduct. You just don't do that."

While Miller's unattributed appropriations from Nathanson's report called his credibility into question, they did not directly undermine the substance of his testimony. Miller had incorporated Nathanson's material because he agreed that religion had shown up on both sides of Prop 8. This stance dovetailed with his testimony at trial.

Yet unfortunately for Miller, it did not square with an article he had published months before he took the stand. Boies cited a 2009 article in which Miller had written: "Churches and religious organizations supplied most of Proposition 8's institutional support, with Catholics, Evangelicals, and Mormons leading the way." The article further stated that "religion was critical in determining voter attitudes towards Proposition 8." On the stand, Miller said he thought there were other "critical" factors as well, but admitted he had neglected to mention any in the article. Boies closed this line of questioning by quoting from Miller's article: "Opportunity to establish gay marriage was lost in large part because California's Democratic coalition divided along religious lines."

Boies sought to show that Miller's 2009 article reflected his real views. He pressed Miller on his earlier argument that "there were churches on both sides of the debate." Under questioning by Boies, Miller estimated the membership of the pro-gay California Council of Churches to be 1.5 million. He estimated the number of Catholics and Evangelicals in California to be about 18 million.

To be sure, Miller's core expertise was not in the power of churches but in direct democracy. But when Boies turned to that subject, one of the most bizarre sequences in the trial unfolded. Boies revealed that in a 2001 article, Miller had asserted that "populist-oriented initiative lawmaking tends to undermine representative government and impose majoritarian values at the expense of minority rights. Racial minorities, illegal immigrants, homosexuals, and criminal defendants have been exposed to the electorate's momentary passions as Californians have adopted a large number of initiatives." That same year, in an contribution to a collection titled *Dangerous Democracy,* Miller had recommended that courts "be more vigilant, not less, when reviewing initiatives." With regard to ballot initiatives, Miller in 2001 could have been a witness for the plaintiffs.

On redirect, Thompson asked Miller to explain the evolution of his thinking since 2001. Miller said he had developed a "more favorable view of the initiative process after having reviewed the entire hundred-plus years of this process, dating back to the very beginning of the twentieth century." On the topic of marriage, he considered that "taking that decision out of the hands of the people in general is an example of the courts taking too strong a position on this issue."

It was not at all obvious, however, that Miller's position had changed. During Miller's deposition, he had been asked, "Do you agree that the direct initiative can be and has been used to disadvantage minorities?" Miller replied: "I believe that's a fair interpretation of the history of the initiative process." During the trial, Boies asked him if he stood by that position. Miller said he did.

Of course, academics do change their positions over time, but usually over a period of decades—not over a period of months (as Miller did in the case of religion) or years (as Miller did in the case of ballot initiatives, if one takes the most generous view). Miller himself would not explain his conflicting testimony—repeating only what he said at trial. Other individuals I spoke with—ranging from a colleague in his postdoctoral program to his dissertation supervisor and coauthor to Segura to the plaintiffs' lawyers—expressed bewilderment. In speaking generally about this topic, Chuck Cooper kept alluding to liberal bias in the social sciences. But there are plenty of conservative political science professors in the academy. Of all those professors, why select the expert on direct democracy who had written that ballot initiatives problematically disadvantaged minorities? It was a mystery.

The final, perhaps most daunting, hurdle that the plaintiffs had to jump was a Supreme Court precedent defining political powerlessness. That precedent had been set in *Cleburne v. Cleburne Living Center,* a case involving intelligence disability, in which the Court defined political powerlessness as the condition of having "no ability to attract the attention of the lawmakers." Finding that individuals with disabilities had garnered the attention of the federal government through the Rehabilitation Act of 1973 (a precursor to the 1990 Americans with Disabilities Act) and related policies, the Court rejected their bid for heightened scrutiny. Under this standard, given the power Miller had described, it would be hard to make the case that gays were politically powerless.

Still, if a court were to deny gays heightened scrutiny based on *Cleburne* alone, it would reveal a profound incoherence at the heart of the standard. Before *Cleburne,* the Court had granted heightened scrutiny to groups that were patently able to "attract the attention of lawmakers." Women had been protected by the Equal Pay Act of 1963 and Civil Rights Act of 1964 for over a decade before gender-based classifications received heightened scrutiny in 1976. Under *Cleburne*'s logic, they should not have received such judicial protection. Yet as recent cases have confirmed, the test announced in *Cleburne* did not mean that gender-based classifications—or the other heightened-scrutiny classifications—were demoted to rational-basis review. The Court could have grandparented in the preexisting classifications because they had made it under the wire before *Cleburne* was decided. Yet it flouts basic fairness—not to say "equal protection"—for a classification to receive heightened scrutiny (or not) based on when it arrived on the Supreme Court's doorstep. There is no reason to suppose that the most worthy oppressed groups got to the Supreme Court first.

If the Court were to look for more coherent alternatives, the most obvious one comes from the case of *United States v. Carolene Products.* In that case, the Court observed that "prejudice against discrete and insular minorities" could warrant greater intervention from the judiciary. This statement is often seen as the fountainhead of the heightened-scrutiny jurisprudence.

As later courts and scholars have elaborated, the theory goes like this: In a democracy, we expect minorities to lose. Yet majorities are not monolithic—they are composed of shifting coalitions of minority groups. For this reason, every minority can be expected to have its day in the sun, because every minority will sometimes find itself in the governing coalition. Prejudice, however, can short-circuit this process—turning one particular minority group into a pariah, with whom other minority groups are loath to deal. When a group finds itself marginalized in this way, the democratic process is not working, and the courts must step in to protect its members. The great virtue of this approach is that it recognizes a link between prejudice and political powerlessness. As legal scholar Bruce Ackerman observes, assessing political powerlessness without addressing the role of prejudice is like putting on *Hamlet* without the prince.

To describe enduring prejudice against gays and lesbians, Segura used what political scientists call a "feeling thermometer." When using this tool, researchers ask individuals how they feel about a group on a scale of 0 to 100. Segura observed dramatic differences in how individuals felt about different minority groups. Racial and religious minorities generally scored between 65 and 70. Gays and lesbians scored a mean of 49. Indeed, Segura pointed out that along some dimensions, anti-gay sentiment was rising. After examining hate-crime statistics from 2003 to 2008, Segura found that violence against gay men and lesbians had increased. In 2008, 71 percent of "hate-motivated" murders were of gays and lesbians. Segura then made a link between prejudice and political powerlessness. Prejudice, Segura argued, upends "the pluralist struggle" between groups in a democracy. "It's very difficult to engage in the give-and-take of the legislative process," he said, "when I think you are an inherently bad person."

Miller, on the other hand, not only ignored the link but also showed little awareness of the prejudice faced by LGBT individuals or of their political powerlessness. He was not aware at deposition that the term *gay bashing* referred to physical violence against gays and lesbians, and he remained unfamiliar at trial with some of the most influential writers on LGBT politics. Asked in his deposition how many states lacked an antidiscrimination law covering sexual orientation, Miller had answered, "I don't know the number." On the stand, Miller defended himself by saying that he had not known whether the question referred only to statewide laws or included local ordinances. Boies said: "And you didn't say that at the deposition, did you sir?" Miller confirmed that he had not. Miller had also touted the passage of federal hate crimes legislation protecting gays—the Matthew Shepard Act—as evidence of political power. Boies suggested that the need for such legislation reflected group vulnerability as much as group influence. Shepard, after all, had been tortured, impaled on a fence, and left to die just for being gay. Boies inquired if the passage of Megan's Law, which protected children from sexual predators, meant children were politically powerful. Miller said, "I don't know."

The Court has also sometimes adopted a third, commonsensical, approach to political powerlessness. When the Supreme Court first advanced the idea of giving women heightened scrutiny, a plurality of the justices relied heavily on analogies between women and racial minorities. The Supreme Court has yet to formally embrace this comparative approach, though many justices have employed it in practice. Segura squarely engaged in the comparative enterprise, while Miller did not.

Segura testified that "gay men and lesbians are more disadvantaged today than women were in the 1970s." He supported this claim by stating that women were a majority of the electorate, that "being a woman is not inherently controversial," and that "there were women in public office." He also noted that women had secured more federal statutory protection, including the Equal Pay Act of 1963 and certain provisions of the Civil Rights Act of 1964.

Segura also compared the political power of gays and lesbians with that of African Americans before the Civil Rights Act. Segura listed a number of ways in which the political situation of African Americans then might have been considered better, including three amendments to the US Constitution protecting their rights and executive orders from Roosevelt and Truman barring discrimination by government contractors and desegregating the military. Moreover, Segura argued that gays and lesbians were in many ways moving in the opposite direction from African Americans in the 1940s. Since 1990, he told the court, a supermajority of states had entrenched LGBT inequality into their constitutions by banning same-sex marriage. Segura also reminded the court that there were more African Americans than gays and lesbians overall, and that they had received more direct representation, including the presidency.

Under cross-examination, Miller admitted that he had not conducted a comparative analysis of whether gays had suffered more prejudice than African Americans. Asked an analogous question about women, Miller answered: "Again, I think women still face a lot of prejudice and stereotyping and I haven't done a comparative analysis." After the trial, Bruce Cain, Miller's former dissertation supervisor and coauthor, defended Miller's refusal to make any comparative claims about political power: "Ken is not an empirical person. He teaches California politics but he was not trained to do this statistical, empirical work that would have been necessary to answer a question like, 'Is the gay community weaker than the African American community?' I actually thought he showed a lot of integrity in refusing to answer that question, because it was not in his scope."

Miller did, however, dip his toe into statistical waters, saying that the reason he hesitated to make a comparison was that gay individuals were hard to identify, making both the numerator and the denominator of the fraction unclear. Boies stood ready to help:

> *Boies:* Well, sir, take California. You know that no openly gay or lesbian person has ever, in the history of the state, been elected to statewide office, correct, sir?
>
> *Miller:* No openly gay person, that's correct.
>
> *Boies:* Not governor, not lieutenant governor, not attorney general, not senator; correct, sir?
>
> *Miller:* That's correct.
>
> *Boies:* So in that case, whatever the denominator would be, the numerator would be zero, correct?
>
> *Miller:* That's correct.

The exchange elicited laughter but made a serious point. The main opinion in the *Frontiero* case had said that women could be considered a vulnerable group despite being a majority of the population because they were "underrepresented in this Nation's decision-making councils." Boies forced Miller to admit that gays, too, were scarce in at least some of those councils.

At some point, the Supreme Court will have to define political powerlessness more clearly. When it does, it could take one of three paths. It could embrace the *Cleburne* standard of "no ability to get the attention of the lawmakers." But then it would have to explain why gender and race received heightened scrutiny at times when they plainly had such attention. It could embrace the *Carolene Products* standard of "prejudice against discrete and insular minorities." This would be a welcome development, as it is difficult to understand power without understanding prejudice. Finally, it could just muddle along with its analogical reasoning, comparing new classifications to those that have already received heightened scrutiny.

As it chooses among these avenues, I would exhort the Court to at least reject the *Cleburne* formulation as incoherent. This was the only standard under which Miller could prevail, as he failed to show that gay people were not subject to prejudice and refused to engage in a comparative analysis. *Cleburne* assumes that only groups that are utterly powerless can receive the attention of the courts. But the truly powerless in our society do not have the attention of any branch of government, including that of the courts. As a practical matter, it requires a massive amount of social mobilization to even get on the Supreme Court's radar—without the gay-rights movement or the disability-rights movement, those groups would never even have been up for consideration. The paradox of political power is that it takes a massive amount of political power to be deemed politically powerless by the Court. It would be a painful irony to deny gays heightened scrutiny because of the gains they have made, when it is precisely those gains that have finally made them candidates for such scrutiny.

10

THE IDEAL FAMILY

If the plaintiffs could establish either that they had a fundamental right to marry or that they deserved heightened scrutiny under the Equal Protection Clause, they would win. But if they did not get heightened scrutiny, they would lose unless they showed that Prop 8 lacked any conceivable rationale. Unfortunately for the plaintiffs, the proponents had a superabundance of rationales. While some of these justifications were fevered (same-sex marriage will lead children to be raised communally in the "persuasively dystopian vision" of *Brave New World*!) or illogical (if we give gays same-sex marriage, we will have to give bisexuals group marriage!), it was not a bad strategy to heave spaghetti at the wall. If even one strand stuck, Prop 8 would stand.

When Judge Walker called for a trial, however, he transformed the litigation by turning on a threshing machine. Factual allegations would not be taken at face value but instead shunted into a device that would separate wheat from chaff. Even with regard to the legislative facts pertaining to marriage or equality, the trial served this crucial function. However, the trial was perhaps at its most powerful with regard to proponents' justifications for banning same-sex marriage, simply because they offered so many of them. The trial would not allow the sheer number of allegations to carry the day—it would examine each and every one. The proponents, of course, found this level of examination to be inconsistent with rational basis review. Yet the Supreme Court had stated in 1993 that even under rational basis review, a justification had to "find some footing in the realities of the subject." Judge Walker's inquiry proceeded in this vein.

Broadly speaking, the proponents' main rationales could be divided into five baskets. The first basket contained the rights of children, focusing on their right to the ideal child-rearing environment. Another encompassed the preservation of the marital institution, which included preventing the deinstitutionalization of marriage; promoting responsible procreation through marriage; honoring tradition; and proceeding with caution. The third basket held the right of people of faith to exercise their religion. The fourth pertained to the right of parents to control the education of their children. Finally, the proponents offered a "catch-all" basket that included any other interest anyone could produce—essentially inviting the court to pull hypothetical reasons for Prop 8 out of a hat.

Even before the trial began, it was obvious that some of these rationales would not fly. Supreme Court precedent holds that tradition, by itself, cannot shield a law from constitutional attack. In a 1970 case, the Court considered a statute that required incarcerated debtors to work off their debts with additional time, even if that time carried them over the maximum sentence for their infraction. The state argued that the long tradition of debtors' prisons bulletproofed the practice. The Court disagreed and invalidated the law. And of course, the authority of the case is supported by logic—as Olson pointed out in opening statements, if courts always bowed to tradition, states could still have bans on interracial marriage.

Similarly, the claim that same-sex marriage would infringe on religious freedoms was misplaced. We often hear of institutions or individuals whose religious freedoms are allegedly violated by the existence of same-sex marriage. NOM, which staunchly opposes marriage equality, often raises the example of a New Mexico photographer who was fined for refusing to photograph a same-sex commitment ceremony in 2006 on religious grounds. The penalty in such cases, however, arises from laws prohibiting discrimination, not laws permitting same-sex marriage. If a state permitted both discrimination against gay people and same-sex marriage, the photographer could lawfully refuse to photograph a same-sex wedding. And if a state prohibited both discrimination against gay people and same-sex marriage, the photographer could *not* lawfully refuse to photograph a same-sex commitment ceremony. (This was the actual scenario confronted by the photographer, as New Mexico did not recognize same-sex marriage at the time she refused.) The aggrieved photographer should seek the repeal of the anti-discrimination laws or a religious exemption from it. She should not oppose laws permitting same-sex marriage, as those laws do not affect whether she can legally refuse service. Because same-sex marriage, by itself, does not affect the religious liberties of people of faith, the proponents could not forward the protection of those liberties as a justification for Prop 8.

The idea that same-sex marriage infringes on the constitutional right of parents to control the education of their children is also misplaced. The Supreme Court recognized that right in 1923, when it held that Nebraska could not ban parents from teaching their children German. (In the wake of World War I, anti-German sentiment ran so high that many states considered or passed such laws.) Yet the legalization of same-sex marriage would not prohibit parents from teaching their children anything, including their views about the superiority of opposite-sex marriage. What it might do is instill doubt regarding the values parents impart; a child who reads *King & King* at school might ask awkward questions about why opposite-sex couples are better than same-sex ones at home.

But the right to control a child's education does not, and could not, extend to banning same-sex marriage on that basis. Yes, parents objecting to a legal ban on teaching German should prevail. Yet parents who demand a ban on teaching Dutch because it prevents them from teaching their children good German should not. And here the proponents' argument was even more extreme—akin to abolishing the Dutch language in the state so schools could not teach it!

These rationales loomed large in the campaign—including in the "Oncoming Train" and "Princess" ads. Once Judge Walker announced a trial, however, the court heard more about these ads from the plaintiffs than from the proponents. Writing about Walker's decision to go to trial, Adam Liptak of the *New York Times* reported: "Voters in California certainly heard a lot about Proposition 8, which was the most expensive referendum battle ever on a social issue. . . . But television commercials are not quite the same thing as evidence." Liptak praised the trial for "subjecting witnesses' factual allegations to cross-examination." Claims that might seem unassailable in a thirty-second spot on television could be dismantled through hours of methodical questioning in the dock.

Judging from the witness roster he put together, Cooper must have agreed that most of his reasons were not worth bringing to trial. None of the proponents' six witnesses (including the ones who withdrew) submitted reports on the threat that same-sex marriage would pose to tradition, religious liberties, or parental control over education. Only three justifications made it down the chute of Judge Walker's thresher. Those three rationales were optimal child rearing, the prevention of the deinstitutionalization of marriage, and the suppression of irresponsible procreation.

The proponents' vision of the ideal family gleamed on the Protect Marriage campaign logo. It featured blue paper-doll cutouts of a figure in pants and a figure in a dress—versions of what one might find on a restroom door, but more fluid and lithe. These figures denoted a husband and wife. Between them were two smaller figures, representing their children, a boy and a girl. The parents held a banner over the children, which said PROTECT MARRIAGE: YES ON 8. The logo showed what the campaign sought to protect: husband, wife, daughter, son.

During the litigation, a pro-gay group covering the trial devised a logo that mimicked the Protect Marriage one. It replaced the male adult figure with a female adult figure. The new logo showed two women holding a banner stating PROP 8 TRIAL TRACKER, over their two children.

Protect Marriage brought a lawsuit claiming trademark infringement, arguing that the two marks were "substantially indistinguishable." The gay-rights group responded that trademark law allows for "parody," and that their mark should be understood as such. The judge ruled for the gay-rights group. I do not know how he restrained himself from remarking on the richness of the ironies here. The opponents of same-sex marriage complained that one could barely tell apart the two family forms. Meanwhile, the advocates of marriage equality said the family with two moms parodied the traditional one. Again, everyone seemed to have switched sides.

The logo conflict teed up a substantive conflict over the ideal family. The proponents believed in the family represented in their campaign logo—the 1950s vision of the family as a married heterosexual couple with children genetically related to both parents. They argued that children fared best when raised in such families. Anything else was, if not a parody, a falling off from there. In contrast, the plaintiffs maintained that a child's best interests are equally served by same-sex parents, who were "substantially indistinguishable" from the opposite-sex parents.

Regardless of which side is right, it was never obvious how the debate related to marriage. Obviously, many factors besides the sex of the parents and a blood tie contribute to optimal child rearing—from the stability of the household to the quality of the parenting. An abusive or dysfunctional opposite-sex family with a genetic connection is surely less beneficial to a child than a stable, nurturing same-sex family. The proponents' argument is, then, best understood not as an absolute claim—married opposite-sex couples always and by definition provide the best environment—but as a comparative one: they provide a better child-rearing environment than equivalent same-sex couples.

The comparative claim, however, reveals the weakness of the argument. If the ability to be an excellent parent and give a child a secure home is the main qualification for marriage, countless prospective parents would fail the test, whether because of financial resources, incarceration, drug addiction, or a whole host of other factors. Lawyers have statistically higher rates of depression and suicide than the general population does, yet they are allowed to marry, and even to marry other lawyers. Logically, the proponents should have had to explain why the optimal-child-rearing rationale supports the exclusion of same-sex couples from marriage but not the exclusion of opposite-sex couples that deviate from their ideal. However, given that both sides felt they could show that their vision of optimal child rearing was the right one, neither side challenged the relevance of the question.

The plaintiffs' parenting expert was Michael Lamb, a professor and the head of the Department of Social and Developmental Psychology at the University of Cambridge in England. LGBT litigation groups had relied on Lamb's expertise in earlier cases, including Lambda Legal's successful marriage-equality case in Iowa and the ACLU's successful challenges to laws in Arkansas and Florida banning gay foster parenting or adoption. The judge in Arkansas had said that Lamb presented "the best example of what an expert witness is supposed to do in a trial." In *Perry,* Lamb testified that he had written more than five hundred articles. A trim man with a neat brown beard, Lamb had the perhaps unfair advantage of his English accent. Gibson Dunn's Matthew McGill conducted the direct examination; Cooper & Kirk's workhorse David Thompson did the cross.

One of Lamb's research areas concerned the factors that affect children's development. He described a well-adjusted child as one "who had no significant behavioral or psychological problems, who was able to interact effectively and smoothly, not only with adults but also with other children, who is able to perform well and achieve appropriately at school." Lamb said substantial evidence shows that children are just as likely to be well adjusted when raised by gay and lesbian parents as by straight parents. Specifically, Lamb testified that three factors have the strongest effect on child development: their relationship with their parents; the relationship between their parents; and the financial and social resources available to them. The parents' gender, on the other hand, was inconsequential.

To head off an inevitable challenge, Lamb acknowledged that his views had evolved. In the 1970s, he was convinced research would show that a child needed a father for proper adjustment. Since then, a large body of research, including his own, had shown his prediction to be wrong. He said that "the overwhelming consensus in the field" today was that effective parenting is the same whether the parent is a mother or father, and that a child does not need a father to be well adjusted. McGill put a bow on this idea by asking Lamb to read several policy statements from leading professional bodies into the record, including those from the American Psychological Association, the American Academy of Pediatrics, the American Psychiatric Association, and the National Association of Social Workers.

McGill then turned to the proponents' model of optimal child rearing. Once again, the proponents' arguments in the courtroom differed dramatically from their arguments in the campaign. One of the key fruits of the plaintiffs' discovery efforts was an eyebrow-raising document titled "21 Reasons Why Gender Matters," widely disseminated by the chair of the Protect Marriage executive committee. The document suggested that gays suffered from a mental disorder, that they were more likely to raise gay children, and that they were more likely to abuse their children sexually. Chauncey could have used "21 Reasons" to show that Anita Bryant's rhetoric still held sway.

McGill set out to discredit "21 Reasons." Under his questioning, Lamb made clear that developmental psychology considers same-sex orientation to be completely normal, not evidence of "gender disorientation pathology"—a faux-scientific term not used by psychologists. The document claimed that children of lesbians were more likely to become "active lesbians themselves," but Lamb pointed out that the study cited, which was written by a colleague of his in the Cambridge psychology department, did not find that to be true. Finally, Lamb vehemently rejected the document's claim that "homosexual abuse" of children is higher than heterosexual abuse, dismissing it as one of the "canards" disproved in the 1970s. When Boies observed, post-trial, how the "junk science" cited in the campaign literature melted away in the courtroom, he surely had this exchange in mind.

In court, the proponents' position on optimal child rearing was based on two ostensible benefits that could only be provided by an opposite-sex couple: "gender-differentiated parenting" and two parents with genetic ties to the child. By definition, same-sex couples could not provide either. Turning to these claims, McGill asked Lamb to describe the concept of "gender-differentiated parenting." Lamb testified that it was the concept that "to be well-adjusted, children need to be raised by a male parent as well as by a female parent." Asked which scholars espoused this theory, Lamb mentioned David Blankenhorn. However, he said, a significant body of evidence had disproved that claim.

Lamb disposed of the genetic tie argument just as swiftly. He elaborated that a number of studies of adoptive children and children conceived through sperm or egg donation from a third party have found them equally likely to be well-adjusted as the children raised by two genetic parents.

D avid Thompson began his cross-examination by casting Lamb's views as those of a "committed liberal." Thompson got Lamb to acknowledge that he was a member of the ACLU, the NAACP, NOW, and the Nature Conservancy. "You have even given money to PBS, is that correct?" Thompson inquired, to some laughter.

This salvo opened an ambitious line of questioning about "the role of politics in modern-day science." Lamb's testimony had summoned the authority of social science to rebut the claims the proponents had made in the campaign. To dispel that authority, Thompson sowed the idea that liberals had captured the social science surrounding gay rights. He began by asking whether the social sciences are "hermetically sealed" from political influence. Lamb cautiously responded that nobody is "hermetically sealed from the world." Thompson then noted that settled social science could often be wrong, raising the example of phrenology, the idea popular in the nineteenth century that a person's character could be read off the shape of his skull. Lamb mildly observed that many advocates of phrenology were not, even at the time, considered scientists.

Thompson moved on to gender-differentiated parenting. He got Lamb to concede that men were more likely than women to be incarcerated, violent, aggressive, alcoholic, short-lived, mentally deficient, and sexually abusive. He appeared to be arguing that because there were statistical differences between men and women, a parent of each gender was necessary to a child's proper development. (This line of argument was susceptible to at least two interpretations Thompson surely did not intend: first, that men were less apt to be fit parents, and second, that lesbian couples were the optimal child-rearing unit, given male inadequacies.) Thompson then reminded Lamb that he had argued for the necessity of fathers in earlier work. Lamb replied that he had conceded on direct that, four decades ago, he thought those issues could be important, but that the theory had "not held up in subsequent research."

"Well, so science was wrong?" Thompson asked.

"Science, as I understand it, is a cumulative process," Lamb replied.

Turning to the importance of the genetic link between parents and children, Thompson quoted from a paper by Kristin Anderson Moore from a publication titled *Child Trends*: "It is not simply the presence of two parents, as some have assumed, but the presence of *two biological parents* that seems to support children's development." Thompson emphasized that "two biological parents" was italicized in the original. Lamb responded that the article was written for a popular, not a scholarly, audience, which perhaps explained why the conclusion stretched beyond the data. Moore's seemingly categorical claim about "two biological parents" was made solely in the context of a comparison to children who grew up with stepparents, not to children who had grown up with adoptive parents of any kind.

Thompson then asked why, if the biological tie was so irrelevant, many gay couples opted to have children who were genetically related to them. Lamb observed that while the genetic tie might be important to the *parents,* it was not important to the outcomes for the *children.*

Panning out, Thompson then challenged the methodology of the studies on which Lamb relied, including the representativeness and size of their samples. At certain points, Thompson ran into difficulties, as when he challenged Lamb's reliance on a study that drew on US Census data concerning children of gay and lesbian parents.

"They don't purport to be a random sample of the entire US population of same-sex couples, correct?" Thompson asked.

"No, you don't have a random sample when you sample the entire population. You have the population," Lamb responded.

Thompson tried to recover. "Right. A random sample of that population, none of them purport to be that, do they?"

"I think most of us would consider this to be better," said Lamb, to laughter.

At other times, Thompson succeeded in putting pressure on Lamb's position. Lamb conceded that a study by sociologist Sotirios Sarantakos conducted in 1996 purported to show that children with same-sex parents face worse outcomes than children with opposite-sex parents. Lamb observed, however, that the study contained design and interpretation problems that even the author had acknowledged. The children of opposite-sex couples had all lived with the same two parents their entire lives, while those raised by same-sex parents had all experienced divorce and separation.

Thompson then went through the studies on which Lamb relied and asked him if each used "married, biological parents" as a control group. In most cases, Lamb conceded that the control group did not exclude unmarried heterosexuals.

On redirect, McGill sprang a surprise. In discussing the genetic tie, Thompson had introduced studies that stressed the benefits accruing from "two married biological parents." McGill asked how the term *biological* is used in the field of developmental psychology. Lamb said it is used in a number of ways, sometimes referring to a genetic DNA link, but often to describe intact families with adopted children. To substantiate this point, McGill asked Lamb to read a disclaimer from a study conducted at the University of Chicago cited repeatedly in the litigation. Lamb dutifully read: "Most studies do not distinguish biological parents from adoptive parents, since the latter is a rare family form in virtually all studies." For at least some of the studies discussing "biological parents," both members of a same-sex couple raising a child from birth would qualify as "biological parents."

McGill also took up Thompson's point about the control group. He asked why it would be appropriate to maintain a control group of unmarried heterosexual parents when making comparisons to gay and lesbian parents. Lamb answered: "Because you have unmarried couples in all of these groups." To compare married opposite-sex couples to unmarried same-sex couples would change two variables at once.

Thompson's claim that a proper parenting study must use married, biological parents as a control group raised a separate issue. Such a study would demand married same-sex couples as a test group—a cohort that was rare, and that would not exist at all if the proponents had their way. In other words, the proponents' position on child rearing was based on an assumption that they refused to put to the test. The absence of such testing was then used as an argument for retaining the status quo.

Gay people have faced this sort of catch-22 in other arenas. Before the repeal of the military's "Don't Ask, Don't Tell" policy, Gen. Norman Schwarzkopf testified to Congress that "in every case I am familiar with, and there are many, whenever it became known in a unit that someone was openly homosexual, polarization occurred, violence sometimes followed, morale broke down, and unit effectiveness suffered." This claim was sustainable only because open homosexuals were immediately discharged. Once gays were permitted to serve openly, the military gave a yawn and moved on.

The proponents' expert on optimal child rearing was David Blankenhorn. Although widely associated with the theory of gender-differentiated parenting, Blankenhorn never mentioned it during his time on the stand. (When I asked him why, he said that he did not recall.) Perhaps his lawyers steered him away from the theory, since basing public policy on it would arguably violate constitutional norms against sex stereotyping. The Supreme Court had already decided in 1982 that men could not be barred from going to a public nursing school, and in 1996 that women could not be barred from attending a state-run academy to train citizen-soldiers. Although these decisions concerned schools and not families, the

Court had used broad language in both cases about how the government could not engage in sex stereotyping. Writing for the majority in the 1996 military-academy decision, Justice Ginsburg stated: "Generalizations about 'the way women are,' estimates of what is appropriate for *most women,* no longer justify denying opportunity to women whose talent and capacity place them outside the average description." In other words, even assuming there *were* broad differences between men and women, such differences could not be used by the state to bar women from doing a job, even if only a few women could do it. Arguments about gender-differentiated parenting may have been stymied by these precedents.

Blankenhorn did testify about the genetic tie, noting that a married opposite-sex couple who are both related to their child created "the optimal environment for children." Cooper asked why being raised by biological parents matters. Blankenhorn responded with "kin altruism": the concept that human beings behave better toward those to whom they are related. Scholars have established that people typically sacrifice more for relatives than non-relatives, Blankenhorn said, in matters ranging from lending money to risking their lives. So, Blankenhorn continued, you would want a child, where possible, to be cared for by the two adults most closely related to that child—the genetic mother and father.

On cross-examination, Boies pushed Blankenhorn: "You were not meaning to imply, were you, that biological parents were any better parents than adoptive parents?" Blankenhorn said no. Boies continued: "In fact, the studies show that all other things being equal, two adoptive parents raising a child from birth will do as well as two biological parents raising a child from birth, correct?" Blankenhorn balked: "No, sir, that's incorrect." He said that because they are so rigorously screened, adoptive parents do *better* on some outcomes than biological parents. Kin altruism suggests that a child will fare better with its genetic parents than with random strangers. Yet Blankenhorn's point was that children are not adopted by random strangers but by adults who have gone through a screening process. The screened parents fare the same as—or "on some outcomes outstrip"—their genetic counterparts.

After some more discussion, Boies suggested that they "jump to the bottom line." He asked if Blankenhorn knew of any studies showing that children raised by a gay or lesbian couple from birth have worse outcomes than those raised by two genetic parents from birth. Blankenhorn did not.

I was riveted by the parenting testimony, as Ron and I became parents during the *Perry* litigation. At about the time the case was filed, an agency matched us with our surrogate, Sara. In her early thirties at the time, Sara had married her high school sweetheart and had given birth to four children of her own. Because she enjoyed being pregnant, she volunteered to be a surrogate for a friend who was having trouble conceiving. The friend managed to get pregnant on her own, but Sara had become intrigued by her research on surrogacy. As a passionate supporter of gay rights, she was particularly interested in helping a gay male couple.

We flew out to Topeka, Kansas, to meet Sara. We were committed to attending every doctor's appointment and to living there for a month before the due date. She and her husband welcomed us into their extended family. Yet we still found ourselves on edge, given that Topeka houses Westboro Baptist Church, nationally famous for its virulent homophobia. On our drives through the city, we sometimes saw demonstrations that included towheaded children who could not have been more than five or six years old, holding signs that said GOD HATES FAGS. As Ron put it: "We're *not* not in Kansas anymore." I am an ardent supporter of free speech of the "Yes, the Nazis get to march in Skokie" variety. Westboro Baptist put that commitment to the test. Neither was the issue hypothetical—a lawsuit had been filed against the church, which had raised a free-speech defense.

Our apprehension about Topeka grew when we searched for a

place to live during the pregnancy. Because a hotel would have been prohibitively expensive, we looked for other options. We found a listing for a bed and breakfast owned by a family with a veterinary practice. To avoid any misunderstandings, Ron was open about why we wanted to rent the property when he contacted the owner, Carol. Carol agreed to rent to us, but Ron heard distinct hesitation in her voice. It crossed my mind that the family occupation was animal husbandry—the management of heterosexual procreation. We worried that she would back out—and that concern resurfaced when we walked into the cottage. In line with Carol's "Americana" theme, everything down to the embroidered, star-shaped coasters was patterned on the Stars and Stripes. I found this decor disquieting. Yet I was uneasy about my own unease. I thought of how Chad Griffin had made a point of incorporating the American flag in AFER's logo—intent on giving the lie to the notion that gays and lesbians were somehow un-American. It seemed a sad incongruity that I could teach constitutional law but still feel that the flag was not entirely my own.

Only after we met Carol and her family, who lived close to the cottage, did our mistrust begin to dissolve. Each time we arrived, they asked for updates on Sara's pregnancy, and Carol turned down more lucrative offers for the cottage to ensure that we never had to stay elsewhere. By the time we drove our daughter home from the hospital, Ron was certain that Carol's family must have done something festive to the cottage while we were away. I tried to manage his expectations, thinking of how far we were from New York City. Yet he was right: the house was bedecked with flowers, balloons, and a sign proclaiming IT'S A GIRL! Soon after that, they asked our family over for dinner. After a long and emotional dinner where we expressed our gratitude, the patriarch of the family clasped our hands and said, "Thank you for teaching us what it means to be a family." They took a picture of our daughter draped in bunting. It now hangs in the dining room of their cottage, as we learned when we repeated the journey with Sara for our son. At least on the walls of that cottage in the heartland, our daughter has been incorporated into the theme of America.

On our second journey to Kansas, we received even more invitations to social events from supportive families in the area. This time, we were taking care of our fourteen-month-old daughter while we waited for our second child, and my nerves were frayed. "It feels like death by a thousand barbecues," I said at one point, only half-joking. Ron rebuked me, reminding me how afraid we had been of Topeka when we started. Yet he was as puzzled as I was by the outpouring of warmth from virtual strangers. We finally asked Sara. She explained that most people were so horrified that Topeka had become associated with Westboro Baptist that they were making an extra effort to show their solidarity with us. The church had forced many people to think through their views on gay rights. Their reaction brought to mind Justice Louis Brandeis's famous statement that "if there be time to expose through discussion the falsehood and fallacies, to avert the evil by the processes of education, the remedy to be applied is more speech, not enforced silence." When Westboro Baptist won its First Amendment case 8–1 in the Supreme Court, I applauded the decision without reservation.

The issue of surrogacy could fill—and has filled—many books. Focusing on the two issues raised in *Perry,* would I say that our children have suffered or will suffer because two men are raising them? Of course my answer is no. Much of my disagreement with the proponents, I think, has to do with our intuitions about whether men and women have more in common than not. In the world of work and education, we are increasingly seeing the repudiation of what the Court calls "archaic and overbroad" ideas. It used to be thought, for instance, that women were unfit for higher education; today women graduate from college at higher rates than men, but few would brandish this point as evidence that men are intrinsically less intelligent. I think the same insight—that alleged differences between the sexes are more socially constructed than innate—is making its way home into the family. But many Americans seem to experience more ambivalence about sex roles in the private realm than in the public one. In a webcast from the Prop 8 campaign, a speaker says:

> When moms are in the park taking care of their kids, they always know where those kids are. They have like a, like a radar around them. They know where those kids are and there's just a, there's a bond between a mom and a kid different from a dad. I'm not saying dads don't have that bond, but they don't.

"I'm not saying dads don't have that bond, but they don't" is a magnificently succinct description of the speaker's ambivalence. Even as he throws a sop to the cultural ideal of sex equality, the speaker insists on the unbridgeable difference between the sexes. My visceral response is that he really needs to meet my husband. Ron is a stay-at-home dad who has a radar so finely tuned and powerful that he could count our children's hairs from space. I love our children as much as he does, but I do not have this capacity. This could certainly be a difference between us as individuals, but I think it has much more to do with our roles.

During his cross-examination, Thompson asked Lamb why, if genetic connection is irrelevant, many couples go through the expensive process of in vitro fertilization rather than adoption. It was a great question. We considered both options but—like the vast majority of straight couples—decided that we wanted to be genetically linked to our children. We wanted the connection not just with ourselves but with our familial past. And we see this already—our daughter has many traits that remind us of Ron's mother, and our son has many traits reminiscent of my own extended family.

At the same time, we have also experienced firsthand Lamb's rejoinder to Thompson, which is that while a couple may cherish their genetic ties to their children, both surrogacy and adoption produce children who are just as well-adjusted as those with two genetic parents. Indeed, surrogacy and adoption are not mutually exclusive. To the contrary, surrogacy usually entails adoption—as a legal matter, I adopted our daughter, while Ron adopted our son. It is an enormous privilege to be an adoptive parent, as it allows one to understand how little the genetic tie matters when it comes to loving a child. Ron's mother captured it best when we told her that our son has an allergy to penicillin. "That makes sense," she said. "Ron and his dad were the same way." Our son is my genetic offspring, not Ron's, but she had forgotten that our son was any different from our daughter. And of course, in Ron's and my eyes, he is not.

Most important, holding my daughter in my arms for the first time was like moving from a geocentric to a heliocentric model of the universe. I had thought the system moved around me, when in fact I was orbiting her—even the possibility of her—all this time. Many parents—straight and gay—have echoed this point, noting that to become a parent is to cease to understand yourself as the center of your own universe. For me, the identity of parent is deeper than the identity of gay man. And while it seems strange to draw a link between the overmastering love I have for my children and the notions of "gender-differentiated parenting" and the "genetic tie," it seems to me that love speaks directly to those theories. When you would give your life for your child, as most parents would, bridging gender norms or genetic difference seems like a small task indeed.

11

A THREAT TO MARRIAGE

When New York legalized same-sex marriage in 2011, a storage company in Manhattan ran an ad campaign declaring, "If you don't like gay marriage, don't get gay married," neatly capturing the sentiments of many liberals flummoxed by conservative opposition to same-sex marriage. As comedian Wanda Sykes has said: "Are straight couples in marriage counseling now? You know, 'We just ain't been workin' together since Bill and Ted hooked up.'"

Intuitively, it is hard to grasp how same-sex marriage might harm opposite-sex couples. After all, gay marriage does not take away any of the rights or duties of straight marriage. But thinking of it this way misses the essence of the conservative complaint about the damaging effects of "redefining" marriage. Opponents usually zoom out from the individual to the communal, claiming not that any particular gay marriage will damage any particular straight marriage, but that allowing same-sex marriage will damage the institution as a whole.

As I have argued, the opponents' intuition may perhaps be better understood through trademark law than through civil-rights law. Companies use trademarks to advertise and distinguish their products or services. A "tarnishment" claim arises when a competitor uses that mark in a way that diminishes its cachet. A well-known example of tarnishment was an "Enjoy Cocaine" slogan, written in the same font and color as the familiar tagline "Enjoy Coke." Coca-Cola sued over that and won, in part because the court felt some consumers might believe it had produced the poster with the offending slogan. Importantly, however, you can win a tarnishment claim even in the absence of such confusion. Judge Richard Posner gives the hypothetical example of a strip club that calls itself "Tiffany." Every time consumers think of "Tiffany," he writes, they will associate the word with the strip club instead of the fine jewelry. The "Gay Olympics" case that got Walker into so much trouble was also based on a tarnishment claim, and the idea that same-sex marriage demeans the institution of marriage follows the same logic. If a man can get married to a man, or a woman to a woman, the value of the marriage "trademark" will go down, or so the argument goes.

There are, however, happier scenarios. Nancy Cott testified that allowing greater equality on the basis of race or gender strengthened rather than weakened marriage. The same could hold true here: same-sex marriage might burnish, rather than tarnish, the institution for everyone. A passage from the 2003 *Goodridge* decision, which brought same-sex marriage to Massachusetts, is often read aloud at weddings both gay and straight. Chief Justice Margaret Marshall, who wrote the *Goodridge* opinion, takes pride in that fact, saying that it makes her feel that she had understood the true meaning of marriage. It begins: "Civil marriage is at once a deeply personal commitment to another human being and a highly public celebration of the ideals of mutuality, companionship, intimacy, fidelity, and family. . . . Because it fulfills yearnings for security, safe haven, and connection that express our common humanity, civil marriage is an esteemed institution, and the decision whether and whom to marry is among life's momentous acts of self-definition." The use of *Goodridge* at straight weddings suggests that, at least for some straight couples, same-sex marriage has reinforced and deepened their respect for the institution, not undermined it.

In that vein, some have argued that same-sex marriages could serve as an exemplar for straight couples. "By providing a new model of how two people can live together equitably, same-sex marriage could help haul matrimony more fully into the twenty-first century," writes Liza Mundy in the *Atlantic*. As Mundy points out, same-sex spouses cannot decide who pays the bills or cooks the meals by falling back on gender norms, a situation that requires them to negotiate a fair arrangement. "In this regard," she writes, "they provide an example that can be enlightening to all couples."

So, same-sex marriage could demean the institution; it could also improve the institution. There is a third possibility: it could do nothing to the institution, leaving society to shrug its shoulders.

In *Perry*, the proponents made what amounted to a tarnishment argument to provide another rational basis for Prop 8. Same-sex marriage, they claimed, would "deinstitutionalize"—or weaken—marriage for everyone, depriving it of public loyalty and respect. For the most part, the plaintiffs did not argue the opposite, though Olson at times hinted that the institution would become stronger if it became more inclusive. Instead, they focused on doing all they needed to do: dispatch the claim of harm.

Lee Badgett, a professor of economics at the University of Massachusetts, testified in support of the plaintiffs' argument that same-sex marriage would have no discernible effect on the institution. Badgett had written extensively on the social and economic consequences of same-sex marriage, including in her 2009 book, *When Gay People Get Married*.

Under direct examination by Boies, Badgett first took up the

legalization of marriage in Spain and Massachusetts. These jurisdictions had experienced no negative societal effects, Badgett said.
Cooper objected to any discussion about the effects of same-sex
marriage in any jurisdiction other than the Netherlands. He argued
that Badgett had not mentioned other jurisdictions in her expert
report. However, as Boies responded, expert reports provided descriptions of opinions to be offered and the bases for those opinions, not "word for word" recitations of future testimony. In
discussing the effects of same-sex marriage, Boies said, Badgett
would predictably canvass all the jurisdictions that had legalized
same-sex marriage—and in fact Badgett *had* discussed Massachusetts in her deposition. Judge Walker overruled Cooper's objections, which seemed more rooted in the fact that Cooper had
prepared most (perhaps only) for a presentation on the Netherlands. Cooper had promised to address the effects of same-sex
marriage in the Netherlands—the first country to legalize same-sex
marriage—during opening statements.

When he cross-examined Badgett, Cooper kept two promises he
had made during opening statements—he explored both the rate
of marriage and the rate of non-marital cohabitation in the Netherlands. Cooper first displayed a chart showing that marriages in
the Netherlands had declined between 1994 and 2001, and had
continued to decline slightly more steeply between 2001 and 2008.
He suggested that the marriage rate had gone down in the wake
of same-sex marriage. Badgett would have none of it, hinting that
Cooper might be cherry picking a starting date that distorted the
evidence. However, Cooper's selections seemed fair—he had picked
the seven years before and after the legalization of marriage equality in the Netherlands.

In contrast, Cooper's presentation of the data on unmarried
couples with children was mystifying. He observed that "the numbers of unmarried couples with children have escalated steeply
and consistently over time." His chart certainly showed a steady
increase. However, as Cooper's phrase "consistently over time"

suggested, the rate of change had remained constant. A red line sliced through 2001, the year the Netherlands legalized same-sex marriage. Badgett said: "If you took that red line out there and showed it to everyone in this courtroom, nobody would be able to tell where same-sex couples got married."

Cooper turned to the next data set, which showed the rate of unmarried couples with children as a percentage of all families in the Netherlands. Cooper noted that in 1994, 1.54 percent of all families were unmarried couples with children. In 2001, the percentage was 2.84. In 2008, the percentage was 4.3. Cooper then asked Badgett to confirm that the "rate" of unmarried couples with children in the Netherlands had increased significantly over this period of time. Badgett responded that she would use the term *rate* differently. Cooper meant *percentage rate,* noting that the percentage of unmarried couples with children had climbed. The relevant rate, she said, was the *rate of change*—whether the advent of same-sex marriage caused unmarried child rearing to accelerate. And she reiterated that "there's no break, whatsoever, to suggest that anything happened of importance in 2001." The exchange gave me uncomfortable flashbacks to calculus class. Perhaps Cooper felt the same way—he concluded his statistical excursion in fairly short order.

On redirect, Boies took up Badgett's hint. He returned to Cooper's chart regarding marriage rates and asked whether it accurately reflected the long-term trends. Badgett answered that the Netherlands had started collecting marriage statistics in the 1960s, and that "what we see is a well-known change in the marriage rate in the Netherlands, which peaked in about 1970, and since then has been on a pretty steady decline with, you know, some variation from year to year." Boies demonstrated that the starting point the proponents had selected—1994—represented an outlier in that year-to-year variation. Boies then put up a chart that went back to 1965, showing "average annual different-sex marriage rates in the Netherlands on a five-year basis." After smoothing out the year-to-year variation, Badgett said, it was clear that the trend after 2001 was no different from the trend before it.

Boies returned to the increase in unmarried couples with children before and after same-sex marriage. Badgett established that the largest increase occurred from 1999 to early 2001, before same-sex marriage was established. The other increases were slightly smaller. "This is about as close to a straight line as you will ever see in a demographic measure," Badgett concluded.

Although skewed presentations of statistics do not usually survive long at trial, other forums are more forgiving. In 2004, Stanley Kurtz, a conservative commentator with a PhD in social anthropology, analyzed Scandinavian marriage and parenting statistics in an ominously titled essay, "The End of Marriage in Scandinavia." He concluded that unmarried cohabitation and out-of-wedlock births had increased there since the rise of same-sex marriage and registered partnerships. "Will same-sex marriage undermine the institution of marriage? It already has," Kurtz lamented. As Badgett pointed out in a response essay, Kurtz's statistical analysis was flawed: rates of cohabitation and nonmarital birth "slowed down or completely stopped rising" after gay partnership laws were introduced, and "the change in nonmarital births was exactly the same in countries with partnership laws as it was in countries without." Yet Kurtz's conclusions had already made their way into newspapers, legal filings, and the congressional record as a reason to oppose marriage for same-sex couples in the United States. Kurtz, however, made no appearance at trial. Statistical claims that circulate for years in the mainstream political arena can be refuted in a matter of minutes on the stand.

The proponents had not neglected the statistical approach altogether—they had solicited the testimony of Douglas Allen, a Canadian professor of economics at Simon Fraser University in Vancouver. However, he was withdrawn long before trial. At trial, Boies suggested why: Allen had stated in his expert report that "in the Netherlands the total number of heterosexual marriages has slowly fallen since the introduction of same-sex unions. Like most Western countries, this is no doubt part of a larger secular trend." Boies asked Badgett if she agreed with this assessment.

She did.

David Blankenhorn again served as a utility infielder for the proponents in offering his views on deinstitutionalization. Unlike Badgett, he did not make his case in empirical terms; his testimony could be called conceptual, or, less kindly, conjectural. Blankenhorn testified that the term *deinstitutionalization* came from the field of sociology. He observed that all social institutions are governed by stable rules and structures. Deinstitutionalization occurs when an institution's structures are weakened. Blankenhorn noted that its effects could be severe—the institution "becomes less and less able to carry out its contributions."

Applying this concept to marriage, Blankenhorn said that in recent decades in the United States, the deinstitutionalization of marriage had led to "numerous and serious consequences for children and for society as a whole." He noted the large increase in numbers of children born to unmarried parents over the previous five or six decades. Although he underscored that "heterosexuals, you know, did the deinstitutionalizing," he believed that same-sex marriage would accelerate this trend, citing the work of sociologist Andrew Cherlin, who favored same-sex marriage, and sociologist Norval Glenn, who opposed it. While Blankenhorn granted that he could not prove that same-sex marriage would undermine the institution as opposed to reinvigorating it, he said that he considered deinstitutionalization the more likely result. Asked to explain what that would entail, Blankenhorn predicted that same-sex marriage would lead to fewer marriages and higher rates of divorce.

Blankenhorn was by far the most recalcitrant witness, and when Boies cross-examined him on this topic, the tension between the two men came to a boil. Attorneys on cross-examination typically ask the witness a series of closed-ended questions, to which the appropriate response is "yes," "no," or "I don't know." While many witnesses chafe under these restrictions, they usually cooperate, knowing that they will have an opportunity to testify with greater nuance when questioned by their own attorney. Not Blankenhorn. The day before, he had watched Kenneth Miller "get kind of dominated" by Boies. Now he was determined not to be "pushed around."

Boies set out to show that Blankenhorn had produced only speculation—not evidence—that same-sex marriage would lead fewer opposite-sex couples to marry. Cooper would later describe Blankenhorn as an "expert on the experts," which sounded like a euphemism for someone who himself had no expertise. But Boies took this a step further in his examination, suggesting that Blankenhorn's reliance on his experts was unfounded, at least on this point.

> *Boies:* My question is whether Mr. Glenn or any scholar that you relied on has asserted that permitting same-sex marriage will result in a lower rate of heterosexual marriage?
>
> *Blankenhorn:* The problem here—I'm not trying to be evasive, but you must let me just say my answer, which is that if they are arguing—
>
> *Boies:* No, no, sir. I don't have to do this. All that's going to happen is you're going to say something, then I'm going to have to follow up. Okay? What I'm trying to do is—this is a very simple question, all right?
>
> *Blankenhorn:* It is not simple to me.

When I first read this exchange, I found myself strangely sympathetic to Blankenhorn. The moment where he said "you must let me just say," only to be instructed that Boies did not have to let him say anything, had a pathos that would have played well in fiction, I thought. I recalled novels I had taught in my law and literature class—A. S. Byatt's *Babel Tower* or Bernhard Schlink's *The*

Reader—in which the heroine resists the strictures of legal proceedings because they force her to simplify things that are not simple. Everyone who takes a law and literature class roots against the law—as the saying goes, "Law closes things that once were open; literature opens things that once were closed." So help me, I even thought of the Oscar Wilde trial, in which Wilde is brought down by an intellectual inferior because he is confined by the rules of the forum. I kept reading:

> *Boies:* Have any of the scholars that you have said you relied on said in words or in substance, "Okay, this permitting same-sex marriage will cause a reduction in heterosexual marriage"? That's "yes," "no," or "I don't know."
>
> *Blankenhorn:* I know the answer. I cannot answer you accurately if the only words I'm allowed to choose from [are] "yes" or "no." I can give you my answer very briefly in one sentence.
>
> *Judge Walker:* If you know the answer, why don't you share it with us?
>
> *Blankenhorn:* I would be happy to, but he is only permitting me to give "yes" and "no," and I cannot do that and be accurate.
>
> *Judge Walker:* He is giving you three choices, "yes," "no," "I don't know."
>
> *Blankenhorn:* But I do know. I do know the answer.
>
> *Judge Walker:* Then is it "yes" or is it "no"?
>
> *Blankenhorn:* Your Honor, I can answer the question, but I cannot give an accurate answer if the only two choices I have are "yes" and "no." I—if you give me a sentence, I can answer it. One sentence is all I'm asking for.
>
> *Judge Walker:* All right. Let's take a sentence. One sentence.
>
> *Blankenhorn:* Can you ask me the question again, please?

I began to have my doubts that Blankenhorn was the reincarnation of Wilde. But I was still rooting for Blankenhorn to speak in his own terms, and happy that the judge saw fit to let him do so.

Boies: Have any of the scholars who you say you relied on asserted, written, that they believe that permitting same-sex marriage will result in a reduction in the heterosexual marriage rate?

Blankenhorn: My answer is that I believe that some of the scholars I have cited have asserted that permitting same-sex marriage would contribute to the deinstitutionalization of marriage, one of the answer—one of the manifestations of which would be a lower marriage rate among heterosexuals. But I do not have sure knowledge that in the exact form of words you are asking me, for they have made the direct assertion that permitting same-sex marriage would directly lower the marriage rate among heterosexuals.

And then it was over. I was not reading a novel about a hero who knew that any accession to the master's language would only announce his capture by it. I was reading a farce about a person who did not know the difference between the phrases "I don't know," and "I do not have sure knowledge." It is true that trials (and law generally) *do* reduce subtlety. Herek, Lamb, and Segura would later complain that lawyers see only black and white, while social scientists see only gray. But by that point, I had read the testimony of a train of professors who had somehow managed to answer the questions posed to them. I kept reading.

Boies: Mr. Blankenhorn?

Blankenhorn: That wasn't so long.

Judge Walker: If I were to take that as an "I don't know," would that be fair?

Blankenhorn: With respect, Your Honor, I would disagree with you. I know exactly my answer to this question, and I have stated it. And I would be happy to restate it.

I felt only relief when Judge Walker hastened to reply: "The record is clear on what you said."

Blankenhorn later gave a rendition of his experience under Boies's cross-examination: "He'll walk up to you and say, 'Are you a good lawyer or a bad lawyer? Yes, no, or you don't know? Are you a good person? Yes, no, or you don't know?' " With every question, he punched the air. But Blankenhorn is in the end an open and genial person, and he went on to admit that he loved watching Boies's technique. He had expected Boies to read down a list of questions but instead watched him be much more improvisational.

Boies has credited his ability to speak extemporaneously to his dyslexia. Unable to work from written notes, Boies learned as a high-school debater to absorb principles and facts completely, a skill that became useful in the courtroom. As he put it, "If you had people over to your apartment, you would never read to them. You would never pull out your notebook and say, 'Well, let me see, we went down to the movie and it was a great movie, and . . .' I mean, you would talk to them."

Boies's skill in cross-examination was an astonishing serendipity for the plaintiffs. Griffin had wanted the lawyers "Microsoft would hire," but had, ironically, hired Boies, who had taken down Microsoft CEO Bill Gates in an epic deposition during a 1998 antitrust trial. Because the plaintiffs originally intended to avoid a trial, Boies's talents in this area could easily have remained dormant.

After some more back-and-forth in which Blankenhorn had difficulty producing a name, Blankenhorn said he relied on most of the scholars he referenced for their "views about the definition of marriage, not about the deinstitutionalization of marriage." Boies eagerly embraced this point, noting that the people on whom Blankenhorn had relied had not discussed same-sex marriage, much less its effects. Blankenhorn agreed, "by and large."

The strain between the two men did not improve on the next day—the last day of the trial. As Boies continued his cross-examination, Blankenhorn kept talking over him. Finally, Judge Walker intervened: "Because I'm sure you would not want your demeanor on the stand to be a negative factor in your testimony, I would urge you to pay close attention to Mr. Boies's questions and to answer them directly, succinctly." He reminded Blankenhorn of Cooper's later opportunity to conduct the redirect.

After this warning, Blankenhorn was noticeably more responsive. Boies produced a list that spelled out positive, negative, and "other" consequences likely to occur from legalizing same-sex marriage, derived from Blankenhorn's book, *The Future of Marriage*. The original list had been drawn from a session Blankenhorn conducted with family scholars. Their methodology consisted of brainstorming ideas and writing them on whiteboards. The "positive" list included such potential benefits as: improving happiness and well-being for many gays and lesbians; contributing to stability and longer-lasting relationships for committed same-sex couples; and signifying the worth and validity of same-sex intimate relationships. Boies asked Blankenhorn to express his agreement or disagreement with them. (Having mastered the genre, Blankenhorn answered "yes" to thirteen, "I don't know" to five, and "no" to five.) Ultimately, Blankenhorn acknowledged that same-sex marriage would have many benefits for gays, and some for straights as well, such as diminishing the number of closeted gay individuals who married straight partners.

As it turned out, deinstitutionalization was not the proponents' main gambit. Over the course of the litigation, they gravitated toward a related argument about "responsible procreation." One purpose of marriage, they claimed in their trial brief, was "promoting stability and responsibility in naturally procreative relationships." According to this argument, because women in opposite-sex relationships may become pregnant accidentally, straight couples may procreate in an irresponsible manner. Marriage promotes responsible procreation, because it props up unstable straight relationships and encourages the partners to raise children within the social and legal protections of the institution.

Under this theory, gay people need not be allowed to marry for two reasons. First, they cannot have children by accident and thus do not require the same social support as straight people. In addition, if the institution of marriage were weakened by same-sex marriage, it would lose its power as a stabilizing force for straight relationships. Lacking respect for the institution, heterosexual couples would procreate irresponsibly by having more children out of wedlock.

As counterintuitive as this rationale may sound, several courts had already adopted it. In 2003, a court in Arizona observed that the state's interest in "ensuring responsible procreation" supported the limitation of marriage to opposite-sex couples. In 2005, an Indiana court similarly adopted the "responsible procreation" rationale to reach the same conclusion. The next year, a plurality of New York's high court adopted this rationale, noting that the legislature could reasonably believe that "unstable relationships between people of the opposite sex present a greater danger that children will be born into or grow up in unstable homes." In contrast, it observed, gays "do not become parents as a result of accident or impulse." Inverting the usual stereotypes, the opinion deplored that straight relationships are "all too often casual or temporary."

In the *Perry* trial, the proponents touched on this line of argumentation with psychologist Letitia Peplau of UCLA. Peplau had already rejected the notion of deinstitutionalization during her direct examination. When asked whether same-sex marriage would lead to fewer cross-sex marriages, Peplau testified, "It is very hard for me to imagine that you would have a happily married couple who would say, 'Gertrude, we've been married for thirty years, but I think we have to throw in the towel because Adam and Stuart down the block got married.'"

When Nicole Moss of Cooper & Kirk cross-examined Peplau, she took a different tack, asking, "Would you agree that gay and lesbian couples do not accidentally have children?"

"If your question is, can two lesbians spontaneously accidentally impregnate each other, not to my knowledge," Peplau answered.

Moss pressed: "It has to be planned; it has to be an intentional birth, isn't that right?"

"I believe that's correct," Peplau said.

Although the proponents only fleetingly explored the responsible procreation rationale during trial, it became their justification of choice by the time they reached the Supreme Court. The advantage of this rationale is that it shifts the focus away from gay people and toward straight people. Straight people are prone to recklessness and need marriage to make them behave responsibly. Gay people need no such incentives. If anyone is being negatively stereotyped in this analysis, it is straights.

The proponents may have reasoned that a Supreme Court decision peppered with respectful nods to gay relationships would survive longer than one, such as *Bowers,* that openly mocked them. This arguably occurred in the area of women's rights in 1873, when the Court deprived women of equality while purporting to compliment them. In *Bradwell v. Illinois,* the Court upheld an Illinois statute prohibiting women from practicing law. Concurring in that judgment, Justice Joseph Bradley observed that the "natural and proper timidity and delicacy" of women better suited them to "the noble and benign offices of wife and mother." It took a century for the Supreme Court to reverse this thinking when, in 1973, a plurality of the Court recognized that confining women in the name of cherishing them put them "not on a pedestal, but in a cage." If women were once too good to be lawyers, gays were now too good for marriage. By focusing on the bad conduct of straights rather than that of gays, the proponents could avoid the bugbear of equal-protection analysis: the charge of animus.

12

THE BARE DESIRE TO HARM

Opponents of same-sex marriage fear a world that will brand them as bigots. Maggie Gallagher, the former president of NOM, said in 2011: "If you want to know how same-sex marriage is going to affect traditional believers, mainstream Christians, and other faith communities, ask yourself, 'How do we treat racists who are opposed to interracial marriage in the public square?' Racists are marginalized, stigmatized, oppressed, and made second-class citizens." While Gallagher of course believes opponents of same-sex marriage differ vastly from opponents of interracial marriage, she does not trust the polity to make that distinction. In 2014, Brian Brown, the executive director of that organization, said that his group was not interested in seeking religious exemptions from antidiscrimination laws because NOM's members "refuse to be treated like bigots in the law." He elaborated: "We're not bigots. It's not bigotry to stand up for marriage." Just as Gallagher and Brown feared, many people today call them by that name.

Such name-calling lumps too many kinds of people together. The members of Westboro Baptist Church (of "God Hates Fags" fame) can fairly be called bigots, given that they attack the mere fact of being gay. It is hard to regard condemnation of even a celibate gay person as anything other than bias.

The members of the ADF carefully distinguish themselves from Westboro Baptist by saying they love the sinner and hate only the sin. But this distinction between status and conduct is cold comfort to many gay people, who believe that the two are inextricably entwined. One of the savviest moves by the liberal wing of the Court was to slip this point into a 2010 opinion, noting that "our decisions have declined to distinguish between status and conduct" in the context of sexual orientation. Justice Ginsburg, writing for the majority, supported this statement with quotations from other cases, one of which was "a tax on wearing yarmulkes is a tax on Jews." The Court suggested that religious opponents of same-sex marriage might not be so enamored of the distinction between status and conduct were it applied to them: *We love that you're Catholic, but hate that you go to Mass.*

Still further along the spectrum are the people who say that it is fine for gay people to act on their homosexuality, but not for them to marry. At the time of the Prop 8 trial, this group included everyone from Blankenhorn to President Obama. If sincerely held, this position seems different in kind from the previous two—often born of passive misunderstanding rather than active hostility. Of course, many individuals who oppose homosexual conduct hide in this category, pretending that their objection is only to same-sex marriage, when their resistance runs deeper. But I suspect that at least in this country, those who accept same-sex sexual conduct will come to accept same-sex marriage. Those who have objections to homosexual conduct will continue to oppose same-sex marriage, but the grounds of their objection will be laid bare.

In the meantime, calling all opponents of same-sex marriage bigots seems counterproductive, not least because it is unnecessary. Individuals on the fence about marriage equality are more likely to be persuaded by rational arguments or human connections than by epithets. Far from being cowed by such charges, opponents of same-sex marriage have ably used the specter of being labeled "bigots" as a rallying cry. Moreover, plaintiffs can win marriage equality cases without showing the other side to be filled with anti-gay hostility. The Supreme Court's precedents hold that only "animus" is required to invalidate a law. As it turns out, animus requires much less than the official positions of either the Westboro Baptist Church or even the ADF. The problem with the current debate is that it suggests that the *only* reason gays could object to opponents of same-sex marriage is by calling them bigots. Both in the courtroom and out, much less should be required. And much less is.

While the rational-basis test is almost absurdly easy, the Supreme Court has held that it is "not a toothless one." One way in which it has teeth is that it does not permit legislation grounded in "animus." The core question is whether outright bigotry is necessary to a finding of animus, or whether softer forms of misunderstanding, fear, or stereotyping are enough. Again, the Court has provided imperfect guidance on this issue.

The Court has repeatedly declared that "bare . . . desire to harm a politically unpopular group" is constitutionally impermissible. On first reading, this suggests active hostility toward a group. However, the phrase comes from the 1973 *Department of Agriculture v. Moreno* case, in which Congress denied food stamps to "any household containing an individual who is unrelated to any other member of the household." A little digging by the Court showed that the purpose behind the restriction was to block "hippies" and "hippie communes" from getting food stamps. The Court concluded that an intention to discriminate against hippies, standing alone, was not an acceptable purpose under the Equal Protection Clause. The case did not involve torch-wielding villagers—just legislators who assumed hippies were freeloaders.

Further evidence that the Court's "bare ... desire to harm" formulation is an easier bar for minorities to clear than it sounds comes from the 1985 *Cleburne* case, often cited for its formulation of political powerlessness. After deeming individuals with disabilities to be politically powerful, the Court denied them heightened scrutiny. But then, in an unusual application of rational-basis review, it struck down the zoning ordinance challenged in the case. The ordinance barred a group home for individuals with intellectual disabilities. Invoking the "bare ... desire to harm" language, the Court observed that "mere negative attitudes or fear" were not permissible bases for the law. When I first read *Cleburne* in law school, I thought of people with disabilities as unsuccessful game-show contestants who had been sent home with macaroni—they had, after all, failed to get heightened scrutiny. Yet over time, I watched the courts use the "bare ... desire to harm" language to protect them and other groups—including gays in the 1996 *Romer* case.

In *Cleburne*, as in *Moreno*, the legislators seemed to be demonstrating less hatred toward the group than discomfort and ignorance about it. In a concurring opinion in a 2001 case concerning individuals with disabilities, Justice Kennedy meditated on the same theme: "Prejudice, we are beginning to understand, rises not from malice or hostile animus alone. It may result as well from insensitivity caused by simple want of careful, rational reflection or from some instinctive mechanism to guard against people who appear to be different in some respects from ourselves." Kennedy did not connect the dots between "prejudice" and "animus." But he was writing about the same group—people with disabilities—involved in *Cleburne*.

In *Perry*, the definition of "animus" was squarely on the table. The proponents said that, by claiming they had acted with animus, the plaintiffs were tarring millions of voters as "bigots." The plaintiffs contended that animus could simply be the insensitivity described by Justice Kennedy. Under either definition, the question of how much discomfort with gays motivated Prop 8 was in play.

To drive a wedge between opposition to same-sex marriage and animus, the proponents relied on the indefatigable David Blankenhorn. Cooper used Blankenhorn, in his guise as a pro-gay opponent of gay marriage, to build the case that traditional marriage was not based in homophobia. He asked whether Blankenhorn believed that anti-gay prejudice undergirded "the customary man-woman definition of marriage." Blankenhorn answered: "I believe that homophobia is a real presence in our society and, I'm pretty confident, in many, many other societies around the world. And I regret it and deplore it, and wish it to go away." However, he could not find any evidence that anti-gay animus was central to the institution's laws and customs.

Cooper's question to Blankenhorn was both ingenious and telling. It attempted to focus the court's attention on the origins of the institution of marriage, rather than how marriage operated today. But while sex-based restrictions on marriage may not have been *conceived* with anti-gay animus, they could be *maintained* because of such animus. In 1982, the Supreme Court was asked to consider whether an electoral system in Georgia violated the equal-protection rights of African Americans by diluting their voting power. The lower courts had found that the policy behind the electoral system was "neutral in origin," but that it was being maintained for racist reasons. The Supreme Court upheld this finding.

On cross-examination, Boies highlighted the tension in Blankenhorn's support for gay rights and his opposition to same-sex marriage. Returning to Blankenhorn's *The Future of Marriage,* Boies quoted: " 'I believe that today the principle of equal human dignity must apply to gay and lesbian persons.' " Boies then read these lines from the book: " 'In that sense insofar as we are a nation founded on this principle, we would be *more* American on the day we permitted same-sex marriage than we were on the day before.' " Blankenhorn stood by these words.

The *"more* American" quotation became public-relations gold for the plaintiffs, akin to Cooper's "I don't know." Yet it would be wrong to characterize the moment as one where Blankenhorn broke. Blankenhorn's position had been—from the publication of his book onward—that same-sex marriage and the interests of children were "competing goods" that must be balanced against each other. He believed the best way of balancing the rights of same-sex couples and the needs of children was to allow gays to enter domestic partnerships, reserving marriage as a distinctively "pro-child" institution headed by a mother and father. After the trial, Blankenhorn admitted that he was "nobody's perfect witness," because his belief in competing goods became distorted in the "fantasy world of forced adversarial roles."

When the plaintiffs tried to prove animus, they slammed up against the opacity of the initiative process, which allowed voters to make law from the secrecy of the ballot booth. The plaintiffs' main strategy was to put on parade the advertisements and webcasts used during the Prop 8 campaign, such as the "Oncoming Train" ad. Yet to make clear that both soft prejudice and hard-core animus were present—and that both were constitutionally problematic—they also called two lay witnesses.

The first was Jerry Sanders, the Republican mayor of San Diego. Sanders testified about his public shift from opposing same-sex marriage to supporting it. City of San Francisco attorney Dennis Herrera handled the examination. A former police chief of San Diego, the straight, married mayor has a lesbian daughter, Lisa. Sanders testified that as a young police officer, he was among the many who mocked gay and lesbian people. His views gradually changed after he witnessed various anti-gay acts, particularly the ouster of a respected sergeant after he came out as gay. These experiences helped Sanders support his daughter when she came out to him during her sophomore year in college.

"I felt overwhelming love," the mayor said. "I realized how difficult this was for her. I realized how difficult it was to tell your parents that you were a lesbian." At the same time, he had concerns: "I thought it was very tough on gay people in society."

In September 2007, the San Diego City Council passed a resolution ordering the city attorney to draft a brief in support of the San Francisco lawsuit advocating for same-sex marriage. Sanders wanted to veto the bill, given his impending campaign for reelection as a Republican. He also thought civil unions were a fair alternative. With Lisa supporting his position, he scheduled a press conference to announce the veto.

Sanders then made a fateful decision. As a courtesy, he invited his gay and lesbian friends and neighbors to his home the night before the press conference. Their outrage stunned him. One of his neighbors said: " 'My partner and I walk by here all the time, with our children. And you always stop, when you're doing yard work, and say hello to them and talk to them. You know, we're a family just like you're a family.' " Another neighbor told Sanders that she loved her children just as much as he did, and that she felt her children deserved to have married parents. "The depth of the feeling was unbelievable," Sanders recalls. "The depth of the hurt. And also I could see the harm that I had done by considering the veto."

At the press conference the next day, Sanders wept as he announced that he had changed his mind and would sign the resolution. The plaintiffs played a video clip of the announcement, which had gone viral, in court. Herrera asked him why he was so emotional in the clip. Sanders replied: "I came very close to making a bad decision; one that would affect, literally, hundreds of thousands of people. I came very close to showing the prejudice that I obviously had to my daughter, to my staff, and to the community in San Diego." Sanders insisted that he never "hated gay people" or actively thought of them as unequal. Rather, he said, he simply "hadn't understood the issue clearly enough" until he came face-to-face with his gay constituents.

On cross-examination, Brian Raum of the ADF probed Sanders's definition of "prejudice." He asked if Sanders believed people could "distinguish between civil unions and same-sex marriage on reasonable grounds that are not based in animus." Sanders said that on the understanding that "animus" means "hatred or bigotry," he believed the distinction could be "grounded in prejudice" rather than animus.

On redirect, Herrera missed an opportunity to sort out a semantic jumble. Sanders manifestly did not understand "animus" as a legal term of art. His "prejudice" may well have met the legal definition of "animus." But the examination did not explore that point.

Like Ryan Kendall, Jerry Sanders told a conversion narrative, but his was a tale of successful transformation. It was a narrative the nation would hear repeatedly in the years to come.

As their last witness, the plaintiffs called Bill Tam, one of the five official proponents of Prop 8. The plaintiffs called him as a "hostile" witness—one who opposes the party putting him or her on the stand. Born in Hong Kong, Tam was an engineer by training and served as the executive director of the Traditional Family Coalition, a Chinese evangelical Christian organization. When California's government officials declined to defend Prop 8, Tam had voluntarily intervened in the case.

Of the five proponents, the plaintiffs chose to call only Tam. (The other four were Martin Gutierrez, Dennis Hollingsworth, Mark Jansson, and Gail Knight.) Tam presented a rich target of opportunity because he did outreach to the Chinese evangelical community. Many of his articles and speeches were in Chinese. As these documents came in through the discovery process, the plaintiffs had them translated and found a cache of smoking guns. The documents used language more redolent of the Anita Bryant campaigns of the 1970s than of the sanitized, focus-group-tested English ballot materials. The language barrier had perhaps provided Tam with the sense that he could speak his mind without being overheard. The trial revealed that sense of security to be baseless.

To be sure, one cannot take a single individual's positions and make them stand for the intent of seven million voters. At the same time, Tam was not a random individual, but an official proponent of the initiative who had campaigned full-time for its passage. His testimony at least raised the question of whether he said in Chinese what others thought but knew better than to say aloud in English. And if his speech represented the dark id of at least enough voters to have gotten the measure over the top, Prop 8 would be an unconstitutional enactment.

On the eve of trial, Tam sought to withdraw as an intervenor. This did not mean he could escape testifying, but it did mean that he was no longer listed as an official proponent. Retaining separate counsel, he argued that he feared "for his personal safety and the safety of his family." The plaintiffs responded that all his claims of retaliation—such as the claim that someone had taken the air out of his tires—were nothing more than "speculative musings." Tam's attorney shot back that such "trivialization" of Tam's concern about "his safety and the safety of his family" was at best "insensitive" and "borders on the shameful." Yet Tam's attorney attached a document to this response that included Tam's address, telephone number, and e-mail. If Tam's lawyer were so concerned about the risk of harm to his client, why did he not redact that information before submitting it to a public database? Against that backdrop, it seems plausible that Tam withdrew simply because the other proponents wished to dissociate themselves and the campaign from his incendiary views.

In his examination of Tam, then, Boies's goal was to tie Tam back to the campaign with unbreakable bonds. He did so with

ease, walking Tam through e-mails that characterized him and his
organization as a "major" or "strong" part of the Protect Marriage
campaign. Having done so, Boies could then just—as he would
later say—"let Tam be Tam." In addition to heading the Traditional
Family Coalition, Tam also served as the secretary of a group of
Chinese pastors known as the America Return to God Prayer
Movement. This group had a website called 1man1woman.net.
Boies observed that the website stated: "Studies show that homosexuality is linked to pedophilia." Tam confirmed that he believed
this statement. Boies then read the next line: "Homosexuals are
twelve times more likely to molest children." Sensing peril, Tam
said he only served as the secretary of the organization that had
posted the link.

"What's the power of the secretary in your company?" Tam
asked.

"Considerable," Boies answered drily.

When Tam continued to disavow his influence, Boies sidestepped
that debate by asking Tam directly whether he believed "homosexuals are twelve times more likely to molest children." Tam said
he believed this to be true. Boies then read from one of the letters
that Tam had written during the campaign, in which he stated that
"San Francisco city government is under the rule of homosexuals."
The letter elaborated: "After legalizing same-sex marriage, they
want to legalize prostitution. What will be next? On their agenda
list is legalizing having sex with children." Boies asked Tam to confirm that he had used that statement to convince people to vote yes
on Prop 8. Tam confirmed it. Boies observed that the letter went on
to say: "If Proposition 8 loses, one by one, other states would fall
into Satan's hand."

Boies then noted that Tam had offered this observation to the
San Jose Mercury News: "We hope to convince Asian Americans
that gay marriage will encourage more children to experiment with
the gay lifestyle, and that that lifestyle comes with all kinds of disease." Tam also acknowledged his agreement with a flyer put out by

1man1woman.net, saying that after legalizing same-sex marriage in 2001, the Netherlands had legalized incest and polygamy. Asked for the source of this statement, Tam said it came from "the Internet." He insisted that the flyer never claimed a causal link, and said he was instead concerned with the "moral decay" of liberal countries.

The zeal of Tam's opposition to same-sex marriage exceeded that of anyone else who testified. "I believe that if the term 'marriage' can be used beyond one man and one woman, then any two person[s] of any age or of any relationships can use the same argument and come and ask for the term 'marriage,' " he told the court. "That would lead to incest. That would lead to polygamy."

During her brief examination, Nicole Moss of Cooper & Kirk made no attempt to cast Tam in a better light. Rather, she threw him under the bus. She drew a distinction between the petition phase to get Prop 8 on the ballot and the campaign phase. Tam said his work had mostly occurred during the former. In other words, her position was that Tam's messages never reached the voters. Lawyers must say *something* when defending a client, and it would have been hard to do better than Moss did.

Still, when Boies returned to the podium, he made short work of her distinction between the petition and campaign phases. He established that many of the quotations Tam had read out on the stand had come from the campaign phase. He then confirmed that Tam had appeared on television during the campaign and had participated in weekly conference calls held by the public-relations firm running the campaign.

The proponents' lawyers broke ranks regarding Tam. Cooper & Kirk completely dissociated themselves from him. In contrast, the ADF embraced him. Blogging on the day of Tam's testimony, ADF attorney Austin Nimocks wrote: "In the courtroom, Dr. Tam represented many of us who are concerned about attempts to re-define marriage in our country." As a blogger, not a court reporter, Nimocks had the luxury of not having to specify what Tam had said, noting only that Tam believed same-sex marriage would "take a grave toll on our communities and children." Nimocks said that there was a great deal of evidence to sustain this belief, including "adultery, no-fault divorce, and fatherlessness."

Of course, Tam had not discussed any of those topics on the stand. Instead, he had spoken of pedophilia, prostitution, and polygamy. However, Nimocks still saw Tam as a martyr, comparing his plight to that of Fred Fisher in the 1954 McCarthy hearings. He invoked attorney Joseph Welch's excoriation of McCarthy: " 'Let us not assassinate this lad further, Senator. . . . You've done enough. Have you no sense of decency, sir, at long last? Have you left no sense of decency?' " Apparently, Boies was McCarthy. "Had someone stood up and said this today during the cross-examination of Dr. Tam," Nimocks wrote, "it wouldn't have come a moment too soon."

13

THE PHANTOM WITNESSES

When David Blankenhorn stepped down from the stand on the twelfth day of the trial, Judge Walker asked Cooper to call his next witness. "Your Honor," Cooper replied, "we have no further witnesses."

So that was it—the final tally was seventeen witnesses (eight lay witnesses and nine expert ones) for the plaintiffs, and two for the proponents. To any observer, the disparity was astonishing. The asymmetry may explain why the proponents engaged in such interminable cross-examinations. As Andy Pugno said when the plaintiffs rested their case: "The time clock tells me that while plaintiffs have logged twenty-eight hours in presenting their case, the defense team has logged nearly as much time—twenty-seven hours—cross-examining the plaintiffs' witnesses and introducing our own evidence into the record." At one point during the marathon cross-examination of child-rearing expert Lamb, Thompson asked him about studies alleging that lesbian mothers had relative difficulty setting limits for their children. Judge Walker interjected: "Perhaps this is not the only area in which setting limits would be helpful." By conducting such examinations, the proponents projected an illusion of parity.

Yet the illusion was fragile. The ADF's gadfly, the Liberty Counsel, issued a public criticism: "After ADF actively opposed Liberty Counsel, ADF presented only two witnesses at trial. . . . Even Judge Walker commented that he was concerned by the lack of evidence presented by ADF on behalf of Prop 8."

The proponents explained that many of their experts had withdrawn from the proceedings before trial. Had they not withdrawn, the parties' witness roster would still have been lopsided, but less so, particularly if one counted only the plaintiffs' nine expert witnesses.

Two competing theories were offered for why these witnesses withdrew. The plaintiffs argued that the proponents' experts had all blown up on deposition. The proponents countered that their experts withdrew because they were intimidated by Judge Walker's proposal to stream a video broadcast of the trial to other courthouses. The proponents must, then, have been excluding economist Douglas Allen from their count, as Allen told me that he "agreed to testify and wanted to testify" only to have been dropped without explanation by Cooper & Kirk. In fairness to the proponents, they did not include Allen in the final witness list submitted to the court. By looking at this list, I could see that four experts—Paul Nathanson, Katherine Young, Daniel Robinson, and Loren Marks—had been officially withdrawn. I reached out to all four.

Paul Nathanson is an untenured scholar—designated a Researcher—at McGill University who holds a PhD in religious studies. He is also gay. He is close to Katherine Young, another McGill professor who was also withdrawn as a witness. The two have written many books and articles together.

Nathanson testified in the Iowa state court proceedings pertaining to same-sex marriage, along with Young and a third McGill academic, Margaret Somerville. The Iowa trial court excluded all three, noting: "Though these experts desire to make statements regarding gender, results of same-sex marriage on children and the universal definition of marriage, they do not appear to possess expertise in relevant fields such as sociology, child development, psychology or psychiatry." As Nathanson and Young both emphasized to me, the Iowa Supreme Court later reversed this decision and admitted their testimony. Yet the Iowa high court admitted their testimony not because the rules of admissibility had been met but because it found that they did not apply. Neither Nathanson nor Young was aware that the Iowa Supreme Court's ruling was not an endorsement of their qualifications or their report.

Nathanson's report argued that religion was not necessarily hostile to same-sex marriage by giving examples of churches arrayed on both sides of the issue. Political scientist Gary Segura, who was responsible for responding to this report for the plaintiffs, offered a cutting assessment of Nathanson's work: "That report comes as close to insanity as I think I have ever read on a piece of paper. He says, well, on the one hand Roman Catholics and Southern Baptists and Mormons and Orthodox Jews oppose marriage equality but on the other hand, the United Church of Christ, the Metropolitan Community Church, the Unitarian Universalists, and Reform Jews favor marriage equality. . . . So that's four in favor and four opposed; four equals four. Well, the first four represent something like 40 percent of American society while the other four represent like 4.2 percent of all Americans." This false equivalence surfaced in Miller's report after Nathanson withdrew. Obviously, churches had appeared on both sides of the Prop 8 debates, but many more people of faith had voted for Prop 8 than against it. Indeed, as Miller had written in his 2009 article, socially conservative churches had played a decisive role in ensuring the passage of Prop 8. And a CNN exit poll cited by Boies in his cross-examination of Miller showed that 84 percent of those who attended church weekly voted yes on Prop 8, while 83 percent of those who never attended church voted no.

I traveled to Montreal to meet Nathanson. A man in his sixties, of medium build and height, he seemed nervous. His office was a dimly lit square, each wall covered with bookshelves. Nathanson began the interview by lying on his couch and crossing his arms behind his head, as if about to begin a session with a psychoanalyst. When he became animated, he inclined toward me; when he calmed down, he lay back down again. Nathanson opened by observing that his "main objective" for the interview "is just to present myself as a gay man who has opposed gay marriage for reasons that have nothing to do with either religion or homosexuality."

Nathanson confirmed that he withdrew because he was intimidated by the threat of being televised, asserting that certain "people made it known to me and Katherine that they had received death threats." At the same time, he added: "The other thing was simply that the deposition—the whole process—was so manipulative and revealed so little about anything that I cared about, that, at one point, I just said to hell with it." He spoke even more candidly to a reporter, stating that he looked "like an idiot" during the deposition.

I encouraged him to talk about what he *did* care about in the marriage debate. Nathanson articulated two arguments against same-sex marriage—the need to protect children and the need to protect men. When asked what harm would come to children from same-sex marriage, he relied heavily on the notion of gender-differentiated parenting. "Fathers don't need to give their children unconditional love," he said. "The message from fathers should be, I will admire you and respect you, *if* you make your own way in the world effectively and honorably. The message of mothers, by contrast, is, I will love you no matter what you say or do." While he acknowledged that these sex roles could be changed, he said it would require a "colossal cultural effort."

Nathanson's second argument was that same-sex marriage

would marginalize men, contributing to a phenomenon called "misandry." He had published three books with Young on this subject—*Spreading Misandry, Legalizing Misandry,* and *Sanctifying Misandry*—with two more volumes on the way. They argue that to have a healthy identity, an individual must be able to make contributions that are "distinctive, necessary, and publicly valued." Nathanson stated that because of the rise of feminism, "the only source of a healthy collective identity for men now would be fatherhood." If two women could marry, they would reinforce the idea that men were unnecessary—at best "assistant mothers," at worst "walking wallets" or "potential molesters."

Somewhere along the way, Nathanson began to describe his childhood. He told me that as a boy he had been subject to relentless, implacable bullying. "Even in grade school, though, I knew that whatever was wrong with me, whatever in my behavior was maladjusted or effeminate or whatever it was, I didn't deserve the brutal treatment that I got every day in school," he said. He told me about the moment he decided to fight back, in tenth grade. Every week he had a chemistry class, in which every two students had to share a Bunsen burner. None of his schoolmates would ever share a burner with him, leading to a ritual of humiliation at the beginning of each class. This led to an epiphany. "Finally, I just told the teacher that I wanted my own burner," he said. "He gave me one, and so I learned at an early age that I had to think for myself and act on my own initiative." He leaned toward me: "No one tells me how to think!" He sank back down. "I don't know where I'm going with all of this," he said. He paused. "I think I was trying to introduce myself to your potential readers as someone who has paid his dues." His voice faded. "I know what bullying means. I know what prejudice means. I know what suffering is. I don't need to take lessons from anybody else."

I reflected that Nathanson would have been a risky witness for the proponents. He was a gentle soul with a tendency to ramble. He had a PhD but remained untenured. His real objections to same-sex

marriage had little to do with the subject of his report or his expertise in religion. He had already been disqualified by a court in Iowa
for ranging beyond his field. In federal court, where the standards
for admissibility are more exacting, he would have been at even
greater risk of having his testimony discounted.

The proponents appeared to have shared this assessment of Nathanson. He filed his report on October 2, 2009 (the deadline for
the initial expert reports). Miller filed his five weeks later, on November 9 (the deadline for rebuttal reports). Had the proponents
intended to put both men on the stand, Miller's report would never
have absorbed so much of Nathanson's. Miller himself noted that
as he was completing his expert report, "it appeared that Dr. Nathanson might be withdrawing from the case."

That night, I called Ron and told him about my interview with
Nathanson. I said that Nathanson reminded me of Ryan Kendall,
the young gay man who had described a similarly traumatic childhood. I floated the idea that these two men could have turned out
much more alike if they had not been separated by a few decades—
Nathanson was in his sixties and Kendall his twenties when their
testimony was solicited. I found Nathanson to be a smart man with
a curious and interesting mind, an impression that was corroborated as we kept in touch after our interview. I became convinced
that he identified with children more than gays because he had felt
more vulnerable as a child than he felt now as an adult gay man.

Unlike Nathanson, Katherine Young held an endowed chair
in religious studies at McGill University at the time of the
trial (she has since retired). She also had done interdisciplinary
work in anthropology. Instead of jettisoning her report from the
Iowa case as Nathanson had, Young revised it for the *Perry* trial to
track her expertise in religion. She cut a section of the report titled
"Anthropological Evidence" as well as a history of mating behavior
in primates detailing the change "from rear mount intercourse to

frontal mount, which placed the couple face to face and increased the possibility of intimacy." Yet the gist of her report remained the same—she claimed that marriage had been, everywhere and always, between one man and one woman.

Boies asked Young early in her deposition whether she considered herself an expert in anthropology. Young answered: "It's not my primary expertise, as I said, but I read extensively in the area." Boies retorted: "I read extensively about films and I go to the movies, but I don't consider myself an expert in film. I'm asking you whether you consider yourself an expert in anthropology."

Young was caught. She would either have to say she was an anthropology buff in the way Boies was a film buff, or she would have to claim expertise in the field. "It is . . . I would say it is a secondary expertise," she said.

With that answer, Young opened herself to the full Boies treatment:

Boies: Have you published peer-reviewed articles in anthropology?

Young: I have published peer-reviewed articles that include anthropological dimensions. I have several books in preparation that will be based on fieldwork in India.

Boies: Well, let me try to take those one at a time, Professor. You say you've published a peer-reviewed article that deals with anthropology. First, let's define for the record what a peer-reviewed article is.

Young: A peer-reviewed article in the academic world is one that is sent out to experts in a given field, usually under anonymous conditions, for a critical review.

Boies: And what was the name of the peer-reviewed article that you say you published?

Young: Well, I think we need to clarify something here and that is that the field of comparative religions includes within it an interest in anthropology.

Boies then asked her repeatedly if she had "his question in mind," and Young responded that she believed she did. However, she could not reproduce it. Whenever she digressed, Boies would doggedly return to ask if she remembered his question. Finally, Young buckled.

> *Young:* Okay, please repeat your question.
> *Boies:* What was the name of the peer-reviewed article that you say you published?
>
> . . .
>
> *Young:* I need to clarify that my publication that includes some anthropology is published in the field of religious studies, not in the field of anthropology per se, because my field overlaps both anthropology and the history of religions.
> *Boies:* If you don't understand my question, please let me know and I'll rephrase the question, but I would ask you to listen to my question and answer my question. What was the name of the peer-reviewed article that you say you published?
>
> . . .
>
> *Young:* Okay . . . if you're asking me what the name of the anthropological journal is in the discipline of anthropology, then I would say that I have not published in the discipline of anthropology or the journals of anthropology. . . . I publish in the field of religious studies and comparative religions, which includes the study of both small-scale societies and large-scale societies. . . .
> *Boies* [to opposing counsel Peter Patterson]: . . . I've asked her three or four times to give me the name of the article that she said that she published, and I ask counsel to instruct her to give that answer. . . . Otherwise, I'm going to take this transcript to the court because what's happening here is I'm asking a simple question and she is giving a speech that's designed to take up time. . . . She said she published a peer-reviewed article that dealt with anthropology; I am asking her the name of that article. I think I'm entitled to that simple

answer. ... Now, please, madam, tell me the name of the peer-reviewed article that you say you published that dealt with anthropology?

...

Young: If you want the peer-reviewed article in anthropology, in an anthropological journal, I have not written such an article. My anthropology is included in general considerations of religion or in the field of India.

Boies: Do you remember telling me this morning, just a few minutes ago, that you had published an article that dealt with anthropology, do you recall telling me that, yes or no?

Young: That dealt with anthropology within a larger context.

Boies: What is the name of that peer-reviewed article?

Young: Well, I'm thinking of the work on marriage where I have looked at anthropological work and of those articles on marriage ... "The Future of an Experiment" and so forth include some anthropological data.

Boies: Is the name of the article that you were referring to in your testimony this morning "Future of an Experiment"?

Young: That's right.

Boies: Okay. Now, where was "Future of an Experiment" published?

Young: In *Divorcing Marriage.*

...

Boies: And is that a peer-reviewed publication?

Young: No.

Boies: Didn't you tell me that the article that you published was peer-reviewed?

Young: I did, so there is a contradiction there.

A Boies Schiller attorney who attended the deposition remembers the acute discomfort in the room. "You couldn't hear anyone breathe," he said. "We were sort of gripping the table just to get through." He lauded Boies for his tenacity. Most lawyers, he said, "wouldn't have perceived the value in pushing the point and be willing to endure the discomfort and tension in the room." City attorney Terry Stewart, who was also in the room, agreed that Boies had an uncanny ability to tell when someone was lying, and to either force them more deeply into the lie or push them up toward the truth. After this exchange, Boies swiftly got Young to acknowledge that she had never taught in McGill's anthropology faculty, and that she did not have any expertise in social science fields such as child development, political science, or sociology. The gap between her field of expertise—religious studies—and the subject of her report yawned wide.

Boies then challenged Young on her assertion that marriage had been universally defined to exclude same-sex couples. Young had distinguished in her report between "universal" and "nearly universal" aspects of marriage. She claimed that one of the "universal" aspects is that marriage "recognizes the interdependence of maleness and femaleness." In contrast, she asserted that "an emphasis on durability" was only a "nearly universal" quality. According to Stewart, Young had made a similar claim—that marriage had always been closed to same-sex couples—in another proceeding where she was matched against Yale Law School's William Eskridge. Eskridge had given a litany of counterexamples. This time Young came prepared with examples of cultures that permitted same-sex marriage that represented many regions around the world—from the Indian reservations of North America to West Africa to India to China to ancient Rome. Young came across as knowledgeable, but her examples undermined her own report's claims about universality.

Like Nathanson, Young said she had withdrawn because she feared the broadcast of her testimony would lead to harassment. When I asked whether she had faced any harassment because of her views, she answered that harassment had led to "the most extreme event" of her academic life. She observed that when she had spoken on a panel on same-sex marriage in 2005, she was "shocked to find that a lawyer in the front row was talking loudly to her friend, incessantly rolling her eyes in contempt for what I was saying, and using provocative body language to indicate extreme displeasure." The heckler ended up screaming and swearing at her, which, Young said, "was highly embarrassing to at least one person in the audience, who passionately argued with the provocateur that decorum must be maintained." Young also said that her cross-examination by Boies "border[ed] on harassment." She said: "Boies almost never engaged me on my research, but played memory games such as asking me about details in my very long CV, which spanned over forty years."

I asked Young why she had strayed so far from her field of expertise, namely religion. She observed that prior affidavits she had submitted to other courts included scriptural sources from Judaism, Islam, and Christianity. This was true. However, her expert report in *Perry* included none of this material. The probable reason for the change arose in deposition. Boies asked her if religious understandings of marriage were relevant to secular definitions of marriage in the United States. Young answered that they were not, "because of the separation of church and state."

Daniel Robinson is a professor of psychology and psychiatry emeritus at Georgetown and a lecturer at Oxford. His Maryland home feels like the residence of an Oxford don—here a statuette of a Greek figure, there a marble sphere mounted on a wooden stand. He welcomed me with a glass of sherry before we trundled up some stairs to his study.

Robinson got involved in the case after receiving a call from his close friend Robert George—the Princeton professor of jurisprudence who was one of the founders of NOM. George had called him from the airport and said with a chuckle that he had committed Robinson to a law firm "to save Western civilization." Robinson had no idea what aspect of civilization he was meant to save. The next day, David Thompson called and told him. Robinson said,

"To my certain knowledge I had not given twenty minutes' thought in a lifetime" to the topic of same-sex marriage. When I asked what Thompson wanted him to testify about, Robinson said George had "grossly misrepresented me as someone who could address pretty much anything." Ultimately, they settled on Robinson's expertise as a social scientist to address the issue of immutability. He said: "I don't think I had ever read any of the publications they sent my way, or even summaries of them."

As he read through the materials, however, Robinson thought he could be of some use. He felt that the studies on the heritability of homosexuality were flawed. He had written about heritability after Richard Herrnstein and Charles Murray wrote *The Bell Curve,* the infamous book arguing that average black IQ was lower than average white IQ "at every level of socioeconomic status." Robinson had avidly critiqued this book. Drawing on the same expertise, he found the studies regarding the heritability of sexual orientation to be "really pathetic." I got the sense that he entered the trial out of this conviction—that "anyone serious about genetics" should not take such studies seriously. I told him that none of the expert witnesses had—that even the plaintiffs' expert on immutability, Gregory Herek, had disavowed reliance on genetics and testified that "we simply don't understand the origins of sexual orientation."

Robinson also argued that the courts could not protect groups they could not define. Gays, he said, could not be defined because they could be categorized based on the different dimensions of self-identification, behavior, or status. Each dimension could lead to a different definition of who counted as a group member. The proponents used this line of attack on Herek at trial. But as Herek observed, the slippage among these definitions occurred for less than 9 percent of the population. I also could not help pushing a version of Justice Ginsburg's point about the tax on yarmulkes—Catholics could similarly be defined according to self-identification, behavior, or status. Would he deny them protection because they, too, were so amorphous that someone might be

Catholic on one dimension but not another? Robinson agreed that this was a "good point."

Robinson also acknowledged that for a significant number of gay individuals, sexual orientation was immutable. I quoted the portions of his deposition that had been used at trial: when asked whether "sexual orientation is readily subject to change," he had answered no. Robinson said he stood by that answer.

From my discussion with Robinson, it appeared that he entered the *Perry* fray with no clear mandate (the proponents settled on him as an immutability expert only *after* he agreed to participate), and that his testimony—had he participated—would have made little difference to any contested issue, given that his real objection was to the "gay gene" studies, on which the plaintiffs did not rely. Nonetheless, Robinson indicated that he was prepared to interrupt the teaching term at Oxford and fly to California if called to testify. When he found out that Judge Walker wanted to record the trial, however, Robinson worried that it would lead to a public firestorm. "I would be spending my toothless years nailing down the barricades," Robinson said. When the Supreme Court ordered that the trial not be broadcast but Judge Walker still decided to record it, this sharpened Robinson's resolve to withdraw: "It struck me that this judge was not behaving responsibly and really shouldn't be encouraged."

O f the four withdrawn witnesses, Loren Marks had come the closest to testifying. Cooper believed he could have persuaded Marks not to withdraw, despite his reservations, but said he had no reason "to twist his arm." At the time of the *Perry* litigation, Marks had just received tenure at Louisiana State University's School of Social Work. His specialties were faith and families and African American families. In his expert report for the proponents, Marks had maintained that according to "available social science that meets established standards, the biological, marriage-based (intact) family is associated with better child outcomes than non-marital, divorced, or step-families."

What immediately jumped out of the report was that it did not mention gay or lesbian parents. Plaintiffs' lawyer Matthew McGill raised this point early in the deposition, asking Marks if he could name anything specific about outcomes of children raised by lesbian and gay parents. Marks said not many such studies had been done. Marks's lawyer, David Thompson, stepped in to play defense, noting that Marks was preparing a rebuttal report (due in ten days, according to the court's deadlines) to address the literature on same-sex parenting. At several junctures in his deposition, Marks referred to his forthcoming rebuttal. He never filed this rebuttal report, suggesting that the proponents' attorneys made the decision to pull Marks before November 9, when the report was due. But it also meant that had Marks participated, he would have testified about the relative shortcomings of gay and lesbian parents with an expert report that made no mention of them.

In fairness to Marks, his report could be construed to state that the married opposite-sex family is the gold standard relative to all other family structures studied to date. The inference might be that because married same-sex couples are not married opposite-sex couples, future studies would show they were more like stepparents or single parents. Yet to draw that inference, one would need a hypothesis about which difference between married opposite-sex couples and married same-sex couples would lead to this result. There were two obvious candidates for such a difference: the genetic tie and gender-differentiated parenting.

During the deposition, McGill dug into both points. He first asked Marks about the genetic tie. Marks obviously believed it was important; he repeatedly italicized the word "biological" in his report. Yet McGill pointed out that some of Marks's sources used the term "biological" to include adoptive parents. (As Lamb testified at trial, many researchers do not distinguish between genetic children and adoptive children raised by two parents since birth.)

McGill asked Marks whether he had correctly relied on a review in his report when he quoted it as saying that "'teens living with *both biological parents* are significantly less likely to [use] illicit drugs, alcohol, tobacco.'" Marks replied: "Taking a close look at these—at these definitions as been presented, I would withdraw that." McGill kept pushing: "Would you also withdraw your emphasis on both biological parents?" Marks responded: "Certainly so." McGill closed it out: "Would you delete the word biological?" Marks said: "I would." That exchange swept one possible difference off the table.

McGill turned to the theory of gender-differentiated parenting. He asked Marks if he relied on that theory. Marks said he did not: "It's highly contested ground, and frankly, it's not a battle that I would fight either way." McGill landed the plane, asking Marks to confirm that his report did not rely on the theory that there are certain parenting activities men can do that women are very unlikely to do. Marks acceded.

McGill then sought to summarize Marks's opinion as resting on two factors: marital structure, and the biological link between parents and children. Marks answered: "That's correct." Thompson quickly intervened: "Do you have anything to add to that?" Marks answered: "No." Thompson perceived the danger: Marks had already withdrawn his claims about the "biological" link. If the only difference between opposite-sex and same-sex couples was marital structure, that distinction could be overcome by allowing same-sex couples to marry.

McGill then returned to the question of whether a report that made no mention of same-sex couples could illuminate their parenting capabilities. Marks admitted that it was a "judgment call, not a black-and-white, straight comparison." McGill asked whether Marks had intended in the report to make such an inference. Marks said no.

Given the limitations of the report, it is puzzling why Marks agreed to participate in the case. One inkling of an answer surfaced at the end of his deposition, when McGill asked Marks about his faith. Early in the deposition, Marks had stated that all researchers had their biases. McGill asked Marks about his biases. Marks observed: "One of my biases is that research should be very, very thoroughly documented." McGill continued: "Any others that you can think of?" Marks replied: "Optimism."

At the end of the deposition, McGill revealed why he had asked those questions. In 2005, Marks had published a book chapter that identified him as a "Latter Day Saint scholar" who was "understanding, appreciative, and supportive of the LDS perspective on fathering." Marks had gone on to write that he was "predisposed to see the positive value of . . . religious beliefs and practices." Thompson broke in to ask whether McGill really wanted to play that game, saying that he would allow McGill to proceed "if we're allowed to ask your witnesses whether they're atheist, whether they're gay, whether they're lesbian, whether they have children." McGill replied: "I will acknowledge that to the extent any of our witnesses acknowledges in their public writings that they have a subject that potentially biases their analyses and research that you are entitled to explore that."

McGill then alluded to an article Marks had written that suggested he adhered to a 1995 Mormon text titled "The Family: A Proclamation to the World." The preamble to the proclamation stated that "it contains principles that are vital to the happiness and well-being of every family." The body of the Proclamation included the statement: "The Family is ordained of God. Marriage between man and woman is essential to His eternal plan. Children are entitled to birth within the bonds of matrimony, and to be reared by a father and mother who honor marital vows with complete fidelity."

After introducing the subject of Marks's article, McGill asked whether Marks agreed "that the principles stated in the proclamation are vital to the happiness and well-being of every family." Marks replied yes, in terms of "personal belief." However, he observed that he was able to distinguish his belief system from his scholarship, noting that in his report "the points that are made are documented not to religious literature, but to empirical scholarship."

In his office at Louisiana State University, Marks described his involvement in the case. He spoke in such soft and measured tones that time seemed to eddy around him. "People say I talk more slowly than John Wayne," he quipped. Marks's wall was covered with teaching awards, and his computer keyboard had a portrait of Jesus slipped into it. He described the same-sex marriage issue as the perfect storm: "God. Truth. Morality. Marriage. Children. Choice. Any one of those six issues, all by itself, is a tinderbox." Averring that as a social scientist he was keenly aware of the dangers of revisionist history, Marks asked if he could read me entries from his journal. An entry on September 6, 2009, described the day he received the call from David Thompson, asking him to serve as an expert witness in *Perry*. It said that he'd had "dreams and premonitions" about getting such a call "for over a decade." It continued:

> I have 25 days to write a comprehensive brief of 30–40 pages. In that time, I will also need to read some 150 journal articles. I am, in part, overwhelmed . . . and, in part, strengthened and comforted because although I feel woefully inadequate, I know the Lord will strengthen me and that He will make up the difference.

Marks then said that because of this time constraint, he could not get several sources from the library in time to check them. He acknowledged the fairness of a post-trial critique that he had cited sources he had not read.

When I asked how he had been selected as a witness, he told me that earlier in 2009, he had received an e-mail addressed to social scientists around the country known to be moderate or conservative. "What I do know is that I was not the first choice," he continued. "I suspect that, all false modesty aside, that I was nowhere near the first choice. But again, my assumption is that there are many people out there far more sane than I am, who ran screaming when they were asked."

Marks took a dim view of our adversarial system of justice. He reflected that the greatest human accomplishments involve harmony and complementarity. "When we move into the courtroom," he said pensively, "we lose the very best of who we are as human beings." Noting how difficult it was to become fully competent in such a short amount of time, Marks believed that he had nonetheless maintained his integrity, even if that did not make him a good witness "in the eyes of the law."

"I wish that there was a better way of arriving at truth," he said. I asked what that might be, and he said he did not know.

Marks hugged me as we parted, saying he thought he had made a new friend. He had asked if I had children, and I told him my husband and I had a young daughter, and another child on the way. He told me to be gentle with myself in my early years as a father. He said he taught parenting classes, and that I should call him if I ever wanted help with my parenting journey. He was so earnest that I could not even imagine stating the obvious way in which he could help me be a better parent—to let me offer my children the protections of marriage in states like the one in which we stood.

As the cab sped me to the airport, I gazed at the spreading oaks for which the bayou is so famous, backlit by the setting sun. I reflected on the strangeness of how family trees are actually upside down, about how they branch down rather than up. I thought about the strangeness of these interviews, which often imbued me with a sneaking fondness for the people who were hurting my family. After a while, my brain turned off. I focused on the oaks holding their burning genealogies up into the shifting, blinding light.

Shortly after the trial, Maggie Gallagher of NOM wrote to Judge Walker, complaining that, because of his original plan to televise the trial, the true outcome of the suit would never be known. By the time the Supreme Court stepped in to block the broad-cast, she said, "witnesses had already dropped out." She stated: "If the Supreme Court should overturn Proposition 8 and find a consti-tutional right to gay marriage, I will never know whether or not that would be a result of the haste to televise the trial."

Gallagher and others repeatedly insisted that the threat of ha-rassment to their side was real, a claim to which the Supreme Court gave its imprimatur. Yet the only documented case of witness ha-rassment related to the trial concerned the plaintiffs, Perry and Stier. A man from an unknown number called their house several times near the start of the trial, "spewing these awful, homophobic statements . . . just the ugliest kind of homophobic things you could say," Perry said. The calls were made at odd times, including the middle of the night, prompting Perry and Stier to lodge a police report and change their phone number.

Judge Walker's insistence on digitally recording the proceedings conferred an enormous boon on the proponents. He gave the wit-nesses a graceful exit, which they wisely took. We can never know how these four individuals would have fared on the stand. But we can make an educated guess.

PART III

AFTER

14

THE TRIAL COURT

Closing arguments in June were a moment of reckoning for both plaintiffs and proponents, who had to make good on promises made at the beginning of the trial. Judge Walker could hardly have been more emphatic about how much he wanted both sides to anchor their claims in the record. He made a copy of the video recording of the trial available to counsel for their presentations and sent each side specific questions asking them "what evidence at trial" supported points they had made.

Olson began by echoing his opening statement: "We conclude this trial, Your Honor, where we began. This case is about marriage and equality. The fundamental constitutional right to marry has been taken away from the plaintiffs and tens of thousands of similarly situated Californians. Their state has rewritten its constitution in order to place them into a special disfavored category where their most intimate personal relationships are not valued, not recognized, and second rate."

He observed that the "deinstitutionalization" message of the proponents at trial was strikingly different from the "protect our children" message of their campaign. Judge Walker asked if this mattered—under rational-basis review, any plausible justification would do. Olson responded that the proponents' case was too weak to meet even that standard. After a three-week trial, he said, the best argument the proponents could muster was that same-sex marriage might encourage heterosexuals to have children out of wedlock.

Olson pointed out that the plaintiffs held the same understanding of marriage that the Supreme Court had articulated in a series of celebrated cases. He played clips of the four plaintiffs from the first day of trial—Zarrillo saying that he loved Katami "probably more than I love myself," Katami saying that he had found the person "I can dedicate the rest of my life to," Perry speaking of putting the next generation of gay kids in Bakersfield "on a higher arc," and Stier talking about spreading hope to "conservative little pockets of the country." Olson said he could have composed a closing argument based solely on the testimony of the plaintiffs and Helen Zia, who described "from their hearts what marriage means to them." He noted, however, that the lay testimony was buttressed by experts in history, political science, sociology, psychology, and economics, whose evidence was "remarkably powerful, persuasive, and very consistent."

The next clips Olson played illuminated the plaintiffs' vision of the case. He began with snippets from Cott's and Meyer's testimony, which he tied to the right to marry and the right to be free from discrimination. He then shifted to the absence of constitutional rationales for Prop 8, using Blankenhorn to make his point. In one clip, Blankenhorn stated that same-sex marriage would likely "improve the well-being of gay and lesbian households and their children." In another, he gave his memorable "*more* American" quote. The plaintiffs downplayed the heightened-scrutiny factors, signaling their confidence that they could win even under rational-basis review.

After this presentation, Judge Walker asked Olson whether he agreed that this case involved "legislative facts," as Cooper had argued—a sly way of asking whether there should have been a trial. Caught between his initial position that a trial was unnecessary and his current belief that it had been invaluable, Olson conceded that Judge Walker's decision to have a trial had been "exceedingly wise," because it had allowed the court to hear the perspectives of experts in addition to hearing how marriage matters "in real life" to the plaintiffs and other witnesses. The trial, he concluded, "has been a great education. I think not just to the people in this room, but the people who read this record."

After lunch, Cooper took the podium, beginning with an appeal to tradition: "The New York Court of Appeals, Your Honor, observed in 2006 that until quite recently it was an accepted truth for almost everyone who ever lived in any society in which marriage existed that there could be marriages only between participants of different sex." Cooper elaborated that the historical record left no doubt that "the central purpose of marriage in virtually all societies and at all times has been to channel the potentially procreative sexual relationships into enduring stable unions to increase the likelihood that any offspring will be raised by the man and woman who brought them into the world."

Cooper underscored, however, that he was not relying on tradition alone. Instead, he suggested that tradition spoke to the strength of the responsible-procreation argument. From all of the possible justifications for Prop 8 offered in the original briefing, this contention had emerged as the leader. To counter Olson, Cooper referred to Supreme Court cases, including *Loving,* that described marriage as "fundamental to the very existence and survival of the human race."

Predictably, the conversation turned to whether the state should allow infertile straight couples to marry. When Cooper said it should, Judge Walker mused that the state must have some interest in marriage apart from procreation. Cooper disagreed—the state, he argued, could use gender as a proxy for fertility because more direct attempts to ascertain fertility would be "Orwellian." Moreover, Cooper stated, it was enough if the state sought to "increase the likelihood" of naturally procreative relationships occurring in an "enduring and stable family environment," even if the means chosen were not the most precise. That understanding of the family had held true, he said, for "millennia."

Cooper's reference to millennia triggered a turn. "Let's move from the millennia to the three weeks in January when we had the trial," Judge Walker said. "What does the evidence show?" Cooper responded, without giving specifics, that the evidence showed overwhelmingly that responsible procreation lay at the heart of society's interest in marriage. Judge Walker asked which witness had offered testimony to support Cooper's thesis. Cooper mentioned Kingsley Davis, a twentieth-century American sociologist, and William Blackstone, an influential eighteenth-century English jurist. Judge Walker seemed unimpressed by these dead authorities.

> *Judge Walker:* I don't mean to be flip, but Blackstone didn't testify. Kingsley Davis didn't testify. What testimony in this case supports the proposition?
>
> *Cooper:* Your Honor, these materials are before you. They are evidence before you. But Mr. Blankenhorn brought forward . . . brought forward these authorities and that's . . . and that's these social scientists and anthropologists and sociologists and others. But, Your Honor, you don't have to have evidence for this from these authorities. This is in the cases themselves. The cases recognize this one after another.
>
> *Judge Walker:* I don't have to have evidence?
>
> *Cooper:* You don't have to have evidence of this point if one court after another has recognized—let me turn to the California cases on this.

Like his "I don't know" gaffe, Cooper's "you don't have to have evidence" claim became fodder for his opponents. In fairness, Cooper was claiming that Judge Walker did not need factual evidence because prior courts had decided the issue as a matter of law.

Yet Judge Walker still had a point. As he had declared at the outset of the case, he wanted to test its core issues through a trial. He was asking why, if the proponents' position on the nature of marriage was so universal, they had offered only Blankenhorn to speak to it. He continued:

Judge Walker: Let me ask: If you have got seven million Californians who took this position, seventy judges, as you pointed out, and this long history that you have described, why in this case did you present but one witness on this subject? One witness. You had a lot to choose from if you had that many people behind you. Why only one witness? And I think it fair to say that his testimony was equivocal in some respects.

Cooper: Certainly not on this one, Your Honor. And his testimony was utterly unnecessary for this proposition, utterly unnecessary for this proposition.

Judge Walker: This goes back to the *you don't need any evidence* point.

Cooper: Well, Your Honor, it goes to, again, these are legislative facts. You need—you need only go back to your chambers, Your Honor, and pull down any dictionary, pull down any book that discusses marriage and you will find this procreative purpose at its heart wherever you go. Unless, unless, Your Honor, that book was written by one of their experts or has been written over the course of the last thirty years.

Cooper's problem was that he tried to satisfy two incompatible imperatives—the imperative to stick to his position about legislative facts and the imperative to put on a case. If he genuinely deemed evidence on legislative facts irrelevant, the principled stance would have been to decline to offer any witnesses. Alternatively, he could have offered an adequate number of witnesses to address the issues. Instead, he split the baby. Having advanced Kenneth Miller and David Blankenhorn, who both testified to legislative facts, Cooper's suggestion that Judge Walker simply look up the word "marriage" in a dictionary rang hollow.

At the end of his closing argument, Cooper drove home his two core points—that changing the definition of marriage would inevitably change the institution, and that it was impossible to predict with certainty what the ramifications would be. Realizing that this path wound back toward "I don't know," Cooper revisited that statement: "I don't know how many times, Your Honor, I had wished I could have those words back. Because, Your Honor, whatever your question is, I damn sure know, whatever it is."

His more serious point was that—again—it was not just he who did not know, but society. Yet as I read Cooper's lament about the words he could not unsay, I thought they expressed a more encompassing regret. The trial was done and could never be undone. I thought of Omar Khayyám:

> *The Moving Finger writes; and, having writ*
> *Moves on: nor all thy Piety nor Wit*
> *Shall lure it back to cancel half a line*
> *Nor all thy tears wash out a Word of it.*

Judge Walker asked whether "I don't know" or even "We don't know" provided adequate reason to impose restrictions on some citizens and not others. Cooper said yes, if there were a "rational basis for that distinction."

When Olson returned for rebuttal, he went directly to Cooper's point about uncertainty: "You can't come in here and say, 'I don't know, and I don't have to prove anything, and I don't need any evidence except for some people writing in books who won't come into court and subject themselves to the judicial process.'" As usual, the plaintiffs had reserved some Parthian shot for rebuttal. Olson observed that Blankenhorn had spoken about the deinstitutionalization of marriage. He played a clip in which Blankenhorn said that "heterosexuals, you know, did the deinstitutionalizing." Olson moved to the state's interest in creating the best environment for children. He played a clip where Blankenhorn testified: "The studies show that adoptive parents, because of the rigorous screening process that they undertake before becoming adoptive parents, actually on some outcomes outstrip the biological parents."

"Well," Olson said to laughter. "There you have it."

Judge Walker then asked if Olson feared a backlash if the court ruled in his favor. Olson asked whether Judge Walker was thinking of *Roe v. Wade*. Judge Walker confirmed that he was. The reference evoked Justice Ginsburg's claim that the right to abortion would have been on stronger footing if the Court had not moved so far and so fast in *Roe*. It also conjured the concerns of the movement lawyers—after all, a win in a Hawaii court had resulted in DOMA. At the end of the closing argument, Judge Walker asked not whether Olson feared *losing* but whether he feared *winning*. A great deal hung on the persuasiveness of Olson's answer. Even a judge sympathetic to marriage equality might believe Olson needed to be saved from himself.

It was a remarkably frank exchange. In general, judges publicly take the "let the heavens fall" posture that they rule without regard to the consequences of their decisions. Of course, the reality is that judges usually have at least one ear tuned to how their rulings will be received. What was rare about Judge Walker's line of questioning was not that he had this concern, but that he made it explicit.

Olson reassured the judge that there was a "political tide running" on same-sex marriage. At the same time, he said, a court is not justified in waiting for the "polls to be just a few points higher" before intervening. "Some judge is going to have to decide what we've asked you to decide," Olson said, "and there will never be a case with a more thorough presentation of the evidence." Olson's final plea was that the trial record not be forgotten, as he predicted—doubtless correctly—that such a trial would never recur.

Olson concluded: "And we submit, at the end of the day, 'I don't know' and 'I don't have to put any evidence,' with all due respect to Mr. Cooper, does not cut it. It does not cut it when you are taking away the constitutional rights, basic human rights, and human decency from a large group of individuals, and you don't know why they are a threat to your definition of a particular institution." The last word, of course, belonged to Blankenhorn. Olson said: "And Mr. Blankenhorn is absolutely right. The day that we end that, we will be more American."

Judge Walker ended by thanking the parties for their "splendid" advocacy, and intoned the ceremonial words that close all trials: "The matter will be submitted."

On August 4, 2010, Judge Walker issued his decision in *Perry v. Schwarzenegger,* holding that Prop 8 violated both the Equal Protection Clause and Due Process Clause of the Fourteenth Amendment. At the end of his introduction, Judge Walker observed:

> An initiative measure adopted by the voters deserves great respect. The considered views and opinions of even the most highly qualified scholars and experts seldom outweigh the determinations of the voters. When challenged, however, the voters' determinations must find at least some support in evidence. This is especially so when those determinations enact into law classifications of persons. Conjecture, speculation and fears are not enough. Still less will the moral disapprobation of a group or class of citizens suffice, no matter how large the majority that shares that view. The evidence demonstrated beyond serious reckoning that Proposition 8 finds support only in such

disapproval. As such, Proposition 8 is beyond the constitutional reach of the voters or their representatives.

Just as remarkable as Judge Walker's holding was the length and density of his opinion, which came in at 136 pages.

Before turning to his substantive analysis, Judge Walker discussed the credibility of the various witnesses. First he deemed the plaintiffs' witnesses qualified. Regarding the proponents' four withdrawn experts, he questioned the claim that the experts had withdrawn out of fear of being broadcast, since the possibility of broadcast had been removed before the proponents had to call their first witness. He diplomatically observed: "The record does not reveal the reason behind proponents' failure to call their expert witnesses." Finally, the judge turned to the two witnesses who did testify for the proponents. He stated that "Blankenhorn's testimony constitutes inadmissible opinion testimony that should be given essentially no weight." Judge Walker pointed out that Blankenhorn had no peer-reviewed publications or education in relevant fields, had no discernible methodology, and had been unwilling to answer many questions on cross-examination. To a lesser extent, Judge Walker expressed reservations about Kenneth Miller. He stated that "while Miller has significant experience with politics generally, he is not sufficiently familiar with gay and lesbian politics specifically to offer opinions on gay and lesbian power." He noted Miller's admission that proponents' counsel provided him with most of the materials in his expert report, and highlighted that 158 sources had shown up on the list of materials for both Miller and Nathanson. Miller's abrupt change in position also came back to haunt him— Judge Walker observed that Miller's 2001 article about how ballot initiatives endangered minorities conflicted with his testimony.

The opinion then spent fifty-five pages enumerating eighty findings of fact. It is hard to convey the heft of this presentation. Finding fifty-two, for example, stated: "Domestic partnerships lack the social meaning associated with marriage, and marriage is widely regarded as the definitive expression of love and commitment in the United States." Under it were eight citations—two to exhibits in the record and six to trial testimony from experts. Some findings listed only a bullet or two of supporting evidence; others listed as many as eighteen.

After presenting his findings of fact, Judge Walker moved to his conclusions of law. He began with the fundamental-rights analysis. Judge Walker observed that the litigants did not dispute that marriage is a fundamental right. He noted that marriage has retained certain characteristics throughout the history of the United States, and that it has always been a civil matter. He defined marriage as the state recognition of committed couples who live together and form a household, supporting each other and any dependents. He observed that the state regulated marriage because it created households, which in turn contributed to a "stable, governable populace."

The judge then reviewed how marriage had evolved over time. He asserted that race-based restrictions on marital partners, once common, are now seen as "archaic, shameful, or even bizarre." He observed that the doctrine of coverture, similarly unquestioned for centuries, is now regarded as "antithetical to the notion of marriage as a union of equals." He linked the rejection of these gender-based roles to the acceptance of same-sex marriage: "Today, gender is not relevant to the state in determining spouses' obligations to each other and to their dependents. Relative gender composition aside, same-sex couples are situated identically to opposite-sex couples in terms of their ability to perform the rights and obligations of marriage under California law."

Judge Walker concluded this analysis by maintaining that the plaintiffs did not seek recognition of a new right. Instead, he said, the "plaintiffs ask California to recognize their relationships for what they are: marriages." He observed that the state had to have a compelling interest to keep individuals from exercising a fundamental right. As he would discuss later in the opinion, the judge found the state had no such interest.

Turning to the equal-protection inquiry, Judge Walker acknowledged that in most cases, the court defers to the judgment of the legislature (or in this case, the people of California) under rational-basis review. However, even within this deferential framework, a classification must do more than disadvantage or harm a group; it must " 'find some footing in the realities.' " In a provocative passage, Judge Walker explored whether Prop 8 discriminated on the basis of sex or sexual orientation. It did both, he concluded. On the one hand, Perry was prohibited from marrying Stier simply because Perry was a woman. This was sex discrimination. On the other hand, Prop 8 targeted gays and lesbians because it eliminated a right only they would seek to exercise. Judge Walker determined that the "plaintiffs' equal protection claim is based on sexual orientation, but this claim is equivalent to a claim of discrimination based on sex." If he had followed this train of logic, he would have had to subject Prop 8 to heightened scrutiny. However, after making this observation, Walker turned away from it.

Judge Walker then declared that classifications disfavoring gays and lesbians met the criteria for heightened scrutiny. In a significant move, he deemed only two factors relevant: "a history of purposeful unequal treatment" and an equal capacity to contribute to society. Nevertheless, he hedged his bets in case an appellate court disagreed. The judge explicitly found that sexual orientation was immutable: "Individuals do not generally choose their sexual orientation. No credible evidence supports a finding that an individual may, through conscious decision, therapeutic intervention or any other method, change his or her sexual orientation." (Ryan Kendall calls this "his" finding of fact.) The judge further stated that Segura had testified that gays and lesbians were politically powerless, and that Miller's rejoinders to this testimony were unpersuasive.

In the crux of his opinion, Judge Walker considered the rationales that might conceivably support Prop 8. He first canvassed all the tradition-related justifications. In rejecting these rationales, Judge Walker observed that "tradition alone . . . cannot form a rational basis for a law," citing the 1970 Supreme Court decision regarding debtors' prisons.

Judge Walker next considered the justification of "proceeding with caution when implementing social changes." Under this heading, he considered the rationales relating to "deinstitutionalization." Judge Walker was at his most brash here—California did not need to be cautious in allowing gays and lesbians to marry, because no significant social change would occur. He cited several findings of fact, including: "Permitting same-sex couples to marry will not affect the number of opposite-sex couples who marry, divorce, cohabit, have children outside of marriage or otherwise affect the stability of opposite-sex marriages."

In keeping with popular debates about same-sex marriage, Judge Walker identified the promotion of opposite-sex parenting as the most significant set of alleged state interests. He found that same-sex and opposite-sex parents are of "equal quality," and that neither the gender of a child's parent nor the parent-child genetic relationship affects a child's adjustment. Studies that compared "outcomes for children raised by married opposite-sex parents to children raised by single or divorced parents," Walker found, could not be used to "inform conclusions about outcomes for children raised by same-sex parents in stable, long-term relationships."

Judge Walker then took up the justification of "protecting the freedom of those who oppose marriage for same-sex couples." He considered the proponents' arguments that Prop 8 preserved the right of parents to control the education of their children and the right of individuals to oppose same-sex marriage on religious grounds. These justifications loomed large in the campaign—as in the "Princess" ad, where a mother expresses consternation that she cannot keep her child from being taught about homosexuality, and in the "Oncoming Train" ad where a pastor exhorts people of faith to stand up for Christ when the devil blurred lines regarding family structure. Yet they all but disappeared during trial. The judge suggested the reason for this vanishing act, observing that "as a matter of law, Proposition 8 does not affect the rights of those opposed to homosexuality or to marriage for couples of the same sex."

As he neared the end of the proponents' assembled justifications, Judge Walker faced down the ultimate requirement of rational-basis review: that the judge consider "any conceivable rationale that would support the law." He discharged this obligation with the following statement: "Proponents, amici and the court, despite ample opportunity and a full trial, have failed to identify any rational basis Proposition 8 could conceivably advance."

After rejecting the proponents' rationales, Judge Walker made the inference, which he described as "amply supported by evidence in the record," that Prop 8 was "premised on the belief that same-sex couples simply are not as good as opposite-sex couples." Whether based on moral disapproval, animus, or merely a belief that opposite-sex relationships are "inherently better," Judge Walker held, "this belief is not a proper basis on which to legislate."

Having found Prop 8 unconstitutional, the judge ordered California to start issuing marriage licenses to gay couples. However, he offered the Ninth Circuit a few days to stay the ruling before it went into effect. The Ninth Circuit promptly did so, keeping Prop 8 in place.

Reactions to Judge Walker's ruling were predictably mixed. "To say we were euphoric would be a massive understatement," wrote Boies and Olson, who noted that the decision gave them "everything we could have hoped for." When Boies and Olson announced the outcome to the four plaintiffs, they tearfully embraced. Despite their initial opposition, the movement lawyers also celebrated the decision. Jennifer Pizer of Lambda Legal observed that Judge Walker had wanted a "detailed factual record" of the public interests served by Prop 8. She concluded: "The meticulous assessment of the Prop 8 defenders' case . . . makes clear: there's no there, there." The ACLU also praised the "landmark" district court opinion as a "huge victory for LGBT Americans."

The proponents' team reacted with equal vigor. Andrew Pugno invited the public to imagine if every state constitutional amendment were "eliminated by small groups of wealthy activists." This would "no longer be America," Pugno stated, but "a tyranny of elitists." Cooper also focused on the issue of democratic legitimacy, as he had done at trial. "Today, a single federal judge has negated the will of the people of California," he announced in a statement, promising to fight the decision on appeal.

To supporters of marriage equality, Judge Walker's decision was exhilarating. Dahlia Lithwick's response in *Slate* on the day of the court's decision was headlined "A Brilliant Ruling," while the *New York Times* editorial board described the opinion as "a stirring and eloquently reasoned denunciation of all forms of irrational discrimination." When I first read the district court's ruling, it read like an electrifying novel—one that sent me to the epic of the trial transcript itself. Eighty findings of fact with supporting bullets may not seem like a riveting read. Yet for me, the document was mesmerizing, not in spite of, but because of, its dry legalisms. The language was austere because it was the language of power. The words were bricks on the page; the pages were the walls of a citadel. It could never be unwritten. What remained to be seen was whether this edifice, built to such a dangerous height that it practically invited destruction, could survive the inevitable appeal.

15

THE COURT OF APPEALS

By the time the proponents filed their appeal in September 2010, they had significantly scaled back their ambitions. They jettisoned all but two of their justifications—the promotion of responsible child rearing and proceeding with caution. It was a bit like watching a hot-air balloonist throw dead weight overboard in the hopes of a smooth ascent.

The appeal did raise two new procedural issues—the issue of standing and the issue of how much deference should be given to the court below. The issue of standing had to do with whether the proponents had the right to appeal the case. The Supreme Court has long held that a federal court cannot hear a case—no matter how important—unless the proper parties are before it. Here, the plaintiffs had sued Governor Schwarzenegger and other California officials. Because the governor still continued to enforce Prop 8, even though he did not defend it, he was the proper person to sue. However, after the state officials declined to appeal Judge Walker's decision, the question arose as to whether sponsors of a ballot initiative—like the proponents—could do so in their stead. If the appellate courts found that the proponents lacked standing, Judge Walker's decision would be the final word on Prop 8. That prospect understandably horrified the proponents: After spending millions of dollars defending the case, they could be told that no court could legitimately hear their appeal.

The other question before the Ninth Circuit was how much weight to give Judge Walker's findings. Appellate courts review issues of law *de novo,* meaning anew. If an appellate court takes a different view of the law from the trial court, it will say so, and override the trial court's decision. In sharp contrast, appellate courts generally treat issues of fact with great deference, reversing only for "clear error." Even if an appellate court takes a different view of the facts from the trial court, it will uphold the trial court's factual determinations unless they were blatantly wrong.

A classroom favorite used to teach the "clear error" standard is a sex-discrimination case called *Anderson v. City of Bessemer City.* In that case, the trial court ruled that the female plaintiff had been wrongly passed over for the job of city recreation director. On appeal, the reviewing court reversed, disagreeing with the trial judge's determination that the plaintiff was the most qualified candidate for the job. The Supreme Court reinstated the trial court's decision. It acknowledged uncertainty about which candidate was most qualified but ruled that the court of appeals had improperly second-guessed the trial court. Because the trial court's finding was not obviously incorrect, the lower appellate court had to accept it.

If the appellate court in *Perry* gave Judge Walker's eighty findings of fact "clear error" deference, it would have to affirm his ruling. Some legal scholars saw Judge Walker's fact-encrusted opinion as a savvy play (or transparent ploy) to preserve his ruling from reversal. The proponents observed in their appellate brief that the district court had attempted "to insulate its decision from review by cloaking it in 'findings of fact' ostensibly derived from the trial record." They once again invoked the difference between "adjudicative" and "legislative" facts, arguing that while the appellate courts should review adjudicative facts for clear error, they should review legislative facts *de novo,* giving the district court's findings no deference. The proponents contended that because legislative facts were generally not amenable to judicial fact-finding, the trial court was not distinctively equipped to decide them. (The Supreme Court has given no binding guidance here, but some appellate courts support the proponents' view.) The proponents also maintained that the trial court's findings should be discounted because four of their witnesses had been intimidated by the prospect of being broadcast.

The plaintiffs shot back that the proponents had already had their chance, stressing the rigor and breadth of the trial. The plaintiffs also skated past the proponents' claim of witness intimidation, saying that these witnesses had simply self-destructed during deposition.

A week before oral arguments, the parties discovered who would sit on the panel: Judge Michael Daly Hawkins, Judge N. "Randy" Smith, and Judge Stephen Reinhardt. Judge Hawkins was a Democratic appointee; Judge Smith was a Republican appointee. Neither was considered particularly extreme. Judge Reinhardt, in contrast, was the liberal lion of the federal judiciary. As early as 1989, Reinhardt had written that future generations would rank *Bowers v. Hardwick* (the 1986 decision upholding sodomy statutes) alongside *Plessy v. Ferguson* (the 1896 decision upholding the "separate but equal" doctrine). The proponents must have wondered if some inauspicious star governed their cause.

The proponents refused to be passive in the face of fate. Two days later, they moved for Judge Reinhardt's disqualification on the basis that he was married to Ramona Ripston, then executive director of the ACLU of Southern California. This claim was implausible—while Ripston had been approached about having the ACLU participate in *Perry,* she had categorically declined to have anything to do with the case. Judge Reinhardt rejected the motion, deeming it to be "based upon an outmoded conception of the relationship between spouses." Far from limiting their opposition to same-sex marriage, the proponents seemed to want to return to the days of coverture, when a husband was responsible for his wife's opinions. Judge Reinhardt was not shy about giving that vision the back of his hand.

At the oral argument, Cooper studiously resisted any mention of the trial, apparently treating the appeal as a fresh start. Olson, on the other hand, repeatedly invoked it. However, the judges seemed leery about relying on the lower court's findings. Judge Hawkins observed that the case involved "legislative facts," where it did not matter "what a whole bunch of people might suggest one way or another." (When I heard Hawkins dismiss the experts below as a "bunch of people," I began to wonder what collective noun he would apply to experts—a "pride of experts," a "mischief of experts," or just an "implausibility of experts." I was confident he would not choose the word "panel.") When Olson said that the evidence undercut the proposition that children are most likely to thrive when raised by their genetic mother and father, Judge Smith gruffly commented that this was true if "the only evidence in this case is that which the judge has suggested is in the record." The oral arguments made me realize how attached I had become to the trial. And if that were not enough, the Ninth Circuit proceedings were fully televised, granting a transparency that would have been more helpful down below.

In January, the Ninth Circuit punted the question of standing over to the California Supreme Court. It asked whether the proponents had authority under state law to represent California on appeal. The panel suggested that an affirmative answer from the California Supreme Court would be necessary but not sufficient to give the proponents standing. While the parties awaited a ruling from the state high court, the federal litigation remained on ice.

∿

Even though the Ninth Circuit seemed skeptical about the trial, the proponents could not resist the temptation to discredit it entirely when the opportunity arose. Long before the case was filed, it had been an open secret that Walker was gay. Yet the media stayed away from his sexual orientation, which the judge had never publicly confirmed. As the trial progressed, this social contract frayed. A couple of weeks after the trial ended in January, the *San Francisco Chronicle* reported that Judge Walker was gay. Days after closing arguments that summer, the *Los Angeles Times* stated that Judge Walker "attends bar functions with a companion, a physician." Writing on the *National Review*'s website several weeks before Walker handed down his decision, prominent conservative lawyer Ed Whelan argued that the potential interest Walker might have in "entering into a same-sex marriage in California" could be a ground on which to contest his impartiality.

After Walker handed down his decision, the accusations of bias intensified. Maggie Gallagher of NOM accused Walker of substituting his personal views as a gay man for those of the American people. Bryan Fischer of the American Family Association called for his impeachment. Counsel for proponents, however, did not touch the issue, publicly insisting that the case "is and always will be about the law and not the judge who decides it."

Far from subsiding, the controversy only intensified with time. Judge Walker retired from the bench shortly after the Prop 8 decision. In April 2011, he held a "farewell meeting" with a cadre of courthouse reporters. In the meeting, he acknowledged that he was gay and "in a ten-year relationship with a physician." The day after Walker's announcement, J. Matt Barber of the Liberty Counsel published an article with a catchy title: "Prop 8, if the Judge Ain't Straight, You Must Vacate."

The proponents agreed that the judge's public acknowledgment made a difference, though they were marginally more restrained in their motion to vacate his ruling. They were "*not* suggesting that a gay or lesbian judge could not sit on this case," the proponents said. Rather, Judge Walker should be disqualified because he was in a long-term same-sex relationship. If Walker wanted to marry his companion, they argued, he would have a direct interest that would be "substantially affected" by the case. To be clear, Walker had never expressed any intention of marrying his partner. And given that the proponents increasingly emphasized the threat gay marriage posed to straight marriage, a straight judge worried about the devaluation of his own marriage would presumably also be compromised.

Olson later said the proponents made a mistake in bringing a motion to vacate, because it gave the plaintiffs another chance to talk about sexual orientation and equality. "Is Thurgood Marshall not entitled to sit on cases involving black people, and Ruth Ginsburg, isn't she entitled to handle a pregnancy disability case?" he said. Judge Walker told me that, at the trial's inception, he had indeed considered whether to recuse himself. But he did not want to suggest that a gay judge could not impartially judge gay issues, especially when he thought of future generations of gay judges. Nor did he find it necessary to disclose his sexuality. He reflected: "In a case that may touch on religious issues, does a judge have to say, 'Well, I am a Bible-thumping Methodist and I think you ought to know'?"

District Judge James Ware, who took over the case after Judge Walker's retirement, denied the motion in a day. He maintained: "A well-informed, thoughtful observer would recognize that the mere fact that a judge is in a relationship with another person—whether of the same or the opposite sex—does not ipso facto imply that the judge must be so interested in marrying that person that he would be unable to exhibit the impartiality which, it is presumed, all federal judges maintain." The proponents appealed this decision to the Ninth Circuit.

Boies Schiller's Jeremy Goldman said that, until the motion to disqualify Judge Walker, the *Perry* litigation had been more civil even than a run-of-the-mill case involving two corporations fighting over a patent. That civility had been expressed throughout the trial—as perhaps best embodied in the hug Olson gave Cooper each morning. Even the witnesses described an atmosphere of decorum and respect. For his part, David Blankenhorn said that the civility of the trial was a "night and day" contrast to the brutality of the debate roiling around it. Friends cut ties with him—one wrote to him to ask what it was like to be "America's most famous bigot." Donors and board members dropped their support of his Institute. Frank Rich, then a *New York Times* columnist, lambasted him repeatedly as a homophobe. Compared to this maelstrom, the courtroom seemed to him a haven of sanity: "You sit on the stand, people are respectful, he asks his questions, I answer them."

The challenge to remove the judge—the keeper of civility—corroded the collegial relationship between the parties. If Cooper felt his friendship with Olson was strained by Olson's treatment of "I don't know," Olson felt similarly about Cooper's recusal motion. "They're lucky we're not asking for sanctions," he grimly observed at the time.

In November, the California Supreme Court unanimously concluded that the proponents had the authority to defend Proposition 8 under state law. The Ninth Circuit could now rule on the constitutionality of the initiative. The Ninth Circuit then merged the original appeal of the opinion invalidating Prop 8 with the appeal regarding the recusal motion.

The Ninth Circuit finally issued its ruling on February 7, 2012, holding in a 2–1 decision that Proposition 8 was unconstitutional. In clarion tones, the introduction to the majority opinion stated: "Proposition 8 serves no purpose, and has no effect, other than to lessen the status and human dignity of gays and lesbians in California, and to officially reclassify their relationships and families as inferior to those of opposite-sex couples. The Constitution simply does not allow for 'laws of this sort.'"

In its analysis, the Ninth Circuit first held that the proponents had standing to bring the appeal, relying heavily on the California Supreme Court's ruling. In what seemed an obvious nod to the states-rights conservatives on the US Supreme Court, the panel underscored—unanimously—that proper respect for the states required deference to the California Supreme Court.

The majority opinion then moved to the standard of review. It was debatable whether some of the district court's findings were legislative or adjudicative facts, the court observed. Having raised the issue, the court then ducked it by giving deference only to facts that were obviously adjudicative—"those concerning the messages in support of Proposition 8 that proponents communicated to the voters to encourage their approval of the measure." The majority observed that the proponents had conceded the only other relevant fact—that a "meaningful" distinction existed between marriages and domestic partnerships. In addressing the magnitude of that distinction, the court stated:

> We need consider only the many ways in which we encounter the word "marriage" in our daily lives and understand it, consciously or not, to convey a sense of significance. We are regularly given forms to complete that ask us whether we are "single" or "married." Newspapers run announcements of births, deaths, and marriages. We are excited to see someone ask, "Will you marry me?", whether on bended knee in a restaurant on in text splashed across a stadium Jumbotron. Certainly it would not have the same effect to see "Will you enter into a registered domestic partnership with me?" Groucho Marx's one-liner, "Marriage is a wonderful institution . . . but who wants to live in an institution?" would lack its punch if the word "marriage" were replaced with the alternative phrase. So too with Shakespeare's "A young man married is a man that's marr'd," Lincoln's "Marriage is neither heaven nor hell, it is simply purgatory," and Sinatra's "A man doesn't know what

happiness is until he's married. By then it's too late." We see tropes like "marrying for love" versus "marrying for money" played out again and again in our films and literature because of the recognized importance and permanence of the marriage relationship. Had Marilyn Monroe's film been called *How to Register a Domestic Partnership with a Millionaire*, it would not have conveyed the same meaning as did her famous movie, even though the underlying drama for same-sex couples is not different. The *name* "marriage" signifies the unique recognition that society gives to harmonious, loyal, enduring, and intimate relationships.

The Ninth Circuit's "Jumbotron" passage is unlikely to replace the soaring language from *Goodridge* as the new ceremonial reading of choice at weddings. Yet in its mixture of high and low registers, the paragraph makes an equally convincing point about the pervasiveness of marriage. With these words, the opinion endorsed Nancy Cott's position at trial that "there is nothing that is like marriage except marriage."

From a legal perspective, however, the Ninth Circuit departed starkly from Judge Walker's opinion. It actively avoided the issue of whether the right to marry extended to same-sex couples, that is, whether the right should be expanded to include gays in the ways it had been expanded to include interracial couples or inmates. Instead, it analyzed the case solely on Equal Protection grounds. The panel also selected the narrowest Equal Protection grounds possible. It did not consider whether sexual orientation deserved heightened scrutiny, nor did it address Judge Walker's finding that Prop 8 was a form of sex discrimination. Instead, the court viewed the controlling precedent to be *Romer v. Evans*, a decision that struck down Colorado's "a pox on all gays" amendment applying only rational-basis review. It argued that California had guaranteed gays and lesbians certain benefits before withdrawing them through a ballot initiative. The court's analysis relied on the fact that California had granted all the substantive "incidents" of marriage (through its domestic partnership law) as well as the label "marriage" (through its legalization of same-sex marriage), and then withdrawn only the label (through Prop 8).

The major problem with this analysis was that Amendment 2 in *Romer* involved a broad panoply of rights, while *Perry* only involved one—marriage. The Court in *Romer* had seemed especially concerned that Amendment 2 imposed a "broad and undifferentiated disability" on a single group. The Ninth Circuit stated that "Proposition 8 is no less problematic than Amendment 2 merely because its effect is narrower; to the contrary, the surgical precision with which it excises a right belonging to gay and lesbian couples makes it even more suspect." Such an action, it observed, also suggested impermissible animus.

Judge Reinhardt's reading bent *Romer* out of recognition. In equating the breadth of Amendment 2 and the narrowness of Prop 8, the court was required to pass lightly over the fact that "broad" and "narrow" are antonyms. The panel, in other words, worked itself into a pretzel to avoid assessing the factual findings at trial.

Until the Supreme Court explicitly rules on the deference to be given to legislative facts, such distortions are bound to recur, especially in high-stakes cases. The circuit courts will not wish to rest any of their rulings on legislative facts, because the Supreme Court could decide that such factual findings draw no deference. Under that view, the Supreme Court could easily knock out the factual foundations of a circuit court's ruling en route to overturning it. So the circuit courts have a strong incentive to rule based solely on adjudicative facts, which they know require "clear error" deference from the Supreme Court. The trouble with that approach is that it will often require the appellate courts to interpret the law so that it rests only on adjudicative facts. This appears to be exactly what happened here—*Romer* was recast so that it called only for the facts that the Supreme Court could not assail.

Judge Smith dissented on the merits. He stated that the right to marry had never encompassed the right to same-sex marriage, and that the right to equal protection only required some conceivable rational basis for the law. He maintained that *Perry* could be distinguished from *Romer,* insofar as Prop 8 did not impose the "broad and undifferentiated" harm imposed by Colorado's Amendment 2. He believed that the "responsible procreation" rationale and the "optimal child-rearing" rationale both passed muster under rational basis review. And he agreed with the proponents that they were not required to advance any evidence.

Almost as an afterthought, the Ninth Circuit panel unanimously affirmed the denial of the motion to vacate Judge Walker's decision. The proponents took their lumps; they did not seek further review on the recusal issue.

In the weeks to follow, legal analysts obsessively dissected the Ninth Circuit's ruling, debating whether Judge Reinhardt had crafted it narrowly enough to avoid being overturned by the Supreme Court. Law professor Jane Schacter argued that while Judge Walker's broad decision had been a "red cape to wave at the Supreme Court's conservative justices," Judge Reinhardt's "incrementalist" approach would be endorsed by the Court or evade review altogether. The Supreme Court grants review (also known as *certiorari*) in about 1 percent of the cases in which litigants petition for a hearing. If the Court declined review, the Reinhardt rule (states cannot grant a right and then take it away on grounds reflective of animus) would control the nine western states in the Ninth Circuit. As a practical matter, the rule would only invalidate Prop 8. Going forward, however, it would prevent any state that granted marriage in the Ninth Circuit, as Washington State then seemed poised to do, from ever taking away that right unless it could produce a rational basis for doing so.

Others were less optimistic. In an article titled "Gambling with Gay Marriage," legal scholar David Cole speculated that the conservatives on the Supreme Court "may well understand that time and momentum" favored the plaintiffs, and would "jump at the opportunity to stop this movement in its tracks." In the immediate term, the debate was deferred—instead of seeking review directly from the Supreme Court, the proponents asked a larger panel of the Ninth Circuit to rehear the case in what is known as an *en banc* review. (The *en banc* process smooths out idiosyncratic panel assignments, so that if a party had drawn three Reinhardts, it would be able to get a broader bench of judges to review that decision.)

As the petition for *en banc* was pending, the fight for marriage equality continued apace. In March, Gov. Martin O'Malley signed legislation to bring same-sex marriage to Maryland, but the movement suffered setbacks elsewhere. In New Jersey, Gov. Chris Christie vetoed legislation that would have allowed same-sex marriage, and in North Carolina, voters passed a constitutional amendment to ban same-sex marriage by a margin of more than 20 percentage points.

The most significant development was a momentous announcement by President Obama. Speaking with Robin Roberts of ABC News on May 9, 2012, he expressed his personal support for marriage equality. As early as October 2010, President Obama had signaled that his views on the issue were "evolving." The public completion of his evolution followed on the heels of Joe Biden's announcement that he, as vice president, was "absolutely comfortable" with same-sex marriage.

There had long been a tension in the president's position. From the first day of the *Perry* trial, President Obama's public stance against same-sex marriage had been cited by the proponents as proof that one could be pro-gay and still oppose same-sex marriage. At the same time, the president had opposed Prop 8 as "divisive and discriminatory" when it was proposed. Opposing both same-sex marriage and Prop 8 simultaneously is, of course, a politician's prerogative. Unlike the witnesses in *Perry,* President Obama would not face cross-examination.

In his ABC interview, President Obama said: "It is important for me to go ahead and affirm that I think same-sex couples should be able to get married." In explaining his shift, Obama cited conversations with family members and gay friends, as well as his religious beliefs: "The thing . . . at root that we think about is, not only Christ sacrificing himself on our behalf, but it's also the golden rule—you know, treat others the way you would want to be treated. And I think that's what we try to impart to our kids, and that's what motivates me as president."

The president invoked the children of gay couples at every turn. He spoke of meeting same-sex couples and seeing "how caring they are, how much love they have in their hearts—how they're taking care of their kids." He wondered whether opponents of same-sex marriage had "had the experience that I have had in seeing same-sex couples who are as committed, as monogamous, as responsible—as loving a group of parents as any heterosexual couple that I know. And in some cases, more so." Indeed, except for his marquee declaration that "same-sex couples should be able to get married," the president never spoke of "gay and lesbian couples" or "same-sex couples" without alluding to their children.

Law professor Jack Balkin calls this process "ideological drift," meaning that an idea that occupies one end of the political spectrum drifts to the other. "Colorblindness," for instance, used to be the mantra of progressives campaigning for civil rights, but is now used by conservatives as a means of challenging affirmative action. In President Obama's speech, the idea of protecting children had now drifted from the right end of the spectrum to the left. During the Prop 8 campaign, it was the core argument against same-sex marriage. Now it was a core argument for it.

The Ninth Circuit denied the *en banc* hearing in June 2012, removing the final obstacle to an appeal to the Supreme Court. Later that month, another surprising evolution occurred: David Blankenhorn wrote an op-ed in the *New York Times* announcing that he now supported same-sex marriage. Blankenhorn took pains not to undermine the case he had made with his lawyers, saying that he was not recanting anything he had said at trial. (He consulted with a state supreme court justice ahead of time to ascertain whether he could change his stance without breaking any legal or ethical obligation to the proponents.) Blankenhorn had apparently reevaluated the relative weight of the "competing goods" at stake, assigning more value to "the equal dignity of homosexual love." He also seemed to have warmed to the plaintiffs' argument that, even if the idea of marriage as exclusively heterosexual had been *conceived* without prejudice toward gays, one had to examine whether animus was keeping it in place. In his op-ed, he observed: "To my deep regret, much of the opposition to gay marriage seems to stem, at least in part, from an underlying anti-gay animus. To me, a Southerner by birth whose formative moral experience was the civil rights movement, this fact is profoundly disturbing." When pressed to explain his change of heart, Blankenhorn cited longtime interlocutors like conservative gay-rights advocate Jonathan Rauch. Yet Boies and Olson were both convinced that the trial had transformed his views.

16

THE SUPREME COURT

In bringing the *Perry* litigation, Boies and Olson had long trained their sights on the United States Supreme Court. However, when the proponents sought review from the high court in July 2012, it was natural that Boies and Olson submitted a brief opposing it, given that they had won in lower courts. Still, their ambivalence was written all over their filing.

They began by pointing out that the *Perry* litigation was "an attractive vehicle for approaching—if not definitively resolving" the question of the constitutionality of same-sex marriage because it offered "a fully-developed factual record—indeed, the most comprehensive record ever developed in a case challenging a restriction on the right to marry." The strength of the trial record was hard to surrender, but as Olson explained to the press, the decision was driven by the needs of the plaintiffs themselves: "In the end, we represent real, live people, and if the Court doesn't take the case, we've won and our clients and thousands of others in California can get married." In short, Boies and Olson did not want to risk losing marriage equality in California for what seemed a slim chance of winning it across the nation.

In December, amid polls showing support for same-sex marriage at an all-time high of 51 percent, the Supreme Court granted review. Boies and Olson swiftly tacked, telling the press that they would seek a broad ruling from the Court. The proponents were just as upbeat, stating that the high court's review "finally gives us a chance at a fair hearing." The proponents were beyond the caprice of the lottery that had given them Judges Walker and Reinhardt. At the Supreme Court, the proponents knew who would decide their case.

On the same day, the Court also granted review in *United States v. Windsor,* a case involving an equal-protection challenge to a key provision of DOMA. *Windsor* was one of several actions coordinated by movement groups and their allies to challenge the federal government's refusal to recognize lawful same-sex marriages. These lawsuits were bold in that they sought to invalidate federal legislation. Nonetheless, they fit within the movement groups' incremental approach. They did not seek to change the marriage law in any state, much less all fifty. The goal was simply to ensure that the federal government recognized same-sex marriages already validly performed in a particular state.

The facts could hardly have been more sympathetic. Edie Windsor had been in a relationship with her partner, Thea Spyer, for more than forty years. In 2007, the couple wed in Canada. Their home state of New York recognized same-sex marriage. In the eyes of New York, the two women were next of kin. In the eyes of the federal government, they were legal strangers. Windsor felt the bite of that mismatch when Spyer died in 2009. New York recognized Spyer as Windsor's wife by, for instance, releasing her remains to Windsor. Yet the federal government levied a $363,000 estate tax on Windsor that she would not have had to pay had Spyer been a man.

Windsor herself was a dynamo—in her ninth decade, she carried our son aloft with total confidence. I was glad that the amount of the estate tax was a figure that many of the justices—who tend to be wealthier than average Americans—could imagine themselves having to pay. I was glad that the ACLU was deeply involved in the case, as was my colleague Robbie Kaplan of Paul Weiss. And I was glad that Kaplan had asked for a trial in the case. I had only one regret: she had not gotten one. The defenders of DOMA had been able to make arguments that were never subjected to the rigors of cross-examination—including a corporate law professor's musing that gay parenting was suboptimal because "in fables, stepparents are typically hostile to their step-children."

Legal analysts had long speculated that *Windsor* would be the easier case for gay-rights advocates to win. Marriage law has historically been left to the states, and DOMA represented a federal intrusion into that traditional state domain. Lower courts had handed the plaintiffs a long string of victories. And *Windsor* also involved two of Justice Kennedy's favorite things: gay rights and state sovereignty.

The Supreme Court's agreement to hear both *Windsor* and *Perry* left many advocates of same-sex marriage fearful that the Court would split the difference between the two cases, striking down the contested part of DOMA but upholding Prop 8. However, the Supreme Court's orders granting certiorari introduced another possibility. In both *Perry* and *Windsor*, the Court asked the parties to address whether the litigants had standing. A ruling that the proponents lacked standing would mean that they had no right to appeal Judge Walker's ruling. As a result, marriage equality would return to California, but no other state would be affected.

Two levels removed from the trial court, the proponents took an even more withering tone toward the district court's factual findings. They cited the same sources they had presented to Judge Walker—including Blackstone, the English jurist, and Kingsley Davis, the American sociologist—to argue that marriage was inextricably linked to procreation. (Cooper later acknowledged that he had stepped up references to Kingsley Davis as an implicit rebuke to Judge Walker's comments at closing argument.) Where the proponents did mention the district court, they dismissively referred to Judge Walker's "findings" in scare quotes.

The plaintiffs, for their part, described the proponents' definition of marriage as "cramped," observing that they did not once use the word "love" in their brief. To be sure, the proponents were only trying to express why the state regulates marriage, not to describe how couples experience it. But by drawing attention to the parties' contrasting understandings of marriage, the plaintiffs homed in on one of their opponents' vulnerabilities. Over the course of the trial, the proponents' conception of marriage's purpose seemed to shrink, ultimately boxed into the uninspiring "utilitarian incentive" of channeling heterosexuals into responsible procreation. Meanwhile, the plaintiffs' definition of marriage resounded with the language of inclusion, commitment, and love.

In another contrast, the plaintiffs relied heavily on the district court, highlighting the "twelve-day bench trial" with "nineteen witnesses" and "hundreds of pages" of briefing. They asked the Supreme Court to adopt the district court's reasoning, which would have legalized same-sex marriage in all fifty states, rather than the narrower reasoning of the Ninth Circuit. Having taken that position, they could avail themselves of the full breadth of Judge Walker's opinion. In arguing that Prop 8 violated the plaintiffs' fundamental right to marry—a line of argument the Ninth Circuit had avoided—the plaintiffs pointed to the "extensive evidence and detailed factual findings of the district court" showing that the regulation of procreation was not the defining purpose of marriage. The plaintiffs similarly cataloged the district court's findings on the four heightened-scrutiny factors, another issue the Ninth Circuit had avoided. Like the Greek giant Antaeus, who regained his strength whenever he touched the ground, the plaintiffs knew that any contact they made with the trial record would strengthen their case.

The proponents hit back hard in their reply brief, arguing that "courtroom fact finding" was entirely irrelevant under rational-basis review. In addition, they contended that the district court's findings warranted no deference. The proponents then turned the tables on the plaintiffs, arguing that *they* had failed to supply enough evidence. They cast the plaintiffs' vision of marriage as "a recent academic invention."

The Obama administration also stepped into the fray, seeking and securing the right to participate in oral arguments in *Perry*. As early as February 2011, the administration had ceased to defend DOMA. By the time the same-sex marriage cases were before the Court, the solicitor general had taken the position that both DOMA and Prop 8 should be invalidated, in part because sexual orientation met the four heightened-scrutiny factors. In *Perry*, the administration introduced another option to the mix. It argued that all states that gave the rights of marriage while withholding only the label violated the Equal Protection Clause. If the Court accepted their argument, the eight states with domestic partnership or civil union laws that met this standard would have to permit same-sex couples to marry.

Going into oral argument, the Supreme Court had at least five logical options. First, it could rule for the proponents, holding that same-sex marriage was not constitutionally required in any state. Second, it could dismiss the case for lack of standing, leaving the district court's ruling in place. Third, it could affirm the judgment as well as the reasoning of the Ninth Circuit's decision, meaning that no state in the country could grant the right to marry and then withdraw it, unless it could show a rational basis for doing so. (As a practical matter, the second and third options would both legalize same-sex marriage in California, but no other states.) Fourth, it could accept the administration's view and compel the eight states with "everything but marriage" statutes to adopt same-sex marriage. Finally, the Court could adopt some version of Judge Walker's reasoning and make same-sex marriage available in all fifty states.

~

To help the Court choose among these options, almost a hundred "friends of the court" filed amicus briefs in *Perry*. Several directly addressed the district-court opinion. Ed Whelan, who had earlier questioned Judge Walker's impartiality in the *National Review*, wrote a brief "to alert this Court to the fact that it should be especially wary of accepting at face value any assertion" by Judge Walker. Whelan again accused Judge Walker of bias, noting Walker's "egregious course of misconduct" and his "failure to disclose that he was in the midst of a long-term same-sex relationship." Whelan argued that this misconduct included Walker's decision to proceed to trial rather than to rule on summary judgment, and his "deeply confused belief that the live trial testimony on matters of legislative fact had an exclusive, or highly privileged, claim on his consideration."

Writing in response to Whelan's brief, a group of constitutional law professors argued that the district court's findings of fact deserved "significant weight." Dean Erwin Chemerinsky of UC Irvine and Professor Arthur Miller of NYU wrote:

> Evidentiary proceedings, and especially trials, subject bare allegations to rigorous review, expert analysis, and cross-examination. They help avoid the danger that courts will rely on preexisting assumptions that have little factual foundation. Regardless of how one categorizes the different kinds of factual findings trial courts make, judicial resolution of constitutional issues must be informed by facts. In our system, disputes over these facts are best resolved through adversarial proceedings before a trial court judge who can oversee the proper presentation of those facts. Here, the district court's factual findings address the core questions that this Court must answer.

Chemerinsky and Miller further argued that trials were particularly useful in civil-rights cases because of the "unfounded inferences" and "longstanding assumptions" that could attach to a minority group. They contended that this danger was particularly acute "in the context of voter initiatives, which are enacted without any formalized hearing or debate" and can allow "each citizen to follow her preconceptions anonymously and unaccountably."

In thinking about this dispute, I find Chemerinsky and Miller's position far more persuasive. Whether Judge Walker ultimately made the right call on any particular fact, the claims made at trial were subject to adversarial testing. The same could not be said of the amicus briefs, which repeatedly made assertions that the proponents failed to substantiate during trial. Regarding the nature of marriage, a brief filed by "scholars of history and related disciplines" stated that same-sex marriage "had never existed in human history" before 2000 (directly contradicting Blankenhorn and Young). On the question of whether gays deserved heightened scrutiny, a brief by the Concerned Women of America argued that gays were not politically powerless. "Many individual members of religious faiths support same-sex marriage regardless of the stance of their faith group," it observed. The brief supported this claim with a reference to Segura's testimony that 10.47 percent of Mormons supported same-sex marriage, which did little to advance their point.

Compared to the testimony at trial, the brief's discussion of the justifications for the bans on same-sex marriage also seemed cursory. On the question of optimal child-rearing, a coalition of social science professors, which included proponents' withdrawn witness Allen, set forth the gender-differentiated parenting argument (which Blankenhorn had eschewed on the stand) with a vengeance. As I read it, I became even more convinced that such blatant sex stereotyping would not have passed muster under existing precedents—and might even have forced Judge Walker to elaborate on his sex discrimination holding. "Mothers help children to understand their own feelings," the brief observed. Fathers, in contrast, teach them "that biting, kicking, and other forms of physical violence are not appropriate." With respect to deinstitutionalization, a law professor wrote a brief arguing in florid terms that "same-sex marriage would be the *coup de grace* to the procreative meanings and social roles of marriage." Perhaps the most colorful brief of all was submitted by the Westboro Baptist Church, aptly captioned "in support of neither party." The brief retold the story of Sodom and Gomorrah and observed that there was no more compelling interest than abiding by God's law.

Reading these amicus briefs, I felt rising concern about the vast majority of cases that do *not* go to trial. Aside from the Westboro Baptist brief, one could imagine any of these assertions making its way into an appellate opinion or, failing that, influencing a justice's view of the case. As the number of trials has declined, the number of amicus briefs submitted to the Supreme Court has swelled by 800 percent in the last fifty years, according to a study by law professor Allison Orr Larsen. This flood is no surprise: The Court needs to get its facts from somewhere, and groups with a stake in the case are happy to provide them. Many amicus briefs are measured and scholarly, submitted by experts and professional bodies with careful citation to reliable sources. Others are flimsy, containing what Larsen describes as "eleventh-hour, untested, advocacy-motivated claims of factual expertise."

As Larsen demonstrates, the Court's reliance on dubious material is not unusual. In 2013, one of the Court's copyright decisions relied on a blog post cited in an amicus brief. The blog has since been discontinued. A 2012 decision referred to the "increasing number of gang fights" in jails and prisons, citing an amicus brief that gave no evidence that such a rise had occurred. And in 2007, the Court cited an amicus brief for the proposition that women can experience "severe depression and loss of self-esteem" after an abortion. The expert cited was not a medical doctor, but an electrical engineer who received his PhD from an unaccredited university. In this case, Judge Walker had at least created a record below that advocates and scholars could mine, both before and after the Court's decision. Indeed, far from demanding a trial because he was biased, Judge Walker may have called for a trial to protect himself from charges of bias. The record showed that he had allowed both sides to put all the witnesses they wanted on the stand (despite motions to exclude Blankenhorn and Miller as unqualified), and also showed the evidence each side had mustered. The record speaks for itself. But in cases without a trial, no such record exists.

On March 26, 2013, the usual crowds of protestors massed outside the Supreme Court in anticipation of oral argument at ten a.m. It was Ron's first time at the Supreme Court. We scanned the protestors from Westboro Baptist to see if we recognized anyone from Topeka. (We did not.) The protests devolved into shouting matches. In the courtroom, however, all was hushed and ceremonious. At the beginning of Cooper's argument, Chief Justice Roberts asked him to discuss the issue of standing. Every justice except Alito and Thomas jumped in with questions, seeming to confirm that members of the Court were considering the most cautious option—dismissal for lack of standing—as the way to resolve the case.

When Cooper turned to the merits, Justice Kagan swiftly went to the question of whether same-sex marriage harmed anyone. Cooper parried by observing that he did not believe that this was the relevant question. Justice Kennedy asked him if he was conceding no harm would occur. When Cooper demurred, Justice Kennedy mildly observed that he thought Justice Kagan deserved an answer. Cooper replied that "it is impossible for anyone to foresee the future accurately enough to know exactly what those real-world consequences would be." It was the summary judgment hearing all over again, but this time Cooper, when pressed to the wall, carefully said "We don't know," rather than "I don't know."

Justice Scalia interrupted, sounding testy as he asked Cooper why he refused to speak about specifics. The justice alluded to the "considerable disagreement" among sociologists about the efficacy of same-sex parenting. His comment suggested that he would grant no deference to the trial court's finding that "children raised by gay or lesbian parents are as likely as children raised by heterosexual parents to be healthy, successful and well-adjusted," and that "the research supporting this conclusion is accepted beyond serious debate in the field of developmental psychology." Responding to Justice Scalia, Justice Ginsburg pointed out that California could not make an argument resting on the consequences of parenting by gay couples because the state already afforded gay couples equal parenting rights under its domestic-partnership law. While clearly on the other side of the debate, she too avoided reliance on the legislative facts established at trial. That avoidance came at a cost: Justice Scalia said that California's domestic-partnership law was irrelevant, because the plaintiffs wanted a ruling covering all fifty states.

Justice Kennedy then spoke. I reflexively leaned forward. Everyone knew this issue was in his hands; Cooper later said he never wrote a sentence or spoke a word without Kennedy in mind. "There's substance to the point that the sociological information is new," the justice said. "We have five years of information to weigh against two thousand years of history." I groaned inwardly. At least on certain key questions—such as the effects of child-rearing by gay couples—we have more than four decades of data showing that even without the benefit of marriage, gay couples are raising their kids just as well as straight couples. Unless allowing same-sex parents to marry would *hurt* their children, that data was relevant.

But as Kennedy took away, so he gave. "On the other hand," he continued, "there are some forty thousand children in California . . . that live with same-sex parents, and they want their parents to have

full recognition and full status. The voice of those children is important in this case, don't you think?" The ideological drift of "Protect
Our Children" was complete. Even at the time of the Prop 8 campaign, any association of gays with children seemed toxic. Five years
later, children were being invoked in the Supreme Court as a reason
to allow same-sex marriage, not to deny it. Cooper responded that
this consideration could be presented to the voters.

Kennedy then said that, based on the sociological evidence, the
plaintiffs were asking the Court to go into "uncharted waters,"
which could lead to a "wonderful destination" or off a "cliff." He
further observed that Olson was bringing a broad claim based on a
narrow Ninth Circuit opinion. He became pensive: "I just wonder
if—if the case was properly granted." On rare occasions, the Court
grants review in a case but then "dismisses certiorari as improvidently granted," which puts the case in the same posture as if the
Court had never granted review. The first interracial marriage case
to make it to the Supreme Court—*Naim v. Naim* in 1955—had been
dismissed in a similar way, leading to a twelve-year gap before the
Court decided *Loving*. The move to dismiss certiorari gives the issue
more time to work through the lower courts and to establish a more
thorough record of the arguments and evidence. Scalia responded,
in a tone that to my ears sounded gleeful, that the Court had already
taken the case. I became convinced that the conservative wing of the
Court had granted review, and felt another twinge of concern.

Soon after that, Justice Alito expressed skepticism about the
Ninth Circuit's reasoning, asking Olson whether the case should
come out differently if it were from a state in which domestic partnerships were unavailable. The problem with Judge Reinhardt's
theory was that it hinged on the state's "generosity"—having gone
so far in granting rights to same-sex couples, California could not
retreat unless it had a rational basis for doing so. A state that had
been less "generous" would be under no such compulsion.

When Solicitor General Donald Verrilli took the podium, it became clear that the justices also had little appetite for the federal

government's argument. Like the Ninth Circuit's theory, the administration's theory required more of states that had done more. Verrilli's proposal was even broader than the Ninth Circuit's because it did not even require the state to grant same-sex couples the right to marry. The administration argued instead that states that allowed gay couples all the rights of marriage could not withhold the label, as there was no reason, other than animus, for doing so. Justice Alito expressed another concern: "Traditional marriage has been around for thousands of years. Same-sex marriage is very new. . . . So there isn't a lot of data about its effect. . . . But you want us to step in and render a decision based on an assessment of the effects of this institution which is newer than cell phones or the Internet?"

It is as dangerous as it is irresistible to make predictions based on oral arguments. Yet my sense after the arguments was that the Court was not prepared to do anything radical. The fifty-state solution seemed vanishingly unlikely, given that even the liberals had expressed doubts about moving too quickly on this issue. Justice Sotomayor had wondered aloud whether it would be better to let the issue percolate in the lower courts, while Justice Ginsburg had made a reference to how the courts had proceeded incrementally in the context of interracial marriage. I had also heard no takers for the two more modest substantive way stations—the Reinhardt theory and Verrilli's eight-state proposal. The case seemed most likely to be decided on procedural grounds, either by a dismissal of certiorari as improvidently granted or by a ruling on standing.

However, I could not exclude the possibility that the Supreme Court would rule for the proponents. I kept thinking of an interview that Michael Hardwick had given about how optimistic he and his lawyers had been after Laurence Tribe's forceful oral arguments in *Bowers v. Hardwick*. One never knew. And we were arguing in the clouds; the careful edifice Judge Walker had built seemed leagues below us.

The *Windsor* case was argued the next day. During the oral arguments, Justice Ginsburg delivered perhaps her best line to date from the bench. Under DOMA, she observed, there were "two kinds of marriage: the full marriage, and then this sort of skim-milk marriage," referring to marriages like Windsor's (or Ron's and mine) that were recognized by the couple's home state but not by the federal government. And after oral argument, Windsor walked down the steps of the Supreme Court to cheering crowds. One of her lawyers, Pam Karlan, said to the press: "A few minutes ago we came out of the front door of the Supreme Court. Over that door is written the words 'Equal Justice Under Law.' . . . We walked down forty-four steps, which coincidentally is how many years Edie Windsor and Thea Spyer spent together as a committed couple. And we ask for equal justice under law here." That was when I knew with utter conviction that we would win *Windsor*.

Most observers expected that the cases would not be resolved until the end of the term in June, when the Court often hands down its biggest decisions in rapid succession. In the meantime, there was nothing to do but wait.

In the three months between oral argument and the end of the Court's term, marriage equality advanced with astonishing speed in the United States and around the world. Rhode Island, Delaware, and Minnesota all legalized same-sex marriage, as did Uruguay, New Zealand, and France. The gay-rights movement progressed in other ways, too: the Boy Scouts announced an end to its ban on gay youth, and NBA player Jason Collins announced that he was gay, making him the first openly gay man to be active in a major American team sport. The Supreme Court was poised to make its own powerful contributions to Olson's running tide.

On June 26, 2013, I woke up knowing that the status of our marriage was likely to change. Chief Justice Roberts had announced the day before that the Court would convene that day to release all remaining opinions—including *Windsor* and *Perry*. I kissed my husband good-bye and headed to the MSNBC studios, where I was scheduled to provide legal commentary. I promised Ron that I would come home after my segment, hopefully to toast him with a glass of whole milk. I remained confident that the Court would convert our "skim milk" marriage into a "whole milk" marriage. My concern centered on *Perry*.

The anchor of the ten a.m. hour, Chris Jansing, had corralled a panel including MSNBC anchor Rachel Maddow, legal strategist Richard Socarides, and Freedom to Marry's Evan Wolfson. The Court handed down *Windsor* first. The producer rushed a copy of the opinion over to us, which we all scanned frantically as Pete Wilson delivered the headlines from the Supreme Court. Once I saw that Kennedy had written the opinion in *Windsor* and that Scalia had written a dissent, I knew that Guido Calabresi would never again have to feel self-conscious when he married same-sex couples in Connecticut. And indeed, Justice Kennedy struck down the contested provision of DOMA with language that even my speed-reading eyes could see was stirring. I also noticed that a separate dissent by Chief Justice Roberts previewed the Court's yet-to-be-announced holding in *Perry*. He had written that Kennedy's opinion did not necessarily affect state bans on same-sex marriage, and that "we hold today that we lack jurisdiction to consider it in the particular context of *Hollingsworth v. Perry*." Minutes later, we got official word in a ruling by Chief Justice Roberts: On a 5–4 vote, *Perry* had gone down on standing, restoring Judge Walker's decision at the district-court level and effectively allowing same-sex marriages to continue in California.

Seated there with colleagues in the gay community, I could hardly contain my emotion. I averted my eyes from my fellow panelists. But then my eyes lit on Wolfson, who was seated before a separate camera at the other end of the room. I thought of the law-school thesis that he had written in 1983, and how, thirty years later, his vision was coming to fruition. I hastily addressed all my remarks to Jansing, who, sharp as she was, had no direct connection to this issue, and somehow made it through the segment.

After I returned home to Ron and the kids, we all solemnly drank whole milk. I then sat down with the two opinions. I could see that for most people, *Perry* would seem anticlimactic. Chief Justice Roberts explained that the district court's decision did not affect the proponents in the "personal and individual way" required to permit them to appeal. It was all pretty technical. But to my eyes, the opinion meant one splendid thing—Judge Walker's opinion was now the "law of the case," its governing and final disposition.

B ecause it focused solely on the issue of standing, Chief Justice Roberts's *Perry* opinion included no discussion of the substantive issues. Instead, the justices battled out the merits of *Perry* in *Windsor*. In ruling that DOMA violated the equal-protection guarantee of the federal Constitution, Justice Kennedy's majority opinion in *Windsor* laid heavy emphasis on principles of federalism. Kennedy noted that the responsibility for defining and regulating marriage had long been the province of state governments, and that DOMA—by withholding federal recognition of same-sex marriages lawfully entered at the state level—violated this precept. At the same time, Kennedy declined to decide the issue solely on federalism grounds. He made almost a dozen references to the "dignity" of gay individuals.

Kennedy's analysis left the case open to two interpretations. On one view, *Windsor* was just about keeping the federal government out of state business, which would mean that states could choose to have same-sex marriage or not. On the other view, it was a case about the dignity of gay people, which would mean that all states would have to provide marriage equality to respect that dignity. In dissent, Chief Justice Roberts underscored that the constitutionality of the state bans remained an open issue. As in *Lawrence*, however, Justice Scalia wrote a blistering dissent noting that the case logically required all fifty states to allow same-sex marriage. In an opinion that *Vanity Fair* compared to a "long Tumblr rant,"

Scalia argued that the majority's conclusion that DOMA had been motivated by animus made it "easy . . . indeed inevitable, to reach the same conclusion with regard to state laws denying same-sex couples marital status." To demonstrate his point, Scalia marked up passages from the majority's opinion to show how "transposable" the language was:

> DOMA's *This state law's* principal effect is to identify a subset of state-sanctioned marriages *constitutionally protected sexual relationships,* see *Lawrence,* and make them unequal. The principal purpose is to impose inequality, not for other reasons like governmental efficiency. Responsibilities, as well as rights, enhance the dignity and integrity of the person. And DOMA *this state law* contrives to deprive some couples married under the laws of their State *enjoying constitutionally protected sexual relationships,* but not other couples, of both rights and responsibilities.

The majority, Justice Scalia argued, had "arm[ed] well every challenger to a state law restricting marriage to its traditional definition," and in the process, promised to lay waste to the ongoing democratic debate over same-sex marriage. Scalia closed angrily: "The Court has cheated both sides, robbing the winners of an honest victory, and the losers of the peace that comes from a fair defeat. We owed both of them better. I dissent."

Justice Alito's dissent in *Windsor* addressed *Perry* directly, with choice words for Judge Walker's trial. He wrote: "At present, no one—including social scientists, philosophers, and historians—can predict with any certainty what the long-term ramifications of widespread acceptance of same-sex marriage will be. And judges are certainly not equipped to make such an assessment." Indeed, Alito argued, the primary question that litigants were seeking to have the Court answer—resolving the debate over "two competing views of marriage"—was entirely outside the competence of the judiciary, best left to "philosophers, historians, social scientists, and theologians."

Evidence of the limitations of judicial decision-making, Alito continued in a footnote, was on display during the *Perry* trial. In keeping with the proponents' use of scare quotes, Alito noted that Judge Walker had "purported to make 'findings of fact' on such questions as why marriage came to be" in a trial that "reached the heights of parody . . . when the trial judge questioned his ability to take into account the views of great thinkers of the past because they were unavailable to testify in person in his courtroom." Alito remarked that "only an arrogant legal culture that has lost all appreciation of its own limitations could take such a suggestion seriously."

Justice Alito's opinion raises provocative questions about what constitutes judicial arrogance. According to multiple canonical opinions, the Constitution protects the right to marry as fundamental. Justice Alito did not suggest that the Court retreat from that view. Everyone also agrees that, as the Court held in *Marbury v. Madison*, "it is emphatically the province and duty of the judiciary to say what the law is." So if the Court were to be properly confronted with the question of whether the right to marry extended to same-sex couples, it would have to answer that question. To decline to do so would not be to avoid the debate, but to settle it by default without taking accountability for the decision.

In fairness, Justice Alito's view—that the definition of marriage is simply outside the power of judges to change—is shared by many others. His dissent repeatedly cited a book coauthored by Robert George, *What Is Marriage? Man and Woman: A Defense,* which was released in 2012 to conservative acclaim. (By publishing the book just as *Perry* was finding its way to the Supreme Court, George continued his involvement in the litigation, after having suggested Cooper as lead counsel to Pugno and Robinson as an expert to Cooper.) The book contends that marriage is a "basic human good" like health, knowledge, play, and friendship. As a basic good, the authors argue that marriage must have an "objective core meaning" fixed by human nature. The book argues that the core of a true marriage is defined by the ability of one man and one woman to achieve "comprehensive union" through coitus—a union that supposedly cannot occur in same-sex relationships. As the law has no power to define marriage in a way that departs from its true meaning, opponents have taken to placing the word "marriage" in scare quotes when referring to same-sex unions.

From this perspective, asking a judge to rule on the meaning of "marriage" is equivalent to asking a judge to rule on the meaning of "friendship," a point Chief Justice Roberts made during oral argument in *Perry*. "If you tell a child that somebody has to be their friend, I suppose you can force the child to say, 'This is my friend,'" Roberts asserted. "But it changes the definition of what it means to be a friend." Yet as of this writing, we have no laws codifying friendship. And if there were such a law, the judges *would* control its meaning, whether they did so explicitly or not.

For the most part, supporters of same-sex marriage applauded the Supreme Court's decisions. True, the Court had not established a broad constitutional right to same-sex marriage, as some had hoped it would, and the rulings in *Windsor* and *Perry* were decidedly careful and incremental. Yet some commentators noted that it was "essential to listen not only to the words of the Court's decisions, but to the music as well." The decisions suggested that future challenges to same-sex marriage bans would be "heard seriously and with respect." Supporters of "traditional marriage" criticized the rulings as unprincipled, and noted that in taking sides in the marriage debate, the majority had put "a thumb on the scale in future cases."

Two days after the decision in *Perry*, the Ninth Circuit lifted the stay on the district court's ruling, and the governor of California ordered all state clerks to begin issuing marriage licenses to same-sex couples immediately. That same day, plaintiffs Perry and Stier, and Katami and Zarrillo, were married in San Francisco and Los Angeles, respectively.

17

CIVIL CEREMONIES

By proceeding incrementally, the Supreme Court had ironically left intact the most sweeping ruling on same-sex marriage imaginable. Yet because Judge Walker's decision was only a district court ruling, what happened over those twelve days in San Francisco could easily fade from public view. That would be a great loss, as the trial record offered an unparalleled discussion of the civil-rights issue of our time.

The great strength of the *Perry* trial, and of our adversarial system generally, is an obsessive commitment to factual accuracy. (Indeed, the concept of a "fact" originated in the legal discourse of early modern England before it penetrated the natural sciences and other intellectual disciplines.) Some adversarial methods, however, are more effective than others at unearthing facts. One major distinction lies between written and spoken exchanges. As Boies has remarked, "Papers never meet each other—it's like people talking past each other. The crucible of cross-examination forces the witness to confront the other side." To be sure, cross-examination can occur without going to trial—Young was subjected to a searing one and was effectively disqualified as an expert witness without setting foot in a courtroom. But trials are much more likely to involve such examinations, and to ratchet up their intensity. When Boies observed that "a witness stand is a lonely place to lie," he meant that it was lonely because it was so public—with the glare of the judge, the parties, and the gallery upon him or her, the witness is in a position that has no ready analogue in our culture.

Legal scholars have challenged this faith in the fact-finding capacities of trials. One of the most persuasive is John Langbein, who argues that cross-examination is a "source of fresh distortion" because of its latitude for bullying and underhanded questioning. Langbein points out that John Henry Wigmore, who famously described cross-examination as "the greatest legal engine ever invented for the discovery of truth," also ceded that it was "almost equally powerful for the creation of false impressions." Trial lawyers, Langbein observes, pride themselves on their ability to "decrease the value of almost any testimony" through cross-examination.

But while any good lawyer can undermine any expert's testimony, she will find some experts more vulnerable than others. In *Perry*, the proponents had tried to paint Nancy Cott as a biased advocate for same-sex marriage. Yet as a professor of history at Harvard who had written a book on marriage grounded in a decade of archival research, she proved difficult to discredit. When David Blankenhorn testified on the same subject, he presented an easier target. Boies successfully attacked weaknesses in Blankenhorn's testimony, such as his claims about the "rule of two."

Trials can also make facts more vivid by putting human faces to abstractions. The lay witnesses in *Perry* arguably gave the most powerful testimony at trial. Like medieval morality plays with allegorical characters like Vice and Virtue, trials use individuals to make facts accessible. Helen Zia embodied the difference between a domestic partnership and a marriage, Ryan Kendall represented the immutability of sexual orientation, and Jerry Sanders and Bill Tam illuminated the legal concept of animus. The four plaintiffs personified the ideas of marriage equality and, perhaps more important, love.

It may seem that testimony of an emotional nature takes us further from the facts rather than bringing us closer to them. The proponents argued that the topics addressed by the plaintiffs' lay witnesses were better left to experts. However, as Judge Walker said in allowing Kendall to testify: "As with so many aspects of testimony in a trial . . . actual firsthand experience to illustrate points that have been raised is very helpful." As Martha Nussbaum has argued, emotions can carry cognitive content; many more people will understand immutability through Kendall's narrative rather than through Herek's statistics.

Finally, trials separate fact from belief. At least in the United States today, the trial requires an innately secular form of argumentation. As such, it operates as a sieve that filters out religious motivations for a law. The *Perry* trial showed that opposition to same-sex marriage is largely rooted in conservative religious beliefs. Beliefs move people to engage passionately in a cause, and passion can often persuade. Yet as the trial showed, a passion is not a reason, much less a reason for a law.

It should therefore not be surprising that trials can make particularly dramatic contributions when religious motives are in play. Opponents of same-sex marriage often compared *Perry* to the famous 1925 Scopes "monkey trial," which concerned a challenge to a ban on teaching evolution in Tennessee public schools. This comparison is unfair, as Scopes could justly be called a "show trial," in which a grandstanding Clarence Darrow asked William Jennings Bryan questions such as where Cain got his wife. The *Perry* trial bears a much closer resemblance to the 2005 trial in *Kitzmiller v. Dover*—often called *Scopes II*—where a court had to determine whether intelligent design was different from creationism. After a five-week trial in a Pennsylvania federal court in 2005, Judge John E. Jones (a George W. Bush appointee) issued a 139-page ruling finding that intelligent design was not science and barring it from being taught as such in public schools. Although this decision did not completely shut down efforts to teach creationism in public schools, it inflicted severe damage on the campaign for intelligent design. In both *Perry* and *Kitzmiller,* the trial distinguished secular fact from religious belief.

People of good will can disagree over the place of religion in public policy. Some insist that religious conviction should play no role in politics at all. Others argue that laws should be grounded in secular reasoning but that broad exemptions should be available to religious objectors. This view was on display in the 2014 *Hobby Lobby* decision, in which the Supreme Court ruled that "closely held" corporations cannot be required to provide health-insurance coverage for contraceptive methods that conflict with the owners' religious beliefs. Still others dispute whether we should be living in a nation where lawmaking requires a secular basis at all. During the same term, in *Town of Greece v. Galloway,* Justice Alito suggested that the Court's "tests" for assessing constitutionality may be invalid if they are inconsistent with the practice of legislative prayer. These comments suggest that Alito might favor overruling the *Lemon* test, which requires state action to be justified by a secular purpose. Unless and until such precedent is overruled, however, trials will continue to discourage the state from advancing laws predicated on religious belief alone.

T he fact-finding benefits of the trial may be clearest in the courtroom, but they reverberate beyond it. One benefit is that other jurisdictions can rely on their findings. Since *Windsor* and *Perry,* same-sex couples have challenged bans on marriage equality in every state that has one, and have prevailed in almost every district-court ruling to date. These courts have taken Justice Scalia's view that *Windsor* demands that state bans on same-sex marriage be overturned. The Supreme Court will almost certainly decide this question by June 2015.

Some have argued that Boies and Olson have claimed too much credit for their victory, when *Windsor,* not *Perry,* governs these lower court cases as precedent on the substantive issues. I agree that *Windsor* has had the greater effect. Yet many of these critiques have failed to recognize the full magnitude of what Boies and Olson accomplished with their trial. Reading subsequent lower court opinions, one sees the imprint of the *Perry* trial everywhere. A Utah court adopted *Perry*'s definition of marriage verbatim. A Texas court quoted *Perry* on the equal capacity of gay people to contribute to society. A Wisconsin court cited *Perry* to support its analysis of the history of discrimination suffered by gays and lesbians. Federal courts in Idaho, Michigan, and Ohio have quoted *Perry* on immutability. An Oregon court quoted *Perry*'s finding that children raised by gay or lesbian parents are as likely to thrive as those raised by straight parents. By the time one of these cases reaches the Supreme Court, there will be a network of courts endorsing Judge Walker's findings, which will make them hard to ignore.

Moreover, Boies and Olson are far from finished with this cause. In *Bostic v. Rainey,* they joined forces again to fight Virginia's ban on same-sex marriage. "Virginia gave us the first marriage equality case," Olson asserted, citing *Loving.* "It's fitting, then, that Virginia be the battleground for another great test of that principle." In striking down the ban, the district court in *Bostic* affirmed the findings in *Perry* that same-sex couples have "happy, satisfying relationships and form deep emotional bonds and strong commitments to their partners," and that their children are just as likely as children of heterosexual parents to be "healthy, successful and well-adjusted." This decision was upheld on appeal, and the Supreme Court declined to review it, thereby bringing same-sex marriage to Virginia.

In addition to influencing other courts, trials have the power to discredit fringe scholars and viewpoints with finality and authority. The witness bank for opponents of same-sex marriage has been greatly depleted, mainly due to the witnesses' poor courtroom performance before, during, and after *Perry.* In the Hawaii trial in the

1990s, one of the state's witnesses, Kyle Pruett, conceded that gay and lesbian parents "are doing a good job" and that "the kids are turning out just fine." The court chose to disregard the testimony of another witness in the same case, Richard Williams, because of his "expressed bias against the social sciences," and his "severe views"—including his belief that there was "no scientific proof that evolution occurred."

George Rekers, a former University of South Carolina psychologist and ordained Baptist minister, had testified against gay and lesbian parenting in Arkansas and Florida. He became public-relations poison for opponents of same-sex marriage after a Miami newspaper reported that he had taken a European vacation with a male prostitute. Even before his hypocrisy was exposed, Rekers had been roundly discredited. In the Arkansas case, the judge concluded from Rekers's testimony that "he was there primarily to promote his own personal ideology." The judge described how Rekers selectively analyzed studies, gave inconsistent testimony, and read from prepared notes instead of answering questions. In the Florida trial, the judge was no less scathing. She found that Rekers's testimony was "far from a neutral and unbiased recitation of the relevant scientific evidence" and that his beliefs were motivated by "strong ideological and theological convictions" inconsistent with social science.

In contrast, experts for the side of marriage equality have almost uniformly survived the rough-and-tumble of litigation and media exposure. The Arkansas judge who slammed George Rekers heaped praise upon Michael Lamb, who testified in the same proceedings. And the plaintiffs' witnesses from *Perry*—including Cott, Chauncey, and Herek—have gone on to participate in other proceedings. The two proponents' witnesses have not reprised their roles.

After *Perry*, the primary champions remaining on the opponents' side were two of the withdrawn witnesses: Douglas Allen and Loren Marks, who, though bruised from *Perry*, was ready to keep fighting with a version of the rebuttal report that he had promised but not filed. Most significant, however, was a new entrant to the battleground—University of Texas sociologist Mark Regnerus. Regnerus published the now infamous "New Family Structures Study," which purported to show statistically significant differences in outcomes between children with "intact biological families" and those with "lesbian mothers" or "gay fathers." Widely touted as the first systematic study done on the issue, it generated a flood of academic criticism, including a repudiation of it by Regnerus's own department at the University of Texas. Nevertheless, it figured in many state legislative debates about same-sex marriage, including those in Hawaii, Illinois, Colorado, Maryland, Minnesota, and Rhode Island. For a time, it seemed unstoppable.

Then, in February 2014, Judge Bernard A. Friedman held a trial in Michigan focused on the issue of optimal child rearing, in which Allen, Marks, and Regnerus all testified. (When Friedman announced that he was going to have a trial—the first and so far only same-sex marriage trial after *Perry*—Judge Walker wrote me a one-line e-mail: "Imitation is the sincerest form of flattery.") A Reagan appointee, Friedman found "Regnerus's testimony entirely unbelievable and not worthy of serious consideration." Among his litany of substantive criticisms, he observed that almost all the children characterized as being raised by "gay fathers" or "lesbian mothers" were the product "of a failed prior heterosexual union." Obviously, that circumstance provided an alternative explanation for negative outcomes. Judge Friedman also lambasted the provenance of the study, noting that it was "hastily concocted at the behest of a third-party funder" concerned that decisions like *Perry* and *Windsor* were threatening the institution of marriage. The court observed: "The funder clearly wanted a certain result, and Regnerus obliged."

Marks and Allen fared no better—they were ultimately lumped in with Regnerus as representatives of a "fringe viewpoint" in the social sciences that should not be accorded "any significant weight." After the Michigan trial, reliance on Regnerus appears to be on the wane. The state of Utah explicitly distanced itself from the Regnerus study in an appeal before the Tenth Circuit, less than a month after the Michigan decision.

Finally, the trial is, as one reporter said of *Perry,* a "great and theatrical classroom." Olson later reflected that *Perry* "was an enormous education to everybody who was in that courtroom, even those who had been laboring in the vineyard for gay rights." Though the proceedings were not broadcast, *Perry* has generated numerous books, articles, TV pieces, a documentary, and a play, all of which have extended the trial's reach. While the purpose of a trial is justice for the parties, not public education, trials have been known to provide that education as a collateral benefit.

The most noteworthy dramatic interpretation came from screenwriter Dustin Lance Black, who won the Academy Award for his biopic of Harvey Milk. Black, who sat on the board of AFER, attended most of the trial. Moved by the power of the testimony and the knowledge that the trial would not be broadcast, he resolved to write a play that would bring the trial to the public. Just over a year after the district-court decision, the play—titled simply *8*— premiered in New York with an all-star cast. A subsequent "West Coast premiere" featured even more celebrities, including Brad Pitt as Judge Walker, George Clooney as David Boies, Martin Sheen as Ted Olson, and Kevin Bacon as Charles Cooper. (Cooper ruefully noted to me that Bacon often plays villains.) In August 2013, AFER announced that the play had surpassed 900,000 views online. Rob Reiner has said that a feature film might also be in the works, with Black writing the screenplay. As of May 2012, there had been more than four hundred staged readings nationwide. A friend in Japan wrote that he had recently been to a sold-out production there.

Black would never have felt similarly inspired by a judicial decision without a trial, even if that decision had had the same legal effect. The shelf of works of literature based on summary judgments remains bare.

～

For all its merits, *Perry* failed to resolve an enduring dilemma: how to treat so-called legislative facts in deeply controversial cases. Walker believed that these facts should be determined at trial; commentators like Whelan felt that submitting such facts to trial was a mistake. Yet while judges need not submit every legislative fact to trial, I believe they should feel free to do so. I see no reason that judicial truth-finding mechanisms will not work as well for legislative facts as they do for the adjudicative facts that everyone agrees trial courts should resolve as a matter of course. After all, some adjudicative facts (such as the reason voters approved a ban on same-sex marriage) can be far more complex than some legislative facts (such as whether gays have suffered a history of discrimination).

It seems equally clear that legislative facts found through trials warrant at least some deference from appellate courts. *De novo* review, which gives no such deference, fails to acknowledge that trial courts are specially designed for fact-finding. Higher courts generally grant deference on questions of adjudicative fact on the grounds that the trial judge was physically present during witness testimony and could therefore make better determinations of credibility. This would seem to be equally true of legislative facts—as when Judge Walker found Blankenhorn to lack credibility in part because of his demeanor on the stand. *De novo* review also creates perverse incentives for circuit-court judges. If the courts know they will receive deference on adjudicative facts but not on legislative facts, they may be tempted to strain the law to rest only on adjudicative facts, as the Ninth Circuit opinion arguably did.

At the same time, the standard of review should be somewhat less stringent than "clear error." Because legislative facts can and do span multiple cases, such a standard would not only be inadvisable, but also impractical. Two district courts in the same circuit could easily take opposite positions with regard to a legislative fact without either being manifestly in the wrong. In that instance, it would be impossible for the court of appeals to grant clear-error deference to both.

The solution must lie somewhere in between. I took the constitutional-law professors' brief, which was also derided by Justice Alito's dissent, to be advocating for such an intermediate standard. It argued that findings of legislative fact should be granted "significant weight," a new term that suggests a standard between *de novo* and clear error review. One of the authors of the brief, Dean Erwin Chemerinsky, corroborated this view.

Perhaps the strongest objection to granting legislative facts significant weight on appeal would be the parade of cases in which courts have erred with regard to social-science issues. A familiar example concerns the famous "doll studies" conducted by Kenneth Clark in the 1930s and '40s. In these studies, Southern children were presented with a black doll and a white doll, then asked which doll they would play with, and which was "nice" or "bad." The studies revealed a strong preference among both black and white children for the white doll. In *Briggs v. Elliott,* a case later merged with *Brown v. Board of Education,* the trial court heard testimony on these studies. In *Brown,* the Supreme Court also cited these studies to conclude that school segregation "generates a feeling of inferiority" in African American students "that may affect their hearts and minds in a way unlikely ever to be undone."

Yet the use of Clark's studies posed a problem—known at the time, but increasingly publicized in the wake of the opinion. Clark had obtained the same results in Northern schools, which were integrated. While Clark's studies supported the claim that *racism* affected children, they did not show that *segregation* had done so. Justice Clarence Thomas has argued that the opinion in *Brown* should have arrived at the same result without relying on "dubious social science." Tellingly, he was also the only justice on the Court to join Justice Alito's opinion criticizing the *Perry* trial for assessing questions best left to "philosophers, historians, social scientists, and theologians."

Of course, if a legal determination does not turn on legislative facts, then the Court should avoid making findings. *Brown* was arguably such a case. Yet if the Court's legal determinations rest on such facts, as they did in *Perry*, it seems strange to say that the Court should not avail itself of the most rigorous fact-finding procedures available. If the courts make a mistake, they should adjust the law accordingly. And not surprisingly, the Supreme Court has mechanisms for correcting its own reliance on incorrect data. In 1992's *Planned Parenthood v. Casey*, the Court summarized the considerations it would take into account when deciding whether to overrule one of its own precedents. One such consideration was whether "facts have so changed or come to be seen so differently" that the earlier case should be overruled. If a holding *did* rest entirely on social-science evidence that was later proven wrong, then the Court's own precedent would demand that the law absorb the new understanding.

But the deeper question about whether trials are the best way to determine legislative facts is—compared to what? Courts, like any fallible institution, will sometimes get facts wrong. Yet here I am reminded of Winston Churchill's comment that democracy is the worst form of government except all the alternatives. Rather than measuring a court's determinations against some unattainable Platonic ideal, we must measure them against the other options at our disposal. When that comparison is made, I see no substitute for litigation that culminates in a trial.

If legislative facts are not determined at trial, judges have to ascertain them in some other way. Summary judgment, for example, requires a court to discern facts based largely on the materials in the record, such as expert reports and depositions. Yet the fact-finding capacity of summary judgment is inferior to that of a full trial. At trial, expert reports are more thoroughly examined, the questioning at deposition is repeated and amplified, and parties are forced to confront their opponents' arguments in front of a judge.

Facts can be, and increasingly are, introduced at the appellate level through amicus briefs. Yet as discussed, "amicus facts" are highly suspect because they are not subjected to *any* form of adversarial testing. The Court's rising use of amicus briefs has been a matter of scholarly consternation—and public parody. Comedian Stephen Colbert suggested in 2014 that the Court should not restrict itself to amicus briefs when there were "so many sources for unverified facts." He himself favored the factoids on the back of Snapple caps.

Judges may also rely on their own research and deliberation. Yet a judge's own research into the history of marriage, for example, is sure to be less comprehensive and accurate than that of a historian who has devoted her career to the topic. A judge, unlike a historian at trial, is not subjected to any adversarial testing. Moreover, once a case has made it to the Supreme Court, the justices' findings are no longer vulnerable to an appeal. Legislative facts become more susceptible to the idiosyncrasies and biases of the justices, and less amenable to correction, than factual assertions made at a trial.

Moving beyond the courtroom, we see that other lawmaking bodies fare no better. Legislatures may have the tools to conduct rigorous inquiries, but if so, they rarely use them. In the typical legislative hearing, as legal scholar Douglas Laycock has noted, committee members wander in and out of the room, each member has just two to three minutes to question a witness, and use of campaign contributions to sway legislators is seen as business as usual. In court, judges preside over the entire proceeding, cross-examinations can go on for hours, and attempts to influence the judge will land one in prison. And of course, once we move from legislative hearings to floor debates, the proceedings rely solely on the intelligence, preparedness, and integrity of the individual legislators.

Minnesota held a legislative hearing and debate on same-sex marriage in 2013, which I followed with some care. Sure enough, the legislative hearing began with the committee chair observing that "some members would have to leave early" and asking witnesses not to take offense. The questioning was brief and haphazard. When the issue reached the floor of the Minnesota House, I found the session an exercise in patience. One representative stated that "redefining marriage has had a chilling effect on the relevance of marriage as it connects to parenthood," citing the "decline in heterosexual marriage" and "increase in out-of-wedlock births" in the Netherlands in the years since same-sex marriage was legalized there. Another stated that the Regnerus study had proven that children do best when they have a mother and father in a stable marriage. Not only had these claims been debunked in earlier trials, there was no systematic testing of any of the arguments. Another representative later rose and said that there appeared to be some problems with the Regnerus study, but the claims and counterclaims just hung in the air. The contrast with the *Perry* trial could not have been starker. And of course, in the Michigan trial, Regnerus himself was subjected to cross-examination.

Ballot initiatives give rise to perhaps the most haphazard factfinding of all. In the free-for-all of an initiative campaign, every kind of misinformation is propagated, ranging from Tam's statements about polygamy gleaned "from the Internet" to the "21 Reasons Why Gender Matters" dictum that homosexuality was a psychological disorder. The only time real rigor is applied to such campaigns is when the outcome becomes a matter of litigation, and a court combs through what the wide world is willing to say.

To be sure, a trial is far from the most democratic decision-making forum. For anyone who cares about both rigorous debate and the democratic process, this raises a painful dilemma. Scholars have written, and will continue to write, extensively on the question of how to balance legislative and judicial decision-making in a constitutional democracy. For my part, I think of the trial as a truth-finding mechanism whose results can then be brought into the public sphere. Just as we can understand texts we never could have written, so too can a polity absorb a debate it could never itself have produced.

Opponents of judicial intervention will point out that trials are not like academic discussions that can simply be dropped into democratic debate—trials actually *resolve* the debate. The people of California cannot appreciate *Perry* as a truth-finding mechanism, because the trial has foreclosed them from debating any further. Yet one virtue of the Supreme Court's decision to proceed incrementally is that other jurisdictions have had the option to live with the *Perry* trial. And even when, as I expect will happen shortly, same-sex marriage becomes a national reality in the United States, the trial can also be exported to the some two hundred nations that still do not have marriage equality, adding another layer to their own legal and political conversations on the topic. Nations can live under the truths of the trial before they are asked to live up to them.

Critics may believe I admire the *Perry* trial simply because the side I favor prevailed, not because of the dialogue it produced. Yet both parties in *Perry* were represented by experienced, capable advocates; they had the entire world of experts in relevant fields at their disposal; they had ample resources and abundant opportunity to test the evidence and arguments of the opposing side. The reason the trial was lopsided and the outcome comprehensively in favor of the plaintiffs was not due to the limitations of the trial's fact-finding procedures, witness intimidation, or judicial bias. It was because the opponents finally had nowhere to turn, and their arguments were revealed for what they are: wholly unpersuasive. So let me pre-commit myself: Next time such a legal controversy arises that implicates thorny "legislative" facts, let it go to trial. Let us try whether women regret their abortions, whether guns deter crime, or whether climate change is occurring. And let the product of the trial be disseminated throughout all forums in which the debate is taking place. For me, the *Perry* trial explored not one, but two civil ceremonies—the ceremony of marriage and the ceremony of the trial. I have come to see that my convictions about the importance of the civil trial are just as consequential as my convictions about marriage. And so I say again—for the next great legal controversy that turns on key legislative facts: *Let there be a trial.*

EPITHALAMIUM

W hen I left New Haven to live with Ron in New York, the dean of NYU School of Law, Richard Revesz, offered me the Earl Warren Professorship of Constitutional Law. It was a good fit for me, he said, given my interests in civil rights and constitutional law. Reluctantly, I declined, saying that as attorney general of California, Earl Warren had approved the internment of individuals of Japanese descent. Dean Revesz said that he completely understood and would get back to me in a few days with the name of a new chair. He called me back and offered me the Chief Justice Earl Warren Professorship of Constitutional Law. Repressing a lot of reactions, I asked him how the addition of "Chief Justice" could possibly make a difference. He answered that he had spent the intervening days rereading a biography of Earl Warren, and learned that as Chief Justice, Warren had expressed regret for his actions during the internment.

"Wouldn't it be great," he asked, "if your chair embodied how much an individual can grow over a single lifetime?" I accepted the chair.

The trial has led me to see a deeper meaning in the title. Chief Justice Warren wrote the opinion in *Loving v. Virginia,* which guaranteed the right of individuals of different races to marry. In large part because of that opinion, I am barely conscious of being in an interracial marriage. I am confident that at some point, same-sex marriage will be as uncontroversial as interracial marriage is in the United States—and, someday, in the world. As same-sex marriage becomes more routine, we are again witnessing how much people can grow over a single lifetime.

This includes me. I remember sitting in the Supreme Court listening to the oral arguments in *Lawrence v. Texas* in 2003. The question before the Court was whether gay people could be deemed outlaws in Texas and twelve other states. When the sodomy statute was struck down, I felt I had taken a huge step forward toward full psychic citizenship in this country. I had grown up, after all, with the story of Sodom and Gomorrah—in which Lot and his wife repel a mob of men who wish to rape the two men (who are angels in disguise) lodging with them. Like Ryan Kendall, I was horrified to learn at a young age that I would be considered a "sodomite," the villain in the story. Of course, it is hard to identify with anyone in that story, as its ostensible hero, Lot, offers his daughters to the would-be rapists instead.

Ten years later to the day, in 2013, I returned to the Court for oral arguments in *Perry.* This time I sat next to my husband. The question before the Court was whether gay people could be denied marriage in states across the land. This time, the answer was not as resoundingly in our favor. Yet the narrative had shifted. Rather than trying in vain to find a place for myself in the Sodom story, I chose to inhabit the Greco-Roman version of it. In this rendition, an old married couple—Philemon and Baucis—are visited by the gods. Like Lot and his wife, they are spared from destruction because of their virtue. Yet unlike the story of Lot and his wife, this story ends happily for its protagonists. After their city is destroyed, the gods grant them a wish.

They wish that they might die in the same moment, so that neither need know the world without the other. They live out long lives as keepers of the temple. But one day, they are nowhere to be seen. In their stead are two trees—an oak and a linden—with interlaced branches.

I loved this story as a child, and saw it anew when I read the poet Thom Gunn's reimagining of it:

> *Two trunks like bodies, bodies like twined trunks*
> *Supported by their wooden hug. Leaves shine*
> *In tender habit at the extremities.*
> *Truly each other's, they have embraced so long*
> *Their barks have met and wedded in one flow*
> *Blanketing both.*

Perhaps because Gunn was gay, I have always read this poem as an epithalamium for a same-sex couple.

I believe we are shaped by our wishes as much as by our actions. If I am right, then Ron and I will take the shape of these trees. We wish this for ourselves, and we wish each of our children will also someday know the same embrace. The law, of course, cannot grant this wish. Yet the law can help us move from imagining ourselves as the antagonists whom the story must destroy to thinking of ourselves as its protagonists. And it can enlarge and ratify our capacity for love so that we are ready to find the person without whom life is unimaginable. Law cannot grant this wish, but it can help us make it.

While *Perry* did not end (and could not have ended) the debate over same-sex marriage, I believe it will stand the test of time as one of the most powerful civil-rights trials in

American history. And although the fight for marriage equality in the United States may soon come to a close, *Perry* is an exemplar of the meaning of human dignity both here and abroad.

There is still much work to be done. Even in the United States, where gay rights appear to be making inexorable progress, battles old and new remain to be won. In twenty-nine states, gays can be lawfully terminated from a job simply for being gay. Indeed, if anyone had told me ten years ago that workplace equality would lag so far behind marriage equality, I would not have believed it. I strongly suspect that the reason for the discrepancy is that the proposed Employment Non-Discrimination Act (ENDA) protects not only lesbians, gays, and bisexuals, but also transgender individuals. Assuring the dignity of individuals who are transgender is one of equality's next frontiers. Another such frontier concerns finding the right balance between religious liberties and gay equality. I view the next key judicial decisions to be those, like *Hobby Lobby,* that determine how broadly people of faith will be exempted from anti-discrimination laws that generally forbid discrimination on the basis of sexual orientation.

When one takes a global perspective, the challenges for the LGBT community look staggering, exposing any progress narrative about gay rights as parochial and premature. More than two hundred nations still lack marriage equality. And many appear to be moving starkly in the opposite direction from the United States. Countries have recently criminalized "propaganda of nontraditional sexual relations" (Russia), introduced a law that imposes prison sentences on gay couples (Nigeria), and reinstated a ban on consensual same-sex intimacy (India). Ron and I would still be deemed criminals in some six dozen countries; we could be put to death for homosexual conduct in eight of them.

I am of course most trenchantly reminded of this when I travel. In December 2013, I joined Justice Albie Sachs for a conversation in Taipei on marriage equality. I had been invited there in part because Taiwan seems likely to become the first East Asian nation to legalize same-sex marriage. Sachs was the Supreme Court justice who wrote the opinion for the Constitutional Court of South Africa that legalized same-sex marriage in that country. His moral authority is written on his body: he lost an eye and an arm to a car bomb while engaged in antiapartheid activism. In his same-sex marriage decision, he observed, as Vaughn Walker later would, that equality could either mean state-sanctioned marriage for gays and straights, or state-sanctioned marriage for no one. He wrote that the law required the "equality of the vineyard and not equality of the graveyard."

Through an interpreter, Sachs and I addressed a packed audience in a dance studio famous as a site of liberal activism. Everyone was polite, but emotions ran high. As one of the young audience members said to me afterward, it was the first time that someone "with an Asian face" had argued against her elders, many of whom seemed deeply opposed to same-sex marriage. I called Ron that night to tell him I felt I had done more for gay rights in that evening than I had in the past year.

If I were to pinpoint the moment in the debate when I grew most impassioned, it would be when I began to tell the story of Philemon and Baucis. I spoke of interlaced trees, of the dream of finding the person without whom life is unimaginable.

As I finished, I could see that while some audience members were moved to tears, others looked nonplussed. "What is the argument," an audience member asked afterward, "for those of us who are not like you?" I could not tell whether the questioner objected to the fact that I was gay, that I was American, or that I was a citer of Western mythologies. But his question was manifestly a challenge to the idiosyncrasy of my perspective. I shifted in my seat.

"Let me tell you," I said, "about a trial."

ACKNOWLEDGMENTS

Emma Berry, Guido Calabresi, Sara Chinn, Denise Cote, Ariela Dubler, Rae Dylan, Priscilla Parkhurst Ferguson, Robert Ferguson, David Glasgow, Simon Howe, Michael Kavey, Julia Kaye, Rachel Klayman, Betsy Lerner, Daryl Levinson, Kristen Loveland, Bernadette Meyler, Trevor Morrison, Meghna Philip, Alexis Piazza, Richard Revesz, Brad Sears, David Shieh, Reva Siegel, Lindsay Friaglia Stankovich, Molly Stern, David Weber, Annmarie Zell.

I gratefully acknowledge financial support from the Filomen D'Agostino and Max E. Greenberg Research Fund.

Final thanks to my family, and most of all to Ron Stoneham, who daily ennobles my life with his kindness, strength, humor, and wisdom.

PERRY TRIAL CHRONOLOGY

Day One—January 11, 2010

Opening Statements

THEODORE "TED" OLSON, Gibson, Dunn & Crutcher, for the plaintiffs

THERESE "TERRY" STEWART, Deputy City Attorney, for the City and County of San Francisco

CHARLES "CHUCK" COOPER, Cooper & Kirk, for the proponents

JEFFREY ZARRILLO, *Plaintiff*
Direct examination by David Boies, Boies Schiller & Flexner

PAUL KATAMI, *Plaintiff*
Direct examination by David Boies. Cross-examination by Brian Raum, Alliance Defense Fund (ADF)

KRISTIN PERRY, *Plaintiff*
Direct examination by Ted Olson

SANDRA STIER, *Plaintiff*
Direct examination by Ted Olson

NANCY COTT, *Jonathan Trumbull Professor of American History, Harvard University*
Direct examination by Theodore "Ted" Boutrous, Gibson, Dunn & Crutcher

Day Two—January 12, 2010

NANCY COTT
Direct and redirect examination by Ted Boutrous. Cross-examination by David Thompson, Cooper & Kirk

GEORGE CHAUNCEY, *Samuel Knight Professor of History and American Studies, Yale University*
Direct examination by Terry Stewart. Cross-examination by David Thompson

Day Three—January 13, 2010

GEORGE CHAUNCEY
Cross-examination by David Thompson. Redirect examination by Terry Stewart

LETITIA ANNE PEPLAU, *Distinguished Research Professor, UCLA*
Direct and redirect examination by Christopher Dusseault, Gibson, Dunn & Crutcher. Cross-examination by Nicole Moss, Cooper & Kirk

Day Four—January 14, 2010

EDMUND EGAN, *Chief Economist, City and County of San Francisco*
Direct and redirect examination by Christine Van Aken, City Attorney. Cross-examination by Peter Patterson, Cooper & Kirk

ILAN MEYER, *Professor of Clinical Sociomedical Sciences, Columbia University*
Direct and redirect examination by Christopher Dusseault. Cross-examination by Howard Nielson, Cooper & Kirk

Day Five—January 15, 2010

MICHAEL LAMB, *Professor of Psychology, University of Cambridge*
Direct and redirect examination by Matthew McGill, Gibson, Dunn & Crutcher. Cross-examination by David Thompson

HELEN ZIA, *author and journalist*
Direct and redirect examination by Danny Chou, Deputy City Attorney. Cross-examination by Brian Raum.

Day Six—January 19, 2010

JERRY SANDERS, *Mayor of San Diego*
Direct and redirect examination by Dennis Herrera, City
Attorney. Cross-examination by Brian Raum

LEE BADGETT, *Professor of Economics, University of
Massachusetts Amherst*
Direct and redirect examination by David Boies. Cross-
examination by Chuck Cooper

Day Seven—January 20, 2010

RYAN KENDALL, *NCIC Agent, Denver Police Department*
Direct and redirect examination by Ronald Flynn, Deputy City
Attorney. Cross-examination by James Campbell, ADF

GARY SEGURA, *Professor of Political Science, Stanford University*
Direct examination by Ted Boutrous. Cross-examination by
David Thompson

Day Eight—January 21, 2010

GARY SEGURA
Cross-examination by David Thompson. Redirect examination
by Ted Boutrous

HAK-SHING "BILL" TAM, *Executive Director of Traditional Family
Coalition* (called by plaintiffs as a hostile witness)
Examination by David Boies. Examination by Nicole Moss

Day Nine—January 22, 2010

GREGORY M. HEREK, *Professor of Psychology at the University of
California–Davis*
Direct and redirect examination by Ethan Dettmer, Gibson,
Dunn & Crutcher. Cross-examination by Howard Nielson

Day Ten—January 25, 2010

KENNETH MILLER, *Associate Professor, Claremont McKenna College*
Direct examination by David Thompson. Cross-examination by David Boies

Day Eleven—January 26, 2010

KENNETH MILLER
  Cross-examination by David Boies and Tamar Pachter, *Deputy Attorney General for the State of California*. Redirect examination by David Thompson
DAVID BLANKENHORN, *President, Institute for American Values*
  Direct examination by David Thompson. Cross-examination by David Boies

Day Twelve—January 27, 2010

DAVID BLANKENHORN
  Cross-examination by David Boies. Redirect examination by Chuck Cooper

June 16, 2010

Closing Arguments
TED OLSON, for the plaintiffs
CHUCK COOPER, for the proponents

1970s

October 15, 1971: The Supreme Court of Minnesota rules against a same-sex couple, Jack Baker and James Michael McConnell, who seek the right to marry.

October 18, 1971: The US Court of Appeals for the Eighth Circuit rejects McConnell's claim that the University of Minnesota's Board of Regents acted unlawfully when it rescinded its offer to employ him based on his attempt to marry Baker. The court calls same-sex marriage a "socially repugnant concept."

October 10, 1972: The US Supreme Court summarily affirms the Supreme Court of Minnesota's 1971 ruling against Baker and McConnell by dismissing their appeal "for want of a substantial federal question."

1973: Maryland becomes the first state to explicitly enact a statute defining marriage as a union of one man and one woman.

November 1973 and May 1974: Appellate courts in Kentucky and Washington rule against same-sex couples seeking the right to marry.

1975–1979: A growing number of municipalities—including Berkeley, Los Angeles, and San Francisco—enact ordinances barring discrimination based on sexual orientation in the private sector.

1977: Reacting to attempts by several same-sex couples to marry, California enacts legislation clarifying that marriage under state law is "between a man and a woman."

1977: Singer Anita Bryant launches the "Save Our Children" campaign to overturn a Dade County, Florida, ordinance banning discrimination based on sexual orientation. Warning of a "hair-raising pattern of recruitment and outright seductions and molestation" by gays, the campaign convinces a majority of voters to rescind the law in a June referendum. Bryant's activism in Florida sparks successful efforts to repeal sexual-orientation discrimination ordinances elsewhere in the country.

January–November 1978: Harvey Milk serves on the San Francisco Board of Supervisors as one of the nation's first openly gay elected officials. Former supervisor Dan White assassinates Milk and mayor George Moscone on November 27.

November 1978: California voters reject the Briggs Initiative, which would have permitted the firing of schoolteachers who engaged in "advocating, soliciting, imposing, encouraging or promoting of private or public homosexual activity directed at, or likely to come to the attention of, schoolchildren and/or other employees."

1980s

February 1982: Wisconsin enacts the nation's first statewide ban on discrimination based on sexual orientation in private-sector employment.

December 1982: San Francisco mayor Dianne Feinstein vetoes an ordinance that would have provided health benefits to the domestic partners, including same-sex partners, of municipal employees.

1984: The City of Berkeley, California, approves the nation's first municipal domestic-partnership registry for government employees. The city expands the law in 1991 to allow members of the general public to register.

June 20, 1986: As head of the Office of Legal Counsel, Charles Cooper authors a memo finding that the Rehabilitation Act does not prohibit discrimination based on a fear of contagion regarding AIDS—"whether reasonable or not."

June 30, 1986: In *Bowers v. Hardwick*, the US Supreme Court votes 5–4 to uphold a Georgia law criminalizing same-sex sexual conduct. The Court declares there is no fundamental right under the Constitution "to engage in homosexual sodomy."

1987–1988: President Ronald Reagan nominates Vaughn Walker to the US District Court for the Northern District of California. The nomination founders over Walker's membership in San Francisco's controversial Olympic Club, as well as over allegations that Walker is anti-gay.

September–November 1989: On September 7, 1989, President George H. W. Bush nominates Vaughn Walker to the US District Court for the Northern District of California. The Senate confirms him on November 21, 1989.

May 1989: With the passage of the Registered Partnership Act, Denmark becomes the first country to provide nationwide legal recognition of same-sex unions, including nearly all the rights of marriage.

1989: An episode of the hit show *thirtysomething* shows two men in bed together. Religious groups boycott the network, sponsors withdraw, and affiliates refuse to air the show.

1990s

1990: President George H. W. Bush signs the Hate Crimes Statistics Act, requiring the federal government to collect data on "crimes that manifest evidence of prejudice based on," among other things, "sexual orientation." It is the first federal statute to address bias based on sexual orientation expressly.

September 1992: California governor Pete Wilson signs a state law banning employment discrimination based on sexual orientation in the public and private sectors.

May 5, 1993: The Supreme Court of Hawaii issues a landmark ruling in favor of same-sex couples seeking the right to marry. The plurality opinion reasons that the denial of marriage licenses to same-sex couples is a form of sex discrimination. The court does not order same-sex marriages to begin but rather sends the case back to the trial court for proceedings under the appropriate standard.

1993: Congress passes the military policy known as "Don't Ask, Don't Tell." The policy requires the discharge of most openly lesbian, gay, and bisexual service members from the US armed forces. It also terminates any service member who "has married or attempted to marry a person known to be of the same biological sex."

October 28, 1994: MTV airs an episode of *The Real World* in which HIV-positive Pedro Zamora, a fan favorite, exchanges rings with his boyfriend.

March 1995: Utah enacts a law denying recognition of marriages performed in other jurisdictions. Other states begin passing laws and constitutional amendments to block the legalization and/or recognition of same-sex marriages.

March 1996: A Gallup poll finds 27 percent of respondents support the recognition of "marriages between homosexuals."

May 20, 1996: The US Supreme Court rules in *Romer v. Evans* that Amendment 2, a 1992 Colorado ballot measure, violates the federal Constitution's Equal Protection Clause. Amendment 2 would have invalidated any law in Colorado, whether state or local, that protected against anti-gay discrimination.

September 21, 1996: President Bill Clinton signs the Defense of Marriage Act. The Act defines marriage as a union between a man and woman for all federal purposes. It also allows states to deny recognition to same-sex marriages lawfully performed in other states.

December 3, 1996: After a bench trial, Hawaii trial court judge Kevin Chang rules that the state's ban on same-sex marriage violates the Hawaiian constitution. He stays his decision pending appeal.

October 1998: Bias-motivated violence against LGBT people receives unprecedented national attention after the brutal murder of Matthew Shepard, a twenty-one-year-old University of Wyoming student.

November 3, 1998: Hawaii voters authorize legislators to amend the state constitution to bar same-sex marriage.

November 1998: California's Proposition 22 qualifies for the March 2000 ballot. The proposal would amend California's Family Code to recognize only heterosexual marriages and to ensure that the state does not recognize same-sex marriages performed outside California.

October 2, 1999: California governor Gray Davis signs legislation legalizing domestic partnerships in California.

December 20, 1999: The Supreme Court of Vermont rules that under the state constitution, same-sex couples cannot be deprived of benefits and protections afforded opposite-sex couples. The court tasks the state legislature with implementing marital or equivalent rights for gay couples.

2000

March 7, 2000: Proposition 22 passes in California with 61 percent of the vote.

April 26, 2000: Vermont becomes the first US state to recognize civil unions.

December 2000: The Netherlands becomes the first country to legalize same-sex marriage. The law takes effect in 2001.

2003

February 2003: Belgium becomes the second country to legalize same-sex marriage.

June 26, 2003: The US Supreme Court strikes down state sodomy laws in *Lawrence v. Texas,* overruling *Bowers v. Hardwick.*

September 19, 2003: California governor Gray Davis signs legislation expanding domestic-partner rights in California. This gives same-sex couples almost all the material benefits of marriage, but still withholds the word "marriage" from their relationships.

November 18, 2003: The Supreme Judicial Court of Massachusetts holds that limiting the protections and benefits of marriage to opposite-sex couples violates the state's constitution. This is the first state to legalize same-sex marriage in the United States.

2004

January–February 2004: In his January 2004 State of the Union address, President George W. Bush condemns "activist judges" for "redefining marriage by court order," and suggests that he would support a federal constitutional amendment on marriage. The next month, he expressly calls for a constitutional amendment restricting marriage to unions between a man and a woman.

January 12, 2004: New Jersey grants limited rights to same-sex domestic partners.

February–March 2004: San Francisco mayor Gavin Newsom directs the City Clerk's Office to issue marriage licenses to same-sex couples. The Proposition 22 Legal Defense Fund, among others, sues to stop the licenses.

February 27, 2004–March 2004: The mayor of New Paltz, New York, begins issuing marriage licenses to gay couples. In the ensuing legal skirmish, a judge bans the mayor from performing same-sex unions not licensed in New York, and the mayor is charged with misdemeanors for conducting gay marriage ceremonies. The district attorney eventually drops the charges.

March 2004: Thirty percent of respondents in an NBC/*Wall Street Journal* poll favor same-sex marriage.

March 11, 2004: The Supreme Court of California orders San Francisco city officials to stop issuing marriage licenses to gay couples pending its review.

May 17, 2004: The first legal gay wedding in United States takes place in Massachusetts.

August 12, 2004: The Supreme Court of California holds that San Francisco officials were not authorized to give marriage licenses to gay couples. An estimated 4,000 marriages, conducted between February and March 2004, are invalidated.

September 8, 2004: The California Superior Court upholds the California domestic-partnership law against challenges that it undermines Proposition 22.

September 2004: Judge Vaughn Walker becomes chief judge in the US District Court for the Northern District of California.

November 2004: Arkansas, Georgia, Kentucky, Michigan, Mississippi, Montana, North Dakota, Ohio, Oklahoma, Oregon, and Utah pass amendments banning same-sex marriages.

2005

March 14, 2005: California Superior Court judge Richard Kramer finds that Prop 22 violates the state constitution.

April 20, 2005: Connecticut enacts a law authorizing civil unions, becoming the second US state to do so after Vermont.

June–July 2005: Spain and Canada become the third and fourth countries, respectively, to legalize same-sex marriage.

September 2005: California's legislature becomes the first US state legislature to pass a bill legalizing same-sex marriage. Governor Arnold Schwarzenegger vetoes the bill.

2006

April 5, 2006: A Fox News/Opinion Dynamics poll shows public support for same-sex marriage at 33 percent.

July 14, 2006: The US Court of Appeals for the Eighth Circuit upholds a state constitutional amendment in Nebraska providing that same-sex marriages and "other similar same-sex relationship[s] shall not be valid or recognized" in the state.

October 5, 2006: The California Court of Appeal upholds the state's ban on same-sex marriage, reversing in part the March 2005 decision of the California Superior Court.

October 25, 2006: The New Jersey Supreme Court gives the state legislature six months to "either amend the marriage statutes to include same-sex couples or enact a parallel statutory structure by another name."

November 2006: Colorado, Idaho, South Carolina, South Dakota, Tennessee, Virginia, and Wisconsin pass amendments banning same-sex marriage. Of the twenty states that have considered constitutional amendments banning same-sex marriage, Arizona is the first to defeat such a measure.

November 2006: South Africa becomes the fifth country to legalize same-sex marriage.

December 14, 2006: New Jersey passes legislation permitting civil unions and recognizing those solemnized in other states.

2007

April 21, 2007: Washington legalizes domestic partnerships.

May 9, 2007: Oregon legalizes domestic partnerships.

May 31, 2007: New Hampshire legalizes civil unions.

October 12, 2007: California governor Arnold Schwarzenegger vetoes another same-sex marriage bill, maintaining that the legislature should allow the California Supreme Court to rule on Proposition 22, and reiterating support for domestic-partnership rights.

2008

April 12, 2008: At an annual meeting of the Log Cabin Republicans, California governor Arnold Schwarzenegger vows to oppose efforts to change the California Constitution to ban same-sex marriage.

May 15, 2008: The Supreme Court of California strikes down Proposition 22—defining marriage as between a man and a woman—as unconstitutional.

May 17, 2008: California governor Arnold Schwarzenegger says he supports the California Supreme Court's decision "even though his personal view is that 'marriage is between a man and a woman.' "

May 22, 2008: Maryland enacts two bills establishing limited domestic-partnership rights in that state.

June 2, 2008: California voter initiative Proposition 8 qualifies for the November 4, 2008, ballot. Proposition 8 proposes amending the California Constitution to read: "Only marriage between a man and a woman is valid or recognized in California." The initiative proponents are Martin Gutierrez, Dennis Hollingsworth, Mark Jansson, Gail Knight, and Hak-Shing "Bill" Tam.

June 17, 2008: California begins issuing licenses to conduct same-sex weddings.

June 17, 2008: Norway passes same-sex marriage legislation. The law takes effect in 2009.

June 2008: Nine LGBT organizations detail their marriage-equality strategy in a statement titled "Make Change, Not Lawsuits."

October 10, 2008: The Connecticut Supreme Court strikes down bans on same-sex marriage. Connecticut becomes the second US state to legalize same-sex marriage through judicial decision.

November 4, 2008: California voters pass Proposition 8 by a vote of 52.3 percent to 47.7 percent.

November 4, 2008: Constitutional amendments banning same-sex marriage pass in Florida and Arizona.

November 5, 2008: The day after Proposition 8 passes, three lawsuits challenging the initiative are filed in California state court. These cases will be consolidated and decided under the case heading *Strauss v. Horton.*

2009

March 3, 2009: Gay & Lesbian Advocates & Defenders files a federal lawsuit in the US District Court for the District of Massachusetts on behalf of several gay individuals and couples, alleging that Section 3 of the federal Defense of Marriage Act, which defines marriage for all federal purposes as a union of a man and a woman, is unconstitutional.

April–May 2009: Sweden becomes the seventh country to legalize same-sex marriage.

April 3, 2009: The Supreme Court of Iowa unanimously finds the state law barring same-sex marriage to be unconstitutional. Iowa becomes the third US state to legalize same-sex marriage by judicial decision.

April 7, 2009: The Vermont legislature overrides Governor Jim Douglas's veto and legalizes same-sex marriage in that state. Vermont is the first US state to pass same-sex marriage by legislative action.

May 6, 2009: Maine governor John Baldacci becomes the first governor to sign a bill legalizing same-sex marriage. Opponents of same-sex marriage respond with an initiative to put the issue before the voters in a referendum, and the law is put on hold pending the outcome.

May 22, 2009: Two same-sex couples in California—Kristin Perry and Sandra Stier, and Paul Katami and Jeffrey Zarrillo—file a lawsuit challenging Proposition 8 in the US District Court for the Northern District of California. The lawsuit—captioned *Perry v. Schwarzenegger*—is assigned to Judge Vaughn Walker.

May 26, 2009: In *Strauss v. Horton,* the Supreme Court of California upholds Proposition 8 as a valid amendment to the state constitution. However, the court does not invalidate the estimated 18,000 same-sex marriages that took place in California between June and November 2008.

May 27, 2009: The *Perry* plaintiffs and their lawyers hold a press conference announcing their lawsuit.

May 27, 2009: A Gallup poll shows public support for same-sex marriage at 40 percent.

May 27, 2009: The plaintiffs file a motion for a preliminary injunction in *Perry,* asking Judge Walker to stop the enforcement of Proposition 8 and permit gay marriages in California while the lawsuit is being decided.

May 28, 2009: The official proponents of Proposition 8 move to intervene to defend Proposition 8 in *Perry.*

May 31, 2009: The Nevada legislature passes a domestic-partnership law, overriding a veto by Governor Jim Gibbons.

June 3, 2009: New Hampshire legalizes same-sex marriage.

June 25, 2009: The Campaign for California Families moves to intervene in *Perry,* alleging that it has a "significant protectable interest" in the lawsuit that the proponents would not adequately represent.

June 29, 2009: Wisconsin enacts a domestic-partnership statute providing limited rights to same-sex couples. Opponents of the law quickly challenge it in court, arguing that it violates a 2006 state constitutional amendment barring same-sex marriage as well as the recognition of any "legal status identical or substantially similar to that of marriage." After years of litigation, the state's high court upholds the domestic-partnership law in 2014.

June 30, 2009: Judge Walker approves the unopposed motion of the proponents to intervene in *Perry* and expresses his inclination to hold a trial.

July 8, 2009: Our Family Coalition; Lavender Seniors of East Bay; and Parents, Families, and Friends of Lesbians and Gays (together, "Our Family Coalition"), represented by the ACLU Foundation of Northern California, Lambda Legal, and the National Center for Lesbian Rights, file a motion to intervene in *Perry.*

July 8, 2009: The Commonwealth of Massachusetts files a suit challenging the federal government's refusal under the Defense of Marriage Act to recognize same-sex marriages.

July 20, 2009: David Boies, an attorney for the plaintiffs, pens an editorial for the *Wall Street Journal* explaining why he and Ted Olson "are working to overturn California's Proposition 8."

July 23, 2009: The City and County of San Francisco files a motion to intervene in *Perry.*

July 29, 2009: Chuck Cooper, lead counsel for the proponents in *Perry,* responds to David Boies with a letter also published by the *Wall Street Journal.*

August 19, 2009: Judge Walker denies the motions to intervene of Our Family Coalition and the Campaign for California Families, but allows the City of San Francisco to intervene.

August 21, 2009: The plaintiffs in *Perry* serve discovery requests on proponents, seeking internal documents and communications from the Proposition 8 campaign.

September 9, 2009: The proponents in *Perry* request summary judgment.

October 11, 2009: Governor Schwarzenegger signs legislation ensuring that California will recognize lawful same-sex marriages from outside the state if they were performed before the passage of Prop 8. The legislation also provides that same-sex marriages from outside the state that were performed after Prop 8 took effect will be recognized in California as domestic partnerships.

October 14, 2009: Judge Walker denies summary judgment, meaning that *Perry* will proceed to trial.

October 28, 2009: President Obama signs the Matthew Shepard and James Byrd Jr. Hate Crimes Prevention Act. The act expands the existing federal hate-crimes law to cover, among other things, certain violent crimes committed based on sexual orientation or gender identity.

November 3, 2009: Maine voters reject the same-sex marriage bill signed by Governor Baldacci, preventing it from becoming law.

December 16–18, 2009: The Council of the District of Columbia passes a law legalizing gay marriage. The law goes into effect on March 30, 2010.

December 17, 2009: The Ninth Circuit announces that it has "approved on an experimental basis, the limited use of cameras in federal district court within the circuit."

December 21, 2009: A coalition of media companies expresses interest in televising the *Perry* trial.

December 28–29, 2009: The proponents in *Perry* object to public broadcast of the trial, citing "harassment against Proposition 8 supporters," and maintain that the courts' alteration of the rules on broadcasting requires a notice and comment period.

2010

January 6, 2010: Judge Walker announces that the trial will be recorded (subject to Ninth Circuit approval), with a live feed going to various federal courthouses and the recording posted on YouTube.

January 8, 2010: Ninth Circuit Chief Judge Alex Kozinski permits live streaming of pre-trial and trial proceedings to federal courthouses.

January 8, 2010: The proponents ask Judge Walker to stay his broadcast order, and they file an emergency petition with the Ninth Circuit to stop the broadcast. The plaintiffs respond with support for Judge Walker's plan.

January 8, 2010: The Ninth Circuit panel denies the proponents' petition to stop the broadcast.

January 8, 2010: Tam, one of the five official proponents, moves to withdraw from the *Perry* litigation because he "is fearful for his personal safety and the safety of his family," because he "does not like the great burden of complying with discovery requests," and because he "is tired and wants peace."

January 9, 2010: The proponents ask the US Supreme Court to halt the broadcasting of the *Perry* trial.

January 11, 2010: Two hours before the trial is scheduled to begin, the US Supreme Court orders a temporary block of the broadcasting of the *Perry* trial. Live streaming to other rooms in the San Francisco courthouse is permitted.

January 11–January 27, 2010: The civil bench trial in *Perry v. Schwarzenegger* occurs.

January 13, 2010: The US Supreme Court, in a 5–4 decision, issues a permanent order blocking video coverage of the *Perry* trial. The high court finds that the courts below did not follow the appropriate procedures before changing their rules to allow the broadcast.

February 7, 2010: Dubbing it the "biggest open secret" in the trial, the *San Francisco Chronicle* reports that Judge Walker is gay.

May 4, 2010: A Gallup poll shows public support for same-sex marriage at 44 percent.

May–June 2010: Portugal and Iceland legalize same-sex marriage, the eighth and ninth countries to do so, respectively.

June 16, 2010: Judge Walker presides over closing arguments in *Perry*.

July 2010: Argentina becomes the first Latin American country to approve marriage equality.

August 4, 2010: In *Perry*, Judge Walker strikes down Proposition 8 under the Due Process and Equal Protection Clauses of the US Constitution.

August 5, 2010: The *New York Times* praises Judge Walker's *Perry* decision as "an instant landmark in American legal history" and a "stirring and eloquently reasoned denunciation of all forms of irrational discrimination."

August 16, 2010: The Ninth Circuit stays enforcement of Judge Walker's decision in *Perry* pending the appeal proceedings.

October 27, 2010: President Barack Obama says of his opposition to same-sex marriage: "Attitudes evolve, including mine."

December 1, 2010: The proponents move to disqualify Ninth Circuit Judge Stephen Reinhardt as a panel member assigned to the *Perry* case based on his wife's position as executive director of the ACLU of Southern California. The Ninth Circuit denies the motion.

December 6, 2010: A Ninth Circuit panel holds oral arguments in *Perry*.

December 22, 2010: President Barack Obama signs legislation repealing "Don't Ask, Don't Tell."

2011

January 4, 2011: In *Perry*, the Ninth Circuit certifies a state-law question to the California Supreme Court: whether proponents of an initiative measure may defend its constitutionality "when the public officials charged with that duty refuse to do so."

January 31, 2011: Illinois legalizes same-sex civil unions. The law takes effect on June 1, 2011.

February 23, 2011: President Obama directs the Department of Justice to stop defending the constitutionality of the Defense of Marriage Act.

February 23, 2011: Hawaii legalizes civil unions. The law takes effect on January 1, 2012.

March 18, 2011: An ABC News/*Washington Post* poll finds majority support for same-sex marriage for the first time in the poll's history (53 percent).

April 7, 2011: Now-retired Judge Walker confirms he is gay and that he has been in a decade-long same-sex relationship.

April 25, 2011: The proponents in *Perry* file a motion to vacate Judge Walker's ruling, arguing that he should have recused himself because of his long-standing same-sex relationship.

May 11, 2011: Delaware legalizes civil unions. The law takes effect on January 1, 2012.

June 14, 2011: In *Perry*, District Judge James Ware rules that Judge Walker did not have to recuse himself from the case and denies the proponents' motion to vacate.

June 24, 2011: New York enacts a marriage equality law through its legislature. The law takes effect thirty days later.

June 24, 2011: The proponents appeal Judge Ware's ruling on the recusal issue in the *Perry* case.

July 2, 2011: Rhode Island legalizes civil unions.

July 19, 2011: President Obama endorses a bill pending in the US Congress designed to repeal the 1996 Defense of Marriage Act.

November 17, 2011: The Supreme Court of California issues its opinion on the question of state law posed by the Ninth Circuit. The court concludes that proponents may defend voter initiatives when state officials decline to do so.

2012

February 7, 2012: A three-judge panel of the Ninth Circuit upholds Judge Walker's decision, but on substantially narrower grounds.

February 17, 2012: New Jersey governor Chris Christie vetoes legislation that would have legalized gay marriage in that state.

March 1, 2012: Maryland legalizes same-sex marriage. Opponents begin gathering signatures to force a referendum.

March 3, 2012: The play *8*, starring George Clooney and Brad Pitt, premieres in Los Angeles and depicts the events of the *Perry* trial.

May 8, 2012: North Carolina voters pass a constitutional amendment that reads, "Marriage between one man and one woman is the only domestic legal union that shall be valid or recognized in this State."

May 9, 2012: In an interview with Robin Roberts of ABC News, President Obama expresses his personal support for marriage equality. Obama becomes the first sitting US president to back marriage equality.

June 5, 2012: The Ninth Circuit votes against rehearing the *Perry* case en banc.

June 2012: Denmark legalizes same-sex marriage.

June 22, 2012: David Blankenhorn, a witness for the proponents during the *Perry* trial, changes his position on same-sex marriage, writing in the *New York Times* that "the time has come for me to accept gay marriage and emphasize the good that it can do."

July 30, 2012: The *Perry* proponents petition for a writ of certiorari in the US Supreme Court over the constitutionality of Proposition 8.

August 24, 2012: The plaintiffs in *Perry* request that the US Supreme Court deny the proponents' certiorari petition.

September 27, 2012: The US Department of Homeland Security clarifies that it will consider long-term same-sex relationships with US citizens as a mitigating factor in an individual's deportation proceeding.

November 6, 2012: On Election Day, voters in Maine, Maryland, and Washington approve same-sex marriage. Minnesota voters reject a state constitutional amendment that would have banned same-sex marriage.

October 18, 2012: In *Windsor v. United States*, the Second Circuit strikes down the provision in the Defense of Marriage Act that defines marriage, for the purposes of federal law, as a legal union between one man and one woman.

December 7, 2012: The Supreme Court grants writs of certiorari in *Perry* and *Windsor*.

December 2012: A majority of respondents (51 percent) support same-sex marriage in an NBC News/*Wall Street Journal* poll—an increase of 21 percentage points in one year.

2013

February 28, 2013: The US Justice Department files a brief in *Perry* urging the Supreme Court to rule that California voters could not ban same-sex marriage. The brief argues that a state already granting gays extensive rights through civil unions cannot discriminate against them by denying them the word "marriage."

March 7, 2013: Former president Bill Clinton writes in the *Washington Post* that the Defense of Marriage Act is inconsistent "with the principles of a nation that honors freedom, equality and justice above all," and that "as the president who signed the act into law," he has come to believe it is unconstitutional.

March 18, 2013: Hillary Clinton endorses gay marriage.

March 21, 2013: Civil unions are made legal in Colorado. Portions of the law become effective on May 1, 2013, and other portions on January 1, 2014.

March 26, 2013: The US Supreme Court hears oral arguments in *Perry*.

March 27, 2013: The US Supreme Court hears oral arguments in *United States v. Windsor*.

April 2013: Uruguay legalizes same-sex marriage.

April 2013: New Zealand approves same-sex marriage, becoming the first Asia-Pacific nation to do so. The law takes effect in August 2013.

April 29, 2013: NBA center Jason Collins announces he is gay and becomes the first openly gay male athlete active in any of the four major North American professional sports leagues.

May 2013: The legislatures of Rhode Island, Delaware, and Minnesota all legalize same-sex marriage.

May 2013: A sweeping judicial decision in Brazil rules that same-sex couples cannot be denied marriage licenses.

May 2013: France legalizes same-sex marriage.

May 23, 2013: The Boy Scouts ends its ban on gay scouts.

June 12, 2013: Fifty-seven percent of respondents in an ABC News/ *Washington Post* poll favor same-sex marriage.

June 26, 2013: In *Windsor,* the US Supreme Court strikes down the provision of the Defense of Marriage Act limiting federal marriage benefits to opposite-sex couples.

June 26, 2013: In *Perry,* the US Supreme Court rules that the proponents lacked standing to appeal the constitutionality of Proposition 8.

June 27, 2013: President Obama directs the attorney general to work with other members of the cabinet and "review all relevant federal statutes" to ensure that the *Windsor* decision "is implemented swiftly and smoothly."

June 28, 2013: The Ninth Circuit dissolves the stay of the district court's ruling striking down Proposition 8, "effective immediately," returning same-sex marriage to California.

July 17, 2013: Queen Elizabeth II gives royal assent to a bill legalizing same-sex marriage in England and Wales.

July 29, 2013: A Gallup poll shows public support for legalizing same-sex marriage across all fifty states at 52 percent, with 43 percent opposed.

July 29, 2013: In a remark many commentators interpret as a softening position in the Vatican, Pope Francis tells reporters, "If someone is gay and he searches for the Lord and has good will, who am I to judge?"

October 21, 2013: The New Jersey State Superior Court rules that the state is required to permit same-sex marriage in light of the *Windsor* decision and a 2006 New Jersey Supreme Court decision mandating equal benefits for gay couples. Gov. Chris Christie decides not to pursue an appeal. New Jersey becomes the fourteenth state to legalize same-sex marriage.

November 13, 2013: Hawaii legalizes same-sex marriage. One week later, Illinois follows suit.

December 19, 2013: A ruling by the New Mexico Supreme Court makes New Mexico the seventeenth state to legalize same-sex marriage.

2014

February 25–March 7, 2014: Bernard Friedman, a district court judge in Michigan, presides over a two-week trial on the constitutionality of a ban on same-sex marriage, the first since the *Perry* trial.

February 26, 2014: A federal judge strikes down Texas's ban on same-sex marriage. The ruling is stayed while the Fifth Circuit considers an appeal. Its decision will bind Louisiana and Mississippi, the two other states in the circuit.

March 5, 2014: A *Washington Post*/ABC News poll shows record-high public support of 59 percent for same-sex marriage.

April 3, 2014: Brendan Eich resigns from his position as chief executive of Internet company Mozilla after protests about his donation of $1,000 to the Yes-on-8 campaign in California in 2008.

May 9, 2014: A state judge strikes down Arkansas's ban on same-sex marriage. The decision is stayed pending appeal.

May 10, 2014: Michael Sam joins the St. Louis Rams, becoming the first openly gay player drafted to the NFL.

May 19, 2014: A federal judge in Oregon strikes down the state's ban on same-sex marriage. Weeks later, the US Supreme Court declines to issue a stay of the decision. Oregon becomes the eighteenth state with marriage equality.

May 20, 2014: A federal judge strikes down Pennsylvania's ban on same-sex marriage. The next day, Gov. Tom Corbett announces that he will not appeal the ruling, making Pennsylvania the nineteenth state to legalize same-sex marriage.

May 21, 2014: A Gallup poll shows support for same-sex marriage at 55 percent, the highest percentage in the poll's history.

June 6, 2014: A lawsuit challenges North Dakota's ban on same-sex marriage. The filing of the suit means that every existing ban on marriage in the United States has been challenged.

June 6, 2014: A documentary depicting the fight against Proposition 8 and the *Perry* litigation, *The Case Against 8,* is released in theaters.

June 18, 2014: The legislature in Luxembourg approves a bill allowing same-sex couples to marry.

June 25, 2014: The Tenth Circuit Court of Appeals affirms an earlier ruling of the district court in Utah, which struck down Utah's ban on same-sex marriage. It becomes the first appeals court after the Supreme Court decisions in *Windsor* and *Perry* to find that a ban on same-sex marriage violates the US Constitution.

July 18, 2014: The same panel of judges on the Tenth Circuit that decided the Utah case strikes down Oklahoma's ban on same-sex marriage.

July 28, 2014: The Fourth Circuit Court of Appeals affirms a lower court's ruling that Virginia's ban on same-sex marriage is unconstitutional.

August 5, 2014: A state judge upholds Tennessee's ban on same-sex marriage and becomes the first judge to uphold a ban since *Perry*.

August 6, 2014: The Sixth Circuit hears appeals from lower court decisions overturning bans on same-sex marriage in Kentucky, Michigan, Ohio, and Tennessee.

August 21, 2014: A federal judge strikes down Florida's ban on same-sex marriage. The ruling is stayed while the Eleventh Circuit considers an appeal. Its decision will bind Alabama and Georgia, the two other states in the circuit.

September 3, 2014: A federal judge upholds Louisiana's ban on same-sex marriage. He is the first federal judge to uphold a ban since *Perry*.

September 17, 2014: A *New York Times*/CBS News poll shows public support for legalizing same-sex marriage at 56 percent, with a record low of 37 percent opposed.

October 6, 2014: The Supreme Court denies writs of certiorari for petitions arising from challenges to five state bans on same-sex marriage. As a result, lower-court decisions striking down bans in Indiana, Oklahoma, Utah, Wisconsin, and Virginia go into effect. Because the appeals came from three appellate circuits (the Fourth, Seventh, and Tenth), same-sex marriage becomes legal in six other states in those circuits—Colorado, Kansas, North Carolina, South Carolina, West Virginia, and Wyoming. The net effect of this momentous decision to deny review is to bring the number of states with marriage equality, not including the District of Columbia, from nineteen to thirty.

October 7, 2014: The Ninth Circuit issues decisions declaring bans on same-sex marriage unconstitutional in Idaho and Nevada. As a result, same-sex marriage becomes legal in the three other states in the circuit to maintain bans—Alaska, Arizona, and Montana.

October 21, 2014: A federal judge in Puerto Rico dismisses a legal challenge to the territory's ban on same-sex marriage.

November 5–7, 2014: A state judge in St. Louis, Missouri, declares unconstitutional the state's ban on same-sex marriage. Two days later, a federal judge in that state does the same. The state court decision, which applies only to St. Louis, is not stayed, while the federal decision is stayed pending appeal.

November 6, 2014: In a 2–1 decision, the Sixth Circuit upholds same-sex marriage bans in Kentucky, Michigan, Ohio, and Tennessee, thereby becoming the first appellate circuit to do so since *Perry*.

The decision creates a "circuit split" that makes the issue ripe for review by the Supreme Court.

November 25, 2014: A federal judge finds Arkansas's ban on same-sex marriage unconstitutional. Another federal judge finds Mississippi's ban unconstitutional. Each ruling is stayed pending appeals to the Eighth Circuit and Fifth Circuit, respectively.

December 3–19, 2014: The Eleventh Circuit, followed by the US Supreme Court, denies Florida's request to extend the stay of the decision striking down the state's ban on same-sex marriage. As a result, same-sex marriages commence in Florida in January 2015, even while an appeal to the Eleventh Circuit remains pending.

December 16, 2014: The Prime Minister of Ireland announces that a public referendum on same-sex marriage will be held in May 2015.

January 1, 2015: Vietnam abolishes its ban on same-sex marriage. While same-sex marriages are no longer technically prohibited, they are still not recognized or given legal protection.

January 12, 2015: A federal judge finds South Dakota's ban on same-sex marriage unconstitutional. The decision is stayed pending appeal. On the same day, the US Supreme Court declines to grant review of the decision upholding Louisiana's ban on same-sex marriage.

January 16, 2015: The Supreme Court grants review in cases arising from the Sixth Circuit, consolidating appeals from Kentucky, Michigan, Ohio, and Tennessee. This grant makes a national resolution of this issue likely by the end of the Court's term in June 2015.

NOTES

In the course of writing this book, I interviewed the following individuals: Douglas Allen, Lee Badgett, David Blankenhorn, David Boies, Mary Bonauto, Bruce Cain, George Chauncey, Erwin Chemerinsky, Danny Chou, Matthew Coles, Chuck Cooper, Nancy Cott, Jon Davidson, James Esseks, Ronald Flynn, Elizabeth Gill, Jeremy Goldman, Gregory Herek, Rick Jacobs, Robbie Kaplan, Paul Katami, Ryan Kendall, Michael Lamb, Mollie Lee, Loren Marks, Ilan Meyer, Kenneth Miller (via e-mail), Paul Nathanson, Julie Nestingen, Ted Olson, Letitia Peplau, Kristin Perry, Jennifer Pizer, Daniel Robinson, Gary Segura, Terry Stewart, Sandra Stier, Donna Stoneham, Vaughn Walker (after his retirement from the bench), Evan Wolfson, Katherine Young, Jeffrey Zarrillo, and Helen Zia. Quotations from these individuals throughout the book are taken from my interviews, unless they were said in court or another source is indicated in an endnote.

In the interest of space, I have omitted citations to the trial transcript, which is available in its entirety at www.kenjiyoshino.com.

Introduction: Embraced by Law

1 the Defense of Marriage Act (DOMA): 1 USC § 7 (1996).

2 "dealing pain and death": Robert M. Cover, "Violence and the Word," *Yale Law Journal* 95 (July 1986): 1609.

2 "you-will-be-straight": Monique Wittig, *The Straight Mind* (Boston: Beacon Press, 1992), 28.

2 "Until I was twenty-five": Paul Monette, *Becoming a Man: Half a Life Story* (New York: HarperCollins, 1992), 1.

2 "The displacement of family": Andrew Sullivan, *Virtually Normal* (New York: Vintage Books, 1996), 201.

7 "throw around opinions": David Boies, interview by John Dickerson, *Face the Nation*, CBS, August 8, 2010, www.cbsnews.com/htdocs/pdf/FTN_080810.pdf.

8 Writing for the *New Yorker*: Margaret Talbot, "The Gay-Marriage Classroom," *New Yorker*, February 1, 2010.

8 law professor Dale Carpenter criticized: Dale Carpenter, "On the Legal Front Lines of Same-Sex Marriage," review of *Redeeming the*

Dream: The Case for Marriage Equality, by David Boies and Theodore B. Olson, *New York Times,* June 29, 2014.

8 **less than 2 percent:** John H. Langbein, "The Disappearance of Civil Trial in the United States," *Yale Law Journal* 122 (December 2012): 524.

8 **triumph of judicial efficiency:** Ibid.

10 **available nationwide in fewer than twenty:** Caroline Winter, "In 14 Years, Same-Sex Marriage Has Spread Around the World," *Business-Week,* December 4, 2014.

10 **still illegal in more than seventy:** Sara Kavemi, "Focus on Uganda's LGBT Bill Is a Lesson in Our Hypocrisy," *The Huffington Post,* December 3, 2014, www.huffingtonpost.com/sara-kavemi-/focus-on-ugandas-lgbt-bil_b_6258036.html.

10 **In eight countries:** Terri Rupar, "Here Are the Ten Countries Where Homosexuality May Be Punished by Death," *Washington Post,* February 24, 2014.

11 **scene in *Jane Eyre*:** Charlotte Brontë, *Jane Eyre* (New York: W. W. Norton, 2001; 1847), 246.

1: The Plaintiffs

15 **One cartoonist portrayed:** Steve Greenberg, "The Prop. 8 Vote," *Ventura County Star,* November 18, 2008, http://blogs.venturacountystar.com/greenberg/archives/2008/11/.

16 **"All I could think about":** Margaret Talbot, "A Risky Proposal: Is It Too Soon to Petition the Supreme Court on Gay Marriage?" *New Yorker,* January 18, 2010.

16 **Griffin grew up:** Jo Becker, *Forcing the Spring: Inside the Fight for Marriage Equality* (New York: Penguin Press, 2014), 3–4.

17 **It passed with 61 percent:** CBS News, "No to Gay Marriage in CA," CBSNews.com, March 7, 2000.

17 **"Only marriage between":** California Defense of Marriage Act (Proposition 22), Cal. Fam. Code § 308.5 (West 2000).

17 **The first couple to be married:** William Grimes, "Del Martin, Lesbian Activist, Dies at 87," *New York Times,* August 27, 2008.

17 **"sworn duty to uphold":** Gavin Newsom to Nancy Alfaro, February 10, 2004, FindLaw, http://news.findlaw.com/cnn/docs/glrts/sfmayor21004ltr.html.

17 **roughly four thousand:** CNN Library, "Fast Facts: Same-Sex Marriage," CNN, May 31, 2012, www.cnn.com/2012/05/31/us/ff-same-sex-marriage.

19 ordered San Francisco to cease: *Lockyer v. City and County of San Francisco*, 2004 WL 473257 (Cal. 2004).

19 the Newsom marriages: *Lockyer v. City and County of San Francisco*, 33 Cal. 4th 1055 (2004).

19 "Del is eighty-three": Miriam Smith, *Political Institutions and Lesbian and Gay Rights in the United States and Canada* (New York: Routledge, 2008), 1.

19 a group of cases: *In re Coordination Proceeding*, 2005 WL 583129 (Cal. Superior 2005).

19 written submissions alone: *In re Marriage Cases*, 49 Cal. Rptr. 3d 675 (Cal. Ct. App. 2006).

20 first in the nation: Michael J. Klarman, *From the Closet to the Altar* (Oxford University Press: New York, 2012), 120.

20 reversed the lower court: *In re Marriage Cases*, 49 Cal.Rptr.3d 675.

20 legislature passed another bill: Jill Tucker, "Schwarzenegger Vetoes Same-Sex Marriage Bill Again," *San Francisco Chronicle*, October 12, 2007.

20 violated the state's constitution: *In re Marriage Cases*, 183 P.3d 384 (Cal. 2008).

20 " 'the most socially productive' ": Ibid. (quoting *Marvin v. Marvin*, 557 P.2d 106, 122 (Cal. 1976)).

20 in 1948, long before: Perez v. Sharp, 198 P.2d 17 (Cal. 1948).

20 in *Loving v. Virginia*: *Loving v. Virginia*, 388 U.S. 1 (1967).

21 "Only marriage between": Proposition—Marriage—California Marriage Protection Act, 2008 Cal. Legis. Serv. Prop. 8. (Proposition 8) (WEST).

21 but a "revision": *Strauss v. Horton*, 107 P.3d 48 (Cal. 2009).

21 more than five hundred times: Lawrence G. Sager, *Justice in Plainclothes: A Theory of American Constitutional Practice* (New Haven: Yale University Press, 2004), 218.

21 passed with 52.3 percent: Debra Bowen, "Statement of Vote: November 4, 2008, General Election," 13.

21 *Strauss v. Horton*: *Strauss*, at 48.

22 federal law trumps: U.S. Const. art. VI, § 2.

22 famous for winning *Bush v. Gore*: *Bush v. Gore*, 531 U.S. 98 (2000).

22 Olson had become: Jo Becker, "A Conservative's Road to Same-Sex Marriage Advocacy," *New York Times*, August 18, 2009.

22 one of a few: Ibid.

23 Olson worked to end race-based: Ibid.

23 argued against allowing women: *United States v. Virginia*, 518 U.S. 515 (1996).

23 executive branch's wartime powers: Becker, "Conservative's Road."

23 *defending* Prop 8: Talbot, "Risky Proposal."

23 got the job: Ibid.

23 "first couple of the legal conservative world": Jeffrey Toobin, *The Nine* (New York: Anchor Books, 2008), 315.

23 "If Hillary Clinton's vast right-wing conspiracy": Ibid.

23 the *Citizens United* case: Citizens United v. FEC, 588 U.S. 310 (2010).

23 wrote a legal opinion: Talbot, "Risky Proposal."

23 slammed a proposed amendment: Becker, "Conservative's Road."

24 justify governmental restrictions: Ibid.

24 "just be some hired gun": Ibid.

24 known as "the devil": Ted Olson, interview by Gloria Borger, CNN, December 8, 2012, http://transcripts.cnn.com/TRANSCRIPTS/1212/08/cnr.06.html.

24 "I'm the devil to a different group": Ibid.

24 Robert Bork declared: Becker, "Conservative's Road."

24 "a betrayal of everything": Robert Barnes, "Stalwart of the Right Presses the Case for Gay Marriage," *Washington Post*, June 14, 2010.

25 Justice Ginsburg had expressed: Ruth Bader Ginsburg, "Speaking in a Judicial Voice," *New York University Law Review* 67 (1992): 1198–1209; Ruth Bader Ginsburg, "Some Thoughts on Autonomy and Equality in Relation to *Roe v. Wade*," N.C. L. Rev 63 (1985): 385–86. Ginsburg's history has recently been contested, with scholars arguing that *Roe* did not create the backlash she believed it did. See Linda Greenhouse and Reva Siegel, "Before (and After) *Roe v. Wade*: New Questions About Backlash," *Yale Law Journal* 120 (2011).

25 the 1996 case of *Romer v. Evans*: Romer v. Evans, 517 U.S. 620 (1996).

25 the law was "unusual": Romer v. Evans, 1995 WL 605822 (U.S.), 30 (U.S. Oral Arg., 1995).

26 "unprecedented in our jurisprudence": *Romer*, 517 U.S. at 633.

26 "it identifies persons by a single trait": Ibid.

26 "raise the inevitable inference": Ibid., 634.

26 "bare . . . desire to harm": Ibid. (citing *Department of Agriculture v. Moreno*, 413 U.S. 528, 534 (1973)).

26 "moral disapproval": Defense of Marriage Act, H.R. Rep.104-664, 16 (1996).

26 "broad and undifferentiated": *Romer*, 517 U.S. at 632.

26 state supreme courts in liberal states: Conaway v. Deane, 932 A.2d 571, 612–13, 625–26, 690 (Md. 2007); Andersen v. King County, 138

P.3d 963, 975–76, 980–81 (Wash. 2006); *Hernandez v. Robles,* 855 N.E.2d 1, 20 (N.Y. 2006) (Graffeo, J., concurring).

26 **2003 case of *Lawrence v. Texas*:** *Lawrence v. Texas,* 539 U.S. 558 (2003).

27 **he overruled *Bowers v. Hardwick*:** *Bowers v. Hardwick,* 478 U.S. 186 (1986).

27 **"at best, facetious":** Ibid., 186.

27 **"formal recognition":** *Lawrence,* 539 U.S. at 578.

27 **"If moral disapprobation of homosexual conduct":** Ibid., 604–05 (Scalia, J., dissenting).

27 **"Plaintiffs here do not":** *Hernandez v. Robles,* 7 N.Y.3d 338, 363 (2006).

28 **"The foundation's website is":** "40 Under Forty," *Advocate,* April 7, 2010, www.advocate.com/politics/marriage-equality/2010/04/07/40 -under-forty-chad-griffin?page=full.

28 **Gibson Dunn donated:** Chuleenan Svetvilas, "Challenging Prop 8: The Hidden Story," *California Lawyer,* January 2010, www.callawyer .com/Clstory.cfm?eid=906575.

28 **"gay *and* straight":** Talbot, "Risky Proposal."

28 **The total fees:** Chris Geidner, "A $6 Million Legal Bill—And a Fight for Credit in the Marriage Equality Movement," BuzzFeed, April 16, 2014, www.buzzfeed.com/chrisgeidner/a-6-million-legal-bill-and-a- fight-for-credit-in-the-marriag#.ylDwJBqQG.

28 **"the lawyers Microsoft is going to want":** Talbot, "Risky Proposal."

28 **Paul Smith:** Celia Llopis-Jepsen, "Jenner Lawyer Who Argued *Lawrence* Sees It Playing into Same-Sex Marriage Fight," *The AmLaw Daily,* June 7, 2012, www.americanlawyer.com/id=1202558371260/ Jenner-Lawyer-Who-Argued-Lawrence-Sees-It-Playing-Into-SameSex -Marriage-Fight.

28 **Robbie Kaplan:** "As Counsel to Edith Windsor, Paul, Weiss Contends that DOMA Is Unconstitutional Before the United States Supreme Court," Paul Weiss, March 27, 2013, www.paulweiss.com/practices/ pro-bono/news/as-counsel-to-edith-windsor,-paul,-weiss-contends -that-doma-is-unconstitutional-before-the-united-states-supreme -court.aspx?id=13003.

28 **Perry had wed Stier:** Eve Conant, "Profile: Plaintiffs in Calif. Gay-Marriage Trial," *Newsweek,* January 11, 2010.

29 **a video titled *The Gathering Storm*:** National Organization for Marriage, "National Organization for Marriage Gathering Storm TV Ad," YouTube video, posted by "political change," April 15, 2012, www.you tube.com/watch?v=xGi2r-M_gQ8.

29 **"Internet camp classic":** Frank Rich, "The Bigots' Last Hurrah," *New York Times,* April 18, 2009.

29 **Stephen Colbert's parody:** Stephen Colbert, "The Colbert Coalition's Anti-Gay Marriage Ad," *Colbert Report* video, 6:11, April 16, 2009, http://thecolbertreport.cc.com/videos/ippmoa/the-colbert-coalition -s-anti-gay-marriage-ad.

29 **a video called *Weathering the Storm*:** "Weathering the Storm (Response to NOM Gathering Storm)," YouTube video, posted by "Love Not Laws," April 22, 2009, www.youtube.com/watch?v= gtcvhqg-sOM.

30 **"gay-marriage fatigue":** Talbot, "Risky Proposal."

30 **"Now I'm really interested":** Ibid.

30 **"put a respectable face":** Ibid.

30 **"Everyone on the call":** Svetvilas, "Challenging Prop 8."

30 **"California's motto, 'Eureka' ":** David Boies and Theodore B. Olson, *Redeeming the Dream* (New York: Penguin Group, 2014), 31.

30 **"was on the wrong side":** Eve Conant, "David Boies on His Case Against Prop 8," *Newsweek,* January 11, 2010.

31 **won an injunction:** Erik Lundegaard and Cindy Larson, "The Dream Team," *Super Lawyers,* April 2014, www.superlawyers.com/wash ington-dc/article/The-Dream-Team/0361eba5-c580-431f-b9c3-0d590 e242c5c.html.

31 **recovered $1.2 billion:** Ibid.

31 **"used to losing cases":** Timothy Harper, "Boies v. *Bush v. Gore,*" *Super Lawyers,* September 2008, www.superlawyers.com/new-york-metro/ article/Boies-v-Bush-v-Gore/37a36d0f-02cc-4efd-b2f4-b37908a4a95c .html.

31 **Boies would joke:** Richard Socarides, "How Would John Roberts Rule on Gay Marriage Cases?" *New Yorker,* July 9, 2012.

31 **"deep into the weeds":** David Boies and Ted Olson, interview by Campbell Brown, *Campbell Brown,* CNN, March 24, 2010, http:// transcripts.cnn.com/TRANSCRIPTS/1003/24/ec.01.html.

31 **upheld Prop 8 against the procedural challenge:** *Strauss v. Horton,* 207 P.3d 48 (Cal. 2009).

32 **"Creating a second class":** Jesse McKinley, "*Bush v. Gore* Foes Join to Fight Gay Marriage Ban," *New York Times,* May 27, 2009; *see also* "AFER—5.27.09 Press Conference (Part 1)," YouTube video, 8:40, posted by "American Foundation for Equal Rights," July 3, 2009, www.youtube.com/watch?v=2MENYT6dpp4.

32 **"you were pro-gay":** "AFER—5.27.09 Press Conference (Part 3—Q&A Continued)," YouTube video, 8:52, posted by "American Foundation

for Equal Rights," July 3, 2009, www.youtube.com/watch?v=oqcDFZ
pFDZQ.

32 **"a temptation we should resist"**: "Why the Ballot Box and Not the
Courts Should Be the Next Step on Marriage in California," ACLU,
May 2009, www.aclu.org/files/pdfs/lgbt/ballot_box_20090527
.pdf.

33 **"We think it's risky"**: McKinley, *"Bush v. Gore* Foes Join to Fight Gay
Marriage Ban."

33 **"Federal court?"**: Ibid.

33 **"an attempt to short-circuit the process"**: Michelle Garcia, "Too
Much, Too Soon," *Advocate*, May 27, 2009, www.advocate.com/
news/2009/05/27/too-much-too-soon?page=full.

2: The Movement Lawyers

34 **"People are born different"**: Evan Wolfson, "Same[-]sex Marriage and
Morality: The Human Rights Vision of the Constitution," thesis, Harvard Law School, 1983, 77, http://freemarry.3cdn.net/73aab4141a80
237ddf_kxm62r3er.pdf.

35 **"a little bit trivial"**: Ruth Marcus, "Ruth Marcus: Wedded to an
Idea," *Washington Post*, July 2, 2013.

35 **three-track strategy**: "Roadmap to Victory," Freedom to Marry,
www.freedomtomarry.org/pages/roadmap-to-victory.

35 **including the 2004 book**: Evan Wolfson, *Why Marriage Matters:
America, Equality, and Gay People's Right to Marry* (New York:
Simon & Schuster, 2005).

35 **only one state—Wisconsin**: William B. Turner, "The Gay Rights
State: Wisconsin's Pioneering Legislation to Prohibit Discrimination
Based on Sexual Orientation," *Wisconsin Women's Law Journal* 22
(2007):91.

35 **brought lawsuits seeking the right to marry**: *Singer v. Hara*, 522 P.2d
1187 (Wash. Ct. App. 1974); *Jones v. Hallahan*, 501 S.W.2d 588 (Ky.
Ct. App. 1973); *Burkett v. Zaablocki*, 54 F.R.D. 626 (E.D. Wis. 1972);
Baker v. Nelson, 191 N.W.2d 185 (Minn. 1971).

36 **denied their application**: Michael Boucai, "Glorious Precedents:
When Gay Marriage Was Radical," *Yale Journal of Law & the Hu-
manities* (forthcoming) 27, no. 1.

36 **"old as the book of Genesis"**: *Baker v. Nelson*, 191 N.W.2d 185, 186
(Minn. 1971).

36 **"The appeal is dismissed"**: *Baker v. Nelson*, 409 U.S. 810, 810 (1972).

36 **In more recent cases**: For the most significant judicial ruling based on

Baker's force as precedent, see *DeBoer v. Snyder,* 772 F.3d 388 (6th cir. 2014).

36 **"Prospective Newlyweds Really"**: Joyce Murdoch and Deb Price, *Courting Justice: Gay Men and Lesbians v. the Supreme Court* (New York: Basic Books, 2002).

36 **an injunction from a federal district court**: *McConnell v. Anderson,* 316 F. Supp. 809 (D. Minn. 1970) rev'd, 451 F.2d 193 (8th Cir. 1971).

36 **"socially repugnant concept"**: *McConnell v. Anderson,* 451 F.2d 193, 196 (8th Cir. 1971).

36 **ACLU did not appear**: Murdoch and Price, *Courting Justice,* 168.

36 **supported gay rights in principle**: Samuel Walker, *In Defense of American Liberties: A History of the ACLU,* 2d ed. (Carbondale: Southern Illinois University Press, 1999), 312.

36 **In an internal memo**: Murdoch and Price, *Courting Justice,* 168.

37 **LGBT litigation shops**: Scott Cummings and Douglas NeJaime, "Lawyering for Marriage Equality," *UCLA Law Review* 57 (2010): 1248.

37 **In the judges' view**: *In re Thom Lambda Legal Def. & Ed. Fund, Inc.,* 337 N.Y.S.2d 588, 589 (N.Y. App. Div. 1st Dept. 1972).

37 **The state's highest court reversed**: *Application of Thom,* 301 N.E.2d 542, 542 (N.Y. 1973).

37 **The organization's first case**: "GLAD Is Founded in 1978 in Response to a Sting Operation at the Boston Public Library," Gay & Lesbian Advocates & Defenders, www.glad.org/about/history/glad-is-founded.

37 **create a ripple effect**: Joseph Landau, "Ripple Effect," *New Republic,* June 23, 2003.

37 ***Bowers* caused many courts**: See, e.g., *High Tech Gays v. Def. Indus. Sec. Clearance Office,* 895 F.2d 563, 571 (9th Cir. 1990); *Ben-Shalom v. Marsh,* 881 F.2d 454, 464–65 (7th Cir. 1989);. *Padula v. Webster,* 822 F.2d 97, 103 (D.C. Cir. 1987).

38 **from adoption to military service**: See, e.g., *Bottoms v. Bottoms,* 457 S.E.2d 102 (Va. 1995) (custody); *State, Dep't of Health & Rehabilitative Servs. v. Cox,* 627 So.2d 1210, 1217–18 (Fla. Dist. Ct. App. 1993), *vacated on other grounds,* 656 So.2d 902 (Fla. 1995) (adoption); *Ben-Shalom v. Marsh,* 881 F.2d 454, 464–65 (7th Cir. 1989) (military service); *Woodward v. United States,* 871 F.2d 1068, 1074–75 (Fed. Cir. 1989) (military service).

38 **an unfit parent**: *Bottoms,* 457 S.E.2d 102, 107 (Va. 1995) (describing trial court findings).

38 **intermediate appellate court**: *Bottoms,* 444 S.E.2d 276 (Va. Ct. App. 1994).

38 **While purporting to agree:** *Bottoms,* 457 S.E.2d 102, 108 (Va. 1995).

38 **Both groups initially declined:** Michael D. Sant'Ambrogio and Sylvia A. Law, "*Baehr v. Lewin* and the Long Road to Marriage Equality," *University of Hawai'i Law Review* 33 (2011): 708.

38 **a watershed decision:** *Baehr v. Lewin,* 852 P.2d 44 (Haw. 1993).

39 **defense was made and rejected:** Andrew Koppelman, "Why Discrimination Against Lesbians and Gay Men Is Sex Discrimination," 69 (May 1994) *New York University Law Review:* 202, 237–40.

39 **"white supremacy":** *Loving v. Virginia,* 388 U.S. 1, 11 (1967).

39 **"homophobia is driven by male supremacy":** Koppelman, "Why Discrimination," 237–380.

40 **"The life of the law":** Oliver Wendell Holmes Jr., *The Common Law* (Cambridge: Harvard University Press, 2009), 3.

40 **more stringent standard:** *Baehr,* 852 P.2d 44 (Haw. 1993).

41 **The trial court found:** *Baehr,* 1996 WL 694235 at *21. See also Evan Wolfson, "Fourteen Years After Hawaii: New Freedom to Marry Case in California; Same Old, Same Old from Opponents," *Huffington Post,* January 21, 2010, www.huffingtonpost.com/evan-wolfson/14 -years-after-hawaii-new_b_431068.html.

41 **enacted a constitutional amendment:** Haw. Const., art. I, §23.

41 **causing Congress to pass DOMA:** Defense of Marriage Act, 1 USC § 7 (1996).

41 **lopsided vote:** U.S. House, Defense of Marriage Act, HR 3396. 104th Cong., 2nd sess., 142 *Congressional Record,* No. 103 (July 12, 1996), H7505.

41 **his "long-standing" opposition:** Eric Schmitt, "Senators Reject Both Job-Bias Ban and Gay Marriage," *New York Times,* September 11, 1996.

41 **it would defuse a push:** Bill Clinton, "It's Time to Overturn DOMA," *Washington Post,* March 7, 2013.

41 **thirty-one states had enacted:** Sant'Ambrogio and Law, "*Baehr v. Lewin* and the Long Road," 705, 726.

41 **long, public, and celebrated debate:** See Thomas B. Stoddard, "Why Gay People Should Seek the Right to Marry," *Out/look* (Fall 1989): 9–13, and Paula Ettelbrick, "Since When Is Marriage a Path to Liberation?" *Out/look* (Fall 1989): 14–16.

42 **Andrew Sullivan published:** Andrew Sullivan, "Here Comes the Groom: A (Conservative) Case for Gay Marriage," *New Republic,* August 28, 1989.

42 **offer "stabilizing influences":** Jonathan Rauch, "For Better or Worse?" *New Republic,* May 6, 1996.

42 **Michael Warner argued:** Michael Warner, *The Trouble with Normal: Sex, Politics and the Ethics of Queer Life* (Cambridge: Harvard University Press, 2000), 121.

42 **Nancy Polikoff expressed concern:** Nancy D. Polikoff, "We Will Get What We Ask For: Why Legalizing Gay and Lesbian Marriage Will Not 'Dismantle the Legal Structure of Gender in Every Marriage,'" *Virginia Law Review* 79 (1993): 1546.

42 **"rigid dividing line":** Nancy D. Polikoff, *Beyond (Straight and Gay) Marriage: Valuing All Families Under the Law* (Boston: Beacon Press, 2008), 5.

42 **took these perspectives seriously:** Ibid., 56–61.

43 **inch-by-inch approach:** Scott L. Cummings and Douglas NeJaime, "Lawyering for Marriage Equality," William B Rubenstein, "Divided We Litigate: Addressing Disputes Among Group Members and Lawyers in Civil Rights Campaigns," *Yale Law Journal* 106 (1997): 1632–33.

43 **"make a federal case":** Cummings and NeJaime, "Lawyering for Marriage Equality," 1269.

43 **voters became increasingly distrustful:** Thomas E. Cronin, *Direct Democracy: The Politics of Initiative, Referendum, and Recall* (Cambridge: Harvard University Press, 1989), 50–54.

43 **Ballot initiatives originally sought:** David B. Magleby, "Ballot Initiatives and Intergovernmental Relations in the United States," *Publius* 28, no. 1, The State of American Federalism, 1997–1998 (Winter 1998), 147.

44 **increasingly been used to hurt minorities:** Todd Donovan, "Direct Democracy and Campaigns Against Minorities," *Minnesota Law Review* 97, no. 5 (2013), 1731.

44 **called the Thurgood Marshall:** Sheryl Gay Stolberg, "In Fight for Marriage Rights, 'She's Our Thurgood Marshall,'" *New York Times*, March 28, 2013.

44 **Supreme Court of Vermont ruled unanimously:** *Baker v. State*, 744 A.2d 864, 867 (Vt. 1999).

44 **Yet a majority of the court:** Ibid.

44 **Vermont enacted a civil-unions law:** Civil Unions, 2000 Vermont Laws P.A. 91 (H. 847).

44 **Massachusetts Supreme Judicial Court:** *Goodridge v. Dep't of Pub. Health*, 798 N.E.2d 941 (Mass. 2003).

45 **A proposed amendment to its constitution:** Mass. Const., art. XLVIII, §IV.

45 **legislature voted 105 to 92:** Pam Belluck, "Governor of Massachusetts

Seeks to Delay Same-Sex Marriages," *New York Times,* April 16, 2004.

45 **majority in the state legislature:** Mass. Const., art. XLVIII, §IV.

45 **prevail in a popular vote:** Terence Neilan, "High Court in Massachusetts Rules Gays Have Right to Marry," *New York Times,* November 18, 2003.

45 **Couples began to marry:** "Same Sex Couples Exchange Vows in Massachusetts," CNN, May 17, 2004.

45 ***USA Today* said it all:** Deb Price, "The Sky Didn't Fall in Mass.," *USA Today,* May 16, 2005.

45 **voted against it the second time:** Pam Belluck, "Massachusetts Rejects Bill to Eliminate Gay Marriage," *New York Times,* September 15, 2005.

45 **In 2007, a separate attempt:** The Massachusetts Family Institute sought to amend the constitution through a citizen initiative, which only required the affirmation of 25 percent of the legislature during each of two consecutive votes. While that bill made it through the first vote, it, too, was blocked, on June 14, 2007, from going before the voters—by five votes. See Frank Phillips and Andrea Estes, "Right of Gays to Marry Set for Years to Come: Vote Keeps Proposed Ban off 2008 State Ballot," *Boston Globe,* June 15, 2007.

45 **"activist judges":** David Stout, "Bush Backs Ban in Constitution on Gay Marriage," *New York Times,* February 24, 2004.

45 **both 2004 and 2006:** 150 *Cong. Rec.* H7888 (daily ed. Sept. 30, 2004); 152 *Cong. Rec.* H5287 (daily ed. July 18, 2006).

45 **eleven out of eleven proposed bans:** James Dao, "Same-Sex Marriage Issue Key to Some G.O.P. Races," *New York Times,* November 4, 2004.

45 **eight more states enacted such prohibitions:** Ibid.

46 **only 8 percent:** Cal. Const. art. II, § 8(b).

46 **California Marriage Litigation Roundtable:** Cummings and NeJaime, "Lawyering for Marriage Equality," 1269.

46 **The roundtable concluded:** Ibid., 1270.

46 **high courts of Washington and New York:** *Conaway v. Deane,* 932 A.2d 571 (Md. 2007); *Hernandez v. Robles,* 855 N.E.2d 1 (N.Y. 2006); *Andersen v. King County,* 138 P.3d 963 (Wash. 2006).

46 **In Connecticut, however:** *Kerrigan v. Comm'r of Pub. Health,* 957 A.2d 407 (Conn. 2008).

46 **The Iowa Supreme Court ruled unanimously:** *Varnum v. Brien,* 763 N.W.2d 862 (Iowa 2009).

46 **Four days later:** Keith B. Richburg, "Vermont Legislature Legalizes Same-Sex Marriage," *Washington Post,* April 7, 2009.

46 **New Hampshire and the District of Columbia:** Abby Goodnough, "New Hampshire Legalizes Same-Sex Marriage," *New York Times,* June 3, 2009; Ian Urbina, "Gay Marriage Is Legal in U.S. Capital," *New York Times,* March 3, 2010.

46 **In several other states:** *Lewis v. Harris,* 908 A.2d 196 (N.J. 2006); Steve Friess, "Nevada Partnership Bill Now Law," *New York Times,* June 1, 2009; and Patrick Marley, "State Supreme Court Hints That It May Strike Down Part of Domestic Partnership Law," *Journal Sentinel,* October 23, 2013.

47 **federal constitutional challenge in Massachusetts:** Complaint, *Gill v. Office of Personnel Management,* 699 F. Supp. 2d 374 (D. Mass. 2010).

47 **historic *Windsor* decision:** *United States v. Windsor,* 133 S. Ct. 2675 (2013).

47 **already permitted interracial marriage:** *Loving,* 388 U.S. 1, 5 footnote 5 (1967) ("After the initiation of this litigation, Maryland repealed its prohibitions against interracial marriage . . . leaving Virginia and 15 other States with statutes outlawing interracial marriage.").

47 **Smith declined to play a role:** Ross Todd, "Marriage Brokers," *American Lawyer,* March 1, 2011.

47 **advised AFER not to file:** Cummings and NeJaime, "Lawyering for Marriage Equality," 1299, 1311.

48 **"we will vigorously oppose":** Letter from Chad H. Griffin, Board President, American Foundation for Equal Rights, to Kate Kendell, Executive Director, National Center for Lesbian Rights, July 8, 2009 (on file with author).

48 **"a little too much zeal":** Boies and Olson, *Redeeming the Dream,* 79.

48 **After *Plessy v. Ferguson*:** *Plessy v. Ferguson,* 163 U.S. 537 (1896).

48 **orchestrated its litigation:** Richard Kluger, *Simple Justice: The History of* Brown v. Board of Education *and Black America's Struggle for Equality,* 2d ed. (New York: Knopf, 2004), 185–92.

48 ***Missouri v. Gaines*:** *Missouri v. Gaines,* 305 U.S. 337 (1938).

49 **Supreme Court ruled for the plaintiffs:** *Sweatt v. Painter,* 339 U.S. 629 (1950).

49 **The Court also rejected:** *McLaurin v. Oklahoma,* 339 U.S. 637 (1950).

49 **When rogue plaintiffs:** Rubenstein, "Divided We Litigate," 1164, footnote 187.

49 **"We've all seen people":** Talbot, "Risky Proposal."

49 **"honorary lesbian":** Svetvilas, "Challenging Prop 8."

49 **an ethical obligation to defer:** Rubenstein, "Divided We Litigate," and sources cited therein.

3: The Proponents

51 **"I learned that you should never":** Arnold Schwarzenegger, interview by John King, *CNN Late Edition with Wolf Blitzer,* CNN, November 9, 2008, http://transcripts.cnn.com/transcripts/0811/09/le.01.html.

51 **Jerry Brown, decided not to defend:** Chris Megerian, "Prop. 8 Battle Gives Jerry Brown Link to His Father," *Los Angeles Times,* June 28, 2013.

52 **Kamala Harris, took the same position:** Matt Baume, Kamala Harris Vows to Abandon Prop 8, *NBC Bay Area,* December 3, 2010, www.nbcbayarea.com/news/local/Harris-Vows-to-Abandon-Prop-8-111191349.html.

52 **only thirty-five years old:** Marcos Breton, "Local Lawyer Helps Starr Back Prop. 8," *Sacramento Bee,* March 4, 2009.

52 **Eagle Scout and Young Republican:** Marcus Breton, "Folsom Lawyer Helps Starr Back Prop. 8 in Court," *Sacramento Bee,* March 4, 2009.

52 **legislative consultant:** Andy Pugno, JoinCalifornia: Election History for the State of California, www.joincalifornia.com/candidate/13702.

52 **chief of staff:** Ibid.

52 **Knight asked Pugno:** Andrew Pugno, "You Can't Just Change Marriage," *L.A. Times,* May 26, 2009.

52 **returned to service:** Ibid.

52 **Prop 22 passed in 2000:** "No to Gay Marriage in CA," CBS News, March 7, 2000.

53 **prevailed at the California Supreme Court:** *Lockyer v. City and County of San Francisco,* 33 Cal.4th 1055 (2004).

53 **bar same-sex marriage:** John Wildermuth, "Prop. 8 Backers Splinter as Court Fight Resumes," *San Francisco Chronicle,* November 24, 2008.

53 **"We were constantly hassled":** Ibid.

53 **founded the ADF:** Associated Press, "War Chest Amassed to Fight Christian Battles," December 2, 1993.

53 **"to raise $25 million a year":** Ibid.

54 **"It was just years of seeing":** Peter Slevin, "Bringing the Church to the Courtroom: Christian Group Becomes Force in Major Legal Battles," *Washington Post,* July 10, 2006.

54 **"out-swamp them":** Associated Press, "War Chest Amassed."

54 **revenues over $39 million:** "Alliance Defending Freedom," Charity Navigator, www.charitynavigator.org/index.cfm?bay=search.summary&orgid=5495#.VBS332SwJNY.

54 **"farm team":** Alliance Defending Freedom, "Training an Alliance to Defend Religious Liberty," ADF, www.alliancedefendingfreedom.org/about/legal-academy.

54 **"defend religious freedom":** "Media Kit," Alliance Defending Freedom, July 12, 2012, www.adfmedia.org/files/adf_media_kit.pdf.

54 **commit to 450 hours:** Alliance Defending Freedom, "Training an Alliance."

54 **the Blackstone Fellowship:** Rob Boston, "The Alliance Defense Fund Agenda," *Church and State,* June 2004, available at www.au.org/church-state/june-2004-church-state/featured/the-alliance-defense-fund-agenda.

54 **"a biblical world view":** "What Does Religious Freedom Mean to You?" Alliance Defending Freedom, www.alliancedefendingfreedom.org/content/docs/resources/Signature-Brochure.pdf.

54 **Such programs have created:** Alliance Defending Freedom, "Media Kit."

54 **including Pugno:** Alliance Defending Freedom, "Proposition 8 Defenders Seek to Intervene Against Hollywood-Backed Lawsuit," news release, May 29, 2009, www.adflegal.org/News/PRDetail/2316.

54 **changed its name:** Alliance Defending Freedom, "Alliance Defense Fund Is Now Alliance Defending Freedom," www.alliancedefendingfreedom.org/page/new-name.

54 **boasted forty-four staff attorneys:** "Media Kit," Alliance Defending Freedom.

54 **"They're for Christian superiority":** Slevin, "Bringing the Church to the Courtroom."

55 **"founded to defend the right":** Alan Sears and Craig Osten, *The Homosexual Agenda* (Nashville: B&H Books, 2003), 11.

55 **allied attorneys must:** ADF, "FAQ," www.adflegal.org/About/FAQ.

55 **"We believe the Bible":** "Statement of Faith & Guiding Principles," Alliance Defending Freedom, www.alliancedefendingfreedom.org/About/Detail/4205.

55 **Establishment Clause:** U.S. Const. amend. I.

55 **"wall of separation":** See, e.g., *Everson v. Bd. of Ed. of Ewing Twp.,* 330 U.S. 1 (1947); *People of State of Ill. ex rel. McCollum v. Bd. of Ed. of Sch. Dist. No. 71, Champaign Cnty., Ill.,* 333 U.S. 203 (1948); *McGowan v. State of Md.,* 366 U.S. 420 (1961).

55 **only Justice Thomas:** See, e.g., *Town of Greece, N.Y. v. Galloway,* 134 S. Ct. 1811(2014), 1835–38.

55 **"a secular legislative purpose":** *Lemon v. Kurtzman,* 403 U.S. 602, 612 (1971).

55 case involving legislative prayer: *Marsh v. Chambers,* 463 U.S. 783 (1983).

55 the Court did the same thing: *Galloway,* 134 S. Ct. 1811 (2014).

55 "more and more bricks": Boston, "Alliance Defense Fund Agenda" (quoting Sears's e-mail to supporters).

55 a vast array of religious-liberties cases: "A History of Success," Alliance Defending Freedom, www.alliancedefendingfreedom.org/about/ history.

55 "no-brainer cases": Lee Romney, "Two Christian Advocacy Groups Put Faith in Courts," *Los Angeles Times,* March 5, 2004, http://articles .latimes.com/2004/mar/05/local/me-legal5.

56 gays from marching openly: *Hurley v. Irish-Am. Gay, Lesbian & Bisexual Grp. of Boston,* 515 U.S. 557 (1995).

56 Boy Scouts could exclude: *Boy Scouts of America v. Dale,* 530 U.S. 640 (2000).

56 "Marriage Litigation Center": Katherine T. Phan, "ADF Launches New DOMAWatch.org Web Site," *Christian Post,* September 8, 2004.

56 an authors' note underscoring: Sears and Osten, *Homosexual Agenda,* viii.

56 "pain and sorrow it has brought to them": Ibid.

56 "who would picket": Ibid., 8.

56 "With God's grace": Ibid., viii.

57 "crystal-clear, non-debatable issues": Ibid., 8–9.

57 one of those issues: Ibid., 9.

57 "we cannot sit idly by": Ibid., 13.

57 "God's plan for marriage": Boston, "Alliance Defense Fund Agenda" (quoting Sears's e-mail to supporters).

57 a circular argument: Evan Gerstmann, *Same-Sex Marriage and the Constitution,* 2d ed. (New York: Cambridge University Press, 2008), 23; David B. Cruz, " 'Just Don't Call It Marriage': The First Amendment and Marriage as an Expressive Resource," *Southern California Law Review* 74 (2001): 1002; Dale Carpenter, "Bad Arguments Against Gay Marriage," *Florida Coastal Law Review* 7 (2005): 189–90.

57 "the first institution": Jeremy Hooper, "Weird, Prop 8 Legal Eagles: Why Didn't You Make 'Rebellion Against God' Claims in Judge Walker's Court?," *Good As You,* June 6, 2011, www.goodasyou. org/good_as_you/2011/06/weird-prop-8-legal-eagles-why-didnt-you -make-rebellion-against-god-claims-in-judge-walkers-court.html.

58 "Let the People Vote": See National Organization for Marriage (NOM)'s blog, www.nomblog.com/category/let-the-people-vote.

58 **"deceptive advertising":** James Taranto, "The New Religious Right?," *Wall Street Journal,* July 25, 2011.

59 **"a good enough lawyer":** Dan Morain, "Prop. 8 Role Continues to Define Assembly Hopeful," *Sacramento Bee,* June 20, 2010.

59 **"so-called homosexual agenda":** *Lawrence v. Texas,* 539 U.S. 558, 602 (2003).

59 **a professional baseball player:** Dan Levine, "A Conservative Choice for Supporters of Calif. Ban on Gay Marriages," *Legal Intelligencer,* October 9, 2009.

59 **editor in chief:** "Charles J. Cooper," Cooper & Kirk, PLLC, http:// cooperkirk.com/lawyers/charles-j-cooper/.

59 **Justice William Rehnquist:** Howard Kurtz, "Reagan's Conservative Law Adviser Finds Courts Going Against Him," *Washington Post,* March 21, 1987.

60 **"a certain libertarian squishiness":** Becker, "Conservative's Road."

60 **hang side by side:** Scott Shane, "Good Friends, Same Party but Legal Opponents," *New York Times,* May 27, 2013.

60 **the firm motto:** Zach Lowe, "Gold Rush: Thompson Hine on Losing End in Landlord/Tenant Case," *AmLaw Daily,* August 28, 2008, http://amlawdaily.typepad.com/amlawdaily/2008/08/pay-in-gold-tho .html.

60 **defended Michigan's Proposal 2:** *Coal. to Defend Affirmative Action v. Regents of Univ. of Michigan,* 701 F.3d 466 (6th Cir. 2012).

60 **represented the Citadel:** *Faulkner v. Jones,* 14 F.3d 3 (4th Cir. 1994).

60 **Political Victory Fund:** *Federal Election Comm'n v. NRA Political Victory Fund,* 513 U.S. 88 (1994).

61 **"The issue is too volatile":** Levine, "A Conservative Choice."

61 **attorney Paul Clement:** Susan Beck, "How Bancroft Became Conservatives' Law Firm of Choice for Hot-Button Cases," *American Lawyer,* November 30, 2012.

61 **"make an educated guess":** Levine, "A Conservative Choice."

61 **1986 policy memorandum:** Memorandum from Charles J. Cooper, Assistant Attorney General, Office of Legal Counsel, to Ronald E. Robertson, General Counsel, Department of Health and Human Services (June 20, 1986), www.bc.edu/content/dam/files/schools/law_sites /library/pdf/content/tremblay_schulman/1986-06-20.Cooper.Meese .Memo.pdf.

61 **The OLC repudiated:** Memorandum from Douglas W. Kmiec, Acting Assistant Attorney General, Office of Legal Counsel, Department of Justice, to Arthur B. Culvahouse, Jr., Counsel to the President (Sept. 27, 1988).

61 **Cooper filed an amicus brief:** Brief for States of Alabama, California, Idaho, Nebraska, South Carolina, South Dakota, and Virginia as Amici Curiae in Support of Petitioner, *Romer v. Evans,* 517 U.S. 620 (1996), available at 1995 WL 17008426.

61 **"known for taking anti-gay positions":** Linda Hosek, "Mainland Expert to Handle State Same-Sex Appeal: The Attorney for the Three Couples Says the Mainland Lawyer Has an Anti-Gay History," *Honolulu Star-Bulletin,* March 14, 1997.

61 **"I would not hesitate":** Levine, "A Conservative Choice."

61 **"demeanor and civilized tone":** Ibid.

62 **Liberty Counsel had been founded:** Hans J. Hacker, *The Culture of Conservative Christian Litigation* (Oxford, UK: Rowman and Littlefield Publishers, Inc., 2005), 58.

62 **ADF support had enabled:** Ibid., 64.

62 **found a new patron:** Ibid., 58.

62 **By 2004, Staver had:** Ibid.

62 **built a replica:** "Liberty University Builds Replica of Highest Court," Associated Press, March 11, 2007, http://fredericksburg.com/News/FLS/2007/032007/03112007/266611.

62 **"Basically, this courtroom":** Laurence Hammack, "Litigating for the Lord: Liberty Counsel Backs Giles County in Ten Commandments Case," *Roanoke Times,* May 6, 2012, http://ww2.roanoke.com/news/roanoke/wb/308431/.

62 **Southern Poverty Law Center:** "Hate Map," Southern Poverty Law Center, www.splcenter.org/get-informed/hate-map#s=FL.

62 **"Witchcraft is a religion":** P. Douglas Filaroski, "Library Accused of Promoting Witchcraft," *Florida Times-Union,* September 13, 2000, http://jacksonville.com/tu-online/stories/091300/met_4050093.html.

62 **guardians of the fetus:** Romney, "Two Christian Advocacy Groups."

63 **represented Lisa Miller:** Rena M. Lindevaldsen, *Only One Mommy: A Woman's Battle for Her Life, Her Daughter, and Her Freedom: The Lisa Miller Story* (Orlando: New Revolution Publishers, 2011).

63 **high courts of Vermont and Virginia:** *Miller-Jenkins v. Miller-Jenkins,* 912 A.2d 951 (Vt. 2006), *cert. denied,* 550 U.S. 918 (2007); *Miller-Jenkins v. Miller-Jenkins,* 661 S.E.2d 822 (Va. 2008), *cert. denied,* 555 U.S. 1069 (2008).

63 **"the higher law—God's law":** Lindevaldsen, *Only One Mommy,* 110.

63 **told the *New York Times*:** Erik Eckholm, "Which Mother for Isabella? Civil Union Ends in an Abduction and Questions," *New York Times,* July 28, 2012.

63 **Staver's organization rushed:** Devin Montgomery, "California Courts Reject Last-Minute Petitions to Block Same-Sex Marriages," *Jurist,* June 18, 2008, http://jurist.org/paperchase/2008/06/california-courts-reject-last-minute.php.

63 **the two organizations sniped:** Romney, "Two Christian Advocacy Groups."

4: Getting to Trial

65 **a nervous Gibson Dunn associate:** Svetvilas, "Challenging Prop 8."

66 **allegations that he was anti-gay:** T. J. Anthony, "Homophobic Judicial Nominee Opposed," *Stonewall Democratic Club Newsletter, San Francisco Chapter,* January 1988, available at www.outhistory.org/wiki/images/e/e9/1988_1_Stonewall_SF.pdf.

66 **partner in 1978:** "Judge Vaughn R. Walker (Retired)—Arbitrator and Mediator," Federal Arbitration, Inc., www.fedarb.com/judges/vaughn-walker.asp.

66 **San Francisco's Olympic Club:** AP, "Beleaguered Nominee Backed," *New York Times,* November 17, 1989; Katherine Bishop, "Exclusionary Club May Pose Problems for Judge Kennedy," *New York Times,* November 14, 1987.

66 **the "Gay Olympics" case:** "Claiming the Title: Gay Olympics on Trial," YouTube video, 1:46, posted by Joel McKenna, June 19, 2011, www.youtube.com/watch?v=KOywCR_Ztes&noredirect=1.

66 **trademark litigation:** *Int'l Olympic Comm. v. San Francisco Arts & Athletics,* C-82-4183 RFP, 1982 WL 52122, at *5 (N.D. Cal., Aug. 20, 1982).

66 **The Olympic Committee prevailed:** *San Francisco Arts & Athletics, Inc. v. U.S. Olympic Comm.,* 483 U.S. 522 (1987).

67 **committee had not objected:** Ricardo Pimentel, "Gays Lose Ruling on Olympics, Justices Bar Term from SF Games," *Sacramento Bee,* June 26, 1987, A3.

67 **"A lawyer acting":** Philip Shenon, "Battle Looming over a Nominee for U.S. Court," *New York Times,* January 14, 1988, www.nytimes.com/1988/01/14/us/battle-looming-over-a-nominee-for-us-court.html.

67 **Walker had a lien:** Bill Mandel, "Golden Child of the Gay Games Turns 27," *San Francisco Chronicle,* September 1, 2010, http://blog.sfgate.com/bmandel/2010/09/01/golden-child-of-the-gay-games-turns-27/.

67 **Waddell's attorney:** Shenon, "Battle Looming," 14.

67 **"any lesbian or gay cases":** Confirmation Hearing on Vaughn R.

Walker: Hearing Before the S. Comm. on the Judiciary, 100th Cong. 458 (1988) (testimony of T. J. Anthony).

67 **Committee voted for Walker 11 to 2:** AP, "Beleaguered Nominee Backed."

67 **alleged warrantless surveillance:** *Hepting v. AT&T Corp.*, 439 F. Supp. 2d 974 (2006).

67 **criminalization of drugs:** Bob Egelko, "Walker Becomes Chief District Judge," *San Francisco Chronicle*, September 1, 2004.

68 **"apart straw by straw":** John Schwartz, "Conservative Jurist, with Independent Streak," *New York Times*, August 5, 2010.

68 **"a lot about fairness":** Maura Dolan, "Distilling the Same-Sex Marriage Case," *Los Angeles Times*, June 21, 2010.

68 **only one federal judge:** Lisa Keen, "Schumer Urges Obama to Appoint Gay Man to Federal Bench," *Bay Area Reporter*, February 18, 2010, www.ebar.com/news/article.php?sec=news&article=4561.

68 **"a meaning unique":** *Int'l Olympic Comm. v. San Francisco Arts & Athletics*, 789 F.2d 1319 (9th Cir. 1986).

69 **only four states had legalized:** The four states, in chronological order, were Massachusetts, Connecticut, Iowa, and Vermont. By May 2009, the Vermont legislature had passed a same-sex marriage bill, even though the law had not yet gone into effect. See Dave Gram, "Vermont Legalizes Gay Marriage, Overrides Governor's Veto," *Huffington Post*, May 25, 2011. Maine had also legalized same-sex marriage, but the bill was put on hold pending a state referendum on the subject. See Abby Goodnough, "Maine Governor Signs Same-Sex Marriage Bill," *New York Times*, May 6, 2009, and Oren Dorell, "State Ballots Tackle Controversial Issues Tuesday," *USA Today*, November 1, 2009. As the referendum was considered part of the legislative process, the determination in Maine, unlike that in Vermont, was not considered final.

69 **requested a preliminary injunction:** Motion for Preliminary Injunction filed by Plaintiffs, *Perry v. Schwarzenegger*, 704 F. Supp. 2d 921 (N.D. Cal. 2010) (No. 09-2292) (Doc. 7).

69 **to restrain California officials:** Ibid.

69 **generally requires the party to show:** *Winter v. Natural Res. Def. Council, Inc.*, 555 U.S. 7, 20 (2008).

70 **the Governor's Office:** Administration's Opposition to Plaintiffs' Motion for Preliminary Injunction, at 1, *Perry*, 704 F. Supp. 2d 921 (No. 09-2292) (Doc. 33).

70 **issued a significant order:** Order Granting 8 Motion to Intervene, Continuing hearing on preliminary injunction in favor of a case

management conference on 7/2/2009 at 10 a.m., *Perry,* 704 F. Supp. 2d 921 (No. 09-2292) (Doc. 76), at 2.

73 **"genuine issue of material fact":** See Fed. R. Civ. P. 56(a); see also *Adickes v. S. H. Kress & Co.,* 398 U.S. 144, 153 (1970); *Celotex Corp. v. Catrett,* 477 U.S. 317 (1986).

74 **a nine-day trial:** Carlos A. Ball, "The Blurring of the Lines: Children and Bans on Interracial and Same-Sex Marriages," *Fordham Law Review* 76 (2008): 2753.

74 **Cooper had handled the appeal:** Evan Wolfson, "Fourteen Years After Hawaii."

74 **Richard Posner:** *Indiana Harbor Belt R. Co. v. Am. Cyanamid Co.,* 916 F.2d 1174, 1182 (7th Cir. 1990).

75 **"shaping a general rule":** Ibid.

75 **psychological evidence:** John Frazier Jackson, "The Brandeis Brief— Too Little, Too Late: The Trial Court as a Superior Forum for Presenting Legislative Facts," *American Journal of Trial Advocacy* 17 (1993): 31–32.

76 **"vast majority of women":** *Planned Parenthood of Southeastern Pennsylvania v. Casey,* 505 U.S. 833, 888–91 (1992).

76 **diverse student body:** *Grutter v. Bollinger,* 539 U.S. 306, 319, and 330 (2003).

76 **"situation sense":** Karl N. Llewellyn, *The Common Law Tradition: Deciding Appeals* (Boston: Little, Brown, 1960), 121–57.

77 **fired off a motion:** Motion to Intervene filed by ACLU Foundation of Northern California, *Perry,* 704 F. Supp. 2d 921 (No. 09-2292) (Doc. 79).

78 **In 2004, a judge:** *Howard v. Child Welfare Agency Review Bd.,* CV 1999-9881, 2004 WL 3154530 (Ark. Cir. Ct. Dec. 29, 2004).

78 **the Arkansas Supreme Court:** *Dep't of Human Servs. & Child Welfare Agency Review Bd. v. Howard,* 238 S.W. 3d 1 (Ark. 2006).

78 **Again, they prevailed:** *Florida Dep't of Children & Families v. Adoption of X.X.G.,* 45 So. 3d 79 (Fla. Dist. Ct. App. 2010).

79 **recommended "careful reading":** *Howard,* 2004 WL 3154530, at *13.

79 **"bears the financial":** Motion to Intervene filed by City and County of San Francisco at 12–13, *Perry,* 704 F. Supp. 2d 921 (No. 09-2292) (Doc. 109).

79 **"A prompt, thorough trial":** Plaintiffs' Case Management Statement, at 1, *Perry,* 704 F. Supp. 2d 921 (No. 09-2292) (Doc. 134).

80 **"stretch on for weeks":** Defendants-Intervenors Proposition 8 proponents and ProjectMarriage.com's Case Management Statement, at 4, *Perry,* 704 F. Supp. 2d 921 (No. 09-2292) (Doc. 139).

80 **to intervene on behalf of the CCF:** Notice of Motion and Motion for Intervention by Campaign for California Families; Memorandum of Points and Authorities in Support, 704 F. Supp. 2d 921 (No. 09-2292) (Doc. 91).

82 **filed a 127-page brief:** Defendant-Intervenors' Notice of Motion and Motion for Summary Judgment, and Memorandum of Points and Authorities in Support of Motion for Summary Judgment, *Perry v. Schwarzenegger,* No. 09-2292 (N.D. Cal. Jan. 8, 2010) (Doc. 172-1).

82 **excused their failure:** Defendant-Intervenors' Motion for Administrative Leave to Exceed Page Limitations at 1, *Perry,* 704 F. Supp. 2d 921 (No. 09-02292) (Doc. 172).

82 **The apoplectic plaintiffs:** Plaintiffs' Opposition to Defendant-Intervenors' Motion for Administrative Leave to Exceed Page Limitations, at 3, *Perry,* 704 F. Supp. 2d 921 (No. 09-02292) (Doc. 174).

82 **"to resist the temptation":** Order Granting Defendant-Intervenors' Motion for Leave to File Their Motion Papers, at 2, *Perry,* 704 F. Supp. 2d 921 (No. 09-02292) (Doc. 183).

82 **The plaintiffs' response clocked:** Plaintiffs' and Plaintiff-Intervenor's Joint Opposition to Defendant-Intervenors' Motion for Summary Judgment, *Perry,* 704 F. Supp. 2d 921 (No. 09-2292) (Doc. 202).

82 **"radical idea":** Defendant-Intervenors' Motion for Summary Judgment, 71.

82 **"severing the link":** Ibid.

84 **"could not think of any":** Theodore B. Olson, "The Conservative Case for Gay Marriage," *Newsweek,* January 8, 2010.

85 **a final skirmish arose:** *Hollingsworth v. Perry,* 558 U.S. 183, 186 (2010).

85 **live video streaming:** Ibid. The court specifically declined to address other forms of broadcast, such as posting a video of the trial online, because the lower court had not yet issued a final decision on that matter. Nevertheless, the Supreme Court's resolution of the dispute over the video transmission to other courthouses appeared to doom any chance of broadcasting the trial through different media.

85 **"witnesses have already said":** Ibid., 195.

85 **exhibit of seventy-one articles:** Ex. K to Defendant-Intervenors' Motion, *Perry,* 704 F. Supp. 2d 921 (No. 09-2292) (Doc. 187-11).

86 **"all experts or advocates":** Ibid., 205–06.

86 ***ProtectMarriage.com v. Bowen:*** *ProtectMarriage.com v. Bowen,* 830 F. Supp. 2d 914, 918 (E.D. Cal. 2011), vacated in part on other grounds, *Protectmarriage.com–Yes on 8 v. Bowen,* 752 F.3d 827, 830 (9th Cir. 2014).

86 "highly repetitive": Ibid., 830.

86 immediate police response: Exs. K-3, K-5, to Defendant-Intervenors' Motion, *Perry,* 704 F. Supp. 2d 921 (No. 09-2292) (Doc. 187-11).

87 Two Mormon temples: Ex. K-9, to Defendant-Intervenors' Motion, *Perry,* 704 F. Supp. 2d 921 (No. 09-2292) (Doc. 187-11).

87 pilfering from both sides: Ex. K-30, to Defendant-Intervenors' Motion, *Perry,* 704 F. Supp. 2d 921 (No. 09-2292) (Doc. 187-11).

87 "mechanisms relied upon": *Bowen,* 830 F. Supp. 2d at 934 (quoting *ProtectMarriage.com v. Bowen,* 599 F. Supp. 2d 1197, 1218 (E.D. Cal. 2009).

87 free rainbow sherbet: Ex. K-47, to Defendant-Intervenors' Motion, *Perry,* 704 F. Supp. 2d 921 (No. 09-2292) (Doc. 187-11).

87 confronted a recall vote: Ex. K-41, to Defendant-Intervenors' Motion, *Perry,* 704 F. Supp. 2d 921 (No. 09-2292) (Doc. 187-11).

87 his musical theater: Exs. K-38, K-40, K-49, to Defendant-Intervenors' Motion, *Perry,* 704 F. Supp. 2d 921 (No. 09-2292) (Doc. 187-11).

87 "phone calls, emails and letters voicing disagreement": *ProtectMarriage .com v. Bowen,* 830 F. Supp. 2d at 917.

87 "donation of a like amount": Lisa Leff, "Gay-Marriage Ban Backers Targeting Opposition Donors," *U-T San Diego,* October 24, 2008.

87 "Harsh criticism": *Doe v. Reed,* 561 U.S. 186, 228 (2010) (Scalia, J., concurring in the judgment).

5: Curtain Up

93 must be group marriage: Defendant-Intervenors' Proposed Findings of Fact at 29, *Perry v. Schwarzenegger,* 704 F. Supp. 2d 921 (N.D. Cal. 2010) (No. 09–2292) (Doc. 606).

94 Elaine Scarry distinguishes: Elaine Scarry, "Speech Acts in Criminal Cases," in *Law's Stories: Narrative and Rhetoric in the Law,* Peter Brooks and Paul Gewirtz, eds. (New Haven: Yale University, 1996), 166.

96 Mary Anne Case observed: Mary Anne Case, "Couples and Coupling in the Public Sphere: A Comment on the Legal History of Litigating for Lesbian and Gay Rights," *Virginia Law Review* 79 (1993): 1644.

97 coming together in "coitus": Amici Curiae Brief of Robert P. George, Sherif Girgis, and Ryan T. Anderson in Support of Hollingsworth and Bipartisan Legal Advisory Group Addressing the Merits and Supporting Reversal, *Hollingsworth v. Perry,* 133 S. Ct. 2652 (2013) (12–144).

97 "negative liberty": Isaiah Berlin, "Two Concepts of Liberty," in *Four Essays on Liberty* (Oxford: Oxford University Press, 1969), 121–31.

97 **"responsibility-right":** Jeremy Waldron, "Dignity, Rights, and Responsibilities," Public Law & Legal Theory Research Paper Series, Working Paper No. 10-83, December 2010, 9.

97 **tangible legal benefits:** See *In re Marriage Cases,* 43 Cal.4th 757, 779 (2008).

98 **brief and commonplace:** Derald Wing Sue, *Microaggressions in Everyday Life: Race, Gender, and Sexual Orientation* (Hoboken: John Wiley & Sons, 2010), 5.

98 **serious cumulative effects:** Ibid., 6.

98 **the tendency to trivialize:** Dale Schowengerdt, *"Perry v. Schwarzenegger* District Court Trial Blog Posts," Alliance Defending Freedom, January 14, 2010, www.alliancedefendingfreedom.org/News/PRDetail/4897.

6: The Right to Marry

101 **"The freedom to marry":** *Loving v. Virginia,* 388 U.S. 1, 12 (1967).

101 **The proponents agreed:** Defendants-Intervenors Proposition 8 proponents and Projectmarriage.com's Supplemental Case Management Statement—Proposed Stipulations, at 1, *Perry v. Schwarzenegger,* 704 F. Supp. 2d 921 (N.D. Cal. 2010) (No. 09-CV-2292 VRW) (Document 159-2).

101 **Due Process Clauses:** U.S. Const. amends. V, XIV.

101 **Less intuitively, the Supreme Court:** This doctrine is known as "substantive due process," and includes cases such as *Meyer v. Nebraska,* 262 U.S. 390 (1923), *Roe v. Wade,* 410 U.S. 113 (1973), and *Lawrence v. Texas,* 539 U.S. 558 (2003).

102 **the right to privacy:** *Griswold v. Connecticut,* 381 U.S. 479 (1965).

102 **"deeply rooted in this Nation's history":** *Washington v. Glucksberg,* 521 U.S. 702, 721 (1997).

102 **prisoners to marry in 1987:** *Turner v. Safley,* 482 U.S. 78 (1987).

102 **rejected that argument:** See, e.g., *Conaway v. Deane,* 932 A.2d. 571, 629 (Md. 2007); *Andersen v. King County,* 138 P.3d 963, 979 (Wash. 2006).

102 **disposed of the case:** See, e.g., *Varnum v. Brien,* 763 N.W.2d 862 (Iowa 2009); *Kerrigan v. Commissioner of Public Health,* 957 A.2d 407 (Conn. 2008).

102 **Hawaii Supreme Court's:** *Baehr v. Lewin,* 852 P.2d 44, 56 (Haw. 1993).

103 **When a 2010 poll:** "American Values Survey 2010," Public Religion Research Institute, September 1-14, 2010, http://publicreligion.org/

site/wp-content/uploads/2010/05/September-2010-American-Values
-Survey.pdf (question 10 and 11).

104 **one ad portrays a train:** "PX0401," available at YouTube, www.you
tube.com/watch?v=xtEuuqPXaKk.

104 **marriage laws made women:** Peggy A. Rabkin, *Fathers to Daughters:
The Legal Foundations of Female Emancipation* (Westport: Green-
wood Press, 1980), 20.

106 **"Almighty God created the races":** *Loving,* 338 U.S. 1, 3 (1967).

107 **series of short opinions:** *Processes of Constitutional Decisionmak-
ing* (Brest et al., eds., 5th ed., New York: Aspen Publishers, 2006),
957.

107 **avoid deciding the case:** *Naim v. Naim,* 350 U.S. 891 (1955). See also
Michael J. Klarman, *From Jim Crow to the Civil Rights Movement*
(New York: Oxford University Press, 2004), 321–23.

110 **"throws a *huge* wrench":** Austin R. Nimocks, "January 27, 2010,
ADF Senior Legal Counsel Austin R. Nimocks," *Perry v. Schwar-
zenegger* district court trial blog posts, www.adfmedia.org/News/
PRDetail/4897.

110 **"record of genuine concern":** Margaret Talbot, "Gay Marriage and
Competing Goods," *New Yorker,* January 27, 2010.

115 **1987 Supreme Court case:** *Turner v. Safley,* 482 U.S. 78 (1987).

7: A History of Discrimination

119 **Equal Protection Clause:** U.S. Const. amend. XIV.

119 **"race, color, or previous condition of servitude":** U.S. Const. amend.
XV.

119 **"most rigid scrutiny":** *Loving v. Virginia,* 388 U.S. 1, 11 (1967).

119 **"exceedingly persuasive justification":** *United States v. Virginia,* 518
U.S. 515, 534 (1996). The Court distinguishes between two forms of
heightened scrutiny. "Strict" scrutiny is given to classifications like
race, national origin, and alienage. "Intermediate" scrutiny is given to
gender and non-marital parentage. The Court has not drawn a strong
distinction between these two forms, particularly after the *Virginia*
case. I use "heightened scrutiny" to encompass both "strict" and "intermediate" scrutiny.

119 **usually uphold the law:** I say that the Court "usually" upholds a law
under rational basis if any conceivable rationale can be given for it,
because sometimes the Court will strike down a law even if such a
rationale exists. In these instances, the Court is sometimes said to be
applying rational basis "with bite." In my view, the instances in which

the Court applies such rational basis "with bite" almost uniformly concern instances in which the Court discerns some form of animus. Rather than casting those cases as instances in which the Court applied a different standard, I discuss them as instances in which animus, which is by definition irrational, failed the extant standard.

120 **a famous 1955 case:** *Williamson v. Lee Optical of Oklahoma Inc.,* 348 U.S. 483 (1955).

120 **dodged the issue twice:** *Romer v. Evans,* 517 U.S. 620 (1996); *Lawrence v. Texas,* 539 U.S. 558 (2003).

120 **pushed for heightened scrutiny:** See, e.g., Plaintiffs' Notice of Motion and Motion for a Preliminary Injunction, and Memorandum of Points and Authorities in Support of Motion for a Preliminary Injunction at 12-16, *Perry v. Schwarzenegger,* 790 F. Supp. 2d 921 (N.D. Cal. 2010) (No. 09–2292 VRW) (Doc. 7).

121 **an opinion in 1973:** *Frontiero v. Richardson,* 411 U.S. 677 (1973).

121 **dangerous to generate criteria:** Kenji Yoshino, "Assimilationist Bias in Equal Protection: The Visibility Presumption and the Case of 'Don't Ask, Don't Tell,'" *Yale Law Journal* 108 (1998): 565.

121 **not granted formal heightened scrutiny:** Kenji Yoshino, "The New Equal Protection," *Harvard Law Review* 124 (2011): 757.

122 **increasing number of state:** *SmithKline Beecham Corp. v. Abbott Laboratories,* 740 F.3d 471 (9th Cir. 2014); *Windsor v. U.S.,* 699 F.3d 169 (2d Cir. 2012); *Varnum v. Brien,* 763 N.W.2d 862 (Iowa 2009); *In re Marriage Cases,* 183 P.3d 384 (Cal. 2008).

122 **Most courts have found it uncontroversial:** *Windsor v. U.S.,* 699 F.3d 169, 182 (2d Cir. 2012) ("It is easy to conclude that homosexuals have suffered a history of discrimination . . . we think it is not much in debate."); *Whitewood v. Wolf,* 992 F. Supp. 2d 410, 427 (M.D. Pa. 2014) ("That the gay and lesbian community has endured historical discrimination at the national level is uncontested."); *De Leon v. Perry,* 975 F. Supp. 2d 632, 650 (W.D. Tex 2014) ("[The] long history of discrimination against homosexuals is widely acknowledged in federal American jurisprudence.").

122 **proponents offered to concede:** Defendants-Intervenors Proposition 8 proponents and Projectmarriage.com's Case Management Statement at 14, *Perry v. Schwarzenegger,* 790 F. Supp. 2d 921 (N.D. Cal. 2010) (No. 09–2292 VRW) (Doc. 139).

122 **Lambda Legal's Kevin Cathcart:** Kevin Cathcart, "Remarks at the Out in Law summit at NYU School of Law," March 13, 2014, http://outleadership.org/out-in-law-2/oil-past-events/2014/out-in-law-2014/.

124 **A 1942 regulation:** Allan Bérubé, *Coming Out Under Fire: The*

History of Gay Men and Women in World War Two (New York: The Free Press, 1990), 19–20.

125 **US Senate policy statement:** "Employment of Homosexuals and Other Sex Perverts in Government," Interim Report Submitted to the Committee on Expenditures in the Executive Departments by Its Subcommittee on Investigations, S. Doc. No. 81-241 (1950).

125 **enact a law in 1977:** Yolanne Almanzar, "Florida Gay Adoption Ban Is Ruled Unconstitutional," *New York Times,* November 25, 2008.

126 **"Have you thought about":** "PX0016," available at YouTube, www.youtube.com/watch?v=JnyEmOf_xzA.

126 **"taught in public schools":** "PX0029," available at YouTube, www.youtube.com/watch?v=yE-bju4VK_w.

126 **"After Massachusetts legalized":** "PX0091," available at YouTube, www.youtube.com/watch?v=e4RcnotnKlc.

126 **Forceful in its simplicity:** "PX0099," available at YouTube, www.youtube.com/watch?v=_qelscOqbQY.

127 **control the school's curriculum:** *Parker v. Hurley,* 474 F. Supp. 2d 261 (D.Mass. 2007), aff'd by *Parker v. Hurley,* 514 F.3d 87 (1st Cir. 2008).

127 **legal scholar Reva Siegel:** Reva B. Siegel, " 'The Rule of Love': Wife Beating as Prerogative and Privacy," *Yale Law Journal* 105 (1996): 2119.

129 **proponents played their own:** "PX0116," available at YouTube, www.youtube.com/watch?v=BmLuDTljuGo.

130 **obscured by a heart:** Linda de Haan and Stern Nijland, *King & King* (New York: Tricycle Press, 2003).

131 **a white rabbit and a black rabbit:** Garth Williams, *The Rabbits' Wedding* (New York: HarperCollins, 1958).

131 **"taken off the shelves":** Patterson Toby Graham, *A Right to Read: Segregation and Civil Rights in Alabama's Public Libraries, 1900–1965* (University of Alabama Press, 2006), 107.

131 **"completely unaware":** Douglas Martin, "Emily W. Reed, 89, Librarian in '59 Alabama Racial Dispute," *New York Times,* May 29, 2000.

8: Immutability

133 **keyed in on immutability:** *Frontiero v. Richardson,* 411 U.S. 677, 686 (1973).

133 **Many scholars (including me):** See, e.g., Kenji Yoshino, "Assimilationist Bias in Equal Protection: The Visibility Presumption and the Case of 'Don't Ask, Don't Tell,' " *Yale Law Journal* 108 (1998): 485, and Anthony R. Enriquez, "Assuming Responsibility for Who You Are:

The Right to Choose 'Immutable' Identity Characteristics," 88 *New York University Law Review* 373 (2013).

133 **legal scholar Laurence Tribe:** Laurence H. Tribe, "The Puzzling Persistence of Process-Based Constitutional Theories," *Yale Law Journal* 89 (1980): 1073–74, footnote 52.

134 **"an innate characteristic":** *Hernandez-Montiel v. I.N.S.*, 225 F.3d 1084, 1093 (9th Cir. 2000) (emphasis added).

134 **one of my colleagues:** I thank David Glasgow for this point.

134 **"Homosexuals exist":** Jonathan Rauch, *Gay Marriage: Why It Is Good for Gays, Good for Straights, and Good for America* (New York: Henry Holt, 1994), 87.

134 **"Things that exist, exist":** Donald Judd, "Black, White, and Gray" (1964), in *Complete Writings 1959–1975* (Halifax: Nova Scotia College of Art and Design, 1975), 117.

136 **two to five times more likely:** Marla E. Eisenberg and Michael D. Resnick, "Suicidality Among Gay, Lesbian and Bisexual Youth: The Role of Protective Factors," *Journal of Adolescent Health* 39, no. 5 (2006): 662–68 (finding LBG youth were more than twice as likely to attempt suicide than heterosexual peers); Mark L. Hatzenbuehler, "The Social Environment and Suicide Attempts in Lesbian, Gay, and Bisexual Youth," *Pediatrics* 127 (2011), 896–903 (finding gay youths more than five times as likely to attempt suicide than heterosexual peers).

9: Political Powerlessness

146 **filed a pre-trial motion:** Plaintiffs' and Plaintiff-Intervenor's Notice of Motion *in Limine* to Exclude Portions of the Expert Report, Opinions, and Testimony of Kenneth P. Miller, *Perry v. Schwarzenegger*, No. 09-2292 (N.D. Cal. Dec. 7, 2009) (Doc. 280).

149 **precedent had been set in *Cleburne*:** *City of Cleburne, Tex. v. Cleburne Living Center*, 473 U.S. 432, 445 (1985).

150 **"prejudice against discrete and insular minorities":** *U.S. v. Carolene Products Co.*, 304 U.S. 144, 152 footnote 4 (1938).

151 *Hamlet* **without the prince:** Bruce A. Ackerman, "Beyond Carolene Products," *Harvard Law Review* 98 (1985): 731.

154 **"Nation's decision-making councils":** *Frontiero v. Richardson*, 411 U.S. 677 (1973), footnote 17.

10: The Ideal Family

156 "find some footing": *Heller v. Doe,* 509 U.S. 312, 321 (1993).

156 offered a "catch-all" basket: Defendant-Intervenors' Trial Memorandum, at 8, *Perry v. Schwarzenegger,* 704 F. Supp. 2d 921 (N.D. Cal. 2010) (No. 09-2292) (Doc. 295).

156 from constitutional attack: *Williams v. Illinois,* 399 U.S. 235, 239–40 (1970).

157 New Mexico photographer: *Elane Photography v. Willock,* 309 P.3d 53 (N.M. 2013), *cert. denied,* 134 S. Ct. 1787 (2014).

157 it held that Nebraska: *Meyer v. Nebraska,* 262 U.S. 390 (1923).

158 "Voters in California": Adam Liptak, "Trial in Same-Sex Marriage Case Is Challenged," *New York Times,* March 22, 2010.

159 The judge ruled: *Protectmarriage.com v. Courage Campaign,* 680 F. Supp. 2d 1225 (E.D. Cal. 2010).

160 statistically higher rates: Rosa Flores and Rose Marie Arce, "Why Are Lawyers Killing Themselves?" CNN, January 20, 2014, www .cnn.com/2014/01/19/us/lawyer-suicides/.

160 "the best example": *Howard v. Child Welfare Agency Review Bd.,* 2004 WL 3154530, 8 (Ark. Cir. Ct. 2004).

161 "21 Reasons": "21 Reasons Why Gender Matters," Fatherhood Foundation, 2007, www.gendermatters.org.au/Home_files/21%20Reasons %20Why%20Gender%20Matters(low%20res).pdf.

164 grew up with stepparents: Kristin Anderson Moore et al., "Marriage from a Child's Perspective: How Does Family Structure Affect Children, and What Can We Do about It?" *Child Trends,* June 2002, www .childtrends.org/wp-content/uploads/2013/03/MarriageRB602.pdf, 1.

165 study conducted at the University of Chicago: Robert A. Johnson et al., *The Relationship Between Family Structure and Adolescent Substance Use* (Rockville: Substance Abuse and Mental Health Services Administration, Office of Applied Studies, U.S. Dept. of Health and Human Services, Public Health Service, 1996).

166 Supreme Court had already decided: *Mississippi University for Women v. Hogan,* 458 U.S. 718 (1982); *United States v. Virginia,* 518 U.S. 515 (1996).

167 the 1996 military-academy decision: *Virginia,* 518 U.S. 550.

170 When Westboro Baptist won: *Snyder v. Phelps,* 131 S. Ct. 1207 (2011).

170 "archaic and overbroad" ideas: *Weinberger v. Wiesenfeldt,* 420 U.S. 636, 643 (1975).

170 graduate from college at higher rates: US Census Bureau, "Degrees Earned by Level and Sex: 1960 to 2009," Statistical Abstract of the

United States Table 299, www.census.gov/compendia/statab/2012/
tables/12s0299.pdf (accessed October 17, 2014).

171 **"When moms are in the park":** *Perry v. Schwarzenegger,* 704 F. Supp.
2d 921, 975 (N.D. Cal. 2010) (quoting Plaintiffs' Exhibit No. 0506, at 6).

11: A Threat to Marriage

173 **storage company in Manhattan:** Zeke Miller, "Here Are the Viral
Subway Ads That Slam Rick Perry, Michele Bachmann, and the Mets,"
Business Insider, October 10, 2011, www.businessinsider.com.au/
here-are-the-viral-subway-ads-that-make-fun-of-rick-perry-michele
-bachmann-and-the-mets-2011-10#-8.

173 **Wanda Sykes has said:** "Wanda Sykes on Gay Marriage," available on
YouTube, www.youtube.com/watch?v=1IHdaJOZe7E.

174 **As I have argued:** Kenji Yoshino, "Marriage, Trademarked," *Slate,*
July 7, 2007, www.slate.com/articles/news_and_politics/jurisprudence
/2007/07/marriage_trademarked.html.

174 **Judge Richard Posner:** *Ty Inc. v. Perryman,* 306 F.3d 509, 511 (7th
Cir. 2002).

174 **aloud at weddings both gay and straight:** Sasha Issenberg, "With
These Words: Gay-Marriage Court Ruling Is a Hit at Straight Weddings," *New York Magazine,* July 27, 2012.

174 **"Civil marriage is at once":** *Goodridge v. Department of Public
Health,* 798 N.E.2d 941, 954–55 (Mass. 2003).

175 **Liza Mundy in the *Atlantic*:** Liza Mundy, "The Gay Guide to Wedded
Bliss," *Atlantic,* May 22, 2013.

178 **ominously titled essay:** Stanley Kurtz, "The End of Marriage in Scandinavia," *Weekly Standard,* February 2, 2004.

178 **Kurtz lamented:** Ibid.

178 **in a response essay:** M. V. Lee Badgett, "Prenuptial Jitters," *Slate,*
May 20, 2004, www.slate.com/articles/news_and_politics/politics/
2004/05/prenuptial_jitters.html.

178 **Yet Kurtz's conclusions:** Ibid. See also *"Conservative Case" for Same-
Sex Marriage Collapses* by Stanley Kurtz reproduced, 108th Congress,
2nd sess., *Congressional Record* 150, Pt. 11: 15356.

180 **novels I had taught:** A. S. Byatt, *Babel Tower* (London: Chatto &
Windus, 1997); Bernhard Schlink, *The Reader* (New York: Vintage
International, 1997).

181 **Oscar Wilde trial:** Merlin Holland, *The Real Trial of Oscar Wilde*
(New York: Fourth Estate, 2003).

183 **a 1998 antitrust trial:** Elizabeth Wasserman, "Gates Deposition

Makes Judge Laugh in Court," CNN, November 17, 1998, accessed
October 17, 2014, http://edition.cnn.com/TECH/computing/9811/17/
judgelaugh.ms.idg/.

184 **brainstorming ideas:** David Blankenhorn, *The Future of Marriage*
(New York: Encounter Books, 2009), 202–09.

184 **"naturally procreative relationships":** Defendant-Intervenors' Trial
Memorandum, at 8, *Perry v. Schwarzenegger,* 704 F. Supp. 2d 921
(N.D. Cal. 2010) (No. 09-CV-2292 VRW) (Document 295).

185 **"ensuring responsible procreation":** *Standhardt v. Superior Court ex
rel. County of Maricopa,* 77 P.3d 451, 463 (Ariz. Ct. App. 2003).

185 **Indiana court similarly:** *Morrison v. Sadler,* 821 N.E.2d 15, 25 (Ind.
App. 2005).

185 **New York's high court:** *Hernandez v. Robles,* 855 N.E.2d 1, 3 (N.Y.
2006). For my response to this decision, in which I develop some of the
ideas in this chapter, see Kenji Yoshino, "Too Good for Marriage?,"
New York Times, July 14, 2006.

185 **"do not become parents":** Ibid.

185 **"often casual or temporary":** Ibid.

186 **"natural and proper timidity":** *Bradwell v. Illinois,* 83 U.S. 130, 141
(1873) (Bradley, J., concurring).

186 **"not on a pedestal":** *Frontiero v. Richardson,* 411 U.S. 677, 684
(1973) (plurality opinion).

12: The Bare Desire to Harm

187 **"If you want to know":** Candace Chellew-Hodge, "NOM's Gallagher: 'Don't Call Me a Bigot!,'" *Religious Dispatches,* April 22, 2011,
http://religiondispatches.org/noms-gallagher-dont-call-me-a-bigot/.

187 **"refuse to be treated like bigots":** Amanda Holpuch, "Foes of Same-Sex
Marriage Fight on as Courts and Public Opinion Turn Against Them,"
Guardian, August 6, 2014, www.theguardian.com/world/2014/aug/
06/same-sex-marriage-foes-fight-courts-opinion-polling.

188 **a 2010 opinion:** *Christian Legal Society v. Martinez,* 561 U.S. 661
(2010).

188 **"a tax on wearing yarmulkes":** Ibid. at 689 (quoting *Bray v. Alexan-
dria Women's Health Clinic,* 506 U. S. 263, 270 [1993].

189 **"not a toothless one":** *Mathews v. Lucas,* 427 U.S. 495, 510 (1976).

189 **"bare . . . desire to harm":** The Court coined the phrase in *Department of Agriculture v. Moreno,* 413 U.S. 528, 534 (1973). The Court
then used the same formulation in numerous other cases, including

City of Cleburne, Tex. v. Cleburne Living Center, 473 U.S. 432, 447 (1985) and *Romer v. Evans,* 517 U.S. 633, 634 (1996).

189 **to block "hippies":** Ibid.

190 **"mere negative attitudes":** *City of Cleburne, Tex. v. Cleburne Living Center,* 473 U.S. 432, 446–48 (1985). For a thoughtful analysis of the Court's treatment of animus, see Susannah W. Pollvogt, "Unconstitutional Animus," *Fordham Law Review* 81 (2012): 900–15.

190 **Justice Kennedy meditated:** *Board of Trustees of University of Alabama v. Garrett,* 531 U.S. 356, 374 (2001) (Kennedy, J., concurring).

191 **The Supreme Court upheld:** *Rogers v. Lodge,* 458 U.S. 613 (1982).

195 **"the safety of his family":** Hak-Shing William Tam's Notice of Motion and Motion to Withdraw, and Memorandum of Points and Authorities in Support of Motion to Withdraw at 3, *Perry,* 704 F. Supp. 2d 921 (No. 09-2292) (Doc. 369).

195 **"speculative musings":** Plaintiffs' Opposition to Hak-Shing William Tam's Motion to Withdraw, *Perry,* 704 F. Supp. 2d 921 (No. 09-2292) (Doc. 441).

195 **"borders on the shameful":** Hak-Shing William Tam's Reply to Plaintiffs' Opposition to Motion to Withdraw at 2, *Perry,* 704 F. Supp. 2d 921 (No. 09-2292) (Doc. 450).

197 **"Dr. Tam represented":** Austin R. Nimocks, "ADF Senior Legal Counsel Austin R. Nimocks: Prop. 8 Trial Update for Thurs. Jan 21, 2009 [sic]," Alliance Defending Freedom, January 21, 2010, www .alliancealert.org/2010/01/22/adf-senior-legal-counsel-austin-r -nimocks-prop-8-trial-update-for-thurs-jan-21-2009/.

13: The Phantom Witnesses

199 **final tally was seventeen witnesses:** I have omitted any discussion of plaintiffs' expert Edmund Egan, who testified on the fourth day of trial about the economic effects of same-sex marriage on jurisdictions that legalized it. Ultimately, both sides agreed that the legalization of same-sex marriage would not have a negative economic effect. Moreover, the proponents did not advance protection of the public fisc as an argument for Prop 8 in any serious way. So Egan's testimony—though cogent—was swiftly shown to be undisputed and irrelevant. Other than Egan, I have discussed all witnesses (including hostile witness Bill Tam) called by the plaintiffs and all witnesses (actual and withdrawn) advanced by the proponents on their formal witness list.

199 **"The time clock tells me":** Jon Fleischman, "Andy Pugno: A Vigorous Defense for Traditional Marriage," *Flash Report,* January 26, 2010, www.flashreport.org/commentaryob.php?postID=201001260345258 8&authID=2005081622025042&post_offsetP=0.

200 **The ADF's gadfly:** "California Judge Strikes Down Prop 8 Marriage Amendment," *Liberty Counsel,* August 4, 2010, www.lc.org/index .cfm?PID=14100&PRID=960.

201 **"Though these experts":** *Varnum v. Brien,* No. CV5965, 2007 WL2468667 (Iowa Dist. Ct. 2007).

201 **reversed this decision:** *Varnum,* 763 N.W. 2d 862 (Iowa 2009).

201 **they did not apply:** Ibid., 881 ("constitutional facts are not subject to the rules of evidence when presented by a party in the form of witness testimony").

201 **Nathanson's report argued:** Declaration of Paul Nathanson, PhD, as Expert Witness for Defendant, *Perry,* 704 F. Supp. 2d 921 (No. 09-2292).

201 **CNN exit poll:** *Perry v. Schwarzenegger,* 704 F. Supp. 2d 921, 952 (N.D. Cal. 2010).

202 **He spoke even more candidly:** Becker, *Forcing the Spring,* 94.

203 **three books with Young:** Paul Nathanson and Katherine Young, *Spreading Misandry: The Teaching of Contempt for Men in Popular Culture* (Montreal: McGill-Queen's University Press, 2001); Paul Nathanson and Katherine Young, *Legalizing Misandry: From Public Shame to Systemic Discrimination Against Men* (Montreal: McGill-Queen's University Press, 2006); Paul Nathanson and Katherine Young, *Sanctifying Misandry: Goddess Ideology and the Fall of Man* (Montreal: McGill-Queen's University Press, 2011).

204 **She cut a section:** Declaration of Katherine Young, PhD, as Expert Witness for Defendant, at 11 footnote 18, *Varnum,* 763 N.W.2d 862 (No. CV-5965).

205 **"It's not my primary":** Examination of Mrs. Katherine K. Young by Mr. David Boies at 7, *Perry* (No. 09-2292).

205 **the full Boies treatment:** Examination of Katherine Young, at 8–9.

206 **"please repeat your question":** Examination of Mrs. Katherine K. Young by Mr. David Boies at 9–14.

208 **never taught in McGill's anthropology faculty:** Ibid., 36.

208 **child development, political science, or sociology:** Ibid., 37–38.

208 **Young had distinguished:** Declaration of Katherine Young, PhD, as Expert Witness for Defendant at 12-15, *Perry,* 704 F. Supp. 2d 921 (No. 09–2292).

208 **"examples of cultures":** Examination of Katherine K. Young by Mr. David Boies, at 44–52. When I asked Young how she would reconcile these examples of same-sex marriage with her claim that opposite-sex marriage was "universal," she replied that the "norm" in all these cultures was still opposite-sex marriage, and that these examples were the "exceptions." Of course, even if the United States (or any jurisdiction) adopted same-sex marriage, such marriages would never be the "norm," given that gays are a small minority in society.

209 **"separation of church and state":** Examination of Mrs. Katherine K. Young by Mr. David Boies, at 7, 233.

210 **average black IQ:** Richard Herrnstein and Charles Murray, *The Bell Curve* (New York: Free Press, 1994), 269.

210 **Robinson had avidly critiqued:** Daniel N. Robinson, "Hereditary Monarchy in the Republic of Virtue," review of *The Bell Curve* by Richard Herrnstein and Charles Murray, *Journal of Blacks in Higher Education* 117 (1994–95): 117–122.

211 **a "good point":** Of course, many would argue that the cases of religion and sexual orientation can be distinguished because the Free Exercise Clause of the Constitution explicitly protects religious conduct, while the Equal Protection Clause does not explicitly protect sexual conduct. However, the point Robinson was making was a logical one, not a doctrinal one. Robinson originally argued that homosexuality was too inchoate an identity to protect. In his interview, he conceded that religious identity suffered from the same issues but was nonetheless a coherent and protected identity.

212 **"nonmarital, divorced, or step-families":** Expert Report of Loren Marks at 11, *Perry*, 704 F. Supp. 2d 921 (No. 09-2292) (Doc. 286-5).

212 **early in the deposition:** Deposition of Loren Marks at 30, *Perry*, 704 F. Supp. 2d 921 (No. 09-2292).

212 **not many such studies:** Ibid.

212 **At several other junctures:** Ibid., 37, 62, 116.

212 **preparing a rebuttal report:** Ibid., 32.

212 **about the genetic tie:** Ibid., 81–112.

212 **Yet McGill pointed out:** Ibid., 144.

213 **McGill asked Marks:** Ibid., 147.

213 **quoted it as saying:** Expert Report of Loren Marks, at 4, as Expert Witness for Defendant, *Perry*, 704 F. Supp. 2d 921 (No. 09-2292) (Doc. 286-5) (citing Institute for American Values, *Why Marriage Matters: Twenty-Six Conclusions from the Social Sciences*, 2d ed.

(New York: 2005), 25). Marks added the emphasis to the phrase "both biological parents" in his Expert Report.

213 "Taking a close look": Deposition of Loren Marks at 147, *Perry,* 704 F. Supp. 2d 921 (No. 09-2292).

213 "Would you also withdraw": Ibid.

213 gender-differentiated parenting: Ibid., 202–205.

213 "It's highly contested ground": Ibid., 204.

213 Marks acceded: Ibid., 204–05.

213 McGill then sought: Ibid., 205.

213 "That's correct": Ibid.

213 Thompson quickly intervened: Ibid.

213 illuminate their parenting: Ibid., 240.

213 a "judgment call": Ibid.

213 to make such an inference: Ibid.

213 Marks said no: Ibid.

214 had their biases: Ibid., 48.

214 "One of my biases": Ibid.

214 "Optimism": Ibid.

214 "Latter Day Saint scholar": Loren D. Marks and David C. Dollahite, "Family Worship in Christian, Jewish, and Muslim Homes," in *Helping and Healing Our Families: Principles and Practices Inspired by the Family,* Craig H. Hart et al., eds. (Salt Lake City: Deseret Book Company, 2005), 259–63.

214 "if we're allowed to ask": Deposition of Loren Marks, at 63–64.

214 "I will acknowledge": Ibid., 64.

214 a 1995 Mormon text: First Presidency and Council of Twelve Apostles (1995, November), "The Family: A Proclamation to the World," *Ensign* 25 (11): 102.

214 preamble to the proclamation: Ibid.

214 "The Family is ordained": Ibid.

214 "that the principles stated": Deposition of Loren Dean Marks at 259, *Perry,* 704 F. Supp. 2d 921 (No. 09-2292).

214 "personal belief": Ibid., 260.

217 "I will never know": Maggie Gallagher, "Letter to Court Regarding Televised Trials," *National Organization for Marriage Blog,* January 28, 2010, www.nomblog.com/719/.

217 "awful, homophobic statements": Jo Becker, *Forcing the Spring,* 201.

14: The Trial Court

221 copy of the video recording: Order to the Parties, at 2, *Perry,* 704 F. Supp. 2d 921 (No. 09-2292) (Doc. 672).

221 sent each side specific questions: Questions for Closing Arguments, *Perry,* 704 F. Supp. 2d 921 (No. 09-2292) (Doc. 677).

226 "The Moving Finger writes": Omar Khayyám, *The Rubaiyat of Omar Khayyám* (Edward FitzGerald, trans., 1st ed. 1859), Quatrain 51.

228 decision in *Perry v. Schwarzenegger:* 704 F. Supp. 2d 921 (N.D. Cal. 2010).

228 "An initiative measure": Ibid., 938.

229 "The record does not reveal": Ibid., 944.

229 "Blankenhorn's testimony constitutes inadmissible": Ibid., 946.

229 "Miller has significant experience": Ibid., 951.

229 "Domestic partnerships lack": Ibid., 970.

230 "stable, governable populace": Ibid., 992.

230 "archaic, shameful": Ibid.

230 "union of equals": Ibid.

230 "gender is not relevant": Ibid., 993.

230 "plaintiffs ask California": Ibid.

231 "footing in the realities": Ibid. (quoting *Heller v. Doe* by Doe, 509 U.S. 312, 321 (1993)).

231 "plaintiffs' equal protection claim": Ibid.

231 "purposeful unequal treatment": Ibid., 997 (quoting *San Antonio Indep. Sch. Dist. v. Rodriguez,* 411 U.S. 1, 28 (1973)).

231 "Individuals do not generally": Ibid., 966.

232 "tradition alone": Ibid., 998 (citing *Williams v. Illinois,* 399 U.S. 235 (1970)).

232 "proceeding with caution": Ibid., 999.

232 "Permitting same-sex couples": Ibid., 972.

232 "equal quality": Ibid., 999.

232 "stable, long-term relationships": Ibid., 981.

232 "protecting the freedom": Ibid., 1000.

233 "as a matter of law": Ibid., 1001.

233 "any conceivable rationale": Ibid., 1001 (quoting Defendant-Intervenors' Trial Memorandum, 15).

233 "failed to identify": Ibid., 1001–02.

233 "premised on the belief": Ibid., 1002.

233 "on which to legislate": Ibid., 1002.

233 "To say we were euphoric": Boies and Olson, *Redeeming the Dream,* 189.

233 **they tearfully embraced:** Ibid., 190.
233 **Jennifer Pizer of Lambda Legal:** "Lambda Legal Applauds *Perry v. Schwarzenegger* Ruling Striking Down Prop 8," Lambda Legal, August 4, 2010, www.lambdalegal.org/news/ca_20100804_perry-ruling -striking-down.
234 **The ACLU also praised:** Elizabeth Gill, "Historic Victory in Prop. 8 Case, and a Call to Action," ACLU, August 5, 2010, www.aclu.org/ blog/lgbt-rights/historic-victory-prop-8-case-and-call-action.
234 **"groups of wealthy activists":** "Defenders of Marriage in Calif. Will Appeal Dangerous Federal Ruling," Alliance Defending Freedom, August 4, 2010, www.alliancedefendingfreedom.org/News/ PRDetail/4249.
234 **"negated the will":** "Lead Defense Counsel Statement on August 4 *Perry v. Schwarzenegger* Decision," Catholics for the Common Good, http://ccgaction.org/node/849.
234 **"A Brilliant Ruling":** Dahlia Lithwick, "A Brilliant Ruling," *Slate,* August 4, 2010, www.slate.com/articles/news_and_politics/jurisprudence/ 2010/08/a_brilliant_ruling.html.
234 **"eloquently reasoned denunciation":** "Marriage Is a Constitutional Right," *New York Times,* August 4, 2010.

15: The Court of Appeals

235 **proponents filed their appeal:** Defendant-Intervenors-Appellants' Opening Brief, *Perry v. Brown,* 671 F.3d 1052 (9th Cir. 2010) (No. 10-16696) (Doc. 21) [hereinafter Proponents' Ninth Circuit Opening Brief].
235 **federal court cannot hear:** See, e.g., *DaimlerChrysler Corp v. Cuno,* 547 U.S. 332 (2006).
236 **issues of law:** *Pierce v. Underwood,* 487 U.S. 552, 558 (1988).
236 **issues of fact:** *Pullman-Standard v. Swint,* 456 U.S. 273, 287 (1982).
236 **classroom favorite:** *Anderson v. City of Bessemer City, N.C.,* 470 U.S. 564 (1985).
236 **a savvy play:** Andrew Koppelman, "Power in the Facts," *New York Times,* August 4, 2010.
236 **"to insulate its decision":** Proponents' Ninth Circuit Opening Brief, 32.
237 **legislative facts *de novo*:** Ibid., 32–42.
237 **no binding guidance:** In *Lockhart v. McCree,* 476 U.S. 162, 168 footnote 3 (1986), the Supreme Court stated that it was "far from persuaded" that the "clear error" standard applied to legislative facts.

However, it explicitly observed that it was not deciding the case on this ground. For a good discussion, see Caitlin E. Borgmann, "Appellate Review of Social Facts in Constitutional Rights Cases," *California Law Review,* 101 (2013): 1244–48.

237 **some appellate courts:** See, e.g., *Free v. Peters,* 12 F.3d 700, 706 (7th Cir. 1993); *Dunagin v. City of Oxford,* 718 F.2d 738, 748-49 n. 8 (5th Cir. 1983).

237 **rigor and breadth:** Brief for Appellees, *Perry v. Brown,* 671 F.3d 1052 (9th Cir. 2010) (No. 145-1).

237 **self-destructed during deposition:** Ibid., 12 n.1.

237 **Reinhardt had written:** *Watkins v. United States Army,* 847 F.2d 1329, 1358 (9th Cir. 1988) (citations omitted), *withdrawn on reh'g,* 875 F.2d 699 (9th Cir. 1989) (en banc).

238 **Reinhardt rejected the motion:** Memorandum Regarding Motion to Disqualify, *Perry,* 671 F.3d 1052 (No. 10-16696) (Doc. 295).

238 **"an outmoded conception":** Ibid., 4.

238 **"bunch of people":** "Perry v. Schwarzenegger Oral Arguments," YouTube video, 2:04, posted by "LawResourceOrg," April 11, 2011, www.youtube.com/watch?v=tO_H0F1EBfw.

238 **"the only evidence":** Ibid., 2:07.

239 *San Francisco Chronicle* **reported:** Phillip Matier and Andrew Ross, "Judge Being Gay a Nonissue During Prop. 8 Trial," *San Francisco Chronicle,* February 7, 2010.

239 *Los Angeles Times* **stated:** Maura Dolan, "Distilling the Same-Sex Marriage Case."

239 *National Review*'s **website:** Ed Whelan, "Judge Walker's Anti-Prop 8 Sham Trial," *National Review Online,* July 12, 2010, www.national review.com/bench-memos/230960/judge-walker-s-anti-prop-8-sham -trial/ed-whelan.

239 **Maggie Gallagher of NOM accused:** Leonard Pitts Jr., "Who Has the Right to Judge?," *Miami Herald,* August 11, 2010.

239 **called for his impeachment:** Ibid.

239 **"about the law and not the judge":** CBS News/Associated Press, "Gay Marriage Judge's Personal Life Debated," CBS News, August 6, 2010.

239 **the controversy only intensified with time:** Dan Levine, "Gay Judge Never Thought to Drop Marriage Case," Reuters, April 6, 2011.

239 **"You Must Vacate":** J. Matt Barber, "Prop 8, If the Judge Ain't Straight You Must Vacate," *Catholic Online,* April 16, 2011.

239 **more restrained in their motion to vacate:** Defendant-Intervenors Dennis Hollingsworth, Gail J. Knight, Martin F. Gutierrez, Mark

A. Jansson, and Protectmarriage.com's Motion to Vacate Judgment, *Perry,* 704 F. Supp. 2d 921 (No. 09-2292) (Doc. 768).

239 **They were "*not* suggesting":** Ibid., 5 (emphasis in original).

240 **"substantially affected":** Ibid., 3.

240 **denied the motion in a day:** Order Denying Defendant-Intervenors' Motion to Vacate Judgment, *Perry,* 704 F. Supp. 2d 921 (No. 09-2292) (Doc. 797).

240 **"well-informed, thoughtful observer":** Order Denying Defendant-Intervenors' Motion to Vacate Judgment at 15, *Perry,* 704 F. Supp. 2d 921 (No. 09-2292) (Doc. 797) (emphasis in original).

241 **"America's most famous bigot":** Mark Oppenheimer, "David Blankenhorn and the Battle over Same-Sex Marriage," NPR, June 22, 2012, http://wnpr.org/post/david-blankenhorn-and-battle-over-same-sex-marriage.

241 **Frank Rich, then a *New York Times*:** See, e.g., Frank Rich, "Two Weddings, A Divorce, and *Glee,*" *New York Times,* June 12, 2010.

241 **unanimously concluded:** *Perry v. Brown,* 265 P.3d 1002 (Cal. 2011).

241 **Ninth Circuit then merged the original appeal:** Order, *Perry v. Brown,* 671 F.3d 1052 (9th Cir. 2010) (Nos. 10–16696, 11–16577) (Doc. 381).

241 **a 2–1 decision:** *Perry v. Brown,* 671 F.3d 1052 (9th Cir. 2012).

241 **"'laws of this sort'":** Ibid., 1063–64 (quoting *Romer v. Evans,* 517 U.S. 620, 633 [1996]).

242 **deference to the California Supreme Court:** Ibid., 1072–73.

242 **debatable whether some:** Ibid., 1075.

242 **"those concerning the messages":** Ibid., 1075 (citation omitted).

242 **"We need consider only":** Ibid., 1078 (emphasis in original).

243 **narrowest Equal Protection grounds:** Ibid., 1064.

244 **"broad and undifferentiated disability":** *Romer v. Evans,* 517 U.S. 620, 632 (1996).

244 **"no less problematic":** *Perry,* 671 F.3d at 1081.

245 **Almost as an afterthought:** Ibid., 1095–96.

245 **"red cape to wave":** Jane Schacter, "Splitting the Difference: Reflections on *Perry v. Brown,*" *Harvard Law Review Forum* 125 (2012): 72, 77, http://cdn.harvardlawreview.org/wp-content/uploads/pdfs/forvol125_schacter.pdf.

245 **"Gambling with Gay Marriage":** David Cole, "Gambling with Gay Marriage," *New York Review of Books,* February 9, 2012.

246 **an *en banc* review:** Appellants' Petition for Rehearing En Banc, *Perry v. Brown* (9th Cir. 2012) (Nos. 10-16696, 11-16577).

246 **same-sex marriage to Maryland:** Ian Duncan, "Maryland Governor Signs Same-Sex Marriage Law," *Los Angeles Times,* March 1, 2012.

246 **Gov. Chris Christie vetoed legislation:** Kate Zernike, "Christie Keeps His Promise to Veto Gay Marriage Bill," *New York Times,* February 17, 2012.

246 **in North Carolina:** Campbell Robertson, "North Carolina Voters Pass Same-Sex Marriage Ban," *New York Times,* May 8, 2012.

246 **expressed his personal support:** "Transcript: Robin Roberts ABC News Interview with President Obama," ABC News, May 9, 2012, http://abcnews.go.com/Politics/transcript-robin-roberts-abc-news -interview-president-obama/story?id=16316043&singlePage=true.

246 **President Obama had signaled:** Joe Sudbay, "Transcript of Q and A with the President about DADT and Same-Sex Marriage," *America-Blog,* October 27, 2010, http://americablog.com/2010/10/transcript -of-q-and-a-with-the-president-about-dadt-and-same-sex-marriage-2 .html.

246 **Joe Biden's announcement:** Michael Barbaro, "A Scramble as Biden Backs Same-Sex Marriage," *New York Times,* May 6, 2012.

246 **"divisive and discriminatory":** John Wildermuth, "Obama Opposes Proposed Ban on Gay Marriage," *San Francisco Chronicle,* July 2, 2008.

247 **"go ahead and affirm":** "Transcript: Robin Roberts ABC News Interview with President Obama," May 9, 2012, http://abcnews.go .com/Politics/transcript-robin-roberts-abc-news-interview-president -obama/story?id=16316043&singlePage=true.

247 **"The thing . . . at root":** Ibid.

247 **"how caring they are":** Ibid.

247 **except for his marquee declaration:** Ibid.

247 **"ideological drift":** Jack M. Balkin, "Ideological Drift and the Struggle over Meaning," *Connecticut Law Review* 25 (1993): 869–91.

247 **Ninth Circuit denied:** Order, *Perry v. Brown,* 671 F.3d 1052 (9th Cir. 2010) (10-16696).

247 **Blankenhorn wrote an op-ed:** David Blankenhorn, "How My View on Gay Marriage Changed," *New York Times,* June 22, 2012.

248 **"profoundly disturbing":** Ibid.

249 **long trained their sights:** Lyle Denniston, "Court Review of Prop. 8 Opposed," *SCOTUSblog*, August 24, 2012, www.scotusblog.com/?p= 150959.

249 **the proponents sought review:** Proponents' Petition for a Writ of Certiorari, *Hollingsworth v. Perry*, 133 S. Ct. 2652 (2013) (No. 12-144) (Doc. 425).

249 **"an attractive vehicle":** Defendants' Brief in Opposition at 2, *Hollingsworth*, 133 S. Ct. 2652 (No. 12-144).

249 **"real, live people":** Robert Barnes, "Same-Sex Marriage Crusaders Ask Supreme Court to Stand Down," *Washington Post*, September 2, 2012.

250 **amid polls showing support:** "Marriage Equality Is a Mainstream Value," American Foundation for Equal Rights, July 11, 2012, www .afer.org/blog/marriage-equality-is-a-mainstream-value-infographic/.

250 **seek a broad ruling:** Jessica Garrison, Matt Stevens, and Ashley Powers, "Prop. 8 Lawyers Seek Broad Ruling at Supreme Court," *Los Angeles Times*, December 7, 2012.

250 **"finally gives us a chance":** Jessica Garrison, Ashley Powers, and Matt Stevens, "Supreme Court Should Allow Gay Marriage, California Politicians Say," *Los Angeles Times*, December 8, 2012.

250 *United States v. Windsor:* *United States v. Windsor*, 133 S. Ct. 2675 (2013).

250 **one of several actions:** Other suits included GLAD's federal challenges to DOMA in Massachusetts and Connecticut—the first of which was filed in early 2009, shortly before *Perry*—and Lambda Legal's federal administrative complaint and subsequent lawsuit on behalf of Karen Golinski in California. See *Pedersen v. Office of Pers. Mgmt.*, 881 F. Supp. 2d 294 (D. Conn. 2012); *Golinksi v. U.S. Office of Pers. Mgmt.*, 824 F. Supp. 2d 968 (N.D. Cal. 2012); *Gill v. Office of Pers. Mgmt.*, 699 F. Supp. 2d 374 (D. Mass. 2010), *aff'd sub nom. Massachusetts v. U.S. Dept. of Health and Human Servs.*, 682 F.3d 1 (1st Cir. 2012).

251 **"stepparents are typically hostile":** George W. Dent Jr., "No Difference?: An Analysis of Same-Sex Parenting," *Ave Maria Law Review* 10 (2011): 58.

251 **a long string of victories:** *Pedersen*, 881 F. Supp. 2d 294 (D. Conn. 2012); *Golinksi*, 824 F. Supp. 2d 968 (N.D. Cal. 2012); *Gill*, 699 F. Supp. 2d 374 (D. Mass. 2010), *aff'd sub nom; Massachusetts v. U.S. Dept. of Health and Human Servs.*, 682 F.3d 1 (1st Cir. 2012).

251 orders granting certiorari: *Hollingsworth,* 133 S. Ct. 786 (Mem) (2012); *Windsor,* 133 S. Ct. 786 (Mem) (2012).

251 Blackstone, the English jurist: Brief of Petitioners at 32–34, *Hollingsworth,* 133 S. Ct. 2652 (2013) (12-144).

252 in scare quotes: Ibid., 52.

252 marriage as "cramped": Brief for Respondents at 2, *Hollingsworth,* 133 S. Ct. 2652, (No. 12-144).

252 "utilitarian incentive": Ibid.

252 "twelve-day bench trial": Ibid., 6–11.

252 "extensive evidence": Ibid., 25.

252 cataloged the district court's findings: Ibid., 28–35.

253 "courtroom fact finding": Reply Brief of Petitioners at 17, *Hollingsworth,* 133 S. Ct. 2652 (12-144).

253 warranted no deference: Ibid., 16.

253 "a recent academic invention": Ibid., 2.

253 ceased to defend DOMA: Charlie Savage and Sheryl Gay Stolberg, "In Shift, U.S. Says Marriage Act Blocks Gay Rights," *New York Times,* February 23, 2011.

253 the administration introduced: Brief for the United States as Amicus Curiae Supporting the Respondents, *Hollingsworth,* 133 S. Ct. 2652 (12-144).

254 Ed Whelan: Amicus Curiae Brief of the Ethics and Public Policy Center in Support of Petitioners and Supporting Reversal or Vacatur at 1–2, *Hollingsworth,* 133 S. Ct. 2652 (12-144).

254 "deeply confused belief": Ibid., 24–25.

254 constitutional law professors argued: Amicus Curiae Brief of Constitutional Law and Civil Procedure Professors Erwin Chemerinsky and Arthur Miller in Support of Plaintiffs-Respondents Urging Affirmance at 1–2, *Hollingsworth,* 133 S. Ct. 2652 (12-144).

254 "Evidentiary proceedings": Ibid., 3.

255 "unfounded inferences": Ibid., 17–19.

255 "scholars of history and related disciplines": Amicus Curiae Brief of Scholars of History and Related Disciplines in Support of Petitioners, *Hollingsworth,* 133 S. Ct. 2652 (No. 12-144).

255 Concerned Women of America: Amicus Curiae Brief of Concerned Women of America in Support of Petitioners at 36, *Hollingsworth,* 133 S. Ct. 2652 (No. 12-144).

255 a coalition of social science professors: Amici Curiae Brief of Social Science Professors in Support of Petitioners at 36, *Hollingsworth,* 133 S. Ct. 2652 (No. 12-144).

255 "Mothers help children": Ibid., 8.

256 "that biting, kicking, and other forms": Ibid., 10.

256 "the *coup de grace*": Brief of Amicus Curiae Helen M. Alvaré in support of *Hollingsworth* and Bipartisan Legal Advisory Group Addressing the Merits and Supporting Reversal at 34–35, *Hollingsworth,* 133 S. Ct. 2652 (No. 12-144).

256 Westboro Baptist Church: Brief of Westboro Baptist Church as Amicus Curiae in Support of Neither Party Suggesting Reversal, *Hollingsworth,* 133 S. Ct. 2652 (12-144).

256 Allison Orr Larsen: Allison Orr Larsen, "The Trouble with Amicus Facts," *Virginia Law Review* 100 (2014): 1757–1818.

256 what Larsen describes: Ibid., 1757.

256 Court's copyright decisions: *Kirtsaeng v. John Wiley & Sons, Inc.,* 133 S. Ct. 1351, 1364 (2013).

256 a blog post: Larsen, "The Trouble with Amicus Facts," 1791–92.

256 "increasing number of gang fights": *Florence v. Board of Chosen Freeholders of County of Burlington,* 132 S. Ct. 1510, 1518 (2012).

256 no evidence: Larsen, "The Trouble with Amicus Facts," 1786.

256 severe depression and loss of self-esteem: *Gonzales v. Carhart,* 550 U.S. 124 (2007).

256 was not a medical doctor: Larsen, "The Trouble with Amicus Facts," 1795–96.

257 devolved into shouting matches: Kelsey Osterman, "Protesters Clash Outside of Supreme Court over Gay Marriage," *Red Alert Politics,* March 26, 2013.

257 At the beginning: Transcript of Oral Arguments in *Hollingsworth v. Perry,* 133 S. Ct. 2652 (No. 12-144). All subsequent quotations from the oral argument may be found in the transcript.

258 no deference to the trial court's finding: *Perry v. Schwarzenegger,* 704 F. Supp. 2d 921, 980 (N.D. Cal. 2010).

259 Solicitor General Donald Verrilli: Brief for the United States on the Merits Question, *Windsor,* 133 S. Ct. 2675 (No. 12-307); Brief for the United States as Amicus Curiae Supporting the Respondents, *Hollingsworth,* 133 S. Ct. 2652 (No. 12-144).

260 Michael Hardwick had given: Peter Irons, "What Are You Doing in My Bedroom?," in *The Courage of Their Convictions: Sixteen Americans Who Fought Their Way to the Supreme Court* (New York: Penguin, 1988).

261 "two kinds of marriage": Transcript of Oral Arguments in *United States v. Windsor,* 133 S. Ct. 2675 (No. 12-307).

261 Pam Karlan, said to the press: "Windsor legal team's remarks on DOMA case at the Supreme Court," YouTube video, 2:56, posted by

"RespectforMarriage," March 27, 2013, www.youtube.com/watch? v=_Tcb_YvavcE.

261 **Rhode Island, Delaware, and Minnesota:** Katharine Q. Seelye, "Rhode Island Joins States That Allow Gay Marriage," *New York Times*, May 2, 2013; Erik Eckholm, "Delaware, Continuing a Trend, Becomes the 11th State to Allow Same-Sex Unions," *New York Times*, May 7, 2013; Monica Davey, "Minnesota: Governor Signs Same-Sex Marriage into Law," *New York Times*, May 14, 2013.

261 **Uruguay, New Zealand, and France:** "Uruguay: Same-Sex Marriage Is Legalized," *New York Times*, April 10, 2013; "New Zealand: Gay Marriage Bill Passes," *New York Times*, April 17, 2013; Scott Sayare, "Amid Much Tumult, France Approves 'Marriage for All,'" *New York Times*, April 23, 2013.

261 **Boy Scouts announced:** Erik Eckholm, "Boy Scouts End Longtime Ban on Openly Gay Youths," *New York Times*, May 23, 2013.

261 **Jason Collins announced:** Howard Beck and John Branch, "With the Words 'I'm Gay,' an N.B.A. Center Breaks a Barrier," *New York Times*, April 29, 2013.

262 **"we lack jurisdiction":** *Windsor*, 133 S. Ct. at 2697 (2013) (Roberts, C. J., dissenting).

263 **"personal and individual way":** *Hollingsworth*, 133 S. Ct. at 2662 (citing *Lujan v. Defenders of Wildlife*, 504 U.S. 555, 560 n.1 [1992]).

263 **responsibility for defining:** *Windsor*, 133 S. Ct. at 2689–91.

263 **"long Tumblr rant":** Josh Duboff, "The Court Is Hungry, but DOMA Is Fresh Bread? The Corniest *Slices* of Antonin Scalia's Metaphor-Riddled Dissent," *Vanity Fair*, June 26, 2013.

264 **"indeed inevitable":** *Windsor*, 133 S. Ct. at 2709 (Scalia, J., dissenting).

264 **"DOMA's *This state law's*":** Ibid., 2709–10.

264 **"arm[ed] well every challenger":** Ibid., 2710.

264 **"Court has cheated":** Ibid., 2711.

264 **"At present, no one":** *Windsor*, 133 S. Ct., 2716 (Alito, J., dissenting).

264 **"two competing views":** Ibid., 2718.

265 **"reached the heights of parody":** Ibid., 2718 n.7.

265 **"arrogant legal culture":** Ibid., 2718 n.7.

265 **Marbury v. Madison:** *Marbury v. Madison*, 5 U.S. 137, 177 (1803).

265 **"basic human good":** Sherif Girgis, Ryan T. Anderson, and Robert P. George, *What Is Marriage? Man and Woman: A Defense* (New York: Encounter Books, 2012), 13–14.

266 **"comprehensive union":** Ibid., 75.

266 **"essential to listen":** Steve Sanders, "Next on the Agenda for Marriage

Equality Litigators," *SCOTUSblog,* June 26, 2013, www.scotusblog
.com/?p=166145.

266 **suggested that future challenges:** Ibid.

266 **"a thumb on the scale":** William Duncan, "Bad News for Marriage,
Good News for Government Power," *SCOTUSblog,* June 26, 2013,
www.scotusblog.com/?p=166120.

266 **lifted the stay:** *Perry v. Brown,* 725 F.3d 968 (9th Cir. 2013).

266 **the governor of California ordered:** "Governor Brown Directs California Department of Public Health to Notify Counties That Same-
Sex Marriages Must Commence," June 28, 2013, http://sblog.s3
.amazonaws.com/wp-content/uploads/2013/06/Calif-marriage-order
-6-28-131.pdf.

266 **That same day:** Jennifer Medina, "Gay Couples Who Sued in California Are Married," *New York Times,* June 28, 2013.

17: Civil Ceremonies

267 **concept of a "fact":** Barbara J. Shapiro, *A Culture of Fact: England,
1550–1720* (Ithaca, NY: Cornell University Press, 2003).

267 **"Papers never meet":** Margaret Talbot, "The Gay-Marriage
Classroom."

268 **"source of fresh distortion":** John H. Langbein, "The German Advantage in Civil Procedure," *University of Chicago Law Review* 52
(1985): 833.

268 **"discovery of truth":** John H. Wigmore, *A Treatise on the Anglo-
American System of Evidence in Trials at Common Law,* 3d ed. (Boston: Little, Brown, 1940), 29.

268 **"decrease the value":** Langbein, "The Disappearance of Civil Trial in
the United States," 538 footnote 67.

269 **Martha Nussbaum has argued:** Martha C. Nussbaum, *Upheavals of
Thought: The Intelligence of Emotions* (New York: Cambridge University Press, 2003).

269 **1925 Scopes "monkey trial":** For an account of this trial, see Edward
J. Larson, *Summer for the Gods: The Scopes Trial and America's
Continuing Debate Over Science and Religion* (New York: Basic
Books, 1997).

269 ***Kitzmiller v. Dover:*** *Kitzmiller v. Dover Area School Dist.,* 400 F.
Supp. 2d 707 (2005).

270 ***Hobby Lobby* decision:** *Burwell v. Hobby Lobby Stores, Inc.,* 134
S. Ct. 2751 (2014).

270 **Justice Alito suggested:** *Town of Greece, N.Y. v. Galloway,* 134 S. Ct. 1811, 1834 (2014).

270 **in every state that has one:** Niraj Chokshi, "The Nation's Last Un-challenged State Same-Sex Marriage Ban Is About to Lose That Sta-tus," *Washington Post,* May 25, 2014.

271 **Some have argued:** See, e.g., Dale Carpenter, "On the Legal Front Lines of Same-Sex Marriage"; Emily Bazelon, "Review: 'Redeeming the Dream,' *On Marriage Equality,* by David Boies and Theodore Olson," *Washington Post,* June 20, 2014.

271 **A Utah court adopted:** *Kitchen v. Herbert,* 961 F. Supp. 2d 1181, 1201 (D. Utah 2013).

271 **A Texas court quoted:** *De Leon v. Perry,* 975 F. Supp. 2d 632, 651 (W.D. Tex. 2014).

271 **A Wisconsin court cited:** *Wolf v. Walker,* 986 F. Supp. 2d 982 (W.D. Wis. 2014), judgment entered (June 13, 2014), *aff'd sub nom. Baskin v. Bogan,* 766 F.3d 648 (7th Cir. 2014).

271 **Idaho, Michigan, and Ohio:** *Latta v. Otter,* 1:13-CV-00482-CWD, 2014 WL 1909999, at *13 n.9 (D. Idaho May 13, 2014); *Bassett v. Snyder,* 951 F. Supp. 2d 939, 960 (E.D. Mich. 2013); *Obergefell v. Wymyslo,* 962 F. Supp. 2d 968, 991 n.15 (S.D. Ohio 2013).

271 **An Oregon court:** *Geiger v. Kitzhaber,* 6:13-CV-01834-MC, 2014 WL 2054264, at *12 (D. Or. May 19, 2014)

271 **"Virginia gave us":** Maura Dolan, "Prop. 8 Legal Team Joins Fight against Virginia's Gay Marriage Ban," *Los Angeles Times,* September 30, 2013.

271 *Bostic* **affirmed the findings:** *Bostic v. Rainey,* 970 F. Supp. 2d 456, 478 (E.D. Va. 2014).

271 **upheld on appeal:** *Bostic v. Schaefer,* 760 F. 3d 352 (4th Cir. 2014).

271 **Supreme Court declined:** Adam Liptak, "Supreme Court Delivers Tacit Win to Gay Marriage," *New York Times,* October 6, 2014.

272 **"are doing a good job":** *Baehr v. Miike,* CIV. 91-1394, 1996 WL 694235, at *5 (Haw. Cir. Ct. Dec. 3, 1996).

272 **"against the social sciences":** Ibid., *8–9.

272 **testified against gay and lesbian parenting:** *Howard v. Child Wel-fare Agency Review Bd.,* CV 1999-9881, 2004 WL 3154530, at *7 (Ark. Cir. Ct. Dec. 29, 2004); *Florida Dept. of Children & Families v. Adoption of X.X.G.,* 45 So. 3d 79, 88–90 (Fla. Dist. Ct. App. 2010).

272 **European vacation:** John Schwartz, "Scandal Stirs Legal Questions in Anti-Gay Cases," *New York Times,* May 18, 2010.

272 **Arkansas case:** *Howard,* 2004 WL 3154530, 8 (Ark. Cir. Ct. 2004).

272 **Florida trial:** In re Adoption of *Doe,* 2008 WL 5006172, 12 (Fla. Cir. Ct. 2008).

272 **praise upon Michael Lamb:** *Howard,* 2004 WL 3154530, 8 (Ark. Cir. Ct. 2004).

273 **"New Family Structures Study":** Mark Regnerus, "How Different Are the Adult Children of Parents Who Have Same-Sex Relationships? Findings from the New Family Structures Study," *Social Science Research* 41 (2012).

273 **flood of academic criticism:** See, e.g., Gary J. Gates et al., "Letter to the Editors and Advisory Editors of *Social Science Research,*" *Social Science Research* 41, no. 6 (November 2012); Brief of Amicus Curiae American Sociological Association in Support of Respondent Kristin M. Perry and Respondent Edith Schlain Windsor at 16-22, *Hollingsworth,* 133 S. Ct. 2652 (No. 12-144); *Windsor,* 133 S. Ct. 2675 (No. 12-307).

273 **repudiation of it:** Department of Sociology, University of Texas at Austin, "Statement from the Chair Regarding Professor Regnerus," March 3, 2014, http://sites.la.utexas.edu/utaustinsoc/2014/03/03/statement-from-the-chair-regarding-professor-regnerus/.

273 **many state legislative debates:** Nora Caplan-Bricker, "In Michigan, Same-Sex Marriage Goes to Trial Today. Opponents Will Cite This Study. Too Bad It's Already Been Discredited," *New Republic,* February 24, 2014.

273 **"entirely unbelievable":** *DeBoer v. Snyder,* 973 F. Supp. 2d 757, 766 (E.D. Mich. 2014).

273 **"failed prior heterosexual union":** Ibid., 765.

273 **"hastily concocted":** Ibid., 766.

273 **"any significant weight":** Ibid., 768.

273 **explicitly distanced itself:** Sunnivie Brydum, "Utah Backs Away from Defense Using Discredited Regnerus Study," *Advocate,* April 10, 2014; Chris Geidner, "Utah Makes Last-Ditch Effort to Drop Criticized Scholar Before Marriage Arguments," BuzzFeed News, April 10, 2014, www.buzzfeed.com/chrisgeidner/utah-makes-last-ditch-effort-to-drop-criticized-scholar-befo#.mkzxx2jn80.

274 **"great and theatrical classroom":** Margaret Talbot, "The Gay Marriage Classroom."

274 **he resolved to write:** David Ng, "Gay Marriage Rulings: Prop. 8 Playwright Dustin Lance Black Reflects," *Los Angeles Times,* June 27, 2013.

274 **an all-star cast:** Dave Itzkoff, "Morgan Freeman and Anthony Edwards Will Appear in '8' Reading on Broadway," *New York Times,* August 17, 2011.

274 "West Coast premiere": Gazelle Emami, "Brad Pitt Joins '8,' Dustin Lance Black's Prop. 8 Play," *Huffington Post,* March 1, 2012, www .huffingtonpost.com/2012/03/01/brad-pitt-8-dustin-lance-black_n _1312996.html.

274 In August 2013: "400th Performance Confirmed of Marriage Play '8,' " American Foundation for Equal Rights, August 2, 2013, www.afer.org/ blog/400th-performance-confirmed-of-marriage-play-8/.

274 Rob Reiner has said: Kia Makarechi, "Prop 8 Movie Could Happen, as Rob Reiner Looks to Adapt Dustin Lance Black's Play," *Huffington Post,* March 27, 2013, www.huffingtonpost.com/2013/03/27/prop-8 -movie-rob-reiner-dustin-lance-black_n_2963358.html.

274 As of May 2012: Megan Suckut, "8 Takes the Stage at Northwestern," *North by Northwestern,* May 24, 2012, www.northbynorthwestern.com/story/8-at-northwestern.

276 so derided by Justice Alito's dissent: While the dissent criticizes this brief for advocating "clear error" deference, the brief itself makes no mention of that phrase or standard of review.

276 "doll studies": Gordon J. Beggs, "Novel Expert Evidence in Federal Civil Rights Litigation," *American University Law Review* 45, no. 1 (1995–1996): 9–11.

276 *Briggs v. Elliott*: Briggs v. Elliott, 98 F. Supp. 529 (E.D.S.C. 1951).

276 "feeling of inferiority": Brown v. Bd. of Ed. of Topeka, Shawnee Cnty., Kan., 347 U.S. 483, 494 (1954).

276 obtained the same results: Gordon J. Beggs, "Novel Expert Evidence," 13.

276 "dubious social science": Clarence Thomas, "The Higher Law Background of the Privileges or Immunities Clause of the Fourteenth Amendment," *Harvard Journal of Law and Public Policy* 63 (1989): 68.

277 "facts have so changed": *Planned Parenthood of Southeastern Pennsylvania v. Casey,* 505 U.S. 833, 854–55 (1992).

277 Winston Churchill's comment: United Kingdom, *Hansard Parliamentary Debates,* vol. 444 (November 11, 1947), 206, http://hansard.mill banksystems.com/commons/1947/nov/11/parliament-bill ("Democracy is the worst form of Government except all those other forms that have been tried from time to time.").

278 Comedian Stephen Colbert: "Victory for Gay Marriage & The Rise of Amicus Briefs," *Colbert Report,* October 6, 2014, http://thecolbert report.cc.com/videos/ssmvma/victory-for-gay-marriage---the-rise-of -amicus-briefs---allison-orr-larsen.

278 wander in and out: Douglas Laycock, "A Syllabus of Errors," Review

of *God vs. the Gavel: Religion and the Rule of Law,* by Marci A. Hamilton, *Michigan Law Review* 105 (2007): 1176.

278 **business as usual:** Ibid.

278 **"have to leave early":** "Same-Sex Marriage Public Testimony Before MN House Civil Law Committee—PM Session," YouTube video, posted by "UpTakeVideo," March 12, 2013, www.youtube.com/watch?v=840Qa02pNoA.

278 **"a chilling effect":** "MN House OKs Same-Sex Marriage—Full Debate and Vote," YouTube video, posted by "UpTakeVideo," March 10, 2013, www.youtube.com/watch?v=840Qa02pNoA.

279 **Regnerus study had proven:** Ibid.

279 **Another representative later rose:** Ibid.

Epilogue: Epithalamium

282 **story of Sodom and Gomorrah:** *Genesis* 19:4-8.

282 **Philemon and Baucis:** Ovid, *The Metamorphoses* (Rolfe Humphries, trans., Bloomington: Indiana University Press, 1955), 200-04.

283 **Thom Gunn's reimagining of it:** Thom Gunn, "Philemon and Baucis," *Collected Poems* (New York: Farrar, Straus & Giroux, 1992), 461.

284 **"propaganda of nontraditional sexual relations":** Mark Gevisser, "Life Under Russia's 'Gay Propaganda' Ban," *New York Times,* December 27, 2013.

284 **prison sentences on gay couples:** Faith Karimi and Vladimir Duthiers, "Group: Nigeria Arrests Gay 'Suspects' under New Law Banning Homosexuality," CNN, January 16, 2014.

284 **reinstated a ban on consensual:** Gardiner Harris, "India's Supreme Court Restores an 1861 Law Banning Gay Sex," *New York Times,* December 11, 2013.

285 **opinion for the Constitutional Court:** *Minister of Home Affairs v. Fourie* 2006 (1) SA 524 (CC) (S. Afr.).

INDEX

ABOUT THE AUTHOR

KENJI YOSHINO is the Chief Justice Earl Warren Professor of Constitutional Law at New York University School of Law. He is the author of *Covering: The Hidden Assault on Our Civil Rights* and *A Thousand Times More Fair: What Shakespeare's Plays Teach Us About Justice*. He lives in New York with his husband and two children.